THE RETURN OF PLANET-X

And Its Effects on Mother Earth

– A Natural Disaster Survivor's Manual –

– THE RESEARCH, BACKGROUND and SCIENCE –

Written by:
JAYSEN Q. RAND, Ph.D
For Futureworld Publishing International, L.L.C.
All Rights Reserved – © 2007
Registered – WGAw 2007

Internet Contact: www.returnofplanet-x.com
Ordering Information: 1-800-247-6553 or 1-800-Book Log
or www.atlasbooks.com/marktplc/01805.htm

Published in the U.S.A. by
Futureworld Publishing International, L.L.C.
Paperback ISBN: 978-0-9779209-1-4
ebook ISBN: 978-0-9779209-2-5

Library of Congress Copyright © 2007
Library of Congress Cataloging-in-Publication Data is available

Color Planet-X Front/Back Covers and Illustrations
Courtesy of Shusei Nagaoka, Japan/Los Angeles

Book and Graphics Design:
Jaysen Q. Rand, Ph.D.

For information please contact:
Futureworld Publishing International, L.L.C.
P O Box 141, Horn Lake, MS 38637, U.S.A.

Printed in United States of America
    First Printing/January 2007
    Second Printing/October 2007
    Third Printing/December 2007

Representation:
Larry Spellman Management
Palm Springs, CA. (760) 327-0238

*P*hilosophy precedes ecology.
What is most needed today are new realizations about
man's place in the universe, a new sense of life,
a new price in the importance of being human, a new
joyousness in the possibilities for essential human unity,
and a new determination to keep this planet
from becoming uninhabitable.

Saturday Review -- March 7, 1970

PLANET-X, A BROWN DWARF STAR. RETURNS FROM ITS 3,600-YEAR ORBITAL CYCLE AROUND THE SUN.

REVELATION

CHAPTER 8

VRS: 10-13

10 And the third angel sounded, and there fell a great star from heaven, burning as it were a lamp, and it fell upon the third part of the rivers, and upon the foundations of waters:

11 And the name of the star is called **Wormwood**: and the third part of the waters became wormwood; and many men died of the waters, because they were made bitter.

12 And the fourth angel sounded, and the third part of the sun was smitten, and the third part of the moon, and the third part of the stars; so as the third part of them was darkened, and the day shone not for a third part of it, and the night likewise.

13 And I beheld, and heard an angel flying through the midst of heaven, saying with a loud voice, Woe, woe, woe, to the inhabiters of the earth by reason of the other voices of the trumpet of the three angels, which are yet to sound! **[End of Chapter Eight]**

The Holy Bible
Authorized King James Version

THE RETURN OF PLANET-X
WORMWOOD
MANKIND'S ONGOING LEGACY WITH A BROWN DWARF STAR
[a working hypothesis based on science and fact]

The most current working hypothesis we have to examine concerning the expected return date of Planet-X coursing through the solar system centers around the prime fact that "X's" extended orbit (approximately every 3,600 years—first passing through the solar system in 'phase-one' —then back out again within 'phase-two') now suggests that "X's" 'destructive cycle' occurs in two separate cosmic events.

This 'first-phase' begins with "X's" 'initial pass-through,' (possibly in 2009), then separated by approximately three years until its 'second-phase' —wherein "X" makes its 'second pass through' the solar system (expected in 2012). This second passage marks "X's" return leg back again into deep space beginning anew its 3,600 year long trek through the heavens. Planet-X's last return visit likely coincided with the Hebrew exodus from Egypt in 1447 B.C.E. under Moses.

The best researched dates include late summer (September 18, 2009) for "X's" 'first-phase' pass through and in early winter (December 21, 2012) for "X's" 'second-phase' pass through the solar system. Major earth changes will occur during both phases of "X's" passage with the most damage resulting in a possible 'pole flip' (a tipping of Earth on its axis of rotation 180 degrees) in "X's" second phase, December 2012. It's also possible that a complete 'pole flip' may not occur, however planet Earth may still suffer major planetary upheavals from "X's" passage.

And the name of the star was Wormwood... Revelation Chap. 8, Vrs. 11

PLANET EARTH - THE CONTINUING SAGA OF A SMALL WATERY WORLD SEEMINGLY LOST IN SPACE ON ITS INTREPID JOURNEY HURTLING THROUGH THE VASTNESS OF THE MILKY WAY GALAXY HERE IN THE 21ST CENTURY.

THE FIRST BOOK OF MOSES, CALLED GENESIS
Chapter 1 Vrs. 1-31 & Chapter 2 Vrs. 1-4

CHAPTER 1

IN the beginning God created the heaven and the earth.

2 And the earth was without form, and void; and darkness *was* upon the face of the deep. And the Spirit of God moved upon the face of the waters.

3 And God said. Let there be light: and there was light.

4 And God saw the light, that *it was* good: and God divided the light from the darkness.

5 And God called the light Day, and the darkness he called Night. And the evening and the morning were the first day.

6 And God said, Let there be a firmament in the midst of the waters, and let it divide the waters from the waters.

7 And God made the firmament, and divided the waters which *were* under the firmament from the waters ~which *were* above the firmament: and it was so.

8 And God called the firmament Heaven. And the evening and the morning were the second day.

9 And God said, Let the waters under the heaven be gathered together unto one place, and let the dry *land* appear: and it was so.

10 And God called the dry *land* Earth; and the gathering together of the waters called he Seas: and God saw that *it was* good.

11 And God said. Let the earth bring forth grass, the herb yielding seed, *and* the fruit tree yielding fruit after his kind, whose seed *is* in itself, upon the earth: and it was so.

12 And the earth brought forth grass, *and* herb yielding seed after his kind, and the tree yielding fruit, whose seed *was* in itself, after his kind: and God saw that *it* was good.

13 And the evening and the morning were the third day.

14 And God said, Let there be lights in the firmament of the heaven to divide the day from the night; and let them be for signs, and for seasons, and for days and years:

15 And let them be for lights in the firmament of the heaven to give light upon the earth: and it was so.

16 And God made two great lights; the greater light to rule the day, and the lesser light to rule the night: *he made* the stars also.

17 And God set them in the firmament of the heaven to give light upon the earth, 18 And to rule over the day and over the night, ~and to divide the light from the darkness: and God saw that *it was* good. 19 And the evening and the morning were the fourth day.

20 And God said, Let the waters bring forth abundantly the moving creature that hath life, and fowl *that* may fly above the earth in the open firmament of heaven.

21 And God created great whales, and every living creature that moveth, which the waters brought forth abundantly, after their kind, and every winged fowl after his kind: and God saw that *it was* good.

22 And God blessed them, saying, Be fruitful, and multiply, and fill the waters in the seas, and let fowl multiply in the earth.

23 And the evening and the morning were the fifth day.

24 And God said, Let the earth bring forth the living creature after his kind, cattle, and creeping thing, and beast of the earth after his kind: and it was so.

25 And God made the beast of the earth after his kind, and cattle after their kind, and every thing that creepeth upon the earth after his kind: and God saw that *it was* good.

26 And God said, Let us make man in our image, after our likeness: and let them have dominion over the fish of the sea, and over the fowl of the air, and over the cattle, and over all the earth, and over every creeping thing that creepeth upon the earth.

27 So God created man in his *own* image, in the image of God created he him; male and female created he them. 28 And God blessed them, and God said unto them, Be fruitful, and multiply, and replenish the earth, and subdue it:

and have dominion over the fish of the sea, and over the fowl of the air, and over every living thing that moveth upon the earth.

29 And God said, Behold, I have given you every herb bearing seed, which is upon the face of all the earth, and every tree, in the which is the fruit of a tree yielding seed; to you it. shall be for meat

30 And to every beast of the earth, and to every fowl of the air, and to every thing that creepeth upon the earth, wherein *there is* life, *I have given* every green herb for meat: and it was so.

31 And God saw every thing that he had made, and, behold, *it was* very good. And the evening and the morning were the sixth day.

CHAPTER 2

THUS the heavens and the earth were finished, and all the host of them.

2 And on the seventh day God ended his work which he had made; and he rested on the seventh day from all his work which he had made.

3 And God blessed the seventh day, and sanctified it: because that in it he had rested from all his work which God created and made.

4 These *are* the generations of the heavens and of the earth when they were created, in the day that the LORD God made the earth and the heavens.

– TABLE OF CONTENTS –

THE RETURN OF PLANET-X
And Its Effects Upon Mother Earth

A Natural Disaster Survivor's Manual

"Every strand is a glimpse into the past.
Every pattern – a link to the spirits of the ancient ones."
- Winona Brown, Navajo Weaver

We never know how far-reaching something
we might think, say or do today
will affect the lives of millions…

-- B. J. Palmer, D.C., Ph.C.

Acknowledgments

-- Acknowledgments --

We would like to express our sincere thanks to the following friends and associates who contributed to the research, editing and artistic preparation of this unique writing project on *Planet-X*. Their dedication and tireless efforts made this book possible.

First and foremost we wish to acknowledge Shusei Nagaoka, Japan/Los Angeles, one of the truly preeminent airbrush artists in the world. Shusei has graced the front/back covers and several sections of this book with his splendid *Planet-X* illustrations. His brilliant vision, grace and encouragement have spurred us on to produce this tome and its concept for the future of planet Earth. Shusei, thanks for being our trusted friend and confidant. We treasure your artistic abilities and look forward to our future projects.

Shirley Greene, our long-time associate, worked tirelessly to edit, correct and advise us on the final copy preparations, served as our main back-stay and was always there to take our questions spending countless hours reading and re-reading the working text in progress until completed. Shirley, you're a gem, and we love you.

Next is Sergio Clough, our trusted research associate and friend also spent countless hours at the computer finding/gathering/sorting out all the great array of Internet research/document information shared with our reading audience. Sergio's dedication to duty/service is greatly appreciated. We would also like to thank Brett Lloyd, our constant source of Internet information and guidance who helped shape the landscape and quality of this timely work; his insight is duly appreciated. And also our magical wizard and friend, Sami Rose, whose kind deeds and words of wisdom provided a constant beacon of light and guidance during the several years of our writing assignments and research.

We'd also like to acknowledge Hal Puthoff, Ph.D., President, *Institute For Advanced Studies* and J. J. Hurtak, Ph.D., President, *The Academy For Future Science,* for their continued belief, support and creative ideas provided for this writing project and for their ever-present guidance and encouragement to get the job done. Thank you, kind Sirs, -- you are gentlemen, scholars and trusted colleagues.

Larry Spellman, our Manager in Palm Springs, California, was ever constant in his vision, encouragement and wisdom guiding the direction of our writing efforts. His boundless enthusiasm and drive greatly helped to keep this book on the 'right track'.., thanks, Larry, and we treasure our long-term association with you.

And it would not have been possible for this book to be written were it not for the courage, insight and dedication of all those exceptional authors from the past to the present, whose courageous writing contributions, research and historical accounts grace this new volume. Many of them bravely 'flew the flag' in the face of object criticism, professional derision, social and religious persecution. Our heartfelt appreciation is extended to each and every one of them --past and present-- in the hope that our mission in *The Return Of Planet-X* will help to carry on the noble journalistic traditions that these early *'Earth Changes'* pioneers selflessly established/shared with the global community.

Our final acknowledgement goes to you, our enlightened readers, whose interest, enthusiasm and support makes this *'Earth Changes'* journal of research a timely and meaningful project. We want to thank everyone for recommending this book to family, friends and associates and for their caring concerns by informing the public of critical matters we feel are important to planet Earth. As we race into the future of 2009/2012, we suspect *Plant-X* will return once again to terrorize our solar system – and our mission is to prepare our world for whatever surprises come our way.

YOU ARE HERE

Our solar system rotates in deep space located approximately half-way from the center of our galaxy, the Milky Way. Planet Earth's mean distance from the sun (during its annual trek through the heavens) is 92,900,000 miles. The planet rotates on its axis from west to east once in each sidereal day (a period of 23 hours/56 minutes) as it revolves completely around the sun once a year traveling along its slightly elliptical path, streaking through the cosmos (with a physical speed in motion) at approximately 18.5 miles per second while speeding away from the very center of the Milky Way.

Existing as an oblate spheroid, planet Earth, as seen from local space, appears to be slightly flattened at both its polar regions while still bulging noticeably along her equatorial plane. Its polar diameter is 7,900 miles and her equatorial diameter is 7,926.7 miles. The area of Earth's exposed land surface is approximately 57.5 million sq. miles, while the total area of the planet's oceans is believed to be 139.4 million square miles or roughly 70% that of Earth's total surface.

Our world exists as a completely self-contained entity with its eco-sphere and eco-systems being self-regenerating needing the thermonuclear light heat/radiation from the sun to maintain her myriad variety of life forms to exist in total harmony and balance. The Earth and moon are approximately 5.5 billion years old with the moon being a dead body visited by human beings on a number of past occasions.

THE RETURN OF PLANET-X
And Its Effects Upon Mother Earth

A Natural Disaster Survivor's Manual

"The vibrancy of the past reflects the pulse of the future." ...Author Unknown...

— INTRODUCTORY OVERVIEW —

EARTHWATCH—THE 21st CENTURY AND BEYOND

Dear Reader: Please fasten your safety belts! The cosmic ride is just beginning...!
Earth date: Wednesday 09/28/05: The Mission: Create Introductory Overview: Time 7:45 PM

Hi, everybody! I'm Dr. Jaysen Q. Rand, author of this timely natural disaster survivor's manual based upon the history/research/background/science into the reality of *Planet-X—Wormwood.*

We've just finished organizing and reassembling the scientific papers, magazine/newspaper articles, *Planet-X* Internet offerings, plus a graphics illustration package designed to present the scope/mission of our work featured within its exhibits/illustrations/bibliography sections.

Major news coverage all day centered upon the horrific wildfires burning over the past 24 hours throughout southern California and the L.A. basin. Many areas like Topanga Canyon, Chatsworth, Thousand Oaks, Tarzana, Burbank, and as far east as the I-10 corridor (heading towards Palm Springs), were plagued with hot burning ash driven by seasonal Santa Ana winds bringing in dry desert air/blistering temperatures. Many million dollar homes and 75,000 acres are ablaze.

Once again Mother Nature is heaping more woe/misery upon the really important domestic/ global issues plaguing this great nation, i.e., Iraq/the ongoing war on global terrorism/high gas prices/damaged refinery/oil drilling operations/new global warming issues and a massive clean-up reconstruction/repopulation of the Gulf States region with its whopping $50+ billion price tag to accomplish it. The 2005 hurricane season exploded setting many new and deadly records.

President Bush and his key advisors were busy making yet a seventh whirlwind tour sweeping across the Gulf Coast while being briefed/networking/meeting with the head of FEMA, state and local politicians and the news media. President Bush's mission: Bringing immediate consolation/ reassurance/help to the hundreds of thousands of recent *Rita* and *Katrina* evacuees now scattered throughout the five storm-ravaged southern states and beyond. *Had FEMA finally kicked in...??*
    —Yes, dear readers, hope abounds and prayer always works! ...Now shifting gears...

As the troubled year 2005 approached its dramatic end—it posed a bold and ominous question:
    —*Was planet Earth suddenly facing a cosmic struggle for its continued existence?*

Badly battered by no less than 28 tropical storms that year alone (just midway through the 2005 season)—14 tempests turned into category 1/2/3 hurricanes with no less than four of them listed as category 4/5 (in their severity/intensity/destruction) begs the question: *So what's going on here? Was there something drastically wrong now with Mother Nature's seasonal weather tantrums*—or were *we completely missing the key elements of an approaching global apocalypse?*

Hurricane *Katrina* (a huge CAT/5) was deemed the most powerful tropical storm ever recorded in the Atlantic Ocean/Gulf of Mexico in modern-day times. It not only flooded/destroyed a large chunk of New Orleans, but also decimated more than 90,000 square miles of the region's vulnerable Gulf Coast, while killing more than 1,100 people with its blinding fury. *Katrina* sent the nation's repair/rebuild/repopulation costs soaring over their estimated $65 billion+ mark.

Then a mere three weeks later hurricane *Rita* strikes—a monstrous CAT/3 event that further tore the region apart instantly re-scattering *Katrina* evacuees to nearly every state in the union. It's key to remember that these two storms struck suddenly representing the worst and most costly natural disasters to ever ravage this proud country in its entire history...

Question: *Was the end of this nightmare hopefully in sight—or was it just beginning?* That's one of the hot-button *Planet-X* questions we'll strive to answer and explore in this tome!

So, what if the contents of this book prove to be correct/right? And what if there really is a giant Planet-X (a brown dwarf star) out there cruising inbound—already disturbing the sun's solar system by altering Earth's normal range and cycle of global weather patterns? And have the charges/claims/conclusions lodged against the destructive effects of 'global warming' now become only the tip of a much larger iceberg? And lastly—could planet Earth already be experiencing these far-distant electromagnetic effects of this approaching brown dwarf star, the Book of Revelation's—Wormwood? ...Always more questions—but never any real answers!!

During the earlier days of the 2004 hurricane season, a successive train of four very powerful destructive hurricanes pounded the Caribbean Islands, Cuba and the Southeastern United States. Especially the beleaguered state of Florida ravaged by a series of category 4s-5s as other powerful weather-related phenomena/water/volcanoes also ravaged vast regions across the planet.

Then in late September, a grouping of six powerful 6.5+ earthquakes began seriously rattling the California landscape. *Are these new quake patterns suggesting a big up-tick in seismic activity along the infamous San Andreas fault system?* The San Andreas ranges off shore from San Francisco then turns inland and southward towards Palm Springs as it dives under the Salton Sea.

All those episodes of recent natural disasters came as no real surprise to the current Republican administration, for in 2002—the White House doubled FEMA's (Federal Emergency Management Agency's) budget—raising it dramatically upwards to a staggering $6.6 billion a year. But apparently this was not sufficient to handle the magnitude of what was soon approaching in 2004 and 2005. During March of 2003, the FEDS merged FEMA (along with 22 other government agencies) creating the new and complicated Department of Homeland Security (DHS)—a bold Bush administration program structured and run by former Pennsylvania Governor, Tom Ridge. A dramatic experiment began in earnest to protect America following the tragic events of 9/11.

In other words—the government created a new "FEMA on steroids" in order to handle the dire consequences of the approaching tempest—a two-headed monster consisting of both *terrorism* and ever-increasing *Earth Changes*. In May of 2003, this newly created DHS staged a mock drill emergency operation, "TOP-OFF-2"—billed by the government as the largest natural disaster exercise in U.S. history. *Strangely, we didn't hear much about it from TV or media? Why not?*

Then in a weird twist of irony that same week—hundreds of 'real life' (unstaged tornadoes) viciously appeared tearing their way across the Midwest/Northwest/West Coast causing massive devastation on a previously unrecorded scale. *Had Mother Nature gone mad? —Tornadoes in Los Angeles?? Had the recent movie 'The Day After Tomorrow' become sudden reality 101?*

And so our mysterious planetary saga continues on with both the weather and geophysical disasters becoming more frequent/much worse every year. All the while the U.S. government (and those of most other developed nations around the globe) are desperately trying to deal with their ever-increasing preparation efforts suddenly costing hundreds of billions of unanticipated clean-up dollars/loss of lives/property damage/insurance costs. Every year since 1992 when hurricane *Andrew,* (a devastating CAT/5) nearly destroyed south Florida, the nation's natural disaster price tag continued rising dramatically by billions of dollars every year! *(Note: <u>Katrina and Rita's</u> storm damage is currently estimated at over $85 billion with final costs yet to be determined).*

Is the cosmic handwriting already on the wall? And does the government know more about Planet-X than they're telling us? Are the answers to our current natural disasters dilemma more obvious than we know or understand? The answers we discovered (to those and many other key questions in this book) produced our guidance to research/study and then write this work. There are hundreds of arcane answers we revealed in this process that may surprise you—maybe not!

The universe through which the human race travels in the 21ˢᵗ century is truly a wondrous mix of ongoing creation and instant destruction! One doesn't have to peer through a NASA lens or telescope to witness these phenomenal mixtures of creative/destructive forces at work. Our very own planet provides us sober testimony to the stark reality of just how simultaneously beautiful yet sinister dear old 'Mother Nature' can be—*like Hawaii's spectacular Mauna Loa volcano?*

In fact, our world has been repeatedly shaped by massive planetary disasters countless times throughout its ancient 5-billion-year history. Today's new 21ˢᵗ century science, however, hasn't always accepted the reality of these periodic planetary disasters. As recently as a few decades ago most modern-day scientists believed that planet Earth was relatively 'static' in her geologic evolution. After all, Earth was a forever concept—many billions of years old and solid as a rock! *Then again—maybe not??* Let's not forget about her inner mega-hot molten lava core.

These same scientists also believed that our world was largely 'unchanging' and that enormous periods of time (involving millions or even billions of years) endlessly pass by with no apparent alterations to our planet's topography (its surface features). Those same scientists believed in the science of what is now called *uniformitarianism*—the idea/concept/theory that our home planet (spinning alone through the cosmos??) remains a largely 'uniform and unchanging' world over vast amounts of Earthian time involving many millions—perhaps billions of years. Thanks to NASA and other scientific agencies—we now understand this planet in greater detail and clarity.

Today, most scientists agree that Earth is not a static environment and is, in fact, undergoing continuous changes. Although most of these geologic changes are subtle/hardly noticed by the vast majority of people as they go about busy lives on their planet—but on rare occasion (once every several thousand years or so), unforeseen cataclysmic events strike at this planet with incomprehensible fury. *Question: Was Plato's account of a decimated Atlantis in 12,500 BC actually true?? And are the ancient legends of 'UFOs' with their ET 'sky people' also true?* Our research uncovered hundreds of references to UFOs and ETs associated with *Earth Changes*.

The idea that Earth remains relatively unchanged for smaller amounts of time and is then punctuated by enormous 'upheavals' (that suddenly/dramatically rearrange the surface topography of our planet)—is known as *catastrophism*. So in other words, *catastrophism,* being an established *opposing scientific doctrine*—believes that these 'major changes' in Earth's crusted topography result from 'numerous periodic' catastrophes—rather than 'gradual' geologic processes and changes. Those modern-day scientists who study these 'periodic upheaval' periods are known in the field today as *catastrophists*.

And even though slow changes to Earth do take place—today's forward thinking scientists are becoming increasingly aware that periodic 'rapid' changes are largely responsible for shaping all life forms on this planet. Recent geologic and archaeological evidence confirms that periodic cataclysms struck Earth repeatedly in the past suddenly and violently rearranging her continental landmasses, creating new mountain ranges (where none existed before), while suddenly sinking others, thus dramatically altering Earth's global climates and weather patterns and wiping out many assorted life forms on truly apocalyptic scales. Many such archaeological, fossil, and social records of these catastrophic events are historically abundant and well researched. The Internet's ablaze! Check it out! Currently a quarter million Websites worship an unfolding *Planet-X* saga.

Unfortunately, most people living today remain largely oblivious to these periodic global catastrophes. The reason for their lack of awareness varies, yet one of its main tenets is that no one living on Earth today has ever personally witnessed such a massive planetary disaster occurring. Nor have their parents or grandparents, or even their 'great-great-great-great-great-great-great grandparents!' For it appears that even our best-recorded human history contains massive information gaps covering long periods of earthian time from [BC >>>> to >>>> Present Day].

It's because these periodic catastrophes happened with great intervals of time spaced between them that we have no real personal *'knowledge,' 'experience'* or *'known record keeping'* of these huge global upheavals. Those events are simply not part of our normal *'waking consciousness'* —and we don't entertain giving these *'unpleasant,' 'infrequent'* events any second thought as we dash about our busy lives totally preoccupied. *So if Planet-X last returned some 3,600 years ago, is 'out of sight' therefore — 'out of mind' from [BC >>>> to >>>> Present Day]?*

QUESTIONS: Because these catastrophic events happened numerous times in the past and will certainly happen again, does our present-day lack of awareness (regarding these periodic planetary disasters), become a truly unwise situation to find ourselves facing in 2007 A.D.? And are we (by not paying better attention to what's going on around us on a grander scale) setting ourselves up to be caught 'off guard' again when the next periodic Planet-X catastrophe strikes Earth? Atlantian legends claim their mid-Atlantic island chain disappeared in a mere fortnight?

It appears that the universal mystic and folklore surrounding the existence of Atlantis never dies!

And it's against this backdrop of a very complicated mix of planetary creation and its subsequent destruction scenario that our *Planet-X Survivor's Manual* focuses its primary creative attention to *The Return of Planet-X* and its ugly aftermath. Our research addresses these important issues to inform you, our readers, of this 'bigger picture'—those recurring periodic cosmic events reshaping all life across this vibrant yet delicate planet—both in the distant past and near future.

Even though there's been many differing catastrophes striking Earth over time, we'll focus on one specific 'recurring cataclysm' largely responsible for major geologic changes to our world.

This recurring calamity is relatively simple to understand, at least in concept. Our hypothesis involves a large 'celestial object' (a brown dwarf star), periodically close-passing our world in space and, as it does so, this object's massive electromagnetic gravitational force field causes enormous physical changes to Earth's topography—occasionally altering its axis of rotation with the end result triggering a potentially catastrophic trans-global 180 degree pole shift.

This incoming object does not hit the Earth—our planet is not totally destroyed by its passage; instead it drastically *'alters'/'affects'* how the world mechanically rotates on its polar axis in space! And aside from just affecting Earth's rotation, this passing celestial object also triggers a series of massive planetary disasters involving catastrophic flooding/monstrous tornadoes/global tidal waves (tsunamis)—with dozens of 9.5+ earthquakes/active volcanoes/howling winds/and planetary wildfires threatening the world—*similar to what was happening during spring 2006!*

It's because of these enormous geologic changes taking place [when this 'celestial object' passes us in space]—that makes reading this work critically important for every American and citizen of planet Earth living today. For when this cosmic 'fly-by' happens again—it will radically/forever change 'life' as we 'know it' for everyone presently living on this world at this time.

The most current hypothesis we have to examine concerning *X's* next return through the solar system centers around the fact that *X's* extended orbit (about every 3,600 years—first passing through the solar system then back out again), suggests that its 'destructive cycle' occurs in two phases. This 'first phase' begins with *X's* 'initial pass-through' in 2009 separated by three years until its 'second phase' wherein it makes its 'second pass-through' the solar system in 2012.

This passage marks *X's* return leg back into deep space beginning again its 3,600-year-long trek through the heavens. *X's* last return visit through the solar system most likely coincided with the Hebrew's exodus from Egypt, estimated around 1447 BC—roughly 3,459 years ago. *Did God somehow come to Moses' aide by staging a cosmic event that no one today understands?*

Recent research now suggests that fall 2009 might be the initial date for *X's* next 'first phase' return surprise. Calculating approximately three-years for its 'second phase' pass-through, we estimate a future winter date in 2012. And therein, dear reader, lays the greatest 'astrological' paradox of modern times—for it now appears that even the cosmos itself is playing a dramatic role... Astrology and all things 'astrological'—represents the study that assumes and attempts to interpret the influence of the heavenly bodies on human affairs—notwithstanding *Planet-X!*

For some unknown and truly mysterious reason, the *Mayan's Sacred Celestial Calendar Codex* inexplicably ends 21 December 2012. According to ancient Mayan cosmology, *'time'* as we know it on Earth will reach its climax on <u>that particular date</u> in *'real time.'* And there are other sources clearly identifying 2012 as the prophesied *'end of time'* sequencing point here on planet Earth. Hopi nation elders proclaim this event will initiate their *'Great Day of Purification.'* And the Hopis traditions/viewpoints into the future endure over the centuries as proof of their beliefs.

Are these reports and dates simply a 'strange coincidence,' just a 'silly legend of time' —or do they now become 'major clues' leading us to wisely unravel/discover this cosmic mystery of time, space and destiny—as Planet-X's next return date surprise in 2009/2012 reveals?

Before we begin our exploration of the 'destructive cycles' periodically altering planet Earth, there are several important points we must consider! But first comes a sober word of warning.

Some readers may believe this *Natural Disaster Survivor's Manual* is scary as they examine the potential for major disruptions to our world. Yes, it's a frightening scenario for even the most adventure-filled souls who are open-minded and brave enough to challenge the following hard-hitting 314 text pages in our full-length book format—but it's a challenge well-worth taking.

Wise words state: Knowledge equals power—but real power, believe it—is in the knowing!

Even though the *Planet-X* subject may appear scary and unpleasant, it is nevertheless important that you be fully informed of this 'larger cosmic picture' of what's been happening in the past, and what's 'gearing up' to happen to Earth again quite possibly in the next three to six years.

If you're alarmed by the topics discussed in this work, your 'fear factor' should motivate you into taking preparatory actions that may allow you and your loved ones to survive this forth-coming cosmic holocaust. Those actions are ones that we probably wouldn't take unless we're motivated by our 'fear' and 'awareness' of *X.* The true purpose of this work is not meant to scare you—but rather to inform our readers by saving their lives, mitigating property damage and to help preserve our nation's long-term heritage and its continued survival beyond 2012.

Put yet another way, once read, this *Manual* will allow our readers to take notice of what's going on around them on a 'larger cosmic level,' then take intelligent steps to protect themselves and their loved ones from what is rapidly approaching Earth. *In this case, your 'fear factor' can have a positive outcome—forewarned is forearmed...* We are all responsible for creating/maintaining our own reality streams of experience and those of our loved ones. Dear reader, this is one of those rare/special opportunities being offered. Please consider it on behalf of our great nation and the world. Your attention and understanding of making certain 'personal preparations' (not only now in your individual daily lives, but also for your futures in 2009/2012)—may and can make all the difference should this dreaded *Planet-X* reality become apparent.

The second important point begging your attention deals with this 'bigger picture'—the galactic mechanisms that periodically affect all life on this planet. In order for us to fully explore such a vast subject we'll carefully examine Earth's ancient history, her archeology, geology, astronomy, prophecy, political/social science and the personal actions we can all take to prepare ourselves and family members should the dire events in question arrive to threaten 'Mother Earth' again.

Because of the diverse subject matter covered in the following narrative and the sheer volume of information we've reviewed gaining a proper/comprehensive perspective on our current *'Earth Changes'* update, we find that it's necessary this *Manual* approach our *Planet-X* return scenario utilizing an 'overview story format.' We'll simply cover the most relevant/appropriate information/research/dialogue relating specifically to the *X* subject matters discussed. For ease of reading each chapter offers a brief introduction to topic then presents the facts—as a recap moves you on.

If we were to take every topic and example presented here and then proceed to explore all the available research pertaining to those examples (to further argue every pertinent scientific point to its fullest potential)—this survivors disaster research *Manual* would certainly be the size of the current version of the 19-20-book *Encyclopedia Britannica* series—or possibly even larger.

We must therefore simply 'scratch the surface' of this fascinating 'outer space paradox'—for a more in-depth scientific examination would not be possible within any single literary volume. Suggested extra reading (supporting our research) is provided for curious strong-hearted readers —so we eagerly encourage you to explore our chapter footnotes and bibliography pages.

Also wherever possible, technical and scientific jargon has been kept to a minimum so as to not overly tax the non-scientific reader. With these several points in mind and your understanding the universe and its complexity—fully prepare yourself to enter into the 'cataclysmic realms' of the cosmos knowing the consequences of *Planet-X's* anticipated return/arrival. As a backdrop to appreciating the true mission of our work—we'll examine Earth's repeated periods of global landmass and societal destruction—both in the distant past (Atlantis) and the very near future (2009/2012).

It's 2007 in the 21ˢᵗ century. We're now witnessing the dramatic effects of our increased global warming/earthquakes/intense tropical storms/extended forest fire seasons/much warmer winters and summers/plus drastic changes in all of our planet's regular weather systems. *Are we now experiencing what could be the forthcoming countdown to the predicted pole shift event in 2012?*

Added to the cataclysmic changes/events expected to occur—this never ending drama unfolds as it attempts to portray (in graphic detail) these biblical end-times prophecies now taking place daily—just as they're being fulfilled into physical reality 2007 A.D.

And as our planet's vibratory rate increases daily we're also beginning to see phenomenal shifts in our personal time-based physical reality streams. If those ancient Sumerian pictographs, revered prophecies and lost legends of time are indeed correct—*'Wormwood'* will return once again from its 3,600-year-long trek through the solar system to haunt us. By reading this *Manual* —each of you is offered a definitive choice concerning your new reality system, America's future, the world's destiny—and the individual survival needs of you and your loved ones.

The informational content of this book is, to the best of our knowledge and ability, both accurate and timely. This writing project originally began several years ago with the idea of our creating an *"Earth Changes Briefing Document."* It was an investigative handbook designed as a tool of basic information to be shared with our readers. This *Manual* is therefore the end result of those many years of dedicated reading, research, interviews and writing assignments.

Was the end result product worthy of our writing task? —We believe so and hope you do, too!

Our final draft seemingly morphed itself into a book-sized volume reflecting careful editing of numerous scientific reports/topical research papers/charts/graphs/books and magazines on the subject. Many such items were gleaned from official government sources/newspapers/magazine reports/scientific commentaries/global Internet offerings. [See reference notes at chapter's end.]

However, we must first warn you!! Should you decide to continue reading this *Manual*—there are specific consequences! Once you've gained the benefit of the knowledge contained herein— the next logical/critical steps for you to decide on as an individual are: *1) how and what to do with this critical information—and 2) if you should share it with your loved ones and friends?*

Although the subject of *Planet-X* is most fascinating—it nevertheless raises more *questions* than *answers*. We fully expect the scientific community, astronomers, geologists, religious groups and *Earth Changes* pundits to vigorously rise up attacking this book's relevant message and theory— along with its author. We'll take it in stride communicating our message—so please E-mail us!

We expect these attacks to become well coordinated, probably from the highest powers that be— both governmental and religious, and without exception, from the scientific communities. *Why, you might wonder??? Well then, you should ask—when has 'bad news' coming on the horizon ever brought about a cheerful response? And further—what 'prophets in the wild' have ever been accepted, or for that matter, allowed to live past delivering his, hers, or their messages??*

The entire subject of *Earth Changes* and *Planet-X* has been the ongoing subject of religious and scientific ridicule/debate/derision. If we're right—so be it!! And if we're wrong—at least we tried to do the right thing and for all the right reasons! Questions: *Currently there are over 20 million global Internet references to the subject of Planet-X and Earth Changes—so why are these hot topics getting a solid million hits every week?* <u>Seemingly—someone out there is interested</u>!!! Today's most popular subject of discussion (other than Iraq) is our wacky weather!

So what's new here? Solon, the famous Greek historian, philosopher and statesman (who lived in Athens between 639-599 BC)—was much disdained/sometimes ridiculed concerning his Atlantis accounts and theories; *Nicholas Copernicus* (1473-1543) Polish astronomer who promulgated the theory that Earth and the other known planets moved around the sun—was terribly persecuted by the Catholic church for his radical views; *Michel de Nostradamus* (1503-66) French astrologer, physician and seer, was practically hunted down and destroyed by the Church hierarchy in Rome for writing his radical beliefs/prognostications into the future; *Galileo Galilei* (1564-1642) Italian astronomer, physicist and mapmaker who demonstrated the 'truth of Copernican theory' with his early invention of the telescope—was soundly discredited, ridiculed and tyrannized by the Roman church for his work and purest theories; *Christopher Columbus* (1446?-1506) Italian navigator, mapmaker, sailor, explorer, theorist in the service of Spain (discovering America in 1492 believing that the world was indeed round)—lies buried on the

Caribbean island of Santo Domingo—dying penniless and in ridicule/dishonor/shame for his gallant efforts; *Sir Isaac Newton* (1642-1727) English mathematician and philosopher who formulated the binomial theorem, the laws of gravity and motion and the true elements of differential calculus—was widely believed by many of his contemporaries and the Holy Roman Church quite certifiably mad/insane—(until he was proven otherwise); *Dr. Immanuel Velikovsky* (1895-1979) Russian born author, researcher, physician and modern-day theorist who penned two seminal books on the subject of *Earth Changes*: *Earth In Upheaval* and *Worlds In Collision* —remains one of the most controversial authors on the subject, and to this day is still vilified for his ground-breaking efforts; *Dr. Zecharia Sitchin,* a Russian Jew born in Palestine in 1920 and most notably recognized for his best-selling tome, *The Twelfth Planet,* and many other excellent books on topic, remains today one of the Internet's most sought/debated/controversial authors of record; *Charles Hapgood (Path Of The Pole - 1999)* and *John White (Pole Shift - 1998),* two contemporary authors who explored the concept of the 'pole shift' hypothesis—still continue largely unaccredited/unrecognized for their splendid ground-breaking theories and literary work on the much globally debated subject of modern-day *Earth Changes*; and *Gordon Michael Scallion,* a prolific writer, teacher and futurist (who has appeared on numerous television and radio network programs throughout the world), has also authored several credible books on the subject including his *Future Map of North America* and *Future Map of the World,* —Michael Scallion persists (as well with all of the above-mentioned personalities), in being a controversial writer/theorist/scientist regarding the subject of *Earth Changes* by him expressing certain purist views concerning the future 'continental makeup' of planet Earth post the 2012 pole shift event.

So there you have it—throughout history those 'brave souls' who dared to speak out expressing their personal theories and research on controversial science/metaphysics/social topics/prophecy —have all been targets of vicious scientific/religious/societal/governmental bias and professional ridicule 'above and beyond their call of duty.' We salute them all and admire their fine works.

If the general premise of our work is correct (and only future events will determine its validity) —at least we've honestly tried to inform the public. If on the other hand we are proven wrong and the brown dwarf star, *Wormwood,* never materializes, at best we've expressed our sincere concerns over the ever-increasing degradation of planet Earth's troubled environment with its radically changing global weather patterns currently taking place, and the truly massive amount of ancient historical prophecies, science, literature and Internet information supporting our work.

Once again, this book was not written to scare the reader—but moreover to fully inform/advise and share in the vast storehouse of available information we've presented, allowing the public to come to its own conclusions/directives regarding the potential return of *Planet-X* in 2009/2012.

The concept of *Earth Changes* (changing physical conditions on this planet) isn't just a far-off abstract idea—but one having greater relevance than most people in the world willingly realize or accept at this time post 2006. And whether you're aware of it or not—'Mother Earth' herself is rapidly/dramatically changing right under your feet—even as you read these very words. Look around on any given day and if one looks carefully at the environment—even the smallest changes will astound you. The magic of seeing nature's wonders at work demands respect!

Earth's calendar date in Spring 2007 will find our fragile blue world in dire crisis. Consider the facts of overpopulation/global warming/a badly depleted ozone layer/rain forest devastation/

uncontrollable wild fires/hurricanes/typhoons/storms/tornadoes bringing global flooding/tsunamis and droughts/Arctic-Antarctic meltdowns/mass extinctions of multiple plant and wildlife species/widespread famines/deadly disease outbreaks of animal and human origins/ever-increasing worldwide earthquake and volcanic activity—all of which are collectively taking a heavy toll on human, plant and animal life—not to mention billions upon billions of dollars in global property damage, lost wages/the economy and major consumer disruptions to the everyday needs of its citizens. Mother Nature takes no prisoners—gives no quarter—and remains uncontrollable.

And, what if most of the world's major governments already know/suspect/believe that planet Earth may well experience a major global catastrophe in the coming years? What if they are already quietly/secretly/expertly preparing for such an event? What if the present-day threat of global terrorism is only the deadly tip of a monster iceberg, this insidious/horrible threat that is no doubt deadly/corrupting/disruptive to the U.N.'s global community at large?

And, what if the many crazed terrorist organizations/networks also know of the potential for a future Planet-X scenario—thus driving them to wrest as much global control/dominance as possible before the real bottom drops out of their insidious/twisted schemes of death and destruction—as the entire planet is suddenly engulfed in a dire struggle for its very survival?

And, what if our government chooses to 'go it alone' in terms of our global politics/economics/ warfare—knowing forthright that America and its citizens must be ultimately responsible for themselves and their future should this celestial event occur in our lifetime? And, could 'all of the above' be just another exampled demonstration of a dire 'gloom and doom philosophy' —or is it an enlightened example of yet another 'prophetic warning' —one based upon the 'history of the past' meeting the 'reality of the future?'

Beginning with tropical storm *Bonnie (8/12/04)*, then followed by hurricanes *Charlie (a CAT/4 8/11-17/04/Frances (a CAT/5 9/1-7/04)/Ivan (a CAT/5 9/9-16/04)* and *Jeanne (a CAT/4 9/25-27/04)*—five of the deadliest tropical storms to trash Florida, North America and the Caribbean in this century 2004—proves the validity of our real-time 'X' hypothesis. *But it all too soon gets much worse.* An intensely bitter cold winter storm dumped ice/snow/frigid temperatures across three-quarters of America just as Christmas Eve/2004 arrived finding a frustrated nation on the move during the holidays with the threat of global terrorism following 9/11 adding to the misery!

Then on 26 December 2004 at exactly 7:00 AM, a mega-powerful 9.0 magnitude undersea earthquake exploded six miles deep along a 620-mile-long subduction plate beneath the Indian Ocean off the coast of North Sumatra near Malaysia. That quake created a series of 50-75 foot (7-story) killer tsunami waves traveling at speeds of 600 mph stalking much of SE Asia and its dozen Island nations killing well-over 285,000 people across thousands of miles of tropical beaches, island resorts, seaports and crowded SE Asian cities; a mega disaster that is only a small hint of what horrors are soon coming to visit our planet again as *Planet-X* returns.

This giant undersea quake event was so powerful that it actually disturbed Earth's rotation in orbit creating additional powerful earthquakes that were felt as far away as 3,500 miles from their epicenters. This 9.0 killer was confirmed as the fourth most powerful in the past century, equal to a million atomic bombs—soon followed by a massive 8.6 magnitude Iranian quake/

devastating 8.5 and 7.8 Japanese quakes—with all of them striking within a 45-day period. We now believe this massive up-tick in powerful 7/8/9.0 global earthquake activity may well-signal the start of *X's* impending gravitational influences affecting planet Earth far in advance of its anticipated arrival in 2009/2012.

Is this not further evidence that something very wrong is now afflicting planet Earth? And could 'global warming' also be a significant factor at play within this enigmatic equation? The Kyoto Accord remains a hotly debated issue here and abroad—with the U.S. still outside the reality box.

ON THE ABOVE HE IS MISTAKEN. THERE IS NO MAN-MADE GLOBAL WARMING!
IN FACT WE ARE NOW IN A COOLING TREND.

Years 2000-2006 claimed more than 795,000 lives worldwide as a direct result of these devastating *'Earth Changes'* keeping in mind that such global disasters are usually considered as being simply 'normal daily occurrences'—or ones not necessarily connected to a major 'global catastrophe,' a major 'pole flip,' or the near passage of a rogue 'celestial object.' And as each year passes, we continue witnessing the human death toll climbing ever higher with only a few global governmental action/reaction plans created/initiated/deployed across the planet to protect its unsuspecting citizens as the 'proverbial bottom drops out' across an unsuspecting world now facing an apocalyptic crisis of truly biblical proportions. *Is anybody out there listening??*

Few scientists today would reasonably argue that everything is *"OK / JUST FINE."* The reality of our current situation is that our world *IS CHANGING RAPIDLY* and on *A GRAND SCALE.*

So, if Earth is already changing, the primary questions should be: *Why, how much will it continue to change, and how fast will it do so??* Most people today believe that mankind's daily activities are responsible for the drastic environmental changes currently taking place on Earth, and to a certain extent, man's activities do play a significant role in what's happening. The hot-button topic of *WRONG.* global warming' is certainly an important factor we examine within this text. However, dear reader, this 'bigger cosmic picture' (of what's happening in outer space) reveals to us yet another mind-opening version of these dreadful 2009/2012 predictions.

Students of philosophy love stating that the only *'constant'* in the universe is *'change'* —and that conclusion bears truth. *'Change'* is a fact of life everywhere on this planet and everywhere in the visible universe. As modern-day astronomers peer outward into the vastness of space—they see *'changes'* taking place everywhere! Unfortunately, the Earth is not exempt/immune from these violent events—*'cosmic happenings'* both on a micro- (planetary) and macro- (universal) scale.

With the dawn of a new age rapidly approaching, tremendous changes are also occurring now within the everyday (personal) reality patterns/systems surrounding us. We owe it to ourselves to open up to the hidden answers/solutions resident within the human race and to act upon them responsibly. Remember, each of us is our own *"Reality Engineer"* solely responsible for our lives! UNDER GOD!

This new awareness of SELF's responsibility will hopefully eliminate much of today's negative atmosphere that promotes fear/doubt/envy/suspicion of the 'future,' whatever 'future' awaits us. As a nation and as a people, Americans have never fled from adversity—regardless of its nature —and in this case it's Mother Nature with all her unpredictable fury unleashed. We applaud *The Weather Channel's* weekly series, *It Could Happen Tomorrow,* detailing potential natural disasters striking this country as must see TV-fare for the entire family—forewarned is forearmed!

✴ POLITICS, NOT GOOD SCIENCE!

Our completed *Planet-X Earth Changes Survivor's Manual* duly explores why these *'Earth Changes'* are taking place at this critical juncture in mankind's odyssey through space/time/destiny. We also examine the many historical perspectives for these anticipated *'Earth Changes'*—and the prophetic warnings of such happenings and the physical mechanisms and science that govern them/the current signs and symptoms for such events/ current governmental preparations for these catastrophes, and how all of these details/dramas/consequences will ultimately affect America, the world, you/your loved ones post—2009-2012.

This was brought home to us with '05s two most recent category 4 and 5 hurricanes (recently experienced across the Gulf Coast region)—plus tropical storm *Ophelia* that tore across New England just before *Katrina* and *Rita* hit. Those recent events may well demonstrate that in all probability, it's highly unlikely either <u>FEMA</u> or <u>DHS</u> or <u>the military</u> will be able to actually save us, or even provide any meaningful assistance immediately following these dire *Planet-X* events, should they occur—*God forbid they should occur!!* And again, dear reader—please know that this *Manual* of disaster survivors' information provides an excellent guidebook in dealing with even a small local disaster—or worse—a major terrorist attack conducted here on U.S. soil.

In chapter ten we'll explore the many specific skills and items you should consider acquiring as preparation for protecting you and your family against catastrophic events. We certainly must acknowledge that once this disaster occurs—most, if not all, of the modern conveniences we take for granted everyday would be stripped away instantly—probably lasting for months to come. New Orleans proved that there's no water, gas, electricity, sewage lines, food, ATMs, police or fire protection—it's just you—and you alone against old Mother Nature and your fellow man!!

If these dire events do happen, everyone will be suddenly and profoundly responsible for all of his/her/family needs, i.e., food, water, fuel, protection, warmth, shelter, health care, money, etc.

As well meaning/dedicated/hard working and sincere our government agencies are (including FEMA/the Red Cross/Salvation Army/religious organizations and private donors), the ball could be dropped—*Katrina, Rita* and *New Orleans* proved it. *"And, dear citizen, too bad, we're sorry that we couldn't get to you in time. But, if you or your loved ones are dead, you're just dead— 100%—no Boardwalk or Park Place or Wal*Mart stores left standing—you're simply dead."*

And unfortunate as this reality appears—our government can't be held responsible for disasters. AMEN!

This may sound cold—but more than 1,300 Gulf Coast lives were lost, many hundreds because they *didn't* or *couldn't* respond in time to local mandatory evacuation orders that should've been issued 24 or more hours <u>before</u> it was way too late. This blame game has lots of people/places/ systems to attack—so let's not waste valuable time/resources/energy by assigning such culpability for our collective shortcomings as stated/debated/argued in countless TV news media reports.

Instead, let's look at these 'recent experiences' as being a 'learning curve into the future' and then apply those 'lessons' to a brighter and safer 'posterity.' These local and regional disasters could further be treated as solid/viable/timely 'learning tools' for whatever *BIG ONES* may be in store for our planet's future. A good motto from the past states: *If you want something done right—do it yourself.* And God only knows—maybe you could be the next hero of the day who saves one block or a whole community or a hundred thousand lives.

Much of the federal government/community preparedness information we've traditionally read advises that you should prepare yourself and family for up to four days—but in true reality, it could be for as long a period that it takes (days/weeks/months/years) for Mother Nature/society and your individual city/state governments to recover, returning to sanity. —*Will New Orleans and the Gulf Coast region ever appear the same again?* Most indicators point towards—NO!!

So please read chapters 7-9 carefully and you'll have an excellent idea of what it may take to prepare yourself/your family/loved ones and your personal situation to cope. In reality, however, there is no real way to tell you how to prepare for the future! *Only you can decide what is right for you and your family!* These chapters provide practical ideas/usable guidelines pointing you in the right direction. But ultimately it's you (and only you) who will have to be the final judge of what personal and family preventive actions 'to take' or 'not take.' As always, the choices are yours. *So—what are your psychic sensors telling you as you read this opening chapter?*

As I continue writing text for this Introduction it's now dinnertime Saturday night, 1 October 2005. The FOX cable news channel is all over the raging wildfires burning out of control in southern California. Having spent more than a dozen years living in the L.A. basin, I can't help but remember living through the devastating 6.8 Northridge earthquake (01/17/94) (that nearly took my life in Studio City), while also experiencing previous wildfires, landslides and flooding that every year seemingly threatens the San Fernando Valley and Santa Monica mountains.

Although unconfirmed—news commentaries are flying about that some—or most of those California wildfires might be arson, or even worse, terrorism related! It never seems to end!

There's also a nasty new Pacific hurricane, *Otis,* now bearing down on Mexico's Baja Peninsula, plus a brand new tropical Gulf depression across the Yucatan and then *Tami,* soon to be the 19ᵗʰ storm destined to become the next hurricane slamming into the weather-beaten Gulf of Mexico.

With all that said, please join us as we begin our *Return of Planet-X* account into the cosmic journey through Earth's space-time-continuum of *'Planetary Changes'* currently taking place. And let's discover if these 'global changes' might be the beginning episode of something much 'bigger' and 'more important' than any of us could possibly imagine here on planet Earth—2007. Poor old Noah understood the drill and was ready when the deluge came! —*Will you be?*

YES, I AM SPIRITUALLY PREPARED. THE ARK IS A TYPE OF THE RAPTURE.

True, the scientific debate over the reality of *Planet-X* continues with harsh rhetoric on all sides.

According to Charles Lada of the *Harvard-Smithsonian Center for Astrophysics—"Most stars found in our Milky Way galaxy are basically single stars, likely red dwarfs."* He argues that: *"Single stars are more likely than double stars to have planets, which means rogue planets may be very common in the galaxy."* During the last decade no less than seven new planets have been discovered in this sector of the galaxy and several of them may be connected to our solar system. Once again, the Internet is rife with this kind of NASA-supplied information that is quite fascinating, very entertaining and always educational—go NASA—the public loves it!!

The next question up for debate centers on Planet-X being a true planet or a spent brown dwarf star? We believe *'X'* is a brown dwarf and further—that *X* is a formidable component of our solar system and lastly, that we're about to experience *X's* return to the solar system in 2009/2012. This book fully explores all aspects of this theory from inside *X's* phenomena.

In 1982, NASA itself officially recognized the possibility of this legendary *Planet-X,* with an announcement that some sort of mystery object was really out there—far beyond the outermost planets. This NASA statement appears to confirm those ancient 6,000-year old Sumerian pictographic descriptions of our parent solar system containing at least one more planet the Sumerians called *"Nibiru"* —which means *"Planet of the Crossing."* Since then, NASA has been rather quiet about *X, which* suggests that something quite mysterious may yet be out there lurking in our collective future. All the indicators are now in place to confirm *X's* existence and only time will tell approaching (2009/2012), if the Sumerians/Mayans and Aztecs were indeed correct!

I BELIEVE THIS IS REAL, BUT WE CANNOT BE SURE OF THE TIMEFRAME.

Should *Planet-X* prove to be a reality—we believe that no other 'story' could ever be 'bigger' or ✳ more 'important.' Future generations in all countries and from all walks of life would forever be affected once again creating a new societal planetary system where the global playing field was drastically leveled again—a place where everybody begins anew as young 'children.' We do know that 'strange' and 'unexplainable' gaps occurred in recorded human history. *Why so?*

YES THERE IS SOMETHING BIGGER. JESUS CHRIST IS COMING BACK! ARE YOU READY

U.S. naturalist and author Henry David Thoreau once said: *"The cost of a thing is the amount of what I call life, which is required to be exchanged for it immediately, or in the long run."* He also stated: *"That if one advances confidently in the direction of his dreams, and endeavors to live the life which he has imagined, he will meet with success unexpected in common hours."*

We'd like to add a few words of wisdom on our own here: *"Life itself is a great canvas—throw all the paint on it you can!"* If life existing here on Earth is as unique as it appears to be in the universe, we must surely realize the limitless gifts we've been given. Every day of our lives is a truly precious commodity—something special to each one of us and in our own unique way! So please—let's not squander our precious 'cosmic gifts of time' on Earth.

We thank you, dear reader, for your valued time/interest/commitment and wish you and yours well on your reading adventure into *The Return of Planet-X.* We encourage and appreciate your loyal support by passing on word of this book's message whenever possible. And remember dear readers—*tempus fugit*… Make every week, day, moment and breath count—that's all we have.

WE ALSO HAVE JESUS AND ETERNAL LIFE!

As the famous futurist and psychic, Kreskin, once said: *"Everyone (it seems) is fascinated by the future, because that is where we'll spend the rest of our lives."*

For some unknown and truly arcane reason, the *Mayan Celestial Calendar Codex* inexplicably ends 21 December 2012. According to ancient Mayan cosmology—'time' as we know it on planet Earth will reach its climax on <u>that date</u>. *—And no one seems to know why!!* Written across the scroll of time and space, we believe *Planet-X* will return in 2012—*X's* power is real—its story is forever—and its time is soon.

And therein lies the greatest paradox of all times as we'll also explore the metaphysics of life.

Are all the stories about UFOs and ETs associated with the return of X true? And could the modern-day mythos surrounding the subject of UFOs, ET's, crashed flying saucers, human contactees/abductees, cattle mutilations, the wheat crop circle phenomenon, the Grays, U.S. astronaut encounters with UFOs on the moon, and those constant nagging rumors that many of the world's major governments are deliberately hiding, or at best covering up the truth about today's UFO/ET phenomenology—giving rise to further speculation that quite possibly the Biblical Nefilim (those ETs often associated with the subject of X's return)—may already be back on Earth a wee bit early perhaps—but back here nevertheless—and with a bold new 'game plan' for helping us out (via the Rapture scenario)—when Revelation's Wormwood returns again?

✱ NO SIR! THE RAPTURE IS REAL! NOT A "SCENARIO".

The mystical calendar date of 2012 is clearly spelled out by the majority of most native North/Central/South American Indian tribes and many Middle/Far-Eastern, Asiatic and Indian sub-cultures. *Could they all be wrong and could they all be based solely upon false supposition?*

With all that said, let's take a look now into the wonders of the universe (the totality of known and supposed objects and phenomena throughout space), as we begin our intrepid journey into discovering the age-old mysteries surrounding the legendary return of *Planet-X* in 2009/2012. The following discourse focuses its attention to the majesty of creation and mankind's future in it.

— *THE KNOWN UNIVERSE — NATURE'S ULTIMATE COSMIC DESIGN* —

Dear Reader, even a casual glance at the nighttime sky hints at a universe of stupendous beauty, size and awe. The unaided eye discerns far distant stars blazing in the vast blackness of space while taking in the majestic white arc seen high above Earth comprising the Milky Way galaxy. Powerful radio telescopes scanning the electromagnetic spectrum reveal a cosmos of intricate structure, unparalleled beauty and quite unimaginable violence. And the known universe, nature's ultimate cosmic design, is a virtual battleground of timeless forces shaping matter and releasing mega-quantities of energy eventually finding their way to Earth as light and other inter-active forms of solar radiation—the cosmic life force on planet Earth that is constantly/perpetually reshaping our existence 24/7/365.

Astronomers can now skillfully detect billions of distant galaxies but have catalogued only a few million that display a variety of shapes, sizes and complexity. Some are elliptical, while others, like our own Milky Way, have magnificent spiral arms. Galaxies tend to cluster on the periphery of gigantic voids in space, giving the universe a frothy and filamentary web-like structure. In addition, galaxies also cluster like fleets of ships, and other clusters of galaxies are found linked to superclusters in intricate and unusual filamentary chains.

Looking at the larger cosmic picture—clusters and superclusters also bound great voids of space that may account for most of the unknown volume of our known universe. The local Super-cluster (closest to Earth) consists of scores of other star arrays like the Virgo Cluster, some 50 million light years away. The Virgo constellation numbers approximately 200 bright galaxies, most of which dominates our local region of galactic space. Some astronomers believe that this Local Supercluster is connected to an even larger feature, the Great Attractor. Its gravitational pull is strong enough to slow—at least in its immediate vicinity—the expansion of the universe —quite possibly due to the presence of this mysterious/illusive dark matter.

✱ ATTESTED TO BY NUMEROUS SCRIPTURES. FAR TOO MANY TO BE LISTED HERE.

One way astronomers estimate density of cosmic/dark matter is by measuring the masses of rich star clusters. If the density is at or below a critical value, the universe will expand forever. However, if the existence of enough dark matter is confirmed—a contraction of the universe will eventually occur. Prime candidates for dark matter include neutrinos or other subatomic particles, objects of sub-stellar mass—similar to giant planets and miniature black holes.

What explains this remarkable cosmic architecture and design? If the original matter forged by the 'big bang' was spread smoothly on all scales, in what possible manner could galaxies and clusters of galaxies and superclusters have been formed? Early on there may have been freak perturbations crinkling up major parts of the universe, triggering the growth of selected structures. Astronomers are still searching for the unique imprint of these density irregularities in the microwave radiation left over from the much debated original 'big bang' event—happening perhaps 15-20 billion years ago.

Any primordial lumpiness would have eventually become amplified as gravity caused these denser regions in space to coalesce until billions of years later when distinct galaxies emerged. This infill of dark material might have been so concentrated that it created monstrous black holes —colossal gravitational gluttons with masses as large as a hundred million suns—mostly concentrated at the core centers of these galaxies. Astronomers have also found galaxies emitting huge bursts of powerful radio-wave energy—quite possibly the cosmic belching of an engorged black hole.

Did stars and galaxies develop first, then aggregate into clusters, superclusters, and ultimately supercluster complexes? Or did these large-scale structures form first, then become fragmented?

The answers lie both in the initial perturbations and the nature of an invisible, but pervasive, cosmic material. We have evidence that in addition to visible matter such as stars/gas, the universe contains vast quantities of a dark matter of unknown form presumably lingering over from the 'big bang' event.

However the galactic structuring of the cosmos occurred—our very existence depends on it for without galaxies there would be no stars, no planets—no life here on Earth, as we know it. The sun, holding our solar system together becomes the primary life-force energy governing our world. And *Planet-X*—Earth's eternal nemesis—may disturb our sun and the entire solar system as 2009 and 2012 brings *X* (once again) into our "earthian field of reality existence."

— *OUR GALACTIC JOURNEY BEGINS HERE IN PART ONE* —

WE ARE LIVING IN THE UNIVERSE'S PRIME, long after most of the exciting things have happened. Simply gaze into the sky on a starry night and you will see what appear to be only a few thousand glittering stars, most straddling the darkness of space in a great swath we call the Milky Way galaxy. This is all the ancients knew of the vast universe—oh, but there is much, much more to this mystery of the ages. One way the entire family can enjoy the magnificence of the heavens above—is by attending a local planetarium show usually displayed across a giant curved screen that will keep the family spellbound, educated and entertained for hours on end.

When projected across a flat disk for graphic purposes, the known universe appears to have a radius across of 20 billion light years. Most astronomers estimate the age of the universe to be between 15 and 20 billion years old. *(Possibly the end product of the original 'big bang'?)*

However long before Earth's 21ˢᵗ century—before our planet was populated with modern-day man—long before religion/science/technology reigned supreme here, certain ancient 6,000-year-old Sumerian pictographs revealed that our solar system contained one more mystery planet called "Marduk" —what they called "The Planet of the Crossing," a rogue brown dwarf body theoretically roaming the Sun's solar system returning time and time again to terrorize planet Earth and her inhabitants.

Fast-forwarding from the past: Gradually as telescopes of greater lens size/resolution/magnitude were developed, we discovered the vast islands of light called galaxies. All around the galaxies is a cool sea of microwaves—the echoing 'big bang'—from an estimated 15-20 billion years ago. Time, space and dark matter all appear to have their origins in this one explosive event from which the present-day universe has emerged—although still in a state of overall expansion —yet slowly cooling and continuously rarifying until one day it may all collapse back into itself or be swallowed up by a gigantic 'black hole.'

In the very beginning the universe was an inferno of radiation, way too not for any atoms to survive. In the first million years it cooled enough for the nuclei of the lightest elements to form. Only millions of years later would the cosmos be cool enough for whole atoms to appear, followed soon by simple molecules and, after more billions of years, the complex sequence of events that saw the condensation of material forming glittering stars that created swirling islands (of stars) into their respective galaxies of light strewn across the visible horizon throughout infinity.

Then, after more billions of years with the appearance of stable environments, mysterious processes we still do not understand nurtured the complicated products of biochemistry. *But how and why did this elaborate sequence of events begin? And what do modern-day cosmologists have to tell us about the origin of the Milky Way—only one of 100 million charted galaxies to date? Could mankind be so egotistical to believe that we humans exist in the universe all alone?*

Answers to these seminal questions help us to unravel the mystical reality of *Planet-X* so let's begin at the beginning by asking a classic question: *As human beings are we truly all alone out there locked into the solar system and Milky Way spinning through space into a vast universe?*

— *OUR STAR TREK ADVENTURE CONTINUES WITH PART TWO* —

More than four decades ago, during the month of November 1961, an unofficial TOP-SECRET meeting was held by many leading government sponsored scientists and researchers. This unprecedented technical and scientific conclave was convened at the National Radio Astronomy Observatory in Green Bank, West Virginia. It was designed to estimate the number of existing planets in our galaxy that might contain the necessary components/potential life zones, to host and maintain sentient intelligent life. These leading scientific experts in the fields of astronomy, astrophysics and science—secretly concluded that there is probably a minimum potential of between 40-50 million intelligence-based extraterrestrial civilizations lying scattered across the vast Milky Way—our local galactic system estimated to be 150,000 light years across at its core center. *What would happen on Earth if one day out of the blue, a fleet of extraterrestrial space-craft openly landed on the White House lawn—mass hysteria or a warm friendly handshake?*

One of the major conclusions they reached was that there is ever-increasing evidence that some of these outer space civilizations may be presently visiting the earth, and in some cases carrying out sophisticated research and telepathic communications with earthian inhabitants—just as they have done in the near and distant past. This conclusion and its relevant connection to *Planet-X* (with its attendant Sumerian cosmology mentioned earlier in this chapter)—is carefully explored in our research *Manual*.

However, in order to more fully comprehend the implications of this 'ET-Hypothesis' and the search for conscious life on other worlds, we must first understand and then explore the unknown vastness of the universe. Consider for a moment the mind-boggling statistics comprising the scope and apparent construction of the cosmos, as we now understand it—early into the 21st century. *How is it that 'Hollywood' seems to 'get it' regarding films like Star Trek and Star Wars?*

One of the ways modern-day astronomers approach the study of the heavens is in terms of measuring (in light-year numbers), the relative distances between planets, suns and their star system's parent galaxy control points. It's accomplished by using a measurement-based calculation applied to Albert Einstein's complicated 'theoretical properties of light' formula.

A light-year is the calibrated unit of length used in interstellar astronomy equal to the total distance light travels in one year (in a vacuo) at the rate of 186,300 miles per second or approximately six trillion (6,000,000,000,000) miles. Any star that's located several thousand light-years away from Earth is only visible by the arrival of its light source. And that star's light was radiated long, long before the advent of any form or discipline of planetary history was known or recorded about our solar system by primitive humankind (a relative real-time period believed to be less than 15,000 years).

So let's take a fascinating journey into the boundless wonders of the heavens suspected of containing an inestimable number of billions, perhaps trillions of celestial objects. And in whatever direction we gaze into deep space, we detect galaxies, clusters of galaxies, superclusters and local superclusters comprising gigantic star groups—all moving away from us across an elliptical plane.

Towards the observable horizon we see quasars—quasi-stellar objects—notwithstanding the uniform glow of radiation from the 'big bang.' On the largest scale the universe looks the same in every direction. Quasars, the most distant celestial objects yet observed, are among the most curious and the most energetic. Each of the brightest quasars emits the combined energy of hundreds of galaxies—yet flow from an energy volume far smaller than that of our local Milky Way. *If the universe is as boundless and vast as it appears why would we be surprised to find evidence of extraterrestrial life visiting Earth—or are they already here in surprising numbers?*

Each is perhaps the violent nucleus of a distant galaxy and may contain a massive black hole. Thought to be a theoretical massive object, they once formed at the beginning of the universe or by the gravitational collapse of a star exploding as a supernova whose own gravitational field is so intense that no electromagnetic radiation can escape—a mega-void into which all things vanish permanently with no evidence, lingering traces, history or possible chance of recovery.

And as the universe expands—the farthest quasars appear to be rushing 'away' at more than 90 per cent the speed of light, with their light traveling billions of years to reach us. These quasars have evolved during many billions of years and we can only guess at what they are like today.

Also visible at great distances are radio galaxies. And unlike quasars, whose dazzling brightness obscures their stars, radio galaxies reveal enough to allow astronomers to estimate the numbers and ages of the stars contained within them. To look at such objects is to see the wonder of the ultimate universe within its youth some 15-20 billion years ago.

— OUR COSMIC MYSTERY CONTINUES WITH PART THREE —

Our galaxy was thought to be the entire universe until significant discoveries were made in the early 20th century. Today we know it is only one of many billions of existing galaxies—a gravitationally bound rotating congregation of thousands of billions of stars. The Milky Way's oval central bulge glows with the light of much older, redder stars and may also harbor a gigantic hungry black hole.

The Milky Way, its sister galaxy Andromeda (M31), and the smaller M33 are both fast-rotating spirals. M32 and NGC-205 are considered elliptical galaxies consisting mainly of older stars.

The Large and Small Magellanic clouds appear to be irregular shaped galaxies, described as haze in the southern sky by Ferdinand Magellan's gallant crew in 1520 and noted in detail in the Captain's log book. Situated some 150,000 light-years away, these two Magellanic clouds appear to be the nearest galaxies to ours and may well be satellites of our own local system. Our parent galaxy most resembles the great spiral nebula M131 in Andromeda—a breathtakingly beautiful galaxy some two million light years away and twice the size of our own Milky Way.

It should be noted that these two sister galaxies are also held together by gravity and orbit one another, even as the universe continues its timeless expansion outward towards infinity.

Globular clusters contain our galaxy's oldest stars—most estimated to be 10-15 million years old. Even now hot gas and dust condensing in the spiral arms are themselves forming brand-new "baby stars." Located all alone in a far-distant outlaying arm—our own sun's solar system circles the galaxy's center about every 20 million years, traveling at 220km/sec or 355mi/sec.

Astronomers now believe that the large halo enveloping our galaxy's central disc contains very old stars and invisible dark matter. Beyond the expansive Milky Way there are galaxies stretching out and expanding in every direction. Our own system is part of a loosely bound cluster containing some 30 galaxies, called the Local Group in astronomical terms. Our galaxy rotates in locomotion like a giant whirlpool and the myriad of stars move around its center control point just as the nine known planets, asteroids, space debris and comets rotate around our central sun system.

Those stars nearest the center point rotate much faster than those located further out. Our sun, all the visible stars, and billions of other star groups form/design the immense flat spiral profile of our galaxy—much of which is seen only through powerful telescopes based on land and in space.

This stupendous star system is believed to be about 150,000 light years in diameter, but less than 7,000 light years thick in our location. Our sun is close to the equatorial (long) plane of the galaxy, but still located well off to one side. The galactic center or nucleus of this star system appears to be about 26,000 light-years away, pointing towards the constellation Sagittarius.

Our galaxy and the universe itself is so vast that its absolute limits are virtually unknown—a hundred billion stars and suns of many differing types ranging from red supergiants (less dense than the Earth's atmosphere), to immense white-hot dwarfs hundreds of times denser than lead, and lastly the lesser known variety called red or brown dwarf suns—those unignited/failed stars containing a relatively small mass and low or average luminosity as our sun.

Planet-X is believed to be a spent brown dwarf—one that is connected to our solar system—but little understood, nor accepted by most astronomers. Brown dwarf stars will be discussed in the complete body of this project with special emphasis placed on one particular 'brown dwarf star' *Planet-X*—referred to in the Bible as *"Wormwood."*
   (Note: See Book of Revelation, Chapter 8, verses 10-13.)

Conservative astronomical estimates place about 200 billion stars in the Milky Way alone, with half of these systems judged to be binaries (double stars), which would practically preclude the actual presence of an organized system of planets, or for that matter, any kind of planets stable enough to create, foster and sustain ecological life-support systems as we know them to function.

Of the five billion non-binary (single) stars, most, if not all of them, would qualify to become host suns to other solar systems with anywhere from one to 25 planets revolving around a central luminary body (like our sun). Out of the remaining potential of 100 billion suns, about half of these would be classified as F, G, or K stars (an alphabetical arrangement according to temperature and size). The sun holding together our vast solar system is a typical G-rated ordinary yellowish star with an absolute magnitude of 5 and is estimated to be approximately 4-5 billion years old; F and K-rated stars are hotter and cooler respectively. Our solar system is believed to be approximately 5-10 billion years old.

Light from the Sun takes a full eight minutes to cross the huge gulf of deep space to Earth—96 million miles or 150 million km. Light travels five hours longer to reach Pluto and after about four years four months, it touches Alpha Centauri, our sun's nearest stellar neighbor, 40 trillion km or 4.3 light years away. If other sentient life is proven to exist in the universe—the Alpha Centauri star system is widely believed by many cosmologists to be our nearest intelligence-based neighbor. A super-advanced ET civilization could traverse space without limitations.

Information gleaned from a variety of UFO/ET contactees appears to confirm this hypothesis. If they're right, of course, this again changes the chessboard of facts regarding the reality of ETs.

Alpha Centauri is a multiple system with three stars locked by gravity in orbit around each other. Many such stars are binary or multiple-grouped and modern-day astronomers like the American ("SETI-Project"--Search for Extraterrestrial Intelligence) and the Russian group—the ("CETI Project" --Communication with Extraterrestrial Intelligence), are both currently searching the heavens for possible stars with planetary systems similar to our own and the ET evidence to support it. *So how is it possible that we haven't, as yet, found any convincing UFO/ET proof?*

However, all life-bearing planets must orbit in a biosphere range (an absolute gradient ranging from about 100° Fahrenheit below zero to 150° above zero) —not too close and not too far from their host suns, or else they won't have liquid water seas or the proper temperature range(s) to support life—human or otherwise. In our solar system, only Earth and Mars exist within this specific life zone with planet Venus a borderline case and probably much too hot to support life.

Therefore our 50-billion Sol-like suns in the Milky Way would, on the average, render us a total of say 500 billion planets of which only 50 billion (one per sun) would be in an Earth-like life-sustaining range. The rest is astronomical caution, the usual leaning over backwards to be ultra-conservative (thereby unrealistic), and thus display no wild ET suppositions/estimates/theories.

On the average, primary stars are usually spaced multiple light years apart. However, there are some star clusters that appear to be much more closely packed toward their centers that actually contain perhaps half a million stars in all. It's now believed a number of these X-factored life-bearing/life sustaining planets may revolve around many of those far-distant star groups.

Our solar system is located approximately halfway from the center of our galaxy. And around our sun revolve the nine known planets beginning with: Mercury, Venus, Earth/Moon, Mars, Jupiter, Saturn, Uranus, Neptune and Pluto, with their 32 moon-like satellites, the mysterious Asteroid Belt located between Mars and Jupiter, and thousands of smaller asteroids with swarms of errant comets and meteors. *Planet-X*—mentioned as *"Wormwood"* in the Christian Bible—may be the missing-link component—a failed 'brown dwarf star' that was quite possibly a sister sun/companion to our own.

— *OUR INTREPID SPACE ODYSSEY CONTINUES IN PART FOUR* —

We've just completed a fascinating excursion into the boundless wonders of the cosmos containing an inestimable number of millions, perhaps billions of giant galaxies, constellations, suns, planets, moons, asteroids, comets, meteors and other marvels and mysteries of cosmic creation.

Zooming back to our space home, Earth, hurtling through the heavens with a physical speed in motion (traveling at 18.5 miles per second within its yearly orbit around the sun), we find the Earth's relative mass is 1/329,390ths that of the Sun's, or 5.887×10^{21} tons, with an average 'real density' measurement of approximately 5.6 times that of ordinary sea water. Earth itself is not great in physical size—but is the only life-bearing orb known to exist in our solar system to date.

Earth's average distance from the sun during its annual trek is 92,900,000 miles. It rotates on its axis from west to east—once in each sidereal day (a period of 23 hours and 56 minutes) as it revolves completely around the sun once a year along its slightly elliptical path. The axis of the Earth (that imaginary line joining the North and South poles about which it rotates) is inclined to the plane of its orbit (the ecliptic—the intersecting plane of Earth's solar orbit with the celestial sphere) at about 23 degrees, 27 minutes.

Existing as an oblate spheroid, planet Earth, as seen from deep space, appears to be slightly flattened at the poles and bulging noticeably along her equatorial plane. The polar diameter is 7,900 miles and its equatorial diameter is 7,926.7 miles. The area of its exposed land surface is approximately 57.5 million square miles while the total area of the world's oceans is believed to be 139.4 million square miles or roughly 70% of Earth's total surface.

And her highest land peak is Mt. Everest situated within Tibet's Himalayas mountain range with the incredible elevation of 29,141 feet, while her greatest ocean depth is the Swire Deep, some 35,640 feet down located deep within the Marianas Trench in the Mariana Islands, a group of 15 tropical islands in the Western Pacific due east of the Philippines.

The Earth is completely enveloped by a gaseous atmosphere at least 600 miles high, and all that is needed to continually operate its unique set of life-support systems is the Sun's perpetual thermonuclear heat and light machine—without which our verdant planet would quickly be reduced to a beautiful blue ball of frozen ice and snow perhaps a mile or more deep.

Earth is the 'Home Planet' of mankind and self-exists as a living spiritual entity often described as a 'closed ecosystem.' This is reflected in the fact that our living world is completely self-contained, capable of totally regenerating/maintaining/supporting all of its own primary ecological support systems. However, as we strive to learn more about our highly sensitive and vulnerable planet, we must also understand that its continuing ability to cleanse and regenerate itself has some very obvious and fixed limitations—our 21st century society with its U.N. politics, wars, global warming and our grossly mismanaged natural resource policies—notwithstanding!

Recent data obtained from radioactive rock indicates that planet Earth is at least 2,260,000,000 years old and may be as much as twice that age. This wonderful globe has endured for some 5.5 billion years, but its future is now clouded by mankind's reckless ways; his overpopulation, *✶* continuous wars, global pollution of water/air/land, wasted resources and the wanton destruction of her natural wildlife habitats and numerous forms of the local/exotic wildlife inhabiting them.

But this is only the proverbial 'tip of the iceberg.' Consider what happens to the normal ebb and flow of earth's life-support systems if something really catastrophic would one day suddenly disrupt our planet—something like a massive asteroid or a series of comets—even the unthinkable scenario of a rogue celestial object/a smoldering brown dwarf star (*like Wormwood*) tearing through our solar system causing major planetary disruptions—and here on earth a major pole shift—with all the continents moving/shifting—2,000-foot tsunamis slamming against and then obliterating the world's seacoasts, also causing global earthquakes, belching volcanoes with huge cinder cones that soon blacken the skies creating the 24-hour night...

I DISAGREE.

Ohh, and it only gets worse from there… If *Planet-X* does arrive in 2009/2012—all bets are off!

If films like *The Day After Tomorrow, Armageddon, The Perfect Storm, Twister, Core, Super Volcano, Deep Impact* and *The Left Behind* series caught your attention—then what the planet experienced in those fictional Hollywood stories is merely a cakewalk into tomorrow's reality.

THE LEFT BEHIND SERIES IS BIBLICALLY BASED, NOT HOLLYWOOD FICTION!

Impossible, unthinkable and beyond the scope of even science fiction?? Think again!! And that dear reader is the purposeful intention/scope/mission of this assignment. What you are about to personally experience by reading this *Manual* will greatly affect your individual conscious, sub-conscious, intellectual and dream-state reality producing systems! It was carefully designed to!

This seminal work respectfully addresses itself to the President's White House science staff exploring certain impending questions/conclusions/directives surrounding the ongoing welfare of mankind and his continued existence here—the future of our world—spaceship Earth. This book is not meant to frighten its readers—but more so to challenge them to fully explore its contents—thus allowing or readers to make correct decisions about their futures and their loved ones.

I myself am a UFO/ET contactee since age 11—given the ET assignment of writing a number of books on topic—and this is just one of them offering our readers a glimpse into Earth's future.

— *OUR COSMOGONIC EXPLORATION CONCLUDES WITH PART FIVE* —

Earth—the continuing saga of a small watery planet seemingly lost in space on an intrepid journey hurtling through the vastness of the Milky Way galaxy. This is the reality that we—the human race—presently find ourselves experiencing upon this world in 2006—the 21ˢᵗ century.

We are an unpredictable war-like species desperately clinging to the surface of this tiny blue orb totally preoccupied with our day-to-day activities. Our work schedules, school, sleeping, meals, chores, paying bills, vacations, enjoying the holidays, raising kids and combating global terror-ism—all keep us busy from cradle to grave. We live in a frantic world where most people are so 'caught up' in meeting life's immediate demands that we seldom pause to take notice of the 'grand universe' through which our planet is passing in terms of cosmic time and circumstance.

Anyone who does pause for a moment peering into the cosmos and infinity through <u>the lens of a telescope</u>—quickly discovers that the vastness of space is a void filled with continuous creation and incredible beauty. Throughout the visible universe, we witness vast clouds of gas and dust birthing new stars, enormous stellar swarms majestically spiraling into newly formed galaxies and countless other examples of cosmic creation taking place on a truly 'divine' scale.

But the universe also has a much more sinister side—a truly 'destructive tendency' permeating the very fabric/structure of this cosmically 'divine' landscape. Anyone peering <u>through the same telescope</u> also discovers a universe filled with dreaded cataclysmic events graded on an equally 'divine' scale. It's quite possible that Earth itself is the end product of some dramatic 'cosmic destiny' that's cast beyond our human comprehension. We seem to take for granted our very

*NOT GOOD. ET IS NOT WHO MOST PEOPLE THINK HE IS!

'existence' and how fragile 'it' might be! *Looking up into the heavens on any given star-filled night have you ever wondered why we're here and what it's all about? Have you ever wondered about your individual role in life, how it came to be, and what's next should it suddenly change?*

Everywhere we look throughout the cosmos, we see whole galaxies colliding with one another—wiping out countless worlds in enormous collisions with black holes tearing apart stars with such overpowering gravitational force—not even 'light' can escape their destruction; comets crashing into planets with such ferocity that if the same objects were to hit planet Earth—they would instantly pulverize our world into countless pieces and there are stars exploding in gigantic events called 'supernovas'—releasing tremendous energy on or at almost incomprehensible radiation levels. The act of 'creation' appears to be an ongoing/never ending cosmic phenomenon.

(Note: Most major cities host state-of-the-art planetariums offering programs on the cosmos.)

As previously mentioned, the universe through which the human race travels is truly a wondrous mix of ongoing creation and destruction! One doesn't have to peer through the lens of a telescope to witness this phenomenal mixture of creative/destructive forces at work. Our very own planet provides us sober testimony to the reality of just how simultaneously beautiful and sinister old 'mother nature' can be. *Are there established 'timelines' in Earthian history to help us demonstrate this premise?* Let's take a look and see…!

As an ancient civilization (8th to 5th centuries BC >>> to the early 2nd / until the late >>> 1st century BC), Sumerian, Babylonian and Mesopotamian cultures had themselves already conquered mathematics, science, astronomy and the conceptual art of research/writing. But more importantly they had also mastered the complex understanding of 'time' and 'timelines'—thereby seemingly mastering the phenomena of 'time' itself.

Let us now continue this section of our research *Manual* by first examining the concept of 'time' and 'timelines,' since the principal objective of our mission is to establish the 'reality' and 'timeline' of event-evidence to formulate *Planet-X's* next rendezvous date with our solar system.

According to the *American Heritage Dictionary,* the meaning of the word 'time' (as a noun) is defined as: *"a non-spatial continuum in which events occur in apparently irreversible succession from the past—to the present—to the future."* Next, the meaning of the word 'line' (for practical purposes here), is defined in geometry as: *"a set of points (x - y) that satisfy the linear equation (ax+by+c=0), where a and b are not both zero."* In other words, more simply stated—a line could be described as being: *"a form of linear measurement or a (set) continuous straight mark—cast in a one-dimension perspective."*

Example: /// begin a line – [------- a timeline -------] – end a line ///

Now let's combine these two words into one thus producing a new word in the English language —'timeline.' Now we may define this new word 'timeline' as being:

A non-spatial continuum – i.e. BC = [------- a timeline to -------] = AD

A 'timeline' occurs in which 'events' happen in apparently irreversible succession moving from the past – to the present – to the future creating an unbroken linear measurement or straight line of events from some unknown point in the past—BC---through the present---AD—to some unknown point in the future. Let us hypothecate our *Planet-X* timeline BCE [-----to-----] AD enigma, as exampled by the demise of Atlantis in 12,500 BCE [jumping] >>> 14,506 years forward to present-day 2006. (The *Planet-X* timeline BCE [----14,506 years----] to 2006 AD.)

Many eastern and middle-eastern philosophies profess a belief system that hypothecates that time is the 'mind of space'—and—'space' is the 'body of time.' The axiom of time itself allows us to establish when an 'event' occurs in relation to other 'events,' and its measurement involves the establishment of the 'timeline' scale to which these 'events' may then be 'referred to' or be 'pinpointed against.' Earth's 'timeline' of existence is believed to be 4.5 – 6 billion (timeline) years. (*Note: There's hot debate in scientific circles about the exact age of Earth's solar system*).

The concept of 'timelines' plays a curious role in the reality of people's lives here on planet Earth—since it is also hypothecated 'scientifically' that the measurement of 'time' and 'time-lines' may be an exclusive component for all that is strictly 'Earthian in nature' and therefore—that 'time' / 'timelines' do not actually exist or apply within the 'pure vacuity of space' once we leave the 'physical environment' of mother Earth.

If the axiom of Earthian 'timelines' is true—they become the essential ingredients of measure against which all other measurements are calculated—everything from the beating of human hearts to the felling of great empires and governments; to the growth of children or economies and the deaths of disease epidemics; to the decline of the human spirit and the morality content of our 21st century societies; and, quite possibly, the very end of our present-day humanity if *Wormwood (Planet-X)* maintains its deadly rendezvous date with Earth in 2009 and again in 2012. Let us now begin to connect the *Planet-X* dots based upon history and present-day media reports and commentaries…

— *PLANET-X's 2007 TIMELINE OF BACKGROUND SCIENCE AND RESEARCH* —

Long before Earth's 21st century, before our planet was populated with modern-day man and before religion/science/technology reigned supreme here—our *Planet-X* roamed the Sun's solar system, a rogue celestial body (believed to be a huge {Jupiter-sized} brown dwarf star), one that the ancient Sumerians called Marduk. *(NOTE: A brown dwarf is a cold-dark star that is too small to initiate its nuclear reactions that generate sufficient heat and light to become a genuine luminary body like our Sun.)* ✳ IT WAS CALLED MARDUK BY THE BABYLONIANS, NIBIRU BY THE SUMERIANS.

Ancient 6,000-year-old Sumerian pictographs and secret documents reveal that our solar system had at least one more planet—what they called The Planet of the Crossing, Planet-X. You see, 'X' is unique in that we believe it maintains a most unusual orbit around our Sun—an exagger-ated ellipse taking approximately 3,600 years to complete its long-predicted orbital return rip-ping through the solar system. (Note: Many Internet websites suggest that Planet-X be referred to as Planet Nibiru—one particular theory about 'X' that we don't ascribe to. This work should be considered solely on its own merit and the research conducted herein is totally independent.)

OK. POSSIBLY COULD BE RIGHT. IN ANY CASE, A MINOR POINT.

During this brown dwarf's apogee (furthest phase of its fixed orbit), its distance is so great from Earth that '*X's*' natural reflected sunlight can't be detected—not even by the Hubble Space Telescope, one of NASA's most powerful satellite-based eyes-in-space orbiting Earth.

— Citing the New York Times: 9 June 1982 —

"Something out there beyond the farthest reaches of the known solar system seems to be tugging at Uranus and Neptune, some gravitational force keeps perturbing these two giant planets, causing irregularities in their orbits. The force suggests a presence far away/unseen, a large object that may be the long-sought Planet-X. The last time a serious search of the skies was made led to the discovery in 1930 of Pluto, the ninth planet.

"But the story begins more than a century before that, after the discovery of Uranus in 1781 by the English astronomer and musician William Herschel. Until then, the planetary system seemed to end with Saturn. Today, scientists accept theories concerning plate tectonics. There are articles and studies showing that, at one time, all of the Earth's continents were on one side of the planet. What the stories don't explore is the question: If all the continents were on one side, what happened to the other side? The other side has been described as being a tremendous gap, matching the Sumerian story of how the Earth came about. The Sumerians said Earth was really only half a planet called Tiamat, which broke up in a collision with Marduk.

"The discovery of new planets has, in the last two hundred years, owed more to the science of mathematics than it does to the design of bigger and better telescopes. The unaccounted-for mathematical irregularities in the orbits of the outer planets have prompted astronomers to speculate upon the existence of a further, yet undiscovered planet. These astronomers are so certain of this other planet's existence that they have already named it 'Planet-X –the 12th Planet.'

"Recent calculations by the United States Naval Observatory have confirmed the orbital perturb-bation exhibited by Uranus and Neptune, which Dr. Thomas C. Van Flandern, an astronomer at the Naval Observatory, says could be explained by a "single undiscovered planet." He and a trusted colleague, Dr. Richard Harrington, calculate this 12th Planet (quite possibly Marduk?) should be two to five times more massive than the earth and have a highly elliptical orbit that takes it some 5-billion miles beyond that of Pluto.

"In 1982, NASA themselves official recognized the possibility of a Planet-X, with an announce-ment later on that some sort of mystery object is really there, far beyond the outer-most solar system planets. And then one year later, the newly launched IRAS (infrared Astronomical Satellite) spotted a large mysterious object in the depths of space. The Washington Post summarized an interview with the chief IRAS scientist from JPL in California, quoting him as follows:

"A heavenly body possibly as large as the giant planet Jupiter, and possibly so close to Earth that it would be part of this solar system, has been found in the direction of the constellation Orion by an orbiting Earth telescope... All I can say is that we don't know what it is!"...stated Gerry Neugebauer, Chief IRAS scientist.

"The 6,000 year old Sumerian descriptions of our solar system include one more planet they called "Marduk," which means "Planet of the Crossing." And the description of this planet by the Sumerians matches precisely the specifications of Planet-X, which is currently being sought by astronomers in the depths of our own solar system. Why has Planet-X not been seen in recent times? Views from modern and ancient astronomy, which both suggest a highly elliptical, comet-like orbit takes Planet-X into the depths of space well beyond the orbit of Pluto (and back again).

We discovered Pluto with our telescopes just recently in 1930. Is it not possible that there are other forces at work in our solar system besides the nine planets we know? Yes! The Sumerian descriptions of our Solar System are being confirmed with modern advances in science. This article demonstrates actual diagrams from Sumerian times and how their accuracy for describing the known planets in ancient times is overwhelming proof that the extraterrestrial hypothesis was at work for the ancient Sumerians and many other cultures of their time!" (END Times Article.)

— *A RESEARCH TIMELINE REGARDING THE ONGOING HUNT FOR PLANET-X* —

In 1841, John Couch Adams began investigating the, by then, quite large residuals in the motion of Uranus, and in 1845 Urban LeVerrier also started investigating them. Adams presented two different solutions to the *Planet-X* problem, assuming that the deviations were caused by powerful electromagnetic fields created by the gravitational waves from an unknown planet.

Sept. 30, 1846—one week after the discovery of Neptune, LeVerrier declared that there might still be another unknown/undiscovered planet out there. On October 10, Neptune's large moon, Triton, was discovered which yielded an easy way to accurately determine the mass of Neptune, which turned out to be 2% larger than expected from its perturbations upon Uranus.

Another attempt to find a trans-Neptunian planet was done in 1877 by David Todd. He used a "graphical method" and despite the inconclusiveness of the residuals of Uranus, he derived elements for a trans-Neptunian planet: mean distance 52 a.u., 35 years, magnitude fainter than 13.

In 1879, Camille Flammaion added yet another hint as to the existence of a *Planet-X* beyond Neptune: the aphelia of periodic comets tend to cluster around the orbits of major planets. Jupiter has the greatest share of such comets and Saturn, Uranus, Neptune each have a few.

Percival Lowell, most well known as a proponent for canals on Mars, built a private observatory in Flagstaff, AZ, at the end of the 19th century. Lowell called his hypothetical planet, *Planet-X* and performed several searches for it without success. Lowell's first search for *Planet-X* came to an end in 1909, but in 1913 he began a second search with a new prediction of *Planet-X: epoch 1850-01-01, mean long 11.67 deg., perih. Long 186, eccentricity 0.228, mean dist 47.5 a.u. long arc node 110.99 deg., inclination 7.30 deg., mass 1/21000 solar masses.* Lowell and others searched in vain for this *Planet-X*. It is ironical that in <u>this very same year</u>, 1915, two faint images of Pluto were first recorded at Lowell Observatory, although they were never recognized as such until after the official discovery of Pluto in 1930.

We would like to point out that this tome does not attempt to compete in <u>theory</u>, <u>format</u> or <u>storyline</u>, with other existing books dealing with *Planet-X*. Our work constitutes a fresh new look into an ongoing mystery that has been plaguing planet Earth for millions, perhaps billions, of years. We would also like to acknowledge the fact that there are many and varied sources of Internet information regarding the topic of *Planet-X* and we respect these differing viewpoints.

The working theorem for our *'The Return of Planet-X'* theory centers itself on numerous historical narratives (of which there are many thousands to examine), offering us 'in exquisite detail' an ongoing saga of massive *Planetary Changes* shaping/reshaping the topographical and historical perspectives of humanity as these repetitive periods of *Earth Change* events affected planet Earth. It's our considered opinion that the 'facts' stated here more than support our case!

Beginning with the ancient Sumerians and other Middle Eastern cultures from the past, it appears that *Planet-X* may well be Earth's ongoing nemesis scheduled to return again in 2009/2012. If we're right about *X's* 3,600-year repetition theory—now you'll know the rest of that story!

Our 'working hypothesis/theory' for the return of *Planet-X* is predicated solely upon our own research and writing, not to be confused with the abundance of other *'X'* material available.

The research process to create this book required me to read a hundred other books with most, if not all of them, dealing with the geophysical history of the planet, mankind's perilous existence upon his world, and science's well-meaning (but flawed) attempts to record and relate the human experience through time and our evolution of spirit and circumstance.

As you read the following chapters one thing becomes crystal clear. Either everything we've come to know about the past is true—or the ongoing history of mankind has been (in part) a fabrication. 'Something' appears drastically wrong with Mother Earth and we believe she's trying to tell us what that 'something' is!! Two questions logically arise: *Is anybody listening? And do we care?*

We find it curious that most network, cable and general information newscasts presented on the *Weather Channel* appear to focus on the most 'extreme weather patterns' and/or the current 'natural disasters' (du jour), plaguing the nation and world at large. If the news isn't about tornadoes, thunderstorms and wildfires—it's about flash flooding, landslides, levies breaking and the government's dire warnings that the upcoming 2006 hurricane season is just about upon us.

Even more curious is the fact that former FEMA Director, Michael Brown, (who resigned his post following the harsh and often critical distain for his handling the devastating *Katrina* and *Rita* Gulf Coast hurricane disasters), publicly stated that FEMA (now under new stewardship) was ill-equipped, under-staffed and under-funded to handle this year's hurricane schedule.

It's been a rocky road but certainly one well worth the effort and we believe that 'time' itself will soon become the new 'currency' of Earth's cosmic future—whether we're ready to accept it or not!

(Editor's note: The ageless Planet-X 'timeline' continues as we zero in on 2009 and 2012 and what could be the beginning of our newest 21ˢᵗ century Wormwood 'timeline enigma.' We invite our readers to explore this book—keeping an open mind to its subject and the future of Earth).

— CHAPTER ONE —

MESSAGES FROM THE PAST

In beginning our exploration of the concept that a large 'celestial object' passes the Earth, periodically affecting our planet's rotation in space, reaping havoc and destruction in its wake— we must ask ourselves if any ancient civilizations ever recorded such an event in the distant past. Surely if such catastrophic events have taken place on Earth before—ancient civilizations would have left an historic record of these events in their 'written histories' and 'oral traditions' that have been handed down to us through the ages.

As we will soon discover, almost every civilization from the ancient world has left us historic records/legends detailing cataclysmic events that have periodically visited the Earth. Throughout these historical records there are numerous accounts of entire civilizations, vast island regions, even whole continents that have been suddenly and violently destroyed by periodic global cataclysms. Often these ancient accounts mention an altering of our planet's rotation, as a strange 'celestial comet' is simultaneously seen hovering in the skies.

There is an old saying, *"To learn about your future you need only study your past."* Let us now take a look at some of these ancient cataclysmic accounts in order to understand what they might tell us about our own near future.

Solon, Atlantis and the ancient Egyptians

Atlantis, the 'lost continent'—its very name conjures up mysterious and legendary visions of a civilization that long ago vanished beneath the ocean waves. Whether Atlantis existed or not is beyond the scope of this book; what has been recorded about the destruction of Atlantis however, is important for us to briefly examine.

Solon was a Greek historian, philosopher and statesmen, who lived in Athens between 639-559 BC, a little over 2500 years ago and was credited with being the wisest of the 'seven sages' of ancient Greece.[1] It is from the writings of Solon (and his interactions with the ancient Egyptians) that the first historical accounts of world cataclysms, including the destruction of Atlantis comes to us through the ages.

While on an extended stay in Egypt, Solon had many opportunities to study and learn from its priests. Ancient Egypt was a very advanced culture for its day and history has documented many Greek scholars who traveled to Egypt in order to study in their temples.

On one such visit, the Egyptian priests conveyed to Solon the following story of the demise of Atlantis and the 'recurring' cataclysm that caused it:

> *O Solon, Solon, you Hellenes (Greeks) are but children. There is no old doctrine handed down among you by ancient traditions or any science, which is hoary with age, and I will tell you the reason behind this. There have been and will be again—many destructions of mankind out of many causes, the greatest having been brought about by 'earth-fire' and 'inundation.'*

> *Whereas you (the Greeks) and other nations did not keep imperishable records of Atlantis we (the Egyptians) did. And then, after a long period of time, the 'usual inundation' visits (the Earth) like a pestilence and leaves only those of you who are destitute of letters and education. And thus you have to 'begin over again as children' and know nothing of what happened in ancient times either among us or among yourselves (about Earth's history).[2]*

Solon then went on to share with the Egyptian priests his knowledge of Greek history (including their account of the great flood), to which the Egyptians replied:

> *As for those genealogies of yours which you have related to us, they are no better than tales of children, for in the first place, you remember one deluge (inundation) only, whereas there were a number of them. And in the next place there dwelt in your land, which you do not know, the fairest and noblest race of men that ever lived of which you (the Greeks) are but a seed or remnant. And you did not know this because for many generations the survivors of that (last) destruction made no records.[3]*

In other words, what the ancient Egyptian priests were telling the Greek historian Solon was that many civilizations throughout the history of our planet have been 'wiped out' by a recurring catastrophe. These civilization-ending cataclysms not only destroyed many ancient cultures, but their written records and recorded history as well—forcing them to literally "*start over again as children.*" This destruction of past civilizations and their 'recorded histories' is one of the main reasons why our 'modern-day' society has so little remembrance of these past global cataclysms.

The Egyptians then went on to tell Solon about one such destroyed civilization called Atlantis, which at one time was a series of magnificent islands that sat in the Atlantic ocean, out beyond the pillars of Hercules (the Straits of Gibraltar). The priests said that the Atlanteans had become a rich and powerful civilization, but their success had made them arrogant and war-like. The Atlanteans started to systematically invade the other cultures of the Mediterranean and at one time had extended their advances to the very borders of Egypt itself.

But then the "*usual inundation*" struck the Earth, involving great earthquakes and floods. With little warning, Atlantis was engulfed by the ravages of the ocean, slipping beneath the waves—never to be seen or heard from again!

The Egyptian priests, surprised by Solon's ignorance of the destruction of Atlantis went on to say:

> *The catastrophe must have escaped the notice of future generations because as a result of the devastation, for many generations, the survivors died with no power to express themselves in writing.[4]*

These ancient Egyptian priests also related to Solon that the destruction of Atlantis took place 'violently' and 'suddenly' as in a 'fortnight':

> *The islands disappeared! All disappeared, due to earthquakes and floods in a 'grievous day and night.'* [5]

The accounts of Solon and the demise of Atlantis are not the only ancient records of massive cataclysms that the Egyptians have left us. In 1828, the Museum of Leiden in the Netherlands, obtained a copy of an ancient text known as the *Ipuwer Papyrus*.[6] This text describes a massive cataclysm that struck Egypt thousands of years ago and sent this remarkably organized civilization into total disarray.

Some excerpts from the *Ipuwer Papyrus* are as follows:

> *Plague is throughout the land...blood is everywhere. The land turns round [over] as does a potter's wheel...Earth turned upside down...land upside down. Human beings thirst after water...what shall we do? All is ruin.*

> *Cattle are left to stray, and there is none to gather them together...Trees are destroyed...No fruits, no herbs are found...Grain has perished on every side...that has perished which yesterday was seen. The land is left to its weariness like the cutting of flax.*

> *Gates, columns, and wall are consumed by fire. The sky is in confusion...and the fire ran along upon the ground. Lower Egypt weeps...the towns are destroyed. Upper Egypt has become waste...all is ruin. The residence is overturned in a minute.*[7]

A. H. Gardiner, in his book *Admonitions of an Egyptian Sage from a Hieratic Papyrus in Leiden;* states: "*It is no merely local disturbance that is here described, but a great and overwhelming national disaster.*" [8]

What type of extreme geophysical event could have lead to such a massively destructive situation? When this ancient manuscript says that the Earth 'turned upside down' and that the 'sky was in confusion'—could it be referring to a time when the Earth altered its rotation in space? Whatever geologic catastrophe the *Ipuwer Papyrus* is describing, laid waste to an entire nation, destroying its cities, agriculture and even its very infrastructure.

In reality, ancient Egypt went through not one, but several total collapses of its civilization throughout its long history. Each one of these collapses was so severe that it took the Egyptian civilization hundreds of years to recover.

A tablet was found at *El Arish*, a monument erected in ancient times between Judea and Egypt. On this tablet was inscribed a hieroglyphic message referring to a time when a great geologic disaster struck ancient Egypt. The tablet read:

> *The land (Egypt) was in great affliction, evil fell upon the Earth...there was a great upheaval in all the residence...nobody could leave the palace during the nine days of upheaval. There was such a tempest that neither men nor gods could see the faces of those beside them.*[9]

Other cultures have also recorded great cataclysms striking ancient Egypt in the past. Certain legends of the Old Testament known as the Ginsberg's Legends state:

> *An exceedingly strong wind endured seven days. On the fourth, fifth and sixth day, the darkness was so dense that they (the people of Egypt) could not stir from their places. The darkness was of such a nature that it could not be dispelled by artificial means. The light of the fire was either extinguished by the violence of the storm, or else it was made invisible and swallowed up in the density of the darkness (possibly due to volcanic ash or blowing dust). Nothing could be discerned...none were able to speak or hear, thus they remained overwhelmed by the affliction.*[10]

Once again, we must ask ourselves what type of massive disaster could have caused such physical disruption to strike ancient Egypt?

The answer is actually handed down to us by the ancient Egyptians themselves. The ancient Egyptians steadfastly maintained that these 'periodic' planetary catastrophes involved, or where associated with, a 'shifting' of the Earth's rotation in space.

Over two thousand years ago the noted Greek historian Herodotus reported:

> *The scribes of Egypt maintained that 'four times' the Earth in its movements reversed itself so that the Sun shifted and rose where it formerly set, and set where it formerly rose.*[11]

The Latin author Pomponius Mela, from the first century wrote:

> *The Egyptians pride themselves on being the most ancient people in the world. In their authentic annals...one may read that since they have been in existence, the course of the stars has changed direction 'four' times, and that the Sun has set twice in the part of the sky where it now rises today.*[12]

Keep in mind that as the Earth alters its axis of rotation, it looks (to an observer standing on the Earth), like the Sun and stars have changed their direction of travel. In reality, it's not the stars that have changed direction, but the rotation of the planet itself.

There are many other examples indicating the ancient Egyptians believed the Earth has altered its rotation in the past. For example, the noted ancient Egyptian architect, 'Senmut,' had one-half of the ceiling of his tomb painted with the constellations as they appear today and the other half of the ceiling painted with the constellations in reverse, as they would have appeared before our planet's last pole shift. This is a strong piece of physical evidence suggesting that the ancient Egyptians truly believed the 'rotational axis' of the Earth has shifted in the past.[13]

Other accounts from ancient Egypt talk about the Earth being plunged into *"days of darkness"* [14] and *"years of famine."* [15] Some of these ancient historic accounts also mention erratic movement of the Sun or Moon in the sky, followed by great 'quaking' of the Earth—once again indicating a shifting of our planet's axis of rotation.

Other ancient accounts recorded strange 'celestial objects' that appeared in the skies over Egypt—reaping havoc, chaos and misery across the land.

Pliney, the Elder, a first-century savant, wrote:

> *A 'terrible comet' was seen by the people of Ethiopia and Egypt...it had a fiery appearance and 'twisted like a coil' and it was very grim to behold. It was not really a 'star' so much as what might be called a ball of fire; it was not of fiery (color), but of 'bloody red.'* [16]

What type of strange 'red' celestial object could this ancient wise sage have been describing? Certainly nothing that has ever been seen in our skies during modern-day times!

Another ancient Greek returning from Egypt wrote:

> *There appeared a 'comet' (in ancient times over Egypt) and there was a conflict between the forces of heaven and of Earth.* [17]

Ancient Egyptian history clearly recalls a time (thousands of years ago) when the Earth shifted on its axis of rotation, causing great geological upheavals throughout the land. *Could this shifting of our planet's rotation and the accompanying geophysical changes to Earth have been ultimately triggered by the passage of this 'terrible' red comet?*

The ancient historian, Pliny the Elder, described this 'terrible comet' seen by the people of Ethiopia and Egypt saying it *"twisted like a coil"* in the sky. One could also say twisting like a 'snake' or a 'serpent' in the sky!

The Egyptians themselves actually left numerous depictions of a 'cosmic serpent' in their literature—often depicted as 'flying' in the sky. The Egyptians attributed this image of a 'serpent in the sky' to the forces of universal destruction and chaos. [18]

Could these Egyptian depictions of a 'cosmic serpent' have been a representation of the 'terrible comet' talked about so frequently by the historians of the ancient world?

In actuality, most ancient civilizations had an irrational fear of 'comets' or 'serpents in the sky.' These objects were universally seen as the harbingers of destruction and ruin. *The question is why?* As far as we know today, comets are merely dirty 'cosmic snowballs' that entail little to worry about. *Did an ancient event involving an object (that at least looked like a comet) once ravage these ancient cultures? Did this catastrophic event forever change the way ancient societies viewed these otherwise harmless objects? And could Wormwood's passing have caused those 'biblical miracles' to flow from the rod of Moses during the Jewish exodus from Egypt?*

Many modern-day scholars have tried to dismiss these ancient accounts of 'terrible comets' or 'serpents in the sky' as being meaningless mythology, silly legends or even fairy tales. But the ancient Egyptians and the other cultures around them—steadfastly maintained that these events actually happened and were an important part of their civilization's history.

As we shall see, many other ancient cultures also maintained similar 'historical accounts.'

The ancient Greeks

After many years of study in Egypt, the scholars of ancient Greece (such as Solon) began to piece together a better understanding of the true 'cataclysmic history' of Earth. Keep in mind that the people we think of as 'the ancient Greeks' were themselves relative newcomers to the ancient world. Once Greece matured as a nation, they left their own 'written accounts' of these past cataclysmic events. Like the ancient Egyptians, many of these Greek accounts involved great geologic upheavals caused by a 'shifting' or 'tipping' of the Earth's rotation in space.

Of all the scholars and historians of ancient Greece, none were more famous that Plato. By the time of his death in 348 BC, he had recorded and preserved an impressive amount of ancient history. In his classic work, *Timaeus*, Plato describes a great cataclysm that took place in ancient times in which the Earth moved, *"forwards and backwards, and again to right and left, and upwards and downwards, wandering every way in all six directions."* [19]

Plato was not describing a normal earthquake; for he goes on to say the destruction was so great throughout the world—that whole continents, such as Atlantis, sank beneath the sea in a catastrophic series of geophysical events.

Plato also records a time when the Earth altered its rotation, rearranging the normal course of the heavens and causing great death and destruction throughout the world:

> *The Sun and the stars once rose in the west and set in the east (the opposite of today)...and of all changes of the heavenly motions, we may consider this to be the greatest and most complete...and it may be supposed to result in the greatest changes to human beings who (were) the inhabitants of the world at that time...few survivors of the race are (were) left.* [20]

In his famous work *Politicus*, Plato went on to say:

> *I mean in the rising and settling of the Sun and other heavenly bodies, how in those times they used to set where they now rise and used to rise where they now set...at certain periods the (Earth) has its present circular motion, and at other periods it revolves in the reverse direction...of all the changes which take place in the heavens this reversal is the greatest and the most complete.* [21]

Other excerpts from Plato's *Politicus* talking about the prior destruction of mankind state:

The world turning round with a sudden shock, having received an opposite impulse at both ends was shaken by a mighty earthquake, producing a new destruction of all manner of animals.[22]

Like the ancient Egyptians, the ancient Greeks clearly describe several episodes in the past when the Earth altered its rotation, spinning on a new geographic axis and making it seem as if the heavens were moving differently.

Many other ancient scholars also believed that the Earth's rotation had in fact shifted numerous times in the past. These same scholars believed that the passage of a large 'celestial object' was the actual cause of these rotational changes.

Well-respected ancient scholars including Lydus, Servius, Hephaestion, and Junctinus all believed that the shifting of Earth's axis of rotation was brought about by the appearance of a large 'celestial object.' These ancient authors repeatedly mention a 'terrible comet' they called *'Typhon'* which had a 'bloody' appearance in the sky and caused great destruction to Earth—involving plagues, evils and hunger.[23]

The ancient Greek historian Plutarch, who also had direct contact with the priests of Egypt and had the opportunity to personally study at the great library of Alexandria—believed that the ancient world had been 'repeatedly' thrown into chaos by the appearance of a large comet called *Typhon*—also referred to as *"the destructive, diseased and disorderly."* [24]

In his writings, Plutarch describes a time when the terrible comet *Typhon* caused a shifting of the Earth's axis of rotation—resulting in a change of the Sun's normal celestial path and a permanent altering of the seasons. Plutarch states:

> *The thickened air concealed the heaven(s) from view, and the stars were confused with disorderly huddle of fire and moisture and violent fluxions of winds. The Sun was not fixed to an unwandering and certain course, so as to distinguish orient and occident, nor did he (the Sun) bring back the seasons in order.[25]*

The classical Greek writer, Hesiod, also described a great planetary conflagration and flood brought about thousands of years ago by the appearance of the celestial body known as *Typhon*.[26] The appearance of this terrible 'celestial object' cause the Earth to 'wobble' in a strange manner and ultimately shift its axis of rotation, causing great destruction and a total altering of the Earth's normal seasons.

It is directly from this 'celestial object' known as *Typhon* that we currently derive the word 'typhoon'—used to describe powerful and destructive tropical storms.

The ancient historian, Diodorus Siculus, who lived in the reign of Julius Caesar (between 60 and 30 BC) also recorded a time in the remote past when a terrible celestial object called *'Aegis'* flew through the sky, raining fire upon the Earth—setting forests and cities ablaze from India to Europe.[27] *Could all of these noted historians have been wrong in reporting those same 'Earth changing' events in time? And why is it that mankind never seems to learn much from his past?*

The ancient Greeks and Egyptians clearly possessed 'historical records' of several great cataclysms that struck our planet in the past. Cataclysms that were so severe, they altered the very rotation of the Earth; making the Moon, Sun and stars appear to move strangely in the sky.

Was the passage of this 'bloody comet,' known as 'Typhon' or 'Aegis,' the ultimate cause of these catastrophic changes to Earth?

Could our society, with all of its modern technology, be largely ignorant of these ancient accounts—accounts that were at one time in our distant past considered common knowledge?

If one reads the historic accounts that these ancient cultures have left us—the answer is a resounding 'yes' on all accounts!

Once again, the ancient Greeks and Egyptians seem to indicate in their written histories that these catastrophes happened 'suddenly' and with little 'advance' warning. These catastrophes were cyclic in nature however, and happened on a fixed timetable, one that was predictable if a civilization's history could remain intact long enough to understand this great 'cosmic cycle' of destruction.

The civilizations of South and Central America

The Maya

The *Mayan* civilization flourished in Central America for thousands of years. This advanced civilization was renown for its culture, art, architecture and astronomy. What were most important to the Maya, however, were astronomy and their understanding of the great 'destructive cycles' of Earth. In fact, the Maya were literally 'obsessed' with astronomy and the movements of planetary bodies. The famed/sacred 'Mayan Codex Calendar' for example, has astonished modern astronomers with its incredible celestial accuracy/sophistication of design.

In their book, *The Mayan Prophecies,* authors Adrian Gilbert and Maurice Cotterell, unlock many of the secrets of this lost civilization including their 'obsession' with astronomy and celestial mechanics.

Gilbert and Maurice go on to write:

> *The Maya...of Central America were very aware of the heavens around them and the movements of the planets. Often doorways or roof-combs, which are a particular feature of classic Maya temples, were placed in such a way that they could mark the rising, culmination or setting of particular stars. They were especially interested in the movements of the Pleiades star-cluster as well as those wandering planets Mercury, Venus, Mars and Jupiter. Needless to say they made close observations of the Sun and Moon, and this enabled them to predict eclipses (incredibly) accurately.*[28]

Did their flawless astronomy predict the Mayan master calendar ending on 21 December 2012?

The *Popul Vuh*, one of the most sacred texts of the Maya, also recalls the sophistication of ancient Mayan astronomy. The *Popul Vuh* states:

> *They (the ancient Maya) saw, and could see instantly far, they succeeded in knowing all that there is in the world (and in the heavens). When they looked, instantly they saw all around them and they contemplated in turn the 'arch of heaven' and the 'round face of the Earth.' The things hidden (in the distance) they saw all, without first having to move; at once they saw the world...great was their wisdom.*[29]

In other words, Mayan astronomers were so advanced, that even thousands of years ago they knew the "*arch of heaven*" (the curvature of space) and the "*round face of the Earth.*"

Why were the ancient Maya so 'obsessed' with astronomy and the motions of the heavens? What information were they seeking—and why?

Like the ancient Egyptians and Greeks, the Maya also recorded a cyclical cataclysm that revisits our planet on a 'regular' and 'predictable' timetable. By studying and keeping careful track of the celestial order of things, the Maya believed they could anticipate the next great global cataclysm.

The *Popul Vuh,* the sacred text of the Mayan, also records a great disaster that struck the ancient Maya and involved a thick dust that fell night and day from heaven—darkening the Earth. This event was accompanied by great fires and tremendous earthquakes, from which only a few (men) escaped to tell about. These events subsequently prompted a 'great flood' that consumed the Earth.

The *Popul Vuh* goes on to say:

> *They (the Maya) were inundated by a thick resin/dust that fell from the sky... The face of the Earth was obscured and a rain of darkness began, raining day and night... and there was a great din of fire above their heads. The men were seen running about, pushing themselves, full of despair; they tried to climb on top of their houses but the houses would collapse making them fall to the Earth; they tried to climb the trees but the trees would shake them far away, then they tried to enter the caves but the caves would close before them.*[30]

According to the Maya, their civilization recorded not 'one,' but 'four' of these great global cataclysms. Each one of these global catastrophes virtually 'wiped-out' the Mayan civilization, leaving only a tattered remnant to carry on and rebuild their society.[31]

The Maya believed that each of these global cataclysms took place approximately four thousand years apart.[32] As an interesting side note, the Maya also believed that the last world-ending catastrophe took place about four thousand years ago—and today, it appears we may be very close to yet another catastrophic event in 2012! Hopefully, this global happening won't repeat itself in our lifetime—but if it does we owe it to ourselves to be ready/aware/prepared to cope!

In the conclusion of their book, Gilbert and Maurice summarized that the Maya believed Earth undergoes a periodic shifting in its geophysical poles—commonly known as a 'pole shift.'

A 'pole shift' is a phenomenon wherein the planet tilts on its axis of rotation—like a spinning top that falls onto its side. These 'pole shifts' are accompanied by violent tectonic activity (earthquakes), volcanic eruptions, windstorms, global fires, floods and great hurricanes.

As the 'poles' of the Earth shift, the normal movement of the heavens also becomes completely altered. Keep in mind, it's not the heavens that change, it's the way in which the Earth is rotating—making it only look as if the Moon, Sun and stars are moving strangely.

The Maya retain an ancient legend that talks about the survivors of the last 'pole shift,' and how they tried to guess the 'new direction' in which the Sun would rise once the dust (thrown up by this catastrophe), began to settle and the sky could once again be seen.

The Maya state:

> *It was not known from where the new Sun would appear. They looked in all directions, but they were unable to say where the Sun would rise. Some thought...the north... others...the south. Some, however, fixed their attention on the orient (east), and maintained that the Sun would come from there. It was their opinion that proved to be correct.*[33]

Like the ancient Egyptians and Greeks, the Maya also seem to have associated 'pole shifts' with abnormal celestial phenomena. And like the Egyptians, the 'sky-serpent' played a key role in Mayan culture and was tied into their concepts of planetary destruction and cataclysmic celestial events.

The Maya were not the only ancient civilization of South and Central America to have recorded past global catastrophes involving 'pole shifts' and strange 'sky serpents.' As we shall see the Inca, Aztec, Toltec, Hopi, Zuni and many other Native American Indian cultures all recorded similar stories of how planet Earth has been violently destroyed numerous times in the past.

All of these remaining civilizations today displayed a strong 'doomsday anxiety,' believing that these catastrophic events will take place once again—in 'our' near future. A clear example of this doomsday anxiety can be observed in the behavior of the Aztecs.

The Aztecs

Upon arriving in the New World several hundred years ago, the Spanish explorer, Hernando Cortez, was greeted by the Aztec king, Montezuma, and given a large gold disk with elaborately carved symbols on it. These symbols represented the cyclical ages of the Aztecs and their predecessors. *Was there a deeper more complex motive hidden in Montezuma's gift that Cortez failed to understand—and did it have something to do with their 'doomsday anxiety complex' connected to their anticipated cyclical return of that certain 'great destroyer' from the heavens?*

According to the Aztecs, we are currently living in the 'fifth age' or 'world'—the preceding 'four' ages having all been 'wiped-out' by a recurring global calamity which strikes the Earth every few thousand years, and involves the destructive forces of water, wind, great earthquakes, violent storms and an altering of the stars in the sky (describing a pole shift).

The Aztecs remember not only 'four' prior destructions of the Earth, but greatly 'feared' another.[34] The Aztecs were so afraid of another global disaster taking place that they would rush into the hills on a specific evening once every 52 years and nervously wait for the nighttime sky to alter its course. The Franciscan missionary, Bernarddino Sahagun, observed one of these paranoid spectacles and wrote:

> *At the end of each 52-year period the Indians (Aztecs) were mortally afraid. On the last night of the old cycle, terrified the world was about to end (again), and the Sun not rise, they took to the hills. There they studied the skies, waiting for the Pleiades star-cluster to reach the southern meridian. When it carried on moving (and did not change course in the sky) there was great rejoicing, for they knew they would be safe for at least another 52 years.[35]*

Like the ancient Egyptians, Greeks and Maya, the Aztecs were waiting for another 'pole shift'—tipping the Earth in space and making the Pleiades star-cluster appear to change directions in the nighttime sky. When the stars did not alter their normal course, the Aztecs celebrated with great festivals and knew they would be safe—at least for the time being!

The Inca

The Spanish priest, Francisco de Avila, recorded the following Inca account of a great disaster that struck their civilization in the past—and how their current civilization came to be:

> *In ancient times this world was in danger of disappearing...the mother sea had decided to overflow, to fall down like a waterfall (upon the land). The ancient ones knew that soon the great ocean would be here and the whole world would be flooded (the usual inundation mentioned by the Egyptians). We will go somewhere to escape (they said). Let us go to the mountains; there we must save ourselves. And after five days the waters began to recede and dry up. The sea retreated...it killed all the men (Inca). Only he of the mountain survived...to multiply, and by him exists mankind today.[36]*

The Inca therefore built the remarkable city called *Machu Picchu*, which sits over 10,000 feet above sea level. This extraordinary city was built at this site because the Inca believe this is where mankind found refuge and escaped destruction during the great flood. *Machu Picchu* also served as a celestial observatory and a fortress/sanctuary protecting their priests from the next impending disaster.[37]

What type of flood could have been so severe that the Inca felt it necessary to construct a sanctuary over 10,000 feet above sea level in order to provide protection/safety from the ocean? And why did they believe that this 'city in the sky' would have saved them from the great red comet?

The Inca, like the Aztecs and Maya, clearly had a 'doomsday anxiety' over changes in the normal motion of the heavens. Because of this fear of another worldwide disaster, the Inca engaged in numerous 'ceremonial rituals' in order to keep the Sun, Moon and stars traveling in their 'present course' and not change direction—thereby bringing destruction to the world once again.

Many other cultures from South and Central America also recorded great planetary disasters in their civilization's history. These same cultures also possess a powerful 'doomsday anxiety' regarding a future repeat of these destructive episodes.

According to the *Larousse Encyclopedia of Mythology,* the Araucanian Indians of Chile believe that a great (global) earthquake once caused the sea to come inland and flood the world. During this flood only a few Indians survived by taking refuge on a high mountain called *Thegtheg.* This belief is so prevalent and powerful—that even today the Araucanian Indians rush into the mountains with their possessions every time there is an earthquake.[38]

The Toltec Indians believed fierce winds swept across the Earth during the past 'four' destructions of mankind. These winds were so fierce that they at first picked up sand, rocks, water and finally trees, houses and human beings. This was followed by a rain of 'fire and gravel' that fell from the sky. Frightening 'celestial' phenomena and a great flood then plunged the Earth into prolonged darkness.[39]

The Vilela Indians of Argentina have an account that tells how their ancient ancestors were enveloped in darkness that lasted for an entire year (most likely due to volcanic ash in the atmosphere). The starvation that resulted was so severe that the Vilela resorted to eating their dogs.[40] The Toba Indians also have an oral tradition that talks about a great darkness that fell over the world—bringing starvation and a great flood.[41]

The ancient cultures of Brazil recall a time when:

> *The lightning's flashed and the thunders roared terribly and all were afraid. Then the heaven(s) burst and the fragments fell down and killed everything and everybody. Heaven and Earth changed places (pole shift). Nothing that had life was left upon the Earth.*[42]

The Chane Indians of Bolivia, the Bogotá Indians of Colombia, the Guarao Indians of Venezuela and many other South American tribes, all have similar catastrophic legends and 'doomsday' anxieties.[43]

It is interesting just how many ancient cultures from around the world have recorded a great cataclysm in the distant past. These same cultures today carry a deep-seated fear of a recurring global catastrophe and express this 'doomsday anxiety' in defensive behavior or religious ritual practices—which in themselves—offer vital evidence to the nature and reality of the original cataclysms.

With all of this mounting evidence to consider, should we wisely dismiss 'Wormwood's threat'?

Some massive and devastating event brought this deep-seated fear and anxiety into the psyche of these ancient cultures, affecting them in ways we cannot appreciate or even fully understand today.

Like the ancient Egyptians and Greeks, the ancient cultures of South and Central America experienced extreme geophysical conditions brought about by a shifting of the Earth's poles. *Were these events so traumatic that they left an emotional scar on these people; a scar that even after thousands of years has not fully healed?*

Are these 'pole shifts' cyclical in nature, bringing death and destruction to mankind—over and over again through the millennia? Could it be that these periodic 'pole shifts' are ultimately triggered by the passage of the 'terrible comet' talked about so frequently by the ancient Greeks and Egyptians?

As we have already mentioned, like the ancient Egyptians, Greeks and others, 'celestial objects' played an important role in the cultures of South and Central America. Many of these ancient cultures also spoke of a 'cloud-serpent' or 'sky-serpent' that heralded 'unbridled warfare' and 'planetary destruction' by its appearance. It may be from these early legends that the famed 'feathered serpent' (associated with both destruction and regeneration) arose.[44]

As we shall see, many other ancient cultures also recorded similar catastrophic events, including most Native American tribes of North America.

Ancient cultures of North America

The Hopi

Hopi Indian mythology speaks of modern-day humans living in the 'fourth' world, the preceding 'three' worlds all having been destroyed by a recurring catastrophe. According to the Hopi, these past global cataclysms caused land and water to 'exchange' places (the usual inundation) when the 'poles' of the Earth 'flipped' and the following events took place:

> *The world then teetered off balance, spun around crazily, and rolled over twice. Mountains plunged into the seas and the land was inundated... With a great shudder... the planet began rotating again.*[45]

Once again, like so many other cultures, the Hopi believe that a shifting of the Earth's poles destroyed these preceding worlds. According to the Hopi, the present *'fourth world'* will also be destroyed by a 'pole shift' in the very near future.

The Hopi also go on to say that these past worlds were completely destroyed immediately after the appearance of a large 'celestial object' they called, "Saquasohah." [46]

Could 'Saquasohah' also be the same celestial object the ancient Greeks and Egyptians called 'Typhon' or the 'terrible comet' that had a fiery, blood-red appearance and 'twisted' like a coil in the sky?

The Cherokee

The sacred teachings of the Cherokee people encompass many thousands of years, during which they have recorded 'four' great upheavals of the Earth. The fact that the Cherokee traditions speak of the 'great flood' and other geological changes brought on by a passing comet, should come as no surprise, since almost every other ancient cultural heritage also recorded legends of this same cataclysm.

In his book, *Voices Of Our Ancestors,* Dhyani Ywahoo, keeper of the Cherokee oral teachings, explains that the Cherokee believe the past destructions of the Earth were caused by a 'pole shift,' distorting the Earth's crust and causing great planetary flooding and volcanic activity. All of these geologic events were brought on by the passage of a strange comet. Mankind only survived these global upheavals by 'living underground' for many years after the passage of this object.[47]

The Cherokee, like the Hopi, believe that the Earth is quickly heading towards another one of these 'cosmic' encounters—and subsequently—another 'pole shift.'

Other accounts from North America

The Pawnee Indians of North America recall a time when the north and south polar stars, 'changed places' or 'went to visit each other,' once again indicating a shifting of the Earth's axis of rotation. They believed that a similar type of 'pole shift' would happen again at the end of the 'current cycle' when there would be a great flood and the stars would alter their course and fall down to Earth again.[48]

The Bella Coola and Tacullies Indians of British Colombia, the Takahlis of the Pacific Northwest, the Ojibwas, the Wyandots and Dogrib of Alberta, the Ute of Utah and dozens of other North American tribes, all have similar stories about great catastrophic events that virtually wiped out their ancestors—often repeatedly throughout the millennia.[49]

Many of these tribes also believe that a 'cosmic serpent' known as *Yurlunggu*, a large 'celestial object' that periodically passed our planet, is ultimately responsible for these past cataclysms.[50]

The native tribes of Southern California describe a 'Sun-like' object called *Ta-vi* that roams the skies and on occasion, comes so close to the Earth in its heavenly wanderings, that our planet is scorched by its passage.[51]

Other native Tribes of North American recall past world catastrophes being caused by a 'celestial monster.' This 'cosmic demon' that appeared in the sky was so terrifying and brought such horror to these ancient tribes, they depicted it as a large menacing 'bat' with its wings spread open.[52] As we shall continue to see, many other civilizations throughout the ancient world recorded these same planetary catastrophes, which seem to be triggered by the appearance of this strange 'red' celestial object. *And is this 'collective terror consciousness' symptomatic of a much 'deeper problem' that has been plaguing mankind since humans first walked this planet?*

The ancient Chinese

One of the oldest historical cultures on Earth are the Chinese. Like other ancient civilizations from around the world the Chinese have maintained their culture for thousands of years, and like so many other cultures, they possess ancient records of great cataclysms 'wiping out' their ancestors.

The ancient Chinese emperor Yahou, who is believed to have lived around the time of the last great cataclysm, (about 3600 to 4000 years ago), recorded the following account of strange cosmic events:

> *At that time the miracle is said to have happened that the Sun during a span of ten days did not set, the forests were ignited and a multitude of abominable vermin were brought forth. In the lifetime of Yahou, the Sun did not set for ten days and the entire land was flooded (inundated).*
>
> *An immense wave that 'reached the sky' fell down on the land of China. The water was well up on the high mountains, and the foothills could not be seen at all.*[53]

Could this ancient account of the Sun not setting be describing a time when the rotation of the Earth actually stopped—making the Sun appear as if it was motionless in the sky?

Another ancient Chinese work consisting of 4,320 volumes, tells of a time when mankind rebelled against the gods and the universe fell into great disorder:

> *The planets altered their courses. The sky sank lower towards the north. The Sun, Moon, and stars changed their motions. The Earth fell to pieces and the waters in its bosom rushed upwards with great violence that overflowed the Earth.*[54]

Other historical accounts from ancient China recall a time when a great celestial battle raged in the sky, causing a massive calamity to befall Earth:

> *Heaven's pillars broke and the bonds with Earth were ruptured. Heaven leaned over to the northwest, hence the Sun, Moon, stars and planets were shifted, and Earth became empty.*[55]

Many other ancient Chinese legends also refer to 'days of darkness' when the light of the Sun vanished from the sky—while still other accounts speak of the Sun not setting for long periods of time. Such stories often refer to an 'age of horror' when the Earth stopped in its rotation—causing continuous darkness during the 'long night' or continuous daylight during the 'long day.'

Once again, could these ancient accounts be referring to a time when the Earth altered its rotation in space, causing the Sun, Moon and stars to "change their motions" in the heavens?

Our in-depth research of the far-eastern cultures appears to indicate that they may have recorded some of the most accurate and timely accounts of past global disasters hidden in their history.

The sacred Buddhist text of the ancient orient known as the *Visuddhi-Magga*, also speaks of a "*sequence of ages*," separated from one another by great global catastrophes. These ages are terminated every few thousand years by destructive forces involving fire/water/violent winds.[56] Interestingly enough, many of these ancient Chinese accounts also talk about the appearance of a large 'red comet' or a 'second sun' appearing in the heavens immediately before the onset of these catastrophic events. The Chinese refer to the periodic arrival of this celestial object as the terrifying return of the "*Red Dragon*," and say that once it appears, there is no distinction between day and night—and the World is enveloped by heat, smoke and fire.[57]

Like many other ancient cultures, the Chinese have recorded great catastrophic events that struck our planet many thousands of years ago. *Could the incredible similarities in all of these ancient accounts (from around the world) be a mere coincidence—or do they all point to a 'pole shift?'*

Ancient Europe

For thousands of years the Teutonic tribes of ancient Europe flourished over an area from what is today Germany extending north to Scandinavia. These ancient tribes, generally known as the Norse, preserved a rich and detailed history of a time when the Earth was shaken and most of its inhabitants perished. One such account from these tribes tells how a 'celestial monster' chased the Sun—trying to take possession of it. Finally the monster caught the Sun and the world was plunged into total chaos:

> *(The Sun's) bright rays were one by one extinguished. It took on a 'blood-red' hue, and then entirely disappeared. Thereafter the world was enveloped in a hideous winter. Snowstorms descended from all points of the horizon. War broke out all over the Earth. Brother slew brother…it was a time when men were no better than wolves, eager to destroy each other. Soon the World was going to sink into the abyss of nothingness.*

> *The World trembled…Mountains crumbled or split from top to bottom…men were driven from their hearths (homes) and the human race was swept from the surface of the Earth. The Earth itself was beginning to lose its shape. Already the stars were coming adrift from the sky (pole shift) and falling into the void. They (the stars) were like swallows, weary from too long a voyage, which drop and sink into the waves.*

> *The giant surt (comet), set the entire Earth on fire, the universe was…an immense furnace. Flames spurted from fissures in the rocks, everywhere there was hissing of steam. All living things, all plant life, were blotted out. Only the naked soil remained, but like the sky itself the Earth was no more than cracks and crevasses.*

> *And now all the rivers, all the seas, rose and overflowed. From every side waves lashed against waves. They swelled and boiled slowly over all things. The Earth sank beneath the sea…*

> *Yet not all men perished in the great catastrophe. Enclosed in the wood itself of the ash tree Yggdrasil—which the devouring flames of the universal conflagration had been unable to consume—the ancestors of a future race of men had escaped death….*

Thus it was, that from the wreckage of the ancient world a new world was born. Slowly the Earth emerged from the waves. Mountains rose again and from them streamed cataracts of singing waters.[58]

This ancient Norse account is important because it contains so many relevant details. Like other cultures, the statement of *"The stars coming adrift from the sky and falling,"* seems to once again indicate a shifting of the Earth's poles. Also, like so many other ancient accounts, these cataclysmic events seem to coincide with a giant 'surt' or 'comet' that is present in the sky. This giant 'comet' turns the world 'red' and produces a great conflagration and flood (the 'Earth fire' and 'inundation' first mentioned by the ancient Egyptians).

Still other accounts from ancient Norse mythology say that in the 'old world,' the Sun rose in the south, not in the east as it currently does—and placed the Earth's 'frigid zone' in the east, whereas now it is in the north. These accounts strongly indicate that the Norse believed there was a time when the Earth rotated differently than it does today.[59]

The ancient tribes of Finland also recall a time when *'hailstones of iron'* fell from the sky and the land was covered with 'blood.' [60] Note: both these *'hailstones of iron'* and the *'red dust'* that falls down to Earth making it look as if it's covered in *'blood,'* are important details that will be addressed later in this book. *Sounds familiar like when Moses turned Egypt's rivers to 'blood'?*

These same ancient tribes of Europe also believed that a similar catastrophe would destroy the world again in the future. This cataclysm will involve a *'great winter'* that will last for three years, accompanied by tremendous *'earthquakes'* that will cause *'mountains to crumble.'* All of this will take place when the great wolf 'Fenrir' (the terrible comet) once again attempts to devour the Sun—and the Moon and stars will again tumble from the sky in a (pole shift).[61]

One of the most startling ancient European accounts of a large 'celestial object' causing massive geologic upheavals however, comes from a document known as the *Kolbrin Manuscript.* Although the exact origin of this enigmatic document is open to debate, its contents are incredibly revealing and worth our consideration.

The legends surrounding the *Kolbrin Manuscript* states that this document was saved from imminent destruction hundreds of years ago, just before the burning of the famous Glastonbury Monastery in the British Isles, and subsequently safeguarded for centuries by a mysterious religious group known as 'The Culdians.' In 1994, a modern English translation of this ancient, controversial and enigmatic document was produced in New Zealand and has since fueled the *Planet-X* and 'pole shift' controversy throughout the modern world.

Part of the *Kolbrin Manuscript* describes the passage of a large 'celestial object' called 'the Destroyer' that took place thousands of years ago, at the time of the Bible's Great Flood. The *Kolbrin Manuscript (also referred to as The Kolbrin Bible)* states:

Then, with the dawning, men saw an awesome sight. There, riding on a black rolling cloud came the Destroyer, newly released from the confines of the sky vaults, and she (the Destroyer) raged about the heavens, for it was her day of judgment. The beast…opened its mouth and belched forth fire and hot stones and a vile of smoke. It covered the whole sky above and the meeting place of Earth and heaven could no longer be seen. In the evening the places of the stars were changed, they rolled across the sky to new stations (pole shift), and then the floodwaters came (the usual inundation)…

The floodgates of Heaven were opened and the foundations of Earth were broken apart.

The surrounding waters poured over the land and broke upon the mountains. The storehouses of the winds burst their bolts asunder, so storms and whirlwinds were loosed, to hurl themselves upon the Earth. In the seething waters and howling gales all buildings were destroyed, trees were uprooted and mountains cast down. There was a time of great heat, then came a bitter cold…

The Doomshape, called the Destroyer in Egypt, was seen in all the lands thereabouts. In color it was bright and fiery, in appearance changing and unstable…

This was the aspect of the Doomshape called the Destroyer, when it appeared in the days long gone by, in olden times. It is thus described in the old records, few of which remain. It is said that when it appears in the Heavens above, Earth splits open from heat…then flames shoot up through the surface and leap about like fiery fiends upon black blood. The moisture inside the land is all dried up, the pastures and cultivated places are consumed in flames, and all trees became white ashes…

Men forget the days of the Destroyer. Only the wise know where it goes and that it will return in its appointed hour.[62]

Like so many other historical records from the ancient world, the *Kolbrin Manuscript* clearly describes a time in the distant past when a terrible celestial object appeared in the sky and unleashed a geophysical tempest across the land.

Additional cataclysmic accounts from other cultures

The Eskimos of Greenland and other northern regions recall a time when the Earth itself tilted over and all of its people were drowned in the sea.[63] These people point to the existence of fish and whalebones on the surrounding mountains as physical evidence of this catastrophe. These northern people also fear that the world will 'turn over' again in the near future.[64]

The cultures of the South Pacific islands including the Hawaiians, Tahitians, Andaman Islanders and Aboriginal people of Australia also tell of disastrous floods in the past.[65] These people (even today) believe these floods are caused by inundations of the sea, and take place at times of universal chaos and disorder—when the Sun, Moon and stars moved strangely in the sky.[66]

The Maoris of New Zealand, talk about *"fiery winds"* and *"furious hailstorms"* that created tidal waves so large—they touched the sky.[67]

The old traditions of Tibet talk about a great cataclysm that was brought about by a *"terrifying comet."* [68]

In Menin (Flanders), the native people fear that the *"sky is going to fall"* and *"the Earth turn over"* every time a 'comet' is seen in the sky. [69]

The Tatars of Central Asia remember a great conflagration that was preceded by a *"rain of blood"* that turned the whole world red. [70]

Middle Eastern cultures

Contrary to much current archaeological understanding, the ancient Babylonian, Hittite, Sumerian, Chilean, Persian and Mesopotamian cultures, possessed a highly evolved astronomical knowledge of the universe that allowed them to record a long history of global cataclysms in great detail and perspective.

Many of these Middle Eastern cultures also tell of a strange 'celestial object' or 'comet' that periodically appears in the sky—followed by great physical changes to our planet.

The *Bundahis,* a sacred text from Persia, tells of an evil spirit that 'appeared' in the heavens at the close of the last 'world age' and waged a war of darkness and ruin against our solar system and the planet Earth. [71] In other ancient Persian texts the world is sent into total chaos by the appearance of a passing star the Persians called *Tistrya.* [72] This object is described as repeatedly changing shapes as it approaches the Earth from space. [73]

The sacred Hindu scriptures known as the V*edas* also tell of 'four' past ages. The Hindus refer to each of these ages as *yugas*, and say that each subsequent *age* or *yuga* is systematically destroyed by global cataclysms called *pralayas*. These destructive cycles involve apocalyptic floods, high winds and global conflagration (fire) brought on by the appearance of a 'fiery object' in the sky. [74] Still other Hindu accounts say that the appearance of this fiery 'celestial object' in the sky produces a dreadful spectacle (upon the Earth). [75]

The Vedas also mention that each one of these 'destructive cycles' is separated by about 3600 to 4000 years. [76]

Could the 3600 - 4000 years separating global disasters be due to the fact that this 'celestial object' always passes our planet at/or about these same intervals of time?

The ancient Babylonians believed that the Earth periodically underwent massive upheavals brought about by the appearance of a 'celestial object' they called *Marduk*. This object is described as being a huge and 'radiant' visitor from more distant (interstellar) regions that revisits the Earth from time to time, spewing great jets of fire as it passes us in space. [77]

In another ancient Babylonian text know as the *Talmud*, a celestial visitor called *Kimah* is reported to be the ultimate cause of Earth's repeated destruction. *Kimah* is often described as being an actual passing 'planet.' [78]

The similarities in all of these ancient accounts should, at this point, be obvious. These cultures were certainly witnessing and recording the same cataclysmic events in our distant past— brought on by the same 'celestial object' often called by different names, at different times, by different cultures (although always the same villain), throughout Earth's ancient history.

One such revered civilization was the Sumerians, who have left us one of the most complete and revealing ancient accounts involving the passage of this object—an account that hints at the cataclysmic events waiting for us in the very near future.

Zecharia Sitchin and the ancient Sumerians

Zecharia Sitchin is a world-renowned scholar, author and historian, who has translated the 6,000-year-old records of the ancient Sumerian civilization. These records tell of a 'celestial object' that the Sumerians believed passed through our solar system approximately every 3600 years. The ancient Sumerians called this object, *Nibiru*, which means *"Planet of The Crossing."* RIGHT.

The ancient Sumerians believed that the periodic passage of this 'celestial object' caused great changes upon the Earth, including massive floods, earthquakes, volcanoes, and at times—even altering our planet's axis of rotation.

The Sumerian's *Book Of Enki*, gives an extremely clear account of the destruction that the periodic passage of *Nibiru* causes planet Earth.

According to this ancient Sumerian text:

> *Now this is the account of the Deluge that over the Earth swept...For days before the day of the Deluge the Earth was rumbling, groan as with pain it did...For nights before the calamity struck, in the heavens 'Nibiru' as a glowing star was seen...Then there was darkness in daytime, and at night the Moon as though by a monster was swallowed...The Earth began to shake...In the glow of dawn, a black cloud arose from the horizon...The morning light to darkness changed.*
>
> *Then the sound of a rolling thunder boomed (as the Earth's poles began to shift), lightning's the skies lit up...In the Whiteland (polar ice cap), at the Earth's bottom (South Pole), the Earth's foundations were shaking...Then with a roar to a thousand thunders equal, off its foundations the ice sheet slipped, by 'Nibiru's' <u>unseen net force</u> it was pulled away, into the South Sea crashing.*
>
> *All at once a tidal wave arose, the very skies was the wall of waters reaching...The tidal wave northward was spreading...No one his fellow man could see...The ground vanished, there was only water...All that once, on the ground stood, by the mighty waters away was swept...No one except us few survived.[79]*

This is an important ancient description because it further illustrates just how powerful and geologically overwhelming the passage of this 'celestial object' becomes. So powerful in fact, that as *'Nibiru'* passes the Earth, its 'net unseen force' (gravitational effect), causes the whole planet to rumble, ripping the Earth's crust to pieces—shifting its axis of rotation and knocking the south polar ice cap into the Arctic Ocean—setting off a giant tsunami (tidal wave).

We will come back to the accounts of the ancient Sumerians later in this book to see what else their historical records can tell us about this *"Planet of The Crossing."* The historical accounts of great cataclysms having happened in the past, and their likelihood of happening again in our near future, can also be found in one of this planet's most sacred books—the Bible. *Are the end-times drawing near as mystically depicted in the Book Of Revelation?* BY FAR!

YES!

The Bible (King James version)

As one studies the Bible, one fact becomes rapidly clear—the Bible is literally filled with accounts of abundant catastrophes. Numerous books throughout the Bible record great floods, earthquakes, fire falling from the skies and a host of other 'apocalyptic' phenomena. The most popular and well-known Biblical disaster story is however, that of Noah and the great flood.

In this Biblical account, God comes to Noah ordering him to prepare for a global flood in which the Earth and all living things will be destroyed. Quoting the Old Testament:

> *(Genesis 7:10-12): And it came to pass after seven days, that the waters of the flood were upon the earth. In the six hundredth year of Noah's life, in the second month, the same day were all the fountains of the great deep broken up, and the windows of heaven were opened. And the rain was upon the earth for forty days and forty nights.*

> *(Genesis 7:17-19 and 24): And the flood was forty days upon the earth; and the waters increased and bare up the ark, and it was lift up above the earth. And the waters prevailed, and were increased greatly upon the earth; and the ark went upon the face of the waters. And the waters prevailed exceedingly upon the earth. And all the high hills that were under the whole heaven were covered. (7:24): And the waters prevailed upon the earth a hundred and fifty days.*

The similarities between the flood account of Noah and that of many other civilizations living on the Earth at that time are obvious. What is not as well known however, is that like other ancient historical records, the Bible seems to make numerous references to a time when the Earth altered its axis of rotation—causing the Moon, Sun and stars to appear as if they were 'behaving' or 'moving' strangely.

> In the *(Book of Enoch 64:1-3)*, we read: *"In those days Noah saw that the Earth became inclined, and that destruction approached. …And he said, "Tell me what is transacting upon the Earth, for the Earth labours, and is violently shaken."*

QUESTION! When the book of Enoch says, "The Earth became inclined," could it be referring to a pole shift? Was this pole shift the actual cause behind the great flood in Noah's time?

> In the Bible (King James Version), we find the following: *(Isaiah 24:1-20): Behold the Lord maketh the Earth empty, and maketh it waste, and turneth it 'upside down,' and*

scattereth abroad the inhabitants thereof. ...The Earth shall reel to and fro like a drunkard.

QUESTION! When the book of Isaiah says that the Lord made the Earth 'turn upside down,' is this still another biblical reference to a time when the Earth tilted on its normal axis of rotation? Other books of the Bible also mention the strange behavior of the Sun or heavens. The following verses are a few examples.

> *In **(Joshua 10:13)**: "so the Sun 'stood still' in the midst of heaven and hastened not to go down about a whole day."*

> *In **(Psalms 68:8)**: "The Earth shook, the heavens also 'dropped' at the presence of God; even Sinai itself was moved at the presence of God."*

> *Within the **(Book of Amos 8:8)** we read: "shall not the land tremble... and everyone mourn that dwelleth therein? And it shall rise up wholly as a flood; and it shall be cast out and drowned as by the flood of Egypt; and it shall come to pass in that day that I (the Lord) will cause the sun to go down at noon, and I will darken the Earth in the clear day."*

Are all these passages in the Bible describing the same catastrophes brought about by the shifting of Earth's poles as described so clearly in the accounts of many other ancient civilizations?

As we shall see in a later section of this book, the Bible makes it perfectly clear that these events have happened before—and will certainly happen again!

The universal record of global disasters

We have looked at only a 'small sample' of the many historical accounts involving a great catastrophe periodically striking our planet. Virtually every ancient culture from around the world retains historical accounts of a passing 'celestial object' triggering great global floods, earthquakes and a 'shifting' of the planet's poles. One recent scientific compilation has shown that there are over 500 global catastrophe stories, recorded from over 250 indigenous peoples and tribes. *Are we to believe that in all of these cases their disaster reports are mere folklore?*

In his book, *Underworld*, journalist, author and ancient historian, Graham Hancock, discusses the prevalence of global disaster accounts within the recorded histories of ancient cultures. Mr. Hancock states:

> *Such stories turn up in Vedic India, in the pre-Columbian Americas and in ancient Egypt. They were told by the Sumerians, the Babylonians, the Greeks, the Arabs and the Jews. They were repeated in China and Southeast Asia, in prehistoric Europe and across the Pacific. Almost universally, where truly ancient traditions have been preserved, even amongst mountain peoples and desert nomads, vivid descriptions have been passed down of global floods in which the majority of mankind perished.[80]*

Many other researchers, scientists and authors have come to this same conclusion regarding the reality of worldwide cataclysms repeatedly striking Earth in the past. These same authors and scientists have also come to the distinct realization that a passing 'celestial visitor' triggers these global upheavals. In their book, *Cataclysm*, D. S. Allan and J. B. Delair write:

However one wants to regard the collective testimony of the world's flood traditions, there is no escaping its almost monotonously recurrent assertion that the Deluge was a worldwide event—precisely what a catastrophe generated by cosmic agencies (a passing celestial object) could be expected to induce.

> *In that connection it is hardly necessary to stress that the juxtaposition (similarity) in numerous traditions of huge terrestrial convulsions and certain celestial bodies (being present) at the very time of the Deluge, can scarcely be a coincidence or the happy product of traditional imagination.[81]*

In his book, *Atlantis Of The West*, author Paul Dunbavin, states:

> *Even in the small sample of flood legends described here it is possible to identify a pattern. From one source or another it is possible to find descriptions of most of the expected features of an impact event (or celestial fly-by). We find monsters, dragons, serpents and powerful demigods (appearing) in the sky.*

> *Sometimes they shake the mountains and are the cause of the flood. There are the references to the permanent shift of the sky above. Memories of a time when the Earth wobbled on its axis, and the seasons and the length of the day were altered. The changing climate is (also) remembered.*

> *In addition, we find not only memories of land deluged beneath the waters of the flood, but also accounts of the creation of (new) land, the rising of mountains, and of rivers changing their courses.[82]*

So, what does all this mean? How can we put all of these individual accounts into context and make sense of what has actually taken place on this planet in the past?

Let us make a few additional observations before we assemble all of these historical accounts to gain a better understanding of what actually transpired in ancient history.

A summary of *Planet-X* accounts from ancient cultures

Before we can take all of these 'individual' accounts from ancient cultures and use them to reconstruct a clear image of the 'big picture,' we should address three important considerations.

Consideration (#1): The catastrophic accounts from ancient cultures must have been describing events that affected 'most of'—if not the 'entire' world. The 'great flood' of Noah's time has been recorded in exact detail in numerous other sources backing up the Bible's Genesis account.

Many of the ancient civilizations that we have examined were vast empires. The extent of their influence, territories and culture extended over huge areas of the Earth. The Maya, Aztecs, Greeks, Egyptians and many others for example, had civilizations that extended over 'hundreds of thousands' of square miles and contained millions of inhabitants. Not unlike what happened to Atlantis, these ancient cultures were all about to experience the after effects of 'Wormwood.'

These ancient civilizations were no 'small-town' tribes—but vast and sophisticated cultures. When these ancient people talk about a cataclysm destroying the world and virtually eliminating their civilizations, they must have been referring to events that were truly monumental in scope. These events therefore were not small, 'isolated disasters' that affected a local area, but rather major catastrophes that affected 'whole continents' at the very least.

Consideration (#2): Even though the individual accounts of global cataclysms from different civilizations have some variation in their 'recorded details,' that doesn't necessarily mean they are describing different events.

The events that struck our ancient ancestors were sudden, extremely violent and tore their civilizations apart—literally overnight. The few humans that did manage to survive had little time to write down every detail of what was transpiring around them. Instead, these few survivors were most likely totally preoccupied with simply staying alive; securing their 'basic necessities' for survival—like food/water/shelter/protection being paramount; and not sitting around recording how many inches of volcanic dust was accumulating outside their caves.

Additionally, these ancient people would have been in absolute 'terror' of the events unfolding before them and in this 'state of fear,' human recollection becomes fuzzy at best. This fact would further lead to certain details becoming slightly altered or completely forgotten.

In addition, many of the accounts of great cataclysms were originally passed on in 'oral traditions' for 'thousands of years' before eventually being recorded by modern anthropologists. It is therefore more than reasonable to assume that over this amount of time, some of the specific details of these past events would have changed, at least slightly. Some details would likely have been totally forgotten, while other details may have become over-emphasized.

For example: Two adjacent civilizations are largely destroyed by the same disaster that consists of strong earthquakes and a great flood. Even though both of these civilizations experienced the same catastrophe, over thousands of years the 'oral traditions' of civilization (#1) recalls that they were destroyed by a 'great wind,' while civilization (#2) recalls that they were destroyed by a 'great flood.' In reality, both civilizations experienced the same disaster, consisting of both <u>a great wind</u> and <u>a great flood</u>.

Also, geographical placement may have played a large part in the experiences of different cultures. When these events in question took place, civilizations that were in low-lying areas, or in areas closer to the sea, may have experienced more flooding, while civilizations located in more mountainous regions may have experienced a 'great darkness' due to more volcanic ash and blowing dust. What we must understand is that these various cultural accounts are all describing the 'same set of planetary events' simply told from their individual fields of experience.

The historic accounts of ancient cultures have an incredible similarity to them, but because of factors like basic survival, fear, oral traditions and geographical variations—it can be expected there would be slight differences in the 'historical memories' of different cultures from around the world. But one thing remains a constant—something terrible, something catastrophic and something unmistakably <u>global in nature</u>—repeatedly came back to haunt these ancient cultures. Those details may have been remembered or experienced differently, but it was always the same! Because no one ancient culture documented 'all' of the details from past global cataclysms, we will put all of these worldwide accounts together in order to gain a better understanding of what has actually transpired in our past.

Consideration (#3): In order to truly understand the 'larger picture' of what has taken place on the Earth, each of the accounts from different cultures must be looked at as <u>a small piece</u> of a much <u>larger puzzle</u>. To truly understand the 'full story' of what took place in our past, we must take all of the various accounts from ancient cultures and put them together to form a larger picture.

A good example of this would be a detective interviewing witnesses at a crime scene. No one witness may have seen the 'whole' crime take place—but by interviewing all of the witnesses and then putting all their testimonies together, the detective gains a 'better' or more 'accurate' picture of the actual event.

A chronological summary of these ancient accounts paints an interesting and thought-provoking picture of the events that struck our planet in the past—and may again be in store for us in the near future. As we place all of the ancient accounts into a logical 'sequence of events' a truly remarkable 'chain of events' begins to emerge.

1. The sighting of a massive 'red' celestial object as it approaches the Earth.
2. The object's effects—causing earthquakes, volcanoes, and violent winds.
3. The falling 'red' dust—causing the Moon, Sun and Earth to turn blood red.
4. The hailstones of fire, gravel and iron.
5. The Sun, Moon and stars appearing to move erratically in the heavens.
6. The deluge—the overwhelming floods that sweep across the land.
7. The changing positions of Sun and Moon changing day/night time sequences.
8. The destruction of civilizations and their ongoing cultures.
9. The great human migration foretelling their struggle to survive.
10. The destruction of ancient records/accounts/traditions—causing a 'blank period' in Earth's recorded history of humankind.

Since it's more than reasonable to conclude that ancient Sumerians, Egyptians, Maya, Toltecs, Inca, Olmecs, Aztecs, Hopi, Cherokee, Norse, Celts, Chinese, Eskimos (and many other global cultures) all recorded the same catastrophic events—then putting all of these accounts together gives us a much better/accurate picture of what has actually happened on this planet in the past.

Original Sumerian writings offer rich details about Earth's past, shedding light on the mystery of *Planet-X*. They suggest that extraterrestrial visitors may have played an important/key role in the evolution and religious destiny of early mankind each time that *X* returned to terrorize Earth.

A modern-day scientific look at these ancient accounts

Fortunately for us, we have the modern sciences of astronomy, geology and geophysics that can be used to form a more complete understanding of past historic accounts. Let us now reexamine the historic records of these ancient cultures and state a 'modern' hypothesis based on our current scientific understanding.

1) A large 'celestial object' traveling at incredible speed from deep space passes through our inner solar system.

2) As this immense 'red' object passes between the Sun and Earth, it develops a large tail—similar to that of a comet but much more lethal. As this tail sweeps across the Earth, a rain of 'red dust' and 'fire' falls from the sky, causing a conflagration to envelop the Earth. The 'red dust' makes the Moon turn red, turns water to 'blood,' and makes it look as if 'blood' has enveloped the land.

3) As this object quickly passes the Earth, its large gravitational effects cause the rotation of our planet to momentarily stop, making the stars, Sun and Moon appear to sit motionless in the sky. As this object continues to pass the Earth, its gravitational effect ultimately causes a complete shift in our planet's axis of rotation—thus making the stars, Sun and Moon appear as if they are now moving strangely in the sky. In reality—it's the Earth that's moving—not the sky.

4) As the Earth tips over in space, violent winds form in the atmosphere, and great stress is placed on the tectonic plates comprising the crust of our planet, resulting in global earthquakes and numerous volcanic eruptions that send huge amounts of volcanic ash into the atmosphere. Both the volcanic ash (and dust from blowing winds), eventually blocks out the light of the Moon and Sun altogether, turning day into night—causing darkness to envelope the land.

5) Also, as the Earth stops rotating and then tips over in space, large volumes of seawater spill out of the oceanic basins, pouring in over the land—producing 'great floods' with giant waves (tsunamis) as *"high as mountains."* This principle can be simplistically demonstrated by filling a bowl full of water and then placing it on a flat table. Now quickly push the bowl away from you and see what happens. Water spills out of the bowl in the opposite direction from which the bowl is pushed. This is essentially what happens to the oceans when our poles shift.

6) Once the object passes the Earth, which may only take several days, it would swing around the Sun and head back out into deep space—only to return again thousands of years later (approximately every 3,600 to 4,000).

7) In the meantime back on Earth, the flood waters would begin to drain back into the oceanic basins (causing land to reemerge from the sea), the earthquakes would subside, the volcanic ash would begin to settle, the sky would clear and the Sun and

Moon would reappear—although in different places due to the new position of the Earth's axis of rotation.

If you were among the few survivors of this event, you would then crawl out of your cave to an awful mess. Your civilization would be gone and you would have to *"begin again as children."* If you could manage to rebuild your society, you would tell future generations stories of a time when the Sun 'changed directions' in the sky causing a 'great flood' to envelop the land— destroying most of the old world and everything in it. The wildlife remnants and human survivors would once again have to begin all over—with human beings facing life like little children.

If you were like the Maya, Aztecs, Sumerians or ancient Chinese, future generations might develop an 'obsession' with the motion of the heavens in order to be able to predict the coming of the next great 'destructive cycle.'

And if you were like the Inca, you just might develop a 'doomsday anxiety' using the ritual of human sacrifice in order to keep the Sun and Moon moving in their current direction thus preventing a recurrence of the end of the world—again. You would turn the land 'red' with human blood, so the 'celestial demon' from <u>above</u> would not turn it 'red' with its blood <u>below</u>.

As days turned into years and years into millennia, the memory of the great 'cycle of destruction' might begin to fade, or be forgotten again all together.

But unfortunately, the return of this 'celestial object' and the destruction it causes is not dependent on human memory, belief or theories; it obeys only the destructive whims of the universe and cares not for human opinion. The (brown dwarf) object is on its own schedule— and will reappear with little warning and once again cause the end of another age/yuga.

In conclusion...

The similarities in the 'historical records' of ancient cultures cannot be denied. The fact that so many of these cultures describe the passage of a terrible 'red' comet, bizarre motions of the Sun, Moon and stars, similar geophysical upheavals, and 'four' past cycles of destruction—cannot be a mere coincidence.

Something terrible <u>has</u> happened on this planet in our past. Something that has happened repeatedly, each time virtually 'wiping out' most of Earth's civilizations and much of their recorded history. These periodic catastrophes seem to be brought about by the passage of a large 'red' celestial object which takes place every few thousand years, altering our planet's axis of rotation—and triggering a series of violent earthquakes, devastating floods, massive volcanic eruptions and ultimately a global flood.

These events have left the ancient cultures of the Earth with a 'doomsday anxiety' because they strongly believe that these catastrophic events happen on a 'periodic' or 'cyclic' basis. And because these catastrophic events are periodic in nature and have happened a number of times in the past, they are surely going to happen again in the future.

This 'doomsday anxiety' of ancient cultures produces an 'obsession' with astronomy. Carefully watching the heavens and monitoring the movements of the stars—looking for any sign of celestial deviation as a 'warning signal' that the 'terrible object' is once again approaching Earth.

How many other ancient civilizations have been destroyed in our past that we are completely unaware of because we do not have any of their written or oral histories to study?

Can our modern-day society be so preoccupied with its busy work-a-day 'activities' that we are largely ignorant of our own planet's true cataclysmic history and the periodic destruction that it undergoes? And let's not forget about the added threat global terrorism brings to this equation? Could many modern-day anthropologists be looking at the ancient records of individual cultures, but not putting together the 'bigger picture' of what's really happened in the past? Will this recurring calamity strike us still again in the near future—catching our species off guard and sleeping—like it has so many times in the past?

As we will soon discover in the following pages of this book—this may be our exact predicament and we hope our insight helps to mitigate the dire consequences of our global inaction or worse—rejection of the facts as presented here.

CHAPTER ONE ENDNOTES

[1] French, J. Wilson, *The Greatest Story Never Told* (Carlton Press, 1969), p. 39.
[2] White, John, *Pole Shift* (A.R.E. Press, 1980), p. 38.
[3] Ibid., p. 38.
[4] French, J. Wilson, *The Greatest Story Never Told* (Carlton Press, 1969), p. 73.
[5] Ibid., p. 43.
[6] Noone, Richard W., *5/5/200* (Three Rivers Press, 1982), p. 44.
[7] Ibid., pp. 45-47.
[8] Ibid., p. 47.
[9] French, J. Wilson, *The Greatest Story Never Told*, (Carlton Press, 1969), p. 83.
[10] Ibid., p. 83.
[11] Ibid., p. 135.
[12] Velikovsky, Immanuel, *Worlds In Collision* (Dell Publishing, 1967), p. 119.
[13] French, J. Wilson, *The Greatest Story Never Told* (Carlton Press, 1969), p. 137.
[14] Ibid., p. 83.
[15] Ibid., p. 84.
[16] Ibid., p. 78.
[17] Ibid., p. 78.
[18] West, John Anthony, *Serpent In The Sky* (Quest Books, 1993), pp. 58-60.
[19] Plato, *Timaeus*
[20] French, J. Wilson, *The Greatest Story Never Told* (Carlton Press, 1969), p. 72.
[21] Ibid., p. 75.
[22] Ibid., p. 136.
[23] Velikovsky, Immanuel, *Worlds In Collision* (Dell Publishing, 1967), p. 98.
[24] Ibid., p. 133.
[25] Ibid., p. 133.
[26] Allan, D. S. and Delair, J.B., *Cataclysm* (Bear and Company, 1997), p. 152.
[27] Dunbavin, Paul, *Atlantis Of The West* (Carroll & Graf Publishers, 2003), p. 52.
[28] Gilbert, Adrian G. and Cotterell, Maurice M., *The Mayan Prophecies* (Element Books, 1995), p. 38.
[29] Ibid., p. 87.
[30] Ibid., p. 102.
[31] Ibid., p. 2.

(CONTINUED)

CHAPTER ONE ENDNOTES CONTINUED

[32] Gilbert, Adrian G. and Cotterell, Maurice M., *The Mayan Prophecies* (Element Books, 1995), p. 71.

[33] Ibid., p. 103.

[34] Ibid., p. 104.

[35] Gilbert, Adrian G. and Cotterell, Maurice M., *The Mayan Prophecies* (Element Books, 1995), p. 100.

[36] Sullivan, William, *The Secret of The Incas* (Crown Publishers, 1996), pp. 16-17.

[37] *The Larousse Encyclopedia of Mythology* (Chancellor Press, 1996), p. 445.

[38] Ibid., p. 445.

[39] Laviolette, Paul, *Earth Under Fire* (Starburst Publications, 1997), p. 152.

[40] Ibid., p. 101.

[41] Ibid., p. 101.

[42] Allan, D. S. and Delair, J.B., *Cataclysm* (Bear and Company, 1997), p. 157.

[43] Laviolette, Paul, *Earth Under Fire* (Starburst Publications, 1997), p. 257.

[44] Coe, Michael D., *The Maya* (Frederick A. Praeger Publishing, 1966), pp. 90-124.

[45] www.TroubledTimes.com

[46] Laviolette, Paul, *Earth Under Fire* (Starburst Publications, 1997), p. 72.

[47] www.TroubledTimes.com

[48] Ibid.

[49] Laviolette, Paul, *Earth Under Fire* (Starburst Publications, 1997), pp. 168-173.

[50] Hancock, Graham, *Fingerprints Of The Gods* (Crown Trade Paperbacks, 1995), p. 194.

[51] Allan, D. S. and Delair, J.B., *Cataclysm* (Bear and Company, 1997), p. 212.

[52] Ibid., p. 279.

[53] Laviolette, Paul, *Earth Under Fire* (Starburst Publications, 1997), p. 242.

[54] www.TroubledTimes.com

[55] Dunbavin, Paul, *Atlantis Of The West* (Carroll & Graf Publishers, 2003), p.134.

[56] Laviolette, Paul, *Earth Under Fire* (Starburst Publications, 1997), p. 307.

[57] Velikovsky, Immanuel, *Worlds in Collision* (Dell Publishing, 1967), pp. 51-52.

[58] Hancock, Graham, *Fingerprints Of The Gods* (Crown Trade Paperbacks, 1995), pp. 204-205.

[59] www.TroubledTimes.com

[60] Allan, D. S. and Delair, J.B., *Cataclysm* (Bear and Company, 1997), p. 160.

[61] Dunbavin, Paul, *Atlantis Of The West* (Carroll & Graf Publishers, 2003), p. 125.

[62] http://helpthebishops.com/TheKolbrinparagraphs.htm

[63] www.TroubledTimes.com

[64] Velikovsky, Immanuel, *Worlds in Collision* (Dell Publishing, 1967), p. 132.

[65] Laviolette, Paul, *Earth Under Fire* (Starburst Publications, 1997), p. 241.

[66] Dunbavin, Paul, *Atlantis Of The West* (Carroll & Graf Publishers, 2003), pp. 130-131.

[67] Velikovsky, Immanuel, *Worlds in Collision* (Dell Publishing, 1967), p. 147.

[68] Ibid., p. 116.

[69] Ibid., p. 119.

[70] Allan, D. S. and Delair, J.B., *Cataclysm* (Bear and Company, 1997), p. 294.

[71] Velikovsky, Immanuel, *Worlds in Collision* (Dell Publishing, 1967), p. 263.

[72] Allan, D. S. and Delair, J.B., *Cataclysm* (Bear and Company, 1997), p. 152.

[73] Ibid., p. 250.

[74] Laviolette, Paul, *Earth Under Fire* (Starburst Publications, 1997), pp. 306-308.

[75] Allan, D. S. and Delair, J.B., *Cataclysm* (Bear and Company, 1997), p. 252.

[76] Hancock, Graham, *Underworld* (Crown Publishers, 2002), p. 250.

[77] Allan, D. S. and Delair, J.B., *Cataclysm* (Bear and Company, 1997), p. 221.

[78] Ibid., p. 315.

[79] Sitchin, Zecharia, *The Lost Book of Enki* (Bear and Company, 2002), pp. 221-227.

[80] Hancock, Graham, *Underworld* (Crown Publishers, 2002), p. 20.

[81] Allan, D. S. and Delair, J.B., *Cataclysm* (Bear and Company, 1997), p. 20.

[82] Dunbavin, Paul, *Atlantis Of The West* (Carroll & Graf Publishers, 2003), p. 138.

This page provided for reader's notes.

— CHAPTER TWO —

FORBIDDEN ARCHEOLOGY

In the last chapter we investigated the 'written histories' and 'oral traditions' of numerous ancient cultures and discovered the universality of catastrophic events in the historical records of our planet. As we discovered, almost every ancient culture possesses accounts of massive disasters virtually 'wiping out' their civilizations in the distant past.

If these accounts are true, however, is there any 'archeological evidence' that supports or verifies these historic claims made by ancient cultures? Despite the fact that thousands of years have passed since the last 'destructive episode,' is there any physical evidence (in the form of actual 'destroyed' ruins) from these ancient cultures that can verify their historical claims?

Before we look into the 'archeological evidence' for past global cataclysms, it is important to keep in mind the vast amount of time involved in our search. We might want to start out the process by asking ourselves a simple question! *If a modern city were to be completely covered by the ocean, what would be left after 3,600 years?* The obvious answer is—not very much!

If a modern city like San Diego were to be suddenly submerged by the ocean, anything made of wood would quickly deteriorate, metal items would rapidly dissolve in the corrosive saltwater and anything made of concrete would erode and be 'covered up' by marine growth. All of these changes would take place in a few short years. In thousands of years, it is likely there would be little left resembling a modern-day city (San Diego)—and the archeologists of that future time would certainly argue that San Diego was, once again, merely a myth—never really existing!

Unfortunately, the 'historical accounts' of catastrophic events handed down to us from ancient cultures are more than mere fables. In spite of the great deal of time that separates us from past catastrophic events, numerous archeological sites have been uncovered over the years and these sites strongly suggest that many civilizations in the past have indeed perished suddenly and violently leaving little trace of its prior existence.

Most people today take for granted the relative 'geologic calm' we have enjoyed and benefited from over the past several thousand years. We assume that this 'state of calmness' has always been (and will always be) the way in which Earth functions. Nothing could be further from the truth, however! As we will soon discover, massive catastrophes have pulverized the ancient civilizations of Earth many times in the past—and will surely do the same again in the near future.

From the sands of the Gobi Desert to the shores of Africa, from South America to the bottom of the Mediterranean Sea, our planet is littered with the 'shattered remains' of many destroyed civilizations. *What can we learn from modern-day archeology? Are we willing to adjust our preconceived thinking to accommodate new facts and evidence as it's being discovered?*

Let us now examine some of these recent 'archeological discoveries' in order to get a better understanding of the true cataclysmic history of Earth and in turn, what may soon be in store for us. *Confucius once said: "If one wishes to learn about the future he must first divine his past."*

Egypt

A classical Egyptian civilization thrived for thousands of years and was considered by other civilizations of the ancient world as being the 'oldest' and 'wisest' culture on Earth. The Egyptians themselves traced their historical records back thousands of years earlier than our own-recorded history—that is, back into the fog of our historic amnesia. Manetho, one of ancient Egypt's leading historians, asserted that his culture possessed 'historic records' going back over 13,542 years ago,[1] far longer than anything our modern society is 'officially' aware of.

In the first chapter, we investigated some of the ancient Egyptian's historical accounts involving the *"usual inundation"* that periodically visits Earth, destroying the civilizations living on the planet at the time and forcing the few survivors to *"start over again as children."*

But can these ancient accounts be relied upon? Is there any 'physical evidence' giving validity to these ancient claims of the "usual inundation?"

In fact, the 'physical evidence' supporting the ancient Egyptian's historical accounts is prevalent and conclusive. At this present date and time in the calm waters of the Mediterranean Sea off the coast of modern-day Alexandria, Egypt, lies a veritable graveyard of underwater ruins.

British author, scholar and historian Gram Hancock has written a number of best selling books on ancient civilizations and the disasters that befell them. In his most recent book, *Underworld*, Hancock describes a series of underwater dives he recently conducted on these ancient ruins located in Qait Bay, off the coast of present-day Alexandria.

Mr. Hancock summarizes the dives as follows:

> *It may be the most beautiful ancient site I have had the privilege to explore. The visibility (underwater) was poor, which added a kind of foggy glamour to the scene, and we had to criss-cross the ruin-field many times over three lengthy dives before I began to appreciate how vast and how heterogeneous it was.[2]*

Mr. Hancock then describes the underwater ruins at the site:

> *There were huge numbers of columns, some broken, some virtually intact, but all tumbled and fallen. There were Doric column bases surrounded by tumbled debris. Here and there one or two courses of a wall could be seen, rising up out of the murk. There were dozens of meter-wide hemispherical stones, hollowed inside, of a type that I had 'never' encountered before in Egypt.*

Continuing, his narrative reads like an *Indiana Jones* thriller—full of excitement/surprise/action.

There were several small sphinxes, one broken jaggedly in half, and large segments of more than one granite obelisk seemed to have been tossed about like matchsticks. There were also quarried granite blocks scattered everywhere. Most were in the 2-3 square meter range but some were much larger—70 tons (in weight) or more. A notable group of these behemoths, some a staggering 11 meters in length, lay in a line running south-west to north-east in the open waters just outside Qait Bay.[3]

From Mr. Hancock's account we can determine two things. First, these underwater ruins off Alexandria are extensive, containing vast amounts of debris and covering a wide geographic area. And secondly, these ruins are badly damaged. Large stone columns and sphinxes 'broken' in half, huge granite obelisks 'tossed' about like matchsticks and large granite blocks tumbled and scattered over the entire area. Whatever cataclysmic event transpired at this ancient city—it was incredibly violent and happened without warning!

Also, when Mr. Hancock is describing the underwater ruins in the above account and states that he identified some objects of: *"a type that I had never encountered before in Egypt,"* this is saying a lot. Mr. Hancock has written several prior books on ancient Egyptian history and has traveled throughout the country extensively. For him to make this observation indicates that these ruins are 'unusual' in their design and may have originated from a time in ancient Egyptian history with which modern-day archeology is completely unfamiliar.

What type of geologic disaster could have sunk this segment of ancient Egypt into the Mediterranean Sea, turning this once magnificent architecture into shattered piles of rubble? Why is there so much ancient debris underwater and why are we (the public) not hearing more about these ancient, mysterious and fascinating ruins?

Then there is the account of Ashraf Bechai, a gentleman who has spent more than 17 years of his life studying the underwater ruins around Alexandria. Mr. Bechai writes:

> *I have seen things underwater in Alexandria during the last 17 years that challenge all our knowledge of the history of this area.[4]*

In 1984, while spear fishing with some friends off Sidi Gaber (a district along Alexandria's coast, about three kilometers to the east of Qait Bay), Mr. Bechai discovered another series of fascinating underwater ruins.

Mr. Bechai gave the following testimony regarding the discovery:

> *We were about two kilometers from shore, diving off a small boat. I remember that the visibility underwater was exceptionally good. Suddenly I saw hundreds of huge sandstone or limestone blocks laid out neatly in three rows, each two courses high that had been exposed on the seabed at a depth of about six to eight meters.*
>
> *The blocks appeared to be of identical dimensions—four meters wide by four meters long by two meters high. They were stacked up on an underwater ridge of some sort, because there was deeper water between them and the shore. All around there were hundreds*

more blocks of similar size that were heavily eroded, or damaged, or had fallen out of line. This group of blocks has been seen on and off by fishermen and divers over at least 25 years and there is still no proper explanation for it.[5]

From this same area off the coast of modern-day Alexandria, there are also accounts of people seeing what has been referred to as the *Kinessa*, which means 'church' or 'temple' in Arabic. Many people in the area of Alexandria say that about one kilometer to the north of Qait Bay, on the bottom of the shallow sea floor, rest the submerged remains of this ancient and mysterious building.[6]

Unfortunately, to this day there has been relatively little underwater archeology in this area. The Egyptian government officially acknowledges that there are indeed ruins in the ocean around Alexandria, but remains strangely reluctant to allow their full exploration. The little archeology that has been done so far has provided only vague, unsatisfactory explanations as to why these ancient and mysterious ruins are lying off the coast of modern-day Alexandria in the first place.

One does not have to look underwater, however, to find archeological mysteries in Egypt. The deserts of present-day Egypt are filled with the ruins of bygone ages that have long since vanished from our memory. It has been estimated that today, less than 5% of ancient Egyptian ruins have actually been uncovered, while 95% of them still lie mysteriously hidden beneath the sands of the shifting Sahara Desert. One can only imagine the fabulous tale these structures would tell if they are ever excavated from their sandy tombs.

Many of the ancient Egyptian structures that have been excavated by modern archeologists show a common practice of 'themselves' having been built over the ruins of still older structures. These older sub-structures (which the more recent ruins are built upon) often show definite signs of destructive influence caused by floodwaters, massive conflagration (fires) and earthquakes.

The physical evidence supporting past cataclysmic events striking ancient Egypt is so compelling in fact, that geologists, archeologists and pre-historians such as Michael Hoffman, Fekri Hassan and Professor Fred Wendorff, have all confirmed that ancient Egypt was definitely struck by a series of immense and devastating natural disasters.[7]

Why are there so many 'shattered ruins' in Egypt, both underwater and beneath the sands of the Sahara? Why are so many of the ancient ruins of Egypt, 'themselves' built upon the rubble of still earlier destroyed structures? Could the accounts of the 'usual inundation' talked about by the ancient Egyptian priests and scribes actually be a reality?

And why hasn't there been more archeology performed in this area? Could there be many other ruins both on the land and in the waters around Egypt that are yet to be discovered?

Today, Egyptian history is divided into three distinct periods, known as the old, middle and new kingdoms. These three kingdoms (long periods in Egyptian history) are themselves separated by what's known as 'intermediate periods.' Intermediate periods each lasted for hundreds of years and were times when this otherwise orderly civilization had totally collapsed degenerating into lawlessness, chaos and social strife.

Could a cyclical disaster brought about by the passage of the 'terrible comet' be responsible for sending Egyptian society into these 'intermediate periods'? Could the 'pole shifts' (caused by the passage of this object) have caused such extreme geologic changes to this area, that it sent much of ancient Egypt into the sea or buried it beneath the sands of the Sahara?

The ancient Egyptians clearly believed that our planet undergoes periodic 'pole shifts' brought about by the passage of a large 'terrible comet' that has a 'bloody' red appearance and causes plagues, pestilence and destruction across the land as it passes. The modern 'archeological evidence' uncovered so far, clearly indicates that the ancient Egyptians were recording events that actually took place during their Three Kingdoms!

The relentless sands of the Sahara Desert have claimed more than just parts of ancient Egypt, however. In 1933, a French soldier accidentally discovered a series of rock paintings in the middle of the Sahara Desert due west of Egypt, near what is today, Algiers. These rock paintings depicted a now vanished culture living in a lush environment surrounded by elephants, hippopotamuses, rhinoceroses, ostriches, giraffes, antelopes, cows and sheep—along with humans (of all ages) working, hunting and worshiping in this pristine paradise.[8]

Archeologists have since determined that this entire region was hit by some type of massive cataclysm (involving enormous earthquakes and extreme climate changes) thousands of years ago, obliterating this ancient civilization from the annals of history. Today, as a result of this past cataclysm, this area of the Sahara is so inhospitable it can't support any life forms whatsoever.[9]

Once again, the physical evidence found in and around Egypt provides compelling support for their historical claims of the *'usual inundation'* bringing death and destruction to the planet. It is important for us to keep in mind that these were not just local disasters taking place, but simply the localized effects of truly global catastrophes. Even modern-day archeologists have recently concluded that whatever catastrophes affected ancient Egypt and the surrounding Mediterranean area—they were in fact—'global' in nature.

Let us now look at some of the other 'archeological discoveries' recently made in other locations around our planet—and see if these will also reveal evidence of Earth's catastrophic past.

Sumer — (ancient Sumeria)

Located between the Tigris and Euphrates rivers, in what is today the area of present-day Iraq, existed the ancient civilization of Sumer. So significant is the Sumerian's contribution to our modern world that Sumeria is often referred to as the real 'cradle of human civilization.

In fact, the Sumerian civilization is credited by many scholars as being the first culture to have a (true) writing system, the wheel, schools, medical science, written proverbs, history, modern government, taxation, laws, social reforms, cosmology, coined money and mathematics.[10]

The Sumerians, like the Egyptians, also left detailed 'historical accounts' of ancient disasters that ravaged their civilization thousands of years ago. All these disasters were brought about by a passing 'celestial object' the Sumerians called *Nibiru*—their *"Planet of The Crossing."* This celestial object (which the Sumerians believed passed through our solar system approximately every 3,600-4,000years) is believed by many researchers to be the actual cause of Earth's 'cycles of destruction' that repeatedly revisit our planet. *[We believe Nibiru is 'Wormwood."]*

Journalist and author Jim Marrs, has written a number of popular books and has extensively investigated this ancient Sumerian culture. In his book, *Rule By Secrecy*, Mr. Marrs discusses the historical accounts of the ancient Sumerians and the role that *'Nibiru'* plays in planetary cataclysms. Mr. Marrs writes:

> *...The Great Flood was not (only) the result of heavy rains. (The Sumerians) described a darkness accompanied by colossal winds, which increased in intensity, destroying buildings and rupturing dikes. Such conditions would be expected by the near passage of a large planetary body (Nibiru). Scattered archeological excavations over many years indicate that what is regarded as the Great Flood was (in reality) a 'planet wide' catastrophe...*

> *One theory of the Flood was that the gravitational forces caused by the passing of 'Nibiru' caused the Antarctic ice sheet...to slip into the ocean, raising sea levels all over the planet. Even today, most of the original (Sumerian) cities in Mesopotamia remain deep under water and silt near the mouth of the Tigris and Euphrates rivers.[11]*

According to the Sumerians, no fewer than five of their major cities were destroyed in the 'Great Flood' thousands of years ago caused by the last passage of *'Nibiru.'*

The famous British archeologist, Sir Leonard Woolley, conducted a series of excavations between 1922 and 1935 in an area of southern Iraq that was believed to be the location of the ancient destroyed city of Ur—although the exact location of this and other ancient Sumerian cities still remains open to some heated debate.

In 1929, Woolley (digging at these ruins) uncovered a layer of ancient mud, which lacked human artifacts of any kind and had clearly been laid down by the action of floodwaters. Even though this layer of silt had no artifacts in it, clear evidence of the Sumerian civilization was found 'under' this layer, indicating that a flood had indeed taken out at least part of ancient Sumer.[12] The ruins of this ancient city found under the layer of silt produced artifacts such as mud-brick walls, broken pottery, kilns and even a potter's wheel.[13]

As further verification of the Sumerian's written history, archeologists excavating near the ancient city of Shurrupak, have found: "sizable deposits of water-borne clay and sand due to a major and prolonged inundation." [14]

Another British archeologist, Sir Max Mallowan (husband of mystery writer Agatha Christie), identified another layer of sediment brought about by a massive flood covering the ruins of the ancient Sumerian city of Kish.[15]

Are we now beginning to see a repetitious pattern of sudden and violent global destruction?

In addition to ancient Sumerian ruins being uncovered beneath layers of flood debris, many Sumerian sites (like those uncovered in Egypt) also show the typical practice of rebuilding on top of older, earlier 'destroyed' structures. In 1946 and 1949, a team of archeologists from the Iraqi Directorate of Antiquities, conducted a series of excavations at the ancient Sumerian city of Eridu. At this site they proceeded to dig a deep trench that uncovered layers of construction and reconstruction, all built one on top of another. Beneath the corner of one excavated temple, the archeologists found that the structure had been rebuilt no less that seventeen times throughout its long history.[16]

To further illustrate this point, archeologists from the University of Pennsylvania excavating at the Sumerian *Temple of Enlil*, uncovered a section of ancient brick pavement that was 'covered' by thirty-five feet of rubble from various destroyed buildings. Under this brick pavement, archeologists went on to uncover another thirty feet of rubble from an even earlier cataclysm.[17]

Once again, this type of 'rebuilding' on top of the rubble of older developments is an extremely common trait found throughout the world. In many cases these older, lower layers, show definite signs of having met with a catastrophic demise. The rebuilding of newer structures on top of the rubble of older 'destroyed' ruins also tends to 'conceal' or 'obscure' just how many civilizations have been violently destroyed in the past—and how much rubble is actually lying around our planet waiting to be discovered!

Like the Egyptians, the ancient Sumerian accounts of great disasters afflicting their civilization is clearly supported by the physical evidence excavated from their ruined sites. The ancient Sumerians were correct in describing great floods and earthquakes that ravaged their civilization many thousands of years ago! Much to their credit they knew and made adequate preparations!

Could all of this destruction have been ultimately caused by the passage of 'Nibiru'—The Planet of The Crossing? And could 'Nibiru' in fact, be the same brown dwarf star called 'Wormwood'?

Turkey

Like the civilizations of ancient Egypt and Sumer, the ancient cultures of what is today Turkey also possessed historic accounts of great geologic disasters periodically revisiting Earth at regular intervals. Often these accounts of periodic disasters were brought about by a 'cosmic visitor' that periodically appeared in the sky—bringing death/destruction/mayhem to mankind.

On 13 September 2000, *CNN News* ran an article regarding an ancient structure found beneath the Black Sea located off the coast of modern-day Turkey.

This *CNN* article stated:

> *The first evidence that humans lived in an area now covered by the Black Sea—perhaps 'inundated' by the biblical flood—has been found by a team of explorers.*

> *"Artifacts at the site are clearly well preserved, with carved wooden beams, wooden branches and stone tools," said lead researcher, Capt. Robert Ballard, of Titanic fame.*

> *"This is a major discovery that will begin to rewrite the history of the cultures in this key area between Europe, Asia and the ancient Middle East," Hiebert said. (Dr. Fredrik Hiebert, is the team's chief archeologist from the University of Pennsylvania).*
>
> *The remnants of human habitation were found in more that 300 feet of water, about 12 miles off the coast of Turkey.*[18]

Once again we find clear physical evidence of the *"usual inundation"* at work, confirming the historical accounts of massive geologic changes mentioned by the ancient cultures of this area.

As one moves further inland, onto Turkey's well-watered Knoya plain (about 130 miles south of Ankara, the Capital) the mysterious buried ruins of *Catal Hüyük* stand as another sober testament to ancient cataclysmic history. In November 1958, British archeologist, James Mellaart, excavated a large segment of this ancient enigmatic site and was amazed by his find.

James Mellaart recalls:

> *Much of the site was covered by turf and ruin weed (peganum harmala) but where the prevailing south-westerly winds had scoured its surface bare, there were unmistakable traces of mud-brick buildings, burned red in a 'conflagration' contrasting with patches of gray ash, broken bones, potshards and obsidian tools and weapons. To our surprise these were found not only at the bottom of the mound, but they continued right up to the top, some 50 feet above the level of the plain.*[19]

According to James Mellaart and other archeologists, *Catal Hüyük* was inhabited by a population that was very organized, sophisticated and numbered in the thousands. These people thrived in this same location for almost a thousand years and then one day—suddenly abandoned their city without a trace or warning. *The key unanswered question is: where did they all go?*

In his book, *Before The Flood*, author Ian Wilson comments on the abandonment of *Catal Hüyük*, wherein Wilson states:

> *Something very powerful indeed had to have affected the Catal Hüyük community in its last hours. As Mellaart's findings showed, after the community had lived peaceably at this prime, well-watered site for upwards of a thousand years, suddenly they uprooted from the site lock, stock and barrel. They gathered what little belongings they could carry with them…and to all appearances vanished into thin air.*[20]

The ruins of *Catal Hüyük* clearly show they'd been through a great 'conflagration,' but very few human bodies have ever been recovered from this site, indicating that most of the inhabitants had left this city sometime before the conflagration (burning) and other damage occurred.

What could have become of these people? Where did they suddenly disappear to and why?

Interestingly, *Catal Hüyük* is not the only ancient Turkish city to have been mysteriously abandoned; the ancient city of *Hacilar* also shows this same type of sudden mass desertion taking place—and at about the same time. As a matter of fact, throughout the country of Turkey, no fewer than 'three hundred' ancient cities have been uncovered—many of which were mysteriously deserted and then subsequently/mysteriously burned to the ground.[21]

Once again we must seriously ask ourselves, where did 'thousands-upon-thousands' of these ancient people flee to—and why? What catastrophic event in their history caused them flight?

The answers may be found a short distance away, where thousands of years ago, the ancient civilizations of Turkey mysteriously built a series of thirty-six 'underground cities' in the center of the old Turkish kingdom known as *Cappadocia*. It has been estimated by modern archeologists that these subterranean cities could have housed as many as 200,000 people. The largest of these cities is called *Derinkuyu*, covering an area of two and one-half square miles and which has twenty known levels. *Derinkuyu* is so large in fact—it could house 20,000 people alone.[22]

For years archeologists have been puzzled by these underground cities because building and then living in them, is simply not practical. It is much easier and more efficient to live above ground —like the rest of the ancient kingdoms that thrived throughout the world. These cities were built with great difficulty, lived in for a number of years and then were simply abandoned by their occupants. Few of these answers have been uncovered with no clues or data left to decipher.

So why were these ancient underground cities built? And who lived in them?

As we have already seen, many ancient civilizations had an absolute 'obsession' with astronomy and the regular movements of the heavens. One of the main reasons for this obsession was to allow these ancient cultures to keep careful track of the great 'cycles of destruction' (brought about by the passage of the 'terrible comet') that they believed revisited our planet on a regular schedule.

More than one modern archeologist has suggested that these ancient underground cities and the people who lived in them, seem to have been 'hiding' from 'something' terrible and uncontrollable—as opposed to 'someone.'

Could the ancient cultures that built these underground cities have been calculating the great 'cycle of destruction' brought about by the passage of the terrible comet? And could these ancient underground cities have been built ahead of time by such cultures in order to escape the destructive effects of a past 'pole shift' brought about by the passage of this large celestial object? Did these ancient people and their underground cities remain intact—while the 'above ground' cities around them either burned to the ground or disappeared beneath giant waves?

It is obvious that these ancient cultures knew about the periodic passage of the 'terrible comet' and the damage this object's periodic 'fly-bys' inflict upon the Earth. It is also reasonable to assume these ancient cultures would have taken measures to save themselves—and building underground cities would be a logical undertaking considering the extreme geophysical and atmospheric disruption the object's passage causes.

It is often said we may learn key lessons regarding the future by looking deeply into our past!

These underground cities could have been built ahead of time as a safe refuge. Then as the 'terrible comet' was approaching our inner solar system, the inhabitants of the 'above ground' cities like *Catal Hüyük* and *Hacilar*, simply picked up and moved 'underground' for a few years —that is until 'things beyond their control' quieted down geologically and atmospherically.

Once these ancient people came back to their original above ground cities however, so much damage had been done through earthquakes, wind and conflagration (fire), that they were forced to simply abandoned these locations altogether and moved on—establishing new communities in other areas throughout that part of their world.

In support of this idea, the ancient people of Turkey actually left numerous 'historical accounts' documenting how they had survived massive global cataclysms in the past by temporarily living underground.[23] These accounts are quite numerous and filled with dramatic details.

As further evidence supporting this scenario, archeologists have recently determined that the 'way of life' and 'cultural heritage' of the people that built those above ground 'abandoned' Turkish cities like *Catal Hüyük* and *Hacilar*—lived on long after their cities were vacated and subsequently destroyed. Their architecture, textiles, pottery and numerous other aspects of their culture survived in other geographic areas, indicating that these people established other cities and continued their 'way of life' after the geologic upheavals died down.

As we shall see later in this book, these same types of massive 'underground cities' are mysteriously being built today in different locations around the world—presumably in preparation for the upcoming passage. Little or no information about them is readily available. *So why is that?*

As in Egypt and Sumer, many of the ancient 'above ground' ruins of Turkey have also been 'rebuilt' over the rubble of earlier destroyed structures. For example, in modern-day Turkey sits the remains of the ancient city of *Troy,* located in NW Asia Minor. Archeologists have now determined that this arcane city was rebuilt six or seven times and as many times destroyed again, throughout its long history. These ancient ruins also show signs of great earthquakes and conflagrations that were so violent, they overturned walls sometimes fifty-feet thick.[24]

A massive and widespread disaster clearly left its signature upon the ancient cultures of Turkey! Structures submerged 300 feet under the Black Sea, hundreds of abandoned cities burned to the ground, and enormous underground shelters built as a refuge for the inhabitants of these abandoned sites still remains a mystery. The evidence from this part of the world simply speaks for itself. *Will we as modern-day inhabitants of Earth learn from these unsolved mysteries of time?*

The Middle East

Just south of present-day Turkey sits the area collectively known as the Middle East. It is from the specific region known today as Jordan and Israel, that modern archeologists have uncovered an ancient and grizzly discovery.

In recent years, archeologists have uncovered entire ancient cities like *Bab edh-Dhra*, *Numerira*, *Feifa* and others—all covered with a thick layer of spongy charcoal, indicating that these cities had all been burned to the ground thousands of years ago by a massive conflagration.[25]

Whatever tragedy befell this part of the ancient world was sudden, violent and unlike the ancient Turkish cities such as *Catal Hüyük* and *Hacilar,* where the human inhabitants of these Middle Eastern cultures constructed underground sanctuaries to help them escape the fiery wrath that suddenly befell them—while most other Turkish cities were completely destroyed.

At the remote site of the ancient city of *Bab edh-Dhra* alone, 20,000 graves have been uncovered containing the chard remains of a half-million individuals. And in other locations throughout the Middle East, unfortunately similar massive deposits of human remains have also been discovered.

Even today, modern archeologists have no idea what could have caused such massive death and destruction over so large a geographic area—and all at the same time without any warning.

What could have burned all these ancient Middle Eastern cities to the ground and left these once thriving civilizations under thick layers of spongy charcoal?

Could the ancient accounts of fire 'raining from the sky' have set these cities of the Middle East ablaze, burning them to the ground as the fiery tail of a passing celestial object swept across this area of Earth? Could these cultures of the Middle East have stayed above ground and perished in the ensuing inferno—while the cultures of ancient Turkey fled underground to survive?

Later in this chapter, we will investigate additional evidence supporting a massive conflagration raining down from the sky over large areas of our planet in the 'vitrified' or 'fused' ruins found throughout the world.

Whatever 'fiery disaster' struck these ancient cities of the Middle East—it permanently put an end to their existence. Once these ancient urban centers were set ablaze, these sites remained uninhabited for literally thousands of years.

China

Like so many other cultures from the ancient world, the Chinese recorded a long string of repeated cataclysms that violently crushed their society. These episodes of massive planetary destruction were the result of Earth's axis of rotation being 'altered' (a pole shift) by the passage of the dreaded 'red dragon,' as they called 'it'.

On 14 January 1896, a twenty-nine-year-old archeologist by the name of Sven Anders Hedin left the remote desert outpost known as *Khotan* with four porters in search of the ancient legendary city of *Takla Makan.* According to legend, *Takla Makan* was a vast urban center that had been destroyed by a global catastrophe thousands of years ago and was subsequently 'swallowed up' by the sands of the relentless Gobi Desert in eastern China.

Exhausted after three weeks of relentless travel through this hostile no-man's land, with sand dunes towering three hundred feet high all around them, Hedin and his porters suddenly came across *"a dead forest of sun-bleached, wind-scoured tree stumps protruding through the sand."* [26]

At the edge of this ghostly forest, Hedin and his team found the remains of several ancient structures, which they then proceeded to excavate from their sandy tomb. The interior of these structures revealed plastered and polished walls, which were painted with colorful murals depicting women with flowing garments and men with black beards and mustaches.

As the excavations continued, Hedin and his men also discovered the wooden keels of boats and the actual docks where they berthed. And further discoveries indicated that at one time this now inhospitable 'sandy inferno' had actually been a large inland lake supporting a thriving ancient civilization possibly a million strong or more.

Mr. Hedin describes the entire area as:

> *One of the most unexpected discoveries that I made throughout the whole of my travels in Asia…Who could have imagined that in the interior of the dreaded Desert of Gobi, and precisely in that part of it which dreariness and desolation exceeds all other deserts on the face of the Earth, (there are) actual cities submerged under the sand, cities wind-driven for thousands of years, the ruined survivals of a once flourishing civilization…and yet there stood I amid the wreckage and devastation of an ancient people.*[27]

Today, archeologists have concluded that these ancient forgotten people were not of Chinese origin—but exactly who these people were—and what could have tragically happened to this area—still remains an 'official' mystery today thousands of years later.

In recent years this area of the Gobi Desert has revealed a number of other startling discoveries, including the remains of several other destroyed communities that also once thrived in this area millennia ago.

The Gobi desert is not the only area of China that has swallowed up ancient cities, other parts of China have revealed this same type of past devastation on an even grander scale.

On 13 January 2003, the *Xinhua News Agency* of China reported the discovery of relics from another ancient city that was suddenly and violently destroyed thousands of years ago.

According to the *Xinhua* article:

> *Relics from a large section of an ancient city have been discovered in Chao Lake, in Tong Yang Town (in) east China's Anhui Province. The relics, recovered from the lake during the dry season, include broken pieces of tube-shaped tiles and earthen jars covering an area of nearly 16,000 square meters.*
>
> *According to local records…the ancient city of Chaozhou, sank (thousands of years ago) without warning (in) one day. Chao Lake, China's fifth largest freshwater lake came into being at a later date—covering the ancient city.*
>
> *Local fishermen report frequent discoveries of relics, and the cultural relics administrative office has collected more than 300 relics from local people, including gold and silver vessels, jade articles and (even) diamonds.*[28]

Clearly this was not a 'small town' or 'village' that was violently destroyed at this location for only 'one section' of this ancient city covered nearly 16,000 square meters—this was truly a large ancient metropolis with many thousands of residents!

What happened to all of the buildings of this sunken city? What type of violent event could have destroyed a whole city, virtually wiping it off the face of the Earth in a single day? Why would this city's ancient inhabitants abandon artifacts made of gold, silver, jade and diamonds?

Once again, it would seem as if ancient Chinese 'historical accounts' of violent and sudden geologic upheavals is clearly supported by recent archeological discoveries.

Could all of this destruction have been caused by the return of the 'red dragon' mentioned so often in ancient Chinese literature? Could this celestial object that appeared as a second 'red sun' have reaped havoc and destruction on ancient China just as their history tells us today?

Let us now leave the ruins scattered across the planet's landmasses and venture once again to the enigmas that are hidden beneath Earth's watery abyss—her oceans...

The Azores

We have seen clear and decisive evidence of the 'shattered ruins' of ancient civilizations off the coasts of Egypt and Turkey. Clearly some type of intense geophysical event 'inundated' these old-world societies many thousands of years ago. But because so little underwater archeological exploration has been done in these areas however, we have only begun to discover what strange and enigmatic ruins still lie hidden in deeper parts of the oceans.

In recent years, a hint of what could be waiting discovery in the mysterious depths of the abyss has started coming to light. Underwater archeology can be both interesting and dangerous.

The Azores is a group of small islands located in the Atlantic Ocean, on top of an underwater volcanic mountain range known as the Mid-Atlantic Ridge. During the 1950's and 1980's, a number of reports were rumored to exist describing a series of large underwater ruins mysteriously lying on the ocean floor around the Azores.

Then on 13 July 2001, *ABC News* picked up an article from *Nature Magazine* and past 'rumors' suddenly became 'reality.' The *ABC* article revealed:

> *More than 2,000 years ago, the Greek philosopher Plato wrote about a splendid city named Atlantis, with fertile soil and glorious temples that "in a single day and night of misfortune...disappeared into the depth of the sea."*

> *Now researchers probing the ocean bottom have found 18-story high towers of stone deep in the ocean near a section of volcanic fault ridges that extends for over 6,200 miles along the Atlantic floor (the Mid-Atlantic Ridge).*

> *The majestic height of the two dozen stone structures and their location on a seafloor mountain named Atlantis Massif, inspired the scientists to name this area "the lost city" in honor of the fabled flooded city referred to by Plato (as Atlantis).*

> *The underwater stone spirals are unusual for their composition and location… "It was clear these (objects) were unlike anything we'd ever seen before," said Deborah Kelly, an oceanographer at the University of Washington…This 'lost City' is also strikingly bright —brighter than the usual conditions in which things can generally be seen using artificial light a half-mile below sea-level…these newly discovered formations are gleaming white because they are made up of materials similar to those of pale concrete.*[29]

What type of strange—out of place structures could these be? Could Atlantians have built them?

This area of the Mid-Atlantic Ridge is very uniform, having been produced by the upwelling of homogeneous molten lava from the Earth's deep inner mantel. *So why are these structures so strikingly different from the surrounding area? Is it possible that these could actually be the remains of vast Atlantian structures that sank to the bottom of the Mid-Atlantic Ridge in a catastrophic geophysical event exactly as described by the ancient Greek philosopher, Plato?*

Modern-day geologists have determined that this area of the Mid-Atlantic Ridge around the Azores has undergone massive geologic changes in the very recent past. And as we will see in chapter four, large areas of Earth's crust are capable of 'rising' or 'dropping' hundreds or even thousands of feet in a single massive geologic event—*possibly the 2012 'pole shift?'*

If these strange underwater structures were the only 'ancient enigma' found on the bottom of this planet's oceans, they might be easier to dismiss. But the fact is, many areas of the ocean's depths contain 'out-of-place' signs of former civilizations. And one of the most famous examples of this phenomenon has been located off the coast of present-day communist Cuba.

Cuba

In 2001, a professional team of scientists and underwater salvage experts secured an exclusive agreement with Fidel Castro's Cuban government to conduct underwater excavations for lost shipwrecks—and the treasures they might contain. What was found there however, was not a shipwreck, but instead the remains of a very ancient city.

On 14 May 2001, the *Reuters News Agency* published a story about a mysterious underwater city that had been discovered by Canadian oceanographic engineer, Pauline Zelitsky, from British Columbia-based *Advanced Digital Communications*. Their report states:

> *Most intriguingly, researchers using sonar equipment have discovered, at a depth of about 2,200 feet, a huge land plateau with clear images of what appears to be urban development, partly covered by sand. From above, the shapes resemble pyramids, roads and buildings.*

"It is stunning. What we see in our high-resolution sonar images are limitless, rolling, white sand plains and, in the middle of this beautiful white sand, there are clear man-made 'large-sized' architectural designs. It looks like when you fly over an urban development in an airplane and you see highways, tunnels and buildings," Zelitsky said.

"We don't know what it is and we don't have the video-taped evidence of this yet, but we do not believe that nature is capable of producing planned symmetrical architecture, unless it is a miracle," she added, in an interview in her office at Tarara, along the coast east of Havana.[30]

Is this further physical evidence of the "usual inundation" mentioned in the oral traditions of the ancient Egyptians and so many other ancient cultures? What type of massive tectonic activity could have sent an ancient city plummeting some 2,200 feet below the mid-Atlantic ocean?

At the time of this writing, *National Geographic* is actively investigating this site. Samples of these mysterious underwater structures have been brought to the surface indicating they are composed of marble and other ancient building materials. Scientists are 'officially' stumped, however, as to 'how' and 'why' these ancient structures are located where they now sit underwater.

India

The ancient civilizations of modern-day India also mention a series of global destructions periodically brought upon the Earth at regular intervals by the passage of a large (red) celestial object. These cultures recorded that once this terrible object appeared in the sky, all manner of tempest was released upon the Earth. And like many other ancient cultures from around the planet, India is also littered with destroyed ruins, abandoned cities and massive gravesites.

In 1993, off the coast of Kadaikadu, India, a strange U-shaped structure made of large blocks was discovered underwater, five-kilometers from shore in 23 meters of water. In this same general area, the heavily eroded remains of numerous other brick and stone structures have also been discovered offshore, along with broken pottery and numerous other ancient artifacts. Archeologists have speculated that these structures may be as much as 10,000 years old or more.[31]

In southern India it is common knowledge amongst local fisherman that another series of underwater ruins including temples, walls and roads lay offshore. Fishermen claim that these structures are so extensive, they often snag their anchors and fishing nets on them.[32]

A number of local fishermen claim to have actually seen these ruins after diving down to free their entangled nets and anchors. This appears to be more evidence of massive planetary change.

On Saturday, 19 May 2001, the *Times of India* reported on still another set of ruins submerged off the coast of this ancient country. The *Times* reported:

In a major marine archeological discovery, Indian scientists have come up with excellent geometric objects below the seabed in the western coast similar to Harappan-like ruins.

"This is the first time such sites have been reported in the Gulf of Cambay," Science and Technology Minister, Murli Manohar Joshi, told reporters.

The discovery was made a few weeks ago when multi-disciplinary underwater surveys carried out by the National Institute of Ocean Technology (NIOT) picked up images of 'excellent geometrical objects,' which were normally man-made, in a nine-kilometer stretch west of Hazira in Gujerat.

"It is important to note that the underwater marine structures discovered in Gulf of Cambay have similarity with the structures found on land on archeological sites of Harappan and pre-Harappan times," Joshi said.

The acoustic (sonar) images showed the area lined with well-laid house basement-like features partially covered by sand waves and sand ripples at 30-40 meter water depth.

At many places channel-like features were also seen indicating the existence of possible drainage in the area. "Possible age of the finds can be anywhere between 4,000 and 6,000 years," Joshi said, adding the site might have been submerged due to a powerful earthquake.[33]

Is this further evidence of the "usual inundation" (talked about by the ancient Egyptians) that periodically strikes our planet—destroying large regions and many past civilizations?

Like countless other ancient cultures, age-old Indian history recorded horrific 'recurring disasters' causing great destruction upon this planet approximately every 3,600 to 4,000 years.

Are these underwater ruins the remains of an old Indian civilization—one that existed before the last great 'cycle of destruction' ravaged this fragile planet spinning through space?

Who built these structures and why they became submerged off the coast of modern-day India, still remains a mystery! Today, several groups of underwater archeologists are trying to continue the exploration of these sites, but funding is scarce and like the Egyptian government, the Indian government seems strangely reluctant to contribute further help/interest/money whatsoever.

As in Egypt, Turkey, Sumer and the Middle East, physical evidence supporting the catastrophic history of India can also be found on land. In what is today the area of Kashmir (the disputed territory with Pakistan) just outside the city of *Srinagar*, the massive ruins of an ancient temple have been uncovered. The temple had been utterly destroyed and its huge blocks scattered over the entire geographic area—as if a huge explosion violently tore apart the original structure.[34]

And not far from these ruined structures under the sands of what is today known as the Thar Desert, archeologists have also discovered a number of ancient cities such as *Mohenjo-Daro*, *Harappa*, *Chanhu Daro*, *Amri* and *Kot Diji*. Today, archeologists believe that a series of devastating earthquakes and floods buried these ancient cities under 'mountains of sand' and 'flood debris' many thousand of years ago.[35] In fact, so devastating were these earthquakes and floods, that today the earliest levels of *Mohenjo-Daro* are inaccessible because they are inundated by groundwater and deeply buried beneath the sands of the Thar Desert.

These civilizations were at one time thriving cultures—the city of *Mohenjo-Daro*, for example, contained around 40,000 inhabitants.[36] *Once again we must ask ourselves; if these ancient civilizations were destroyed by such ravenous geological changes—then what happened to the inhabitants, artifacts and animals of these ancient cities?*

When archeologists excavated the ancient Indian cities of *Mohenjo-Daro* and *Harappa*, they discovered its streets were littered with human skeletons; many still holding hands as if some sudden, 'horrible doom' overtook them as they went about their daily lives.[37] These cities also contained thousands of clay vessels scattered everywhere that had seemingly 'melted' together by some type of intense heat. *Does this description sound like shades of Sodom and Gomorra?*

The melting together of these clay vessels may well be an important clue as to what caused the destruction in this area. At several other ancient Indian cities located between the River Ganges and the Rajmahal Mountains, huge segments of ancient 'walls' and 'building foundations' have also been found seemingly 'fused together' (vitrified) by some form of intense heat process.

Could this area (like those of Turkey and the Middle East), have also passed through the tail of a large celestial 'comet' that rained "fire from the sky," causing a conflagration to envelop the land—fusing the massive stones of ancient walls together, exactly as the ancient Egyptians described ('it') in the Ipuwer Papyrus?

If you'll recall from the last chapter, these ancient papyrus talked about the red sky *"being in confusion,"* followed by a *"rain of fire"* that ran upon the ground—causing gates, columns and walls, (stone structures) to burst into flames. Many other ancient cultures also mention a *"rain of fire and gravel"* from the sky. Also recall from the last chapter that the ancient European cultures say that a large 'red comet' appeared in the sky and set the entire Earth on fire!

If the passage of this large 'celestial object' did in fact rain 'fire from the sky,' there must be other physical evidence to support this event? Is this 'fire from the sky' threat found elsewhere?

Scotland

Just to the north of England sits the picturesque nation of Scotland. Throughout the country of Scotland, archeologists have discovered the remains of at least sixty ancient structures that also show signs of massive 'vitrification.' Vitrification is a process where intense heat is applied to large blocks of stone, which fuse with smaller gravel to form a hard glassy mass. The stones that comprise these mysterious ruins in Scotland were subjected to such intense heat that rivers of molten rock once ran down their walls.[38]

And Scotland is not the only location where such 'vitrified' ruins have been uncovered. Other 'vitrified' sites have also been discovered in France, Turkey, and India and throughout the Middle East including Iran and Iraq.[39]

Once again, what could have caused such intense heat to affect so large a geographic area? Could all of these 'vitrified' ruins be the result of Earth passing through the fiery tail of a passing celestial object? And could these charred ruins in ancient Turkey and the Middle East also be the result of these same horrific sources of conflagration?

As we shall soon see, the 'celestial object' in question contains a lot of carbon and hydrogen. As this object passes between the Earth and our Sun, a flammable 'hydrocarbon tail' develops. As long as this flammable 'hydrocarbon tail' remains in space, it poses no real threat to Earth, but as soon as this 'hydrocarbon tail' sweeps into Earth's oxygen-rich atmosphere it ignites anything/everything it encounters. In a sense, this hydrocarbon tail forms a giant cosmic 'blow-torch,' sweeping over the planet—setting everything in its pathway on fire.

This is why the ancient Egyptians claimed that even 'stone columns' were set ablaze and why so many ancient civilizations said that the Earth was enveloped by a conflagration (fire) from the sky. This is why the ancient inhabitants of the Turkish kingdom of *Cappadocia* built such extensive underground cities, capable of housing 'hundreds of thousands' of residents and their taking refuge underground would be the only way of them surviving this cosmic flame-thrower.

This area of the world was affected by more than just this passing celestial object's tail however. In both England and Ireland (adjacent to the country of Scotland) numerous other ruins exist today—all indicating that a great cataclysm once ravaged this part of the world.

The local inhabitants of Wales still talk about 'sunken cities' and 'lost lands' lying off the British coast and ancient 'palaces' that were drowned beneath welsh lakes in the distant past. Similar accounts can be found in the area of Cardigan Bay, where local legends say that a lost kingdom called *Cantre'r Gwaelod* was destroyed long, long ago. Today the ruins of this ancient city are said to exist between the Lleyn Peninsula and the Cardiganshire coast.[40]

Other British legions talk about the ancient 'lost civilization' of *Lyonesse*. According to local Cornish tradition this once rich and powerful kingdom was obliterated from the annals of history when the sea suddenly rose up and inundated this great city/state.[41]

Today, modern-day archeologists are giving increasing credence to these ancient accounts as submerged walls, building foundations and agricultural field boundaries are clearly discernable in the shallow waters around these locations.

South and Central America

The cultures of South and Central America have left numerous accounts of great cataclysms repeatedly striking Earth in the past. These cyclic catastrophes often involved a shifting of the Earth's poles brought about by the periodic passage of the 'sky serpent' or 'cloud serpent.' And, just like so many other areas from around the world, archeologists have found solid physical evidence supporting these ancient claims.

One such example can be found in Peru, on the shores of Lake Titicaca. This area is where Professor Arthur Posnansky conducted an archeological dig that turned up a large assortment of human and animal remains chaotically mixed together with other artifacts, all strongly suggestive of a great cataclysm having struck this region in the past.

Professor Posnansky writes:

In chaotic disorder among wrought stones, utensils, tools and an endless variety of other things are found. All of this has been moved, broken and accumulated in a confused heap. Anyone who would dig a trench here two meters deep could not deny that the destructive force of water, in combination with brusque movements of the Earth, must have accumulated those many different kinds of bones, mixing them with pottery, jewels, tools and utensils. Layers of alluvium (flood debris) cover the whole field of the ruins and lacustrine sand mixed with shells from Titicaca, decomposed feldspar and volcanic ashes have accumulated in places surrounded by large walls.[42]

This event must have been so severe that it literally dragged people, their possessions, and the local animals that inhabited this area depositing them in a chaotic fashion—along with mud and other flood debris—out of the shattered remains of their dwellings.

Once again, this is clear evidence that a great and sudden disaster took place in the past—solid 'physical evidence' supporting the 'historic accounts' of those people who once lived in this part of the world.

This excavation at Lake Titicaca and the calamity that befell these ancient people is in no way an isolated incident. In fact, in a recent archeological survey it was concluded that the country of Peru alone, contains the remnants of over 10,000 violently destroyed ancient sites most of which have yet to be fully excavated or explored.

Further north, at the ancient cities of the Mayan civilization, recent archeological discoveries indicate that many of these Mayan cities were hit by a series of devastating and powerful earthquakes causing major damage and disruption to the Mayan empire. In fact, so powerful and disruptive were these quakes on the Mayan civilization—that the extensive damage inflicted was never repaired by the Maya, indicating that after these catastrophic earthquakes happened, Mayan culture was in such disarray they could not even organize the efforts to repair their own cities.

The Island of Malta

Malta is a large, picturesque island located in the Mediterranean Sea. This island was inhabited thousands of years ago by a mysterious culture that seems to have vanished off the face of the Earth. Today, Malta holds many unexplained mysteries, both on land and underwater.

On 31 October 1999, the *Maltese National Newspaper* reported:

Recently, structures that resemble megalithic temples have been discovered on the seabed in Maltese waters. These (underwater ruins) are currently being studied to establish whether they are actually unique megalithic temples.

This discovery has been considered to be of great archeological importance, and has raised great interest among foreign archeologists...the discovery was made on the 13th of July 1999, at 10 a.m. and was extensively photographed.[43]

And in other areas off the coast of Malta, underwater video has revealed the presence of large 'canals' and worn 'cart ruts' indicating that these areas were once above water—on dry land.

In addition to many enigmatic underwater ruins, the island of Malta itself also contains evidence that a massive cataclysm took place.

Archeologists have uncovered the remains of 'twenty-three' ancient megalithic structures throughout the island. Exactly who built these structures, and why, remains a mystery. What is clear however is that these structures and the people who built them seem to have met with a most sudden and tragic catastrophic ending of their lives.

According to senior archeologist, Dr. David Trump, regarding the current state of these ancient structures:

> *Six (structures) stand alone, ten are in pairs, and there is one group of three, and one of four...there are at least twenty scatterings of megalithic blocks...which could represent the last vestiges of former temples...It is on the whole unlikely that many more remain to be discovered. The number destroyed without trace we shall never know.*[44]

Who built these strange megalithic structures? How did these massive structures become so badly damaged? And—what happened to their builders who seem to have just mysteriously vanished?

One explanation of what happened to the inhabitants of this ancient culture can be found in the work of the renowned godfather of Maltese archeology, Sir Themistocles Zammit. At the turn of the twentieth century, Zammit excavated an enormous underground structure known as the *Hypogeum of Hal Saflieni*, and found the broken remains of 7,000 human corpses buried in a matrix of 'red earth' on the island.[45] This was no ordinary burial, for the remains showed the classic signs of having been interned 'violently' and 'suddenly.'

A few years later, T. E. Peet and R. N. Bradley, co-authored a publication about this 'grizzly' find within the *Hypogeum of Hal Saflieni* saying:

> *No complete (human) skeletons came to light and the bones lay in confusion throughout the soils in the rest of the Hypogeum, except that occasionally an arm with fingers, and a complete foot, and several vertebrae would be found lying with the parts in situ. From the upright position of an isolated radius it might be judged that the filling up of the cave was of a wholesale nature, rather than that individual burials took place in it...unrelated bones and also implements were found in the interior of skulls...animal bones were found mingled with human.*[46]

W. A. Griffiths wrote a report about this underground *Hypogeum* for *National Geographic Magazine*. In his report Griffith recalculated the number of human remains found and determined that they were much more numerous than originally thought. Griffith's report stated:

> *Most of the rooms (of the Hypogeum) were found to be half-filled with earth, human bones and broken pottery. It has (now) been estimated that the ruins contained the bones of 33,000 persons...Practically all were found in the greatest disorder...*[47]

So how did so many human remains become violently and suddenly entombed within this underground structure? Was this once again the direct result of a sudden/violent/end-stopping event?

Anton Mifsud, an archeologist on the island of Malta, states quite clearly how the *Hypogeum* came to be filled with human remains. According to Mifsud:

> *The accumulation of human remains at Hypogeum...were not related to primary ritual burial, but were brought down into the Hypogeum labyrinth through the action of flood-water in a matrix of 'red earth' and soil.*[48]

In another underground structure known as the *Hypogeum of Santa Lucia*, a similar 'chaotic deposit' of human remains, broken pottery and 'red soil' was found on Malta in the early 1970s.[49]

Other caves on Malta also show similar signs of flood deposits brought on by some type of massive cataclysm which deposited muddy earth, clay and pebbles mixed with a huge assortment of animal and human remains.[50]

Were the builders of the megalithic structures of Malta destroyed in a great disaster that 'wiped out' their civilization, destroying buildings and entombing 'tens of thousands' of individuals in these underground Hypogeums? Could the ancient inhabitants of Malta have built these underground Hypogeums in order to escape the ravages of the last 'cycle of destruction,' but instead became entombed in them as a giant wave suddenly washed over their island?

What type of severe geologic event could have sent ancient Maltese structures to the bottom of the sea? Why are there ancient 'cart ruts' that were once used to move items around the island, now found offshore—underwater?

Is the ancient Egyptian description of the "usual inundation" once again at work here?

As we will investigate later in this chapter, these are questions in which the current Maltese government is trying very hard to avoid answering. *Of course the key question is: WHY?*

Chaotic graveyards

The island of Malta in the Mediterranean and Lake Titicaca in Peru, are unfortunately not the only locations on Earth where large numbers of human remains have been violently and chaotically entombed for the ages.

In a large cave near Peking, China, the bones of mammoths, buffaloes and humans have been uncovered, once again all chaotically mixed together as if deposited by a great flood.[51]

Chaotic deposits of human remains have been uncovered at *Lagoa de Sumidouro* near Santa Lucia, in *Bishop's Cap Cave* in New Mexico, in *Gypsum Cave* near Las Vegas, Nevada, and in numerous other locations throughout the world. These human remains are often badly smashed and disarticulated—showing classic signs of having undergone powerful geologic forces.[52]

The global cataclysms we are investigating in this book, however, are indiscriminate in their destructive influence—and affect both animal and human alike without prejudice. It is therefore not surprising that massive 'chaotic graveyards' of only animals should also be found throughout the world as well.

In Siberia, Alaska and numerous other places around the Arctic Circle, 'appalling deposits' of mammoths, mastodons, super-bison, lions, horses, hippopotamuses, elephants, rhinoceroses and many other species, including humans, have recently been uncovered. These mass graveyards lie frozen in tangled chaos along with broken and splintered tree trunks that are heaped into piles many 'hundreds of feet' high.[53]

In Europe, similar chaotic deposits have been uncovered in dozens of locations. These morbid animal graveyards often include the remains of horses, hippopotamuses, mammoths, red deer and bovids, all chaotically mixed with shattered tree trunks including maple, coniferous, fir, oak, alder and hazel. Researchers that have uncovered these deposits concluded that: *"A great (and violent) flood had overwhelmed these organisms."* [54]

These same types of 'chaotic' animal graveyards are also found in dozens of other locations around the Mediterranean, including Crete, Corsica, Sardinia, mainland Greece, Cyprus, Italy and Sicily to name a few. These chaotic piles of animal remains often include those of hyenas, lions, bears, elephants, hippopotamuses and dozens of other mammals—all in 'apocalyptic' numbers and in total disarray.

So numerous and in such quantity are the animal remains in these Mediterranean graveyards, that from one cave alone on the island of Sicily, over twenty tons of bones were removed within a six month period. All of these Mediterranean sites also showed the classic signs of having been entombed under exceptionally violent and sudden geologic conditions.[55]

Not only have massive graveyards of large animal and human remains been uncovered in recent years, but also so have huge deposits of insects, birds, reptiles, rodents, plants and a plethora of sea creatures of all types—heaped into chaotic piles throughout the world. These morbid collections of animal remains often contain countless numbers of their carcasses—all showing signs of having been torn apart by the action of high winds and water.

The physical placement of these animal remains also offers some idea as to the extreme geologic upheavals that lead to their demise. In North America for example, around Lake Michigan, the bones of whales have been uncovered in soil 582 feet above today's sea level. North of Lake Ontario, whale skeletons have been found 440 feet above sea level, in Vermont, 500 feet above, and in Montreal-Quebec, 600 feet.[56]

Since whales do not come ashore and climb hills, the presence of these skeletons can only be explained in one of two ways. Either these areas were at one time (in the recent past) hundreds of feet underwater, or some form of massive oceanic 'inundation' brought these sea creatures to their current resting places.

Archeologists have determined that many of these massive animal gravesites were formed in the recent past, possibly just a few thousand years ago. These mass graveyards are most definitely <u>not</u> the result of a slow accumulation of animal remains. In fact, these enormous piles of broken animal carcasses were formed so recently that skin, ligaments, hair and even flesh, can still be clearly seen clinging to these animals—but the bodies have all been 'torn apart' and 'dismembered' under the most extreme catastrophic conditions.[57]

In their book *Cataclysm*, scientists, D. S. Allan and J. B. Delair, concluded that these worldwide graveyards were formed after the passage of a giant 'celestial object' which tore our entire planet apart virtually overnight and once again, without warning.

Allan and Delair go on to say:

> *Only some closely approaching 'cosmic object' of considerable size could activate these titanic forces...and would be necessary to produce such gargantuan topographical and biological changes so rapidly and extensively on Earth.*[58]

The passing of this celestial object produced:

> *A hurricane and a deluge operating on a scale and with ferocity far beyond that of which modern humanity has any experience...it acted globally and indiscriminately...a repeating pattern of wholesale destruction...put bluntly, it was a time of unbridled turmoil.*[59]

In fact, these past cataclysmic events were so violent and widespread, they have lead to the extinction of thousands of species each time they transpire. Species such as mammoths, mastodons, saber-tooth tigers, ground sloth's, pigmy horses, dwarf elephants and thousands of other exotic species are no longer with us today—because countless numbers of their carcasses are entombed around this planet in massive chaotic graveyards.

Other ancient enigmatic sites from around the world

We've investigated only a tiny fraction of the mysterious archeological sites hidden away around the world vindicating ancient accounts of those cosmic violent events destroying civilizations. And quite fortunately for us, there are many other camouflaged sites around the planet also demonstrating similar evidence of civilizations that have been suddenly and violently destroyed.

Undersea off the two tiny atoll-like islands of Bimini, 45 miles east of Fort Lauderdale, Florida, lays a megalithic carved stonewall structure called the 'Bimini Road.' This enigmatic formation was discovered in shallow 15-20 foot waters off North Bimini Island in 1968, by Dr. J. Manson Valentine and his brilliant diving crew—fueling heated scientific controversy ever since.

This information was documented in a series of (on topic) books with the *New York Times* best selling book of all time—*The Bermuda Triangle,* (Double Day Publishing Co., 1974). It was instantly translated into more than 62 world languages, getting United Nations recognition and numerous book awards with all (language versions) of them becoming 'number one best-selling' hits around the world. No book of its 'nature' has ever enjoyed that kind of success in print.

The 'Bimini Road' as the locals called it—consisted of a series of large, wide, flat, beach stones forming what 'looks like' the giant construction of a mysterious underwater highway leading off (in a westerly direction) as it approaches the steep precipice of the powerfully moving, thousands of foot deep, where the Gulf Stream begins. Some of the stones in this road are monstrously huge weighing over fifteen tons each and seemingly perfectly aligned—while in some places they appeared to be perfectly 'cemented/linked' together.[60]

This road extends for some distance off shore and when viewed, especially from the air, certainly looks man-made. We scuba-dived this site in 1976-75 and were amazed by what we found there.

In the same area, just a short distance from the Bimini road, we discovered several rather strange rock formations. One of these structures in particular when viewed from the air, clearly resembles the shape of a large prehistoric shark. And off another near by island we also discovered a series of neatly aligned, carved stone 'turtle pens' and what could be 'fish farm' containment complexes built to harvest fish, etc.

From 1974 until Dr. Valentine died in 1982, I had the distinct pleasure of diving, researching and working with my good friend and teacher, a triple Ph.D., earning a B.A. and his first Doctorate in Zoology (1928) from Yale University. Valentine was a world-renowned authority in speleology, marine/land archeology, entomology, a certified scuba diver, photographer, oceanographer, explorer, flyer, cartographer, artist, teacher and a prolific writer.

Along with his sometimes co-writer, Charles Berlitz, they wrote the great mega-*New York Times* number one hit, *The Bermuda Triangle*, followed later by three other hot best sellers, *Doomsday 1999 A.D., Mysteries From Forgotten Worlds*, and *Without a Trace*.

Having received a special diving charter and permission from the Bahamian government, Dr. Valentine headed up a research diving group sponsored by Dr. Doris L. Johnson (President of the Bahamian Senate from 1971-1979). Dr. Johnson lead a coalition of top business executives and government leaders interested in establishing a new tourist attraction, *The Bahamas Antiquities Museum,* in Nassau, their Bahamian capital).

Jim Richardson, a veteran pilot from WWII, owned and operated *Opa Locka Flight Center*—one of east Florida's premier air charter and flight service operations. Jim served as our veteran pilot, flying a host of different aircraft and equipment as needed. Our land base was his flight operations center at *Opa Loca International Airport* near *Ft. Lauderdale International*. Our sea base was his world-class fly-in fishing and diving resort—the premier Bahamian yacht club— called *The Perfect Angler*. He owned and managed this *tropical* beds and breakfast, motel, hotel, night club all week, all month, or forever holiday hideaway—situated on tropical South Bimini—just a five-minute ferry ride across the sometimes treacherous Bimini Channel— crossing over to its sister town, North Bimini.

During the course of our exciting and sometimes dangerous five-year escapade cruising the southernmost apex of the now infamous *Bermuda Triangle*, we saw, openly witnessed, filmed, recorded, discovered, wrote about dozens of incredible 'construction anomalies' we uncovered on the floor of the ocean around the Biminis and other Bahamian Islands.

For instance, after several years of perfectly planning to recreate the exact 'course,' 'timing' and 'anniversary date flight' of the 'lost patrol,' (one of the Bermuda's Triangle's most infamous tales)—*whatever ever happened to "Flight 19?"*

On 5 December 1945, a squadron of five U.S. Avenger Torpedo Bombers, seemingly disappeared/vanished on a routine training flight into the Bermuda Triangle. They were flying a pre-plotted triangular course taking them eastward out over the Bahamian Islands just off Ft. Lauderdale—their original departure point.

Their normal 'flying time' would have been 2.5 - 3.0 hours in duration—depending on weather conditions. All five planes with their flight crews plus an 11-member search and rescue flying amphibian plane—all mysteriously/completely disappeared late that afternoon about 6:00 pm—without a trace to this day.

Well, we believe all that changed on the blustery afternoon of Sunday, December 5, 1980. That date was the 40th anniversary (right to the day of Sunday) of Flight 19's haunting demise. With Jim, the captain of his ship and myself acting as co-pilot/flight engineer/navigator, we were joined by my friend and associate, Aaron Paul Dey—a brave-hearted soul indeed.

With the official weather data as solid evidence of a 'go flight' that day—the first 'factor' (exact matching weather patterns as they were in 1945), hatched itself into a very strange/unfolding/ compelling/spellbinding drama—as N3357Lima—(Pilot Richardson's favorite airplane's license plate), was about to launch <u>herself</u> into <u>her own</u> 'survival drama' pitted against the dreaded Bermuda Triangle. The sturdy Cessna-182 filled with enough gas to comfortably navigate our objective of recreating 'Flight 19's' several hundred mile 1945 flight plan and back stood ready idling at the end of the same runway <u>they'd</u> lifted off from—40 years ago (12/05/45) to the day.

The entire story of our 'Flight 19' recreated anniversary flight and our perilous mission that day, (based on exactly what happened to us during that flight) leads us to discover where we believe the remains of at least four of those lost Avenger bombers lay buried beneath the sand in the Atlantic ocean—is contained in yet another book under writing.

And what happened to us really happens only in sci-fi stories—unless of course you've survived the *Triangle of Death* and lived to tell about it! We now think Flight 19 lies about three miles offshore submerged in water 400-550 feet deep, waiting to be found in a loose 'crash pattern' possible a mile-wide at most. *OK—so where are they??* The answer to that key question might 'surprise' you, making 'it' the ideal subject for a proposed fascinating new *National Geographic* undersea TV special: **Flight 19's Coming Home.** *Here's a hint: Grand Bahama Island saved us.*

In September 1976, a close friend and an old army buddy of mine from Chicago, Gary Freund, joined me in South Bimini for several days of diving and relaxation. One afternoon with the tide running out the main entrance to the two Biminis (and the small channel leading into the harbor itself), we had enough shallow water (6-8 feet) for free diving on artifacts. Digging into the loose sand we discovered one of the most important modern-day archeological finds in the islands. Suddenly protruding up from the channel's bottom was a 4.5-foot section of a *Doric Capital Relief* cut marble column (pure white/shiny) and weighing nearly three thousand pounds.

This white marble stone piece and its architecture were not indigenous to the Bahamian Islands! And how it got 'there' from 'wherever ' it 'came from' still remains a mystery. However, we should note that we did raise the heavy stone column from the Bimini Channel. It was turned over to Dr. Johnson who was quite thrilled, proudly adding 'it' to the many other 'found treasures' we'd discovered over the years for her impassioned, *Bahamas Antiquities Museum.*

Oh, and one further note! This 'treasured antiquities find' got a lot of press and attention in the Islands—maybe a little 'too much'! Because late one night it mysteriously disappeared from the museum—*all 4.5 thousand pounds of it*—*probably into the hands of some rich private antiquities collector seeking genuine Atlantian artifacts??* We also believe there is much more of this same Atlantian marble waiting to be found in that 'current-swept' channel, but more on that idea later.

Could these curious granite columns be fragments of a once great civilization that lived in this area before it was largely 'ripped apart' by the great cycle of destruction? Strangely, local Bimini folklore does mention that this area was the home of an advanced civilization that long ago vanished after a great global cataclysm struck.

Was this discovery yet another remnant of Plato's Atlantis? And was the sunken stone Lithium spring we discovered hidden out in the mangrove swap (due east of North Bimini), the infamous "Fountain of Youth" that Spanish explorer, Juan Ponce de Leon (1474-1521), so desperately sought in 1513 on his first expedition to the 'New World?' No wonder Earnest Hemingway chose Bimini as the place he penned one of his most beloved books, *The Old Man And the Sea.*

Now moving on—we're off to the Maldives Islands, where divers have reported finding strange stairways and other step-like structures leading off into the deep abyss as well.[61]

On the Island of Crete, the historic home of the ancient Minoan culture, archeologists have just uncovered ruins that indicate an 'overwhelming' catastrophe essentially ended this once great civilization—sending many of their elegantly designed structures to the bottom of the sea.[62]

And on the volcanic Island of Thera archeologist, Doctor K. T. Frost, a studies professor from the University of Belfast, recently uncovered 'street after street' of ancient Minoan houses—all blanketed by thick layers of volcanic ash and dust.[63]

Off the coast of modern-day Yonaguni, Japan, in relatively shallow water, lay the monumental ruins of another mysterious civilization—one that long ago vanished beneath Pacific waves.[64]

In the calm waters of the Gulf of Morbihan, off a small island called Er-Lannic, sit the remains of an ancient structure known as the *Cromlech*—whose massive walls can still be seen from the ocean's surface at low tide.[65]

Other ancient walls and building structures can be found in the waters of the north Atlantic including areas around the Scilly Isles, the Channel Islands, Kernic, Ireland and Rostellan near Cork Harbor.[66] England and the European North Atlantic region appear to have concentrated areas of megalithic constructions. Stonehenge, a prehistoric megalithic monument located on the Salisbury Plain in South England, is probably the most visible (still standing) evidence on land.

The legendary underwater archeologist, Nicholas Flemming, recently discovered the submerged ruins of an ancient city called *Elaphonisos* lying off the coast of Greece. From numerous discoveries made at this eerie and tragic site, it was determined that *Elaphonisos* was destroyed and submerged beneath the sea suddenly—and violently.[67]

Recently, archeologists also discovered the remains of a destroyed ancient civilization in the area of modern-day Brazil that once may have supported as many as 200-million inhabitants. This civilization was wiped out thousands of years ago leaving virtually no trace of its existence. One archeologist was recently quoted as saying, *"It's as if a giant wave (had) swept across the entire country of what is today Brazil, leaving nothing of this former great civilization except for their canals and fields."* [68]

There are literally hundreds—even thousands of other sites from around the world (both above and below water), which also contain the 'shattered remains' of civilizations that were long ago destroyed by an ongoing catastrophic process.

Once again, keep in mind that some of the most famous ancient structures (that are still standing on 'dry land' today) cover the remains of earlier destroyed structures that lay buried beneath them. —Let's note the same pattern of sudden destruction followed by rebuilding as a common theme.

These famous structures include such sites as the *Temple Mount* in Jerusalem, the *Cadiz* in Spain, the *Lixus* in Morocco, the *Acropolis* in Athens, *Cuzco* in Peru and *Ba'albek* in Lebanon, just to name a few. And it's widely believed that most of the Mexican pyramids are similar sites.

The remains of the older structures underlying these famous edifices often show signs of large stones having been smashed to pieces by extreme geophysical forces, walls that have been knocked sideways off their foundations—as if hit by some mysterious and violent force and 'vitrified' rubble that has been fused together by intense heat. This practice of rebuilding on the rubble of earlier 'destroyed ruins' is the end result of repeated destructions that have transpired over and over again throughout history in those regions.

Many other sites from around the world have also been uncovered with 'volcanic ash' and 'flood debris' submerging whole buildings, streets and tragically—piles of human remains. Clearly, all of this physical evidence strongly suggests that these ancient civilizations truly met with cataclysmic fates exactly as their 'oral traditions' would indicate.

In his groundbreaking book, *The Greatest Story Never Told*, author J. Wilson French states:

> *One of the more pronounced facts is that within this century many a buried or destroyed city of an ancient civilization has been exhumed (uncovered). In each and all instances they are covered with silt and soils as from a flood. To name a few of these destroyed cities; in the Aegean Sea there are the cities of Connasus, Phaestus, Troy, Tylissus, Gournia, as well as the mythical lost (continent of) Atlantis.*
>
> *In the Near East there are the cities of Eridu, Ur, Urak, Lagash, Lasa, Nippur, and Nisin. In India there are the cities of Mohenjo-daro and Harappa. And in Eqypt, are the most*

grand and magnificent constructions that likewise have the same apparent conditions of being buried beneath soils. All these exhumed cities have the appearance of having passed through fire, earthquakes, and having been covered up by water and soils.

A hundred cities on the island of Crete and the deleted Etruscans, Carthaginians and southern Italians are all mute evidence of a great calamity. The same general picture is prevalent in Mexico, Honduras, South America and elsewhere.[69]

Many archeologists in recent years have concluded that these ancient sites have in fact been 'decimated' by geophysical disasters. However, some of these same archeologists have tried to argue that these disasters were merely local events, not affecting wide areas of the planet at the same time. Upon closer examination however, researchers have conceded that the events that wiped out many of these ancient civilizations were truly global and monumental in scope, both in their intensity and size. *Absolute and utter destruction was the norm—not the exception!*

J. Wilson French, who also maintained that such widespread damage to Earth could only have resulted from the passing of a large celestial object, goes on to say:

The Event (that simultaneously destroyed these ancient cities) was not localized in any one section, but was "worldwide." [70]

Archeologist, Claude Schaeffer, who spent a great deal of his life excavating the ruins of ancient cities throughout the Middle East, determined that a great catastrophe virtually wiped out most of this area. In his book, *Earth in Upheaval*, Dr. Immanuel Velikovsky echoes Mr. Schaeffer's findings when he writes:

All of these catastrophes (involving) earthquakes and fire (conflagration) were of such encompassing extent that Asia Minor, Mesopotamia, the Caucasus, the Iranian Plateau, Syria, Palestine, Cyprus and Egypt were simultaneously overwhelmed.[71]

In his findings, Claude Schaeffer cites dozens of examples in which cities throughout the Middle East were hit by such a violent upheaval, that: *"walls were thrown from their foundations"* and populations were *"markedly decreased."* [72]

These are only a few examples of the mounting body of evidence that definitively demonstrates many ancient civilizations have indeed met with a violent and untimely demise. As a matter of fact, there are so many recent archeological finds along these lines, that a thorough discussion of them would fill an entire library of books.

Suffice it to say that these 'catastrophic accounts' (within the 'recorded histories' of our planet's ancient civilizations) are more than adequately supported by a plethora of physical archeological evidence we find scattered across the planet.

But if our ancient ancestors have left so many accurate 'historic accounts' of massive planetary disasters taking place, and the 'physical evidence' uncovered strongly supports this catastrophic past—why is our modern-day society not more aware of these past events? Aside from a few popular examples of past cataclysms, like the story of Noah in the Bible, why is our modern-day world so ignorant of our planet's true cataclysmic history? Are there geopolitical reasons?

As we will see in the next section of this chapter—this ignorance may not be entirely accidental.

Re-burying the past

All things considered, it is surprising just how much current archeological evidence has surfaced over the recent years supporting the idea that ancient civilizations have met with sudden and catastrophic endings. *But if there is so much archeological evidence around the world indicating past cataclysms having affected ancient cultures, why is this cataclysmic past not more common in knowledge/understanding/acceptance?*

There seems to be several different reasons for this lack of critical awareness.

The first reason is simply a matter of 'prejudice' and 'bias' on the part of modern archeologists. Archeologists have an old saying that goes something like: *"It's a good thing we <u>knew</u> what we were looking for—or we <u>wouldn't</u> have found it."*

The problem arises in that many archeologists do not fully 'understand' or 'appreciate' the concept of catastrophism, (the idea that the evolution of civilizations is shaped by catastrophes).

Many archeologists therefore simply dismiss ancient histories and oral traditions as 'fairy-tales' and don't give these ancient accounts the credit they truly deserve. Because of this, many archeologists also dismiss the physical evidence relating to Earth's catastrophic past. In other words, if an archeologist doesn't <u>believe in</u> or <u>know about</u> the cataclysmic history of the Earth, they simply <u>dismiss</u> or <u>ignore</u> the mounting evidence relating to the planet's catastrophic past.

In their must-read book, *The Hidden History of the Human Race* authors, Michael Cremo and Richard Thompson, discuss this concept and call it the *"knowledge filter."* This is a term that describes the tendency for mainstream scientists to 'filter out' certain evidence that doesn't fit into their current/accepted theories or preconceived ideas of the way events in the past unfolded.

Michael Cremo and Richard Thompson go on to say:

> *We looked closely at the vast amount of controversial evidence that contradicts current ideas about human evolution (history). We recount in detail how this evidence has been systematically suppressed, ignored or forgotten, even though it is qualitatively (and quantitatively) equivalent to the evidence favoring currently accepted views on human origins.*
>
> *We are talking about an ongoing social process of 'knowledge filtration' that appears quite innocuous but has a substantial cumulative effect on society and science.[73]*

In other words, what this so-called *"knowledge filter"* does is allow archeologists to accept some 'evidence' as <u>being true</u> (and therefore important), but other equally valid 'evidence' as <u>not being true</u> (and therefore not important). If certain facts do not fit into a scientist's favored scientific theory, then these facts are 'discarded' and/or 'swept under the carpet,' removing them from any further discussion or research.

This type of *"knowledge filter"* happens all the time on archeological digs and has been a major factor in keeping the true cataclysmic history of the Earth from being fully realized/understood. Even if an ancient site shows clear evidence of having met with a violent end, many archeologists simply dismiss this evidence because it <u>does not fit</u> into their 'understanding' or 'preconceived ideas' about the past. Often this evidence is simply ignored and neither addressed nor dealt with further— *(the "knowledge filter" at work?)*

As a hypothetical example, a modern archeologist uncovers an ancient building and conducts a lengthy excavation of the site. While working at this hypothetical ancient site he carefully dates it, catalogues every small item found within it, and writes up a detailed report—which is then released in archeological journals throughout the world.

The fact that they had to dig down through 30 feet of solid mud, which apparently overran this ancient structure so quickly and with such force, that it knocked the structure from its foundation—is 'under emphasized' or even simply 'left out' of the final analysis/report all together.

Even though this ancient culture may have left detailed historic records of having been destroyed by a great 'muddy' disaster, archeologists simply dismiss these historic records (and often the physical evidence discovered) as being irrelevant and/or totally unimportant to the overall understanding of the site. *What is the true purpose of archeology if not to uncover <u>all of the facts</u>?*

So this is the *"knowledge filter"* creatively at work—seen selectively screening the evidence that is found—and then molding it into a personal/preconceived notion of the way things were/or not!

And this *"knowledge filter"* is not the only factor that stands in the way of a better understanding of our past. Many archeologists and other scientists simple do not want to study the catastrophic history of our planet because they find it <u>unsavory</u> or even <u>depressing</u>. Because of this, the vast amount of research efforts and dollars, are channeled away from archeological projects dealing with cataclysms and into other 'more pleasant' areas of academia—ones far less stressful.

In addition, many of the archeologists that are willing to study or entertain Earth's cataclysmic past, do not understand two important facts. First, these cataclysms take place globally and second, that they take place on a 'periodic' or 'cyclical' timetable.

Many archeologists believe that any ancient civilization that was catastrophically destroyed in the past—simply involved an isolated incident that affected that one civilization alone. They often do not look at the 'bigger picture' and fail to recognize that the ancient site they are studying is simply an isolated 'piece' of a global disaster 'puzzle' beyond their understanding.

Many archeologists also fail to realize the past destruction to planet Earth is 'cyclic' in nature and happens over and over again. Because they fail to recognize this periodic pattern of global destruction, they believe past disasters bare no relevance to our current day and age! Because of this dismissive attitude they fail to recognize that these past events are, in reality—harbingers of what's in store for us in the near future. Years 2000-2006 should ring the planetary 'panic bell!'

One of the most important reasons our modern society is largely ignorant of our disastrous past however, is going to sound a little conspiratorial, but it's relevant/therefore important to mention at this time. New Orleans was a prime example of a nation unprepared for Mother Nature's fury.

After studying the catastrophic history of our planet for years, many researchers firmly believe that governments throughout the world have repeatedly 'stone-walled,' delayed or flat out denied archeological investigations of important ancient sites. These sites could have shed volumes of light on Earth's true apocalyptic history if they were more open to full investigations. These sites however, have mostly been kept 'secret,' 'buried,' 'out of sight,' from serious archeological investigation—yet another example of the *"knowledge filter"* at work in this field…

Many governments including those of Greece, Egypt, the Caribbean, South and Central America, the Middle East and the Orient, have all come under criticism for deliberately standing in the way of organized excavations of their important/ancient/invaluable archeological sites.

As a personal example, a few years ago in Greece we inquired about scuba diving around the small island we were visiting. We were however, 'adamantly' told by the local authorities that: *"diving anywhere around these islands, and under 'any' circumstances, was strictly forbidden by the Greek government."* A strange attitude for a government that makes much of its revenue from tourism and the allure of its past history! Admittedly, we were confused from the start.

Was there something lying in the waters of this Greek island that we weren't supposed to see? And were they afraid of what we might find and/or report? And when asked why we weren't permitted to dive the local 'hot spot' locations—their answer was simply: *"Forget about it!"*

Unfortunately, the Greek government is hardly alone in forbidding or strictly limiting scuba diving in its territorial waters. Many other governments from around the world have reacted, sometimes even violently, to any inquiries regarding underwater exploration off their coastal waters. *Once again, we are asking why? What secrets are they hiding from their people?*

If a person wishes to dive in the waters around Alexandria, Egypt, one must first endure a long complicated process of red tape bureaucracy. Permissions must first be obtained from the Ministry of Information, the Ministry of National Security, the Supreme Council of Antiquities, the Police, and Customs—even the Egyptian Navy.[74] *Who are they trying to frighten away and why?*

If one does manage to complete this long application process—most requests in the end are simply flat-out denied. If you do manage to obtain permission, you're likely to be accompanied by 'official watchers' from the Egyptian government—who probably won't allow photography of anything 'suspect' or 'archeological' in nature while diving on these ancient sites.

Why all the red tape? According to the Egyptian government—*"There's nothing of importance or anything worth investigating off the coast of Alexandria in the first place!"* Or <u>*might there be*</u> *something important lying off Alexandria's coast that Egyptian officials aren't telling us about?*

Many other governments from around the world seem to have this same, strange 'phobia' (that often borders on 'paranoia') regarding diving in their waters. And it's these same governments who also steadfastly maintain: *"There's 'nothing of real interest' in their seas in the first place!"*

The limiting of underwater exploration is not the only form of 'strange behavior' on the part of many governments. Some/if not most governments have fiercely stood in the way of any archeological progress undertaken on land as well.

The government of Malta for example, maintains a long history of 'stone-walling' important archeological finds. The Maltese government has been accused of losing, stealing and lying about 'critical evidence' found at many of their archeological sites. They have permanently 'buried' important sites in hasty landfills and deliberately allowed developers to bury other sites beneath tons of concrete. They have permanently sealed many important archeological digs behind locked gates, while deliberately and repeatedly destroying evidence from others.[75]

The Maltese government is not alone in this type of obstructive behavior however; many other reports have surfaced through the years about similar destruction of important sites by other governments—including the U.S. government and its agents.

A recent *60 Minutes* TV segment aired a fascinating story on an archeological site in the U.S. Pacific Northwest producing artifacts that were so important, local archeologists working at the site stated: *"The history of this country may have to be rewritten."*

As the U.S. Congress was passing an urgent congressional order to preserve this site—the U.S. Army seized the location, physically removed the archeologists from the area and immediately dumped 'hundreds of thousands' of tons of gravel and earth over the location, essentially putting an end to any further excavation of this find. The Army then confiscated the artifacts already found and locked them away—forbidding any future investigation of this site.

After a highly publicized protest from the archeologists and members of the U.S. Congress, the Army released a public relations statement claiming that they had to cover the site in such a hurry because of 'erosion problems' and then refused to comment on the incident any further.

Unfortunately, literally dozens of other stories have surfaced in recent years regarding this same destruction of important archeological sites pertaining to Earth's ancient history. Different governments have gone so far as expelling archeologists from specific sites where major discoveries were being uncovered and then 'blowing up' these sites with dynamite—or encasing them under of concrete.

Why are so many governments around the world destroying or limiting access to these important archeological finds? What are they hiding? What are they attempting to 'cover up'—and why?

The answer in fact just may be surprisingly simple. Many governments throughout the world currently have to contend with great 'difficulties' in running their countries. Political and religious strife, global terrorism, hard-core military dictators, recent natural disasters, escalating shortages of food/water, rampant malnutrition, increasing hunger, lack of clean drinking water, improper sanitation, diminishing natural resources, economic and financial hardships, crumbling infrastructures, civil and racial unrest, religious fanaticism, global/domestic epidemics, pandemics, the new bird flu and social uprisings—are only some of the many/varied problems which most governments around the world are currently facing on a daily basis.

Many governments today feel that with all of the problems they are currently facing, they are barely able to maintain reasonable 'law and order' as it is. These governments constantly fear losing political control of their countries by having things 'come apart at the seams.' Governments around the world have learned that once societies start to become unraveled, they are very difficult to put back together. Many governments are therefore 'paranoid' of anything that may have a further destabilizing influence or effect on their countries.

The cataclysmic history of our planet is not very difficult to figure out, especially if you look at, or 'seek out' the right information. It would be naive to think that most governments don't have some idea that their country (geographic area), has been affected by destructive geological forces in the past—and will likely be affected by *"catastrophism"* in the near future.

If 'scientifically organized' or even 'accidental archeological discoveries' start publicly revealing the true 'cataclysmic history' of Earth and the 'destructive cycles' that we periodically undergo —this knowledge could prove to be extremely destabilizing/destructive to an already highly unstable environment/situation.

If you add in the fact that we may be rapidly approaching one of these 'destructive cycles' and if the general public in these countries were to learn that 'the world' as we 'know it' was in for some really big changes, 'social chaos' would erupt—long before any geophysical chaos did.

We believe this to be the main reason that many governments have been 'covering up' important archeological discoveries, and why they're so uncomfortable granting access to their country's archeological sites. Their collective motto seemingly reads: *"Keep our catastrophic past hidden —and we won't have to answer difficult questions about our catastrophic future."*

With keeping this rationale in mind, governmental 'stonewalling' of so many archeological sites throughout the world suddenly starts to make a lot more sense in a really confused world—2006.

Missing links

Before we conclude this chapter there is one important point that we should make clear!

Many of the ancient civilizations that existed at the beginning of our 'recorded history' (only several thousand years ago) seem to have appeared out of nowhere! In other words, many of the oldest civilizations that we are aware of today, appeared on the historical stage fully developed— with all of the trappings of civilization fully formed and functioning prior to their launch dates.

As we trace our understanding of history back in time, the very earliest civilizations that we are aware of—had remarkably developed understandings of architecture, metallurgy, mathematics, astronomy, cosmology, writing, animal husbandry, agriculture, textiles, ceramic manufacturing and a litany of other skills that are usually reserved for older more advanced cultures.

How is it that these early civilizations were so developed at the very beginnings of our recorded history? And how did these early cultures get this special knowledge and where did they get it?

Many scholars believe there were fully developed 'proto-civilizations' in existence for thousands of years before the earliest civilizations that we are aware of today. Historical scholars such as Gram Hancock, John Anthony West, Zecharia Sitchin, J.J. Hurtak, Dr. J. Manson Valentine and many countless others, have all come to this conclusion in their recent works.

According to Mr. Hancock for example:

> *The archeological evidence suggests that rather than developing slowly and painfully…(our earliest known civilizations)…emerged all at once and fully formed. Indeed, this period of transition from primitive to advanced society appears to have been so short that it makes no kind of historic sense.*

> *Technological skills that should have taken hundreds or even thousands of years to evolve were suddenly brought into use almost overnight—and with no apparent antecedents (predecessors) whatever.*[76]

Historian John Anthony West, a noted authority on ancient Egyptian civilization, has come to the same conclusion stating:

> *How does a complex civilization spring full-blown into being? Look at a 1905 automobile and then compare it to a modern one. There is no mistaking the process of 'development.' But in Egypt there are no parallels. Everything is right there at the start.*

> *The answer to <u>this mystery</u> is of course <u>obvious</u> but, because it is repellent to the prevailing cast of modern thinking, it is seldom considered. Egyptian civilization was not a 'development'—it was a 'legacy.'*[77]

In other words, the most ancient civilizations that we are familiar with today (from only a few thousand years ago) are in fact, simply the remnants of much earlier 'proto-civilizations' that existed on Earth long before 'them…' and then the ones before 'them.'

These 'proto-civilizations' that existed before our recorded history began, had very developed cultures, but still could not stop the ravages of the *'usual inundation'* from wiping them off the map—leaving only a few survivors that gave rise to these earlier 'proto-civilizations' that we are familiar with today.

The idea that 'proto-civilizations' have existed on this planet before our recorded history began, is supported by more that just cultural enigmas, however. For centuries, strange 'out of place' remnants of long forgotten technology/science have been uncovered throughout the world.

In the eighteenth century, French workmen quarrying limestone very near the town of *Aix-en Province* uncovered mysterious stone columns, coins, and the petrified wooden handles of tools buried beneath massive layers of sandy sediments and limestone. These strange, enigmatic remnants of a past civilization represent the forgotten remains of a people who were wiped off the face of the Earth 'tens,' or even 'hundreds of thousands' of years before our recorded history began.[78]

In South Africa, miners have uncovered hundreds of strange metallic spheres with parallel grooves around their equators—deep within mine shafts. *Where these metallic spheres came from and how they became located deep underground is a total mystery?* Once again, these metallic spheres are thought to be 'hundreds of thousands' of years old—possibly even older.[79]

In 1852, a bell-shaped vessel was blown out of 15 feet of solid stone by workmen while excavating just outside Boston, Massachusetts. This enigmatic object was beautifully inlaid with pure silver and decorated with imagery of flowers and flowing vines. Pictures of this incredibly well-crafted object still hang in several 'curio' museums today, but exactly how this unusual vessel had become entombed in solid rock, possibly 'hundreds or thousands' of years ago still remains a puzzling riddle.[80]

In 1871, the *Smithsonian Institution* reported that miners uncovered copper coins in a mineshaft 114 feet beneath the surface of Marshall County, Illinois. In 1889, a small human figurine was unearthed 300 feet below the surface of Nampa, Idaho. In 1891, *The Morrisonville Times* in Illinois reported that a Mrs. S. W. Culp broke open a large piece of coal while stoking a furnace and found a ten-inch gold chain of exquisite workmanship embedded deep inside it.[81] Lucky her!

On 2 April 1897, the *Daily News* of Omaha, Nebraska reported that coal miners had found large intricate stone carvings, some displaying human faces, at a depth of 130 feet. In 1912 a large iron cup was discovered embedded in a large chunk of coal in Oklahoma.[82]

In 1928, coal miners uncovered a solid wall of perfectly polished stone blocks two miles beneath the surface of Heavener, Oklahoma. In 1868, a similar wall of smooth, polished stone blocks was uncovered in a coal mine located near Hammondville, Ohio.[83] *Could all of these strange anomalies be a mere coincidence or is there a more compelling answer we've not yet discovered?*

In the Middle East, an ancient clay vessel with inserted copper rods has been uncovered that remarkably produces electricity. This strange object has been affectionately termed the 'Baghdad Battery' and is believed to be thousands of years old.

Complicated parts of machinery with intricate gears have been discovered lying on the bottom of the Mediterranean Sea, encrusted by thousands of years of marine growth. In the 1950s, a 50 thousand-year-old geode was sliced open to reveal what appears to be an embedded spark plug.

These are only a few examples of the hundreds of 'out of place' remnants of technology and artifacts that have been uncovered over the years. All conclusively demonstrating that advanced civilizations lived on this planet before our recorded history began. Clearly, there is much more detail about the past history of our world that we do not understand!

Unfortunately, most, if not all of these arcane discoveries have been 'swept' under the carpet by modern-day scientists—who refuse to consider that our current version of history is willfully incomplete and myopic. These examples of discovered 'past technology' are a blatant reminder of our current historic inadequacy (with the 'knowledge filter' at work).

Recall from the last chapter how the ancient cultures from the start of our recorded history said that: *"We currently live in the 'fourth' incarnation of this world and that the preceding 'three' incarnations were all extinguished by the passage of the terrible "red" comet."*

The ancient civilizations that we are familiar with from the beginnings of this 'fourth world' (the one in which we currently live), were merely the recipients of some of the cultural knowledge and technology from the exterminated 'third world' civilizations preceding us. That is why the earliest civilizations from our own 'fourth world' seem to have suddenly appeared on the world-scene so fully developed and apparently schooled with specific knowledge and skills.

The fact that these 'proto-civilizations' are no longer with us today is still further evidence of their fate. They were obliterated from the world-stage by the destructive power of the passing terrible comet—leaving a cultural 'missing link' and a 'blank period' in Earth's history as their legacy. Civilized 'starts' and sudden 'stops' appear to permeate the fabric of many lost cultures.

In conclusion…

Let us indulge ourselves for a moment with a hypothetical scenario; envision an image, a 'motion picture' in our minds if you will. Let us look back into the past, thousands of years ago—before the start of our brief recorded history. The Earth at this distant time is inhabited with numerous sprawling and thriving civilizations. These individual civilizations enjoy a mild, calm climate—and life for them is generally good—not perfect—but good.

Because of their recorded histories—some of these past civilizations' are aware of the periodic passage of a 'celestial object' that causes great destruction to Earth. However, some of these ancient civilizations have forgotten their catastrophic history and aren't aware of this great 'cycle of destruction.' *Remember, there's a 3,600-4,000 year interval between 'Wormwood's return.*

Civilizations that are aware of this 'great cycle' through their history and astronomy build underground cities and provision them in preparation for the coming destructive events. These civilizations, like those of ancient Turkey, build large underground complexes like those at *Cappadocia* and ultimately survive the passage of this 'terrible comet'—establishing new civilizations throughout the area after the geologic tempest settles down returning stability to Earth.

Unfortunately, other ancient civilizations, like those on the Island of Malta, also built underground structures (the *Hypogeums*). But because of Malta's proximity to the ocean, large inundations of water suddenly turned these ancient Maltese shelters into vast gravesites!

Other civilizations (like those of Noah's time in the Bible) laughed at the idea of approaching disaster going about their merry way—way too 'caught up' in their immediate day-to-day life to worry about situations they cared to know nothing about in the first place. Little did these people know that their civilization stood a zero chance against the ravages of the 'terrible comet' and would soon be totally obliterated by its passage! *Except for Noah and his fabled ark, of course.*

Then one day, just as predicted, the 'terrible comet' suddenly appears in the sky. The object's approach begins to place great strain on the Earth's crusted skin. The ground begins to tremble and numerous volcanoes erupt, filling the sky with volcanic ash and cinder. Light from the Moon, Sun and stars becomes obscured by both volcanic ash and blowing dust which is produced by fierce winds. As this unholy tempest continues to build day quickly turns to night.

As the object passes between the Earth and the Sun, its fiery 'hydrocarbon tail' sweeps across the planet, causing a conflagration from the sky that sets entire cities ablaze, burning wood structures to the ground and 'vitrifying' stone buildings.

As the object continues its passage—the shaking of the planet becomes ever greater and the Earth begins to 'tip over' in space making the Moon, Sun and stars appear to 'come adrift,' suddenly changing direction in the sky. As this happens—great walls of water pour in from the sea, 'inundating' the land and sending an unstoppable wall of mud, people and animals cascading into huge chaotic landfills.

As the Earth's axis of rotation shifts, the planet's tectonic plates begin to buckle, large areas of coastal cities fall off into the oceans' abyss where they will lay undisturbed becoming largely forgotten by future generations to come.

Then, just as suddenly as it began, the event begins to settle down. And as the few survivors exit their underground shelters and caves—they are in shock at what they've just experienced and grieve for the devastating losses seen all around them. But the damage has now been done! The 'old-world' and all that it stood for is now gone forever—its buildings, history and 'way of life' have largely been obliterated—it is now time to face the future and start anew—again.

These few survivors take their 'old-world' skills and then 'start all over again' as mere cultural children—finding other survivors and forming new family units, which eventually become villages, then towns, then cities and finally, many years later, thriving civilizations once more.

This continuing cycle of global destruction with human and animal rebirth begins anew—again. After several generations pass, the rubble of 'old structures' begins to be collected and new structures are rebuilt on top of these old ones. 'Mythology' and 'oral traditions' begin to evolve about a 'great flood,' brought on by a terrible event in the sky that wiped the 'old world' away in a devastating global catastrophe.

But once again, as centuries turn into millennia, these historical accounts become vague and many of these important 'oral traditions' are simply forgotten about or totally discarded by future generations as foolishness. Unfortunately, *"ignorance of the past equals ignorance of the future."*

Then, thousands of years later, these 'new world' civilizations are once again revisited by the "usual inundation" scenario, and caught off guard again—are tragically destroyed just like the 'old world' civilizations before them—and the ones before them—and those before them.

And so it goes—over and over and over. Destruction, followed by rebuilding, followed by destruction, again! The ancient Indian cultures were right when they said: *"We live in the 'fourth world' and that the preceding 'three worlds' have all been destroyed by global cataclysms."*

We know very little about our actual recorded history! The true history of the human race was in existence long before the start of our meager 'modern-day' recorded history! *Why is that?*

Our planet is littered with the remains of violently destroyed civilizations! The ruins lying underwater off present-day Egypt, Greece, Malta, Japan, India, Cuba, the Bahamas, Azores, Bermuda and many other locations around the world, are calling out to us—trying to send us a clear warning of the great 'cycles of destruction' and the 'usual inundation' that has claimed the lives of so many in the past—and is once again rapidly headed our way.

The shattered remains of ancient buildings scattered over the landscapes of our planet are screaming at us to 'wake up,' and tune into the 'bigger picture' of what has transpired on our world in the past and what will soon transpire again in the near future—possibly 2009-2012.

The enormous piles of human and animal remains (chaotically entombed in so many locations throughout the world) is a blatant telegraph message—spelling out for us the reality of the situation we are once again rapidly approaching if our theory about *'Wormwood's'* return is correct.

The destructive events that have taken place in our past have cut us off from our ancestry however—and we do not hear their warnings. These past cataclysmic events are so geologically powerful and destructive that (like the ancient Egyptians said), they force us to *"start over again as children"* every several thousand years. We have therefore lost our legacy and the ability to understand our past—we are truly a species aimlessly adrift in space on a small watery planet!

Where we are today...

Our species is not very good at preserving accurate information over thousands of years. We have tried, although unsuccessfully, through the formation of the great libraries of the past like those in Alexandria, South America and China, as our ancient ancestors attempted to leave us an important historic legacy. It's a pity that none of those great repositories of knowledge survived.

These ancient libraries were great storehouses for vast amounts of information regarding the 'true cataclysmic history' of Earth. Many of these ancient libraries where so vast they literally contained 'hundreds of thousands' of documents, manuscripts, scrolls and books, many dealing with the great 'cycles of destruction' that repeatedly revisits this fragile blue world.

Unfortunately, through war, religious fanaticism and terrorism, carelessness and political strife—we've managed to burn all of these grand libraries to the ground. Most of the valuable information contained in these ancient repositories has been lost forever, information that we are in desperate need of today—whether we know it/or not and accept it/or not.

As a result of our inability to 'keep track' of our past, we are a 'species with amnesia.' Modern humans have existed on this planet for tens—maybe even hundreds of thousands of years. And yet, despite all of this time in which we have inhabited this planet, we can only trace our history back a few thousand years before we hit a solid 'wall of ignorance' regarding our own vital past.

Are we to truly believe that only within the past few millennia our species has been able to pro-duce the likes of Einstein, Galileo, Newton, Copernicus, Julius Caesar and Cleopatra, Magellan, Columbus, Montezuma, Lincoln, Kennedy and Genghis Kahn (just for grins)—but for tens, or even 'hundreds of thousands' of years before this—we could only grunt, gather firewood, sleep in caves and eat bugs? The human species has a long and brilliant 'hidden history' on this planet.

Many of our ancient ancestors accomplished technological feats that continue to 'boggle' even the greatest scientific minds of today. *How dare we think that this is all there is or was before?*

We understand virtually nothing of this distant past however, and because of this ignorance, we may be doomed to repeat the same mistakes that our ancient ancestors made! Once again we've lost that arcane knowledge of the past great 'cycles of destruction' brought about by the periodic passage of the *'terrible comet—Wormwood.'* We've forgotten all that has come before us and for this lack of understanding and our inability to preserve our own dynamic history we're about to pay the ultimate price—again!

We dedicate this volume to planet Earth's inhabitants hoping that its message of hope and know-ledge will save us from another dismal struggle for survival as 2009-2012 rapidly approaches.

The Book of Revelation Chapter 8, vs. 10 – 13 states:

10: And the third angel sounded, and there fell a great star from heaven, burning as it were a lamp, and it fell upon the third part of the rivers, and upon the foundations of waters:

11: And the name of the star is called **Wormwood***: and the third part of the waters became* **Wormwood***; and many men died of the waters, because they were made bitter.*

12: And the fourth angel sounded, and the third part of the sun was smitten, the third part of the moon, and the third part of the stars; so as the third part of them was darkened, and the day shone not for a third part of it, and the night likewise.

13: And I beheld, and heard an angel flying through the midst of heaven, saying with a loud voice, Woe, woe, woe, to the inhabiters of the earth by reason of the other voices of the trumpet of the three angels, which are yet to sound! [*End of Chapter Eight – The Holy Bible*]

CHAPTER TWO ENDNOTES

[1] Allen, D. S. and Delair, J. B. *Cataclysm* (Bear and Company, 1995), p. 15.
[2] Hancock, Graham. *Underworld* (Crown Publishing, 2002), p. 14-15.
[3] Ibid. p. 14-15.
[4] Ibid. p.18.
[5] Ibid. p.18.
[6] Ibid. p.18.
[7] Hancock, Graham. *Fingerprints Of The Gods* ((Crown Trade Paperbacks, 1995), p. 411-421
[8] James, Peter and Thorpe, Nick. *Ancient Mysteries* (Ballantine Books, 1999), p. 11.
[9] Ibid. P.11.
[10] Mars, Jim. *Rule by Secrecy* (Harper Collins, 2000), p. 376.

(CONTINUED)

CHAPTER TWO ENDNOTES CONTINUED

[11] Ibid. p. 291-292.
[12] Hancock, Graham. *Underworld* (Crown Publishing, 2002), p. 30.
[13] Wilson, Ian. *Before the Flood* (St. Martin's Press, 2001), p. 29.
[14] Hancock, Graham. *Underworld* (Crown Publishing, 2002), p. 33.
[15] James, Peter and Thorpe, Nick. *Ancient Mysteries* (Ballantine Books, 1999), p. 13.
[16] Hancock, Graham. *Underworld* (Crown Publishing, 2002), p.32.
[17] Sitchin, Zecharia. *When Time Began* (Avon Books, 1993), p. 97
[18] http://www.cnn.com/2000/NATURE/09/13/great.flood.finds.ap/
[19] Wilson, Ian. *Before the Flood* (St. Martin's Press, 2001), p. 108.
[20] Ibid. p. 124.
[21] James, Peter and Thorpe, Nick. *Ancient Mysteries* (Ballantine Books, 1999), p. 56.
[22] Hand Clow, Barbara. *Catastrophobia* (Bear & Company, 2001), p. 161.
[23] Ibid. p. 161.
[24] Velikovsky, Immanuel. *Earth In Upheaval* (Pocket Books, 1977), p. 175-176.
[25] James, Peter and Thorpe, Nick. *Ancient Mysteries* (Ballantine Books, 1999), p. 50.
[26] Ryan, William and Pitman, Walter. *Noah's Flood* (Simon & Schuster, 2000), p. 213.
[27] Ibid. p. 214.
[28] Article taken from Earth Changes Television (www.ectv.com)
[29] Hancock, Graham. *Underworld* (Crown Publishing, 2002), p. 514-515.
[30] Ibid. p. 528.
[31] Hancock, Graham. *Underworld* (Crown Publishing, 2002), p. 220-221.
[32] Ibid. p. 259-260.
[33] Ibid. p. 305.
[34] Childress, David Hatcher. *Technology Of The Gods* (Adventures Unlimited Press, 2000), p. 239.
[35] Feuerstein, Georg, and Kak, Subhash. *In Search of the Cradle of Civilization* (Quest Books, 1995), p.88.
[36] Bowden, Hugh. *Ancient Civilizations* (Barnes and Noble Books, 2002), p. 39.
[37] Childress, David Hatcher. *Technology Of The Gods* (Adventures Unlimited Press, 2000), p.238.
[38] Ibid. p. 221.
[39] Ibid. p. 222.
[40] Dunbavin, Paul. *Atlantis Of The West* (Carroll & Graf Publishers, 2003), pp. 241-143.
[41] Ibid.
[42] Hancock, Graham. *Fingerprints Of The Gods* ((Crown Trade Paperbacks, 1995), p. 89.
[43] Hancock, Graham. *Underworld* (Crown Publishing, 2002), p. 311.
[44] Ibid. p. 336.
[45] Ibid. p. 314.
[46] Ibid. p. 342.
[47] Ibid. p. 342-343.
[48] Ibid. p. 357-358.
[49] Ibid. p. 357-358.
[50] Ibid. p. 381.
[51] Hancock, Graham. *Fingerprints Of The Gods* ((Crown Trade Paperbacks, 1995), p. 221.
[52] Allen, D. S. and Delair. J. B., *Cataclysm* (Bear and Company, 1995), p. 114-118.
[53] Velikovsky, Immanuel. *Earth In Upheaval* (Pocket Books, 1977), p. 253.
[54] Allen, D. S. and Delair. J. B., *Cataclysm* (Bear and Company, 1995), p. 86.
[55] Ibid. p. 105-106.
[56] Velikovsky, Immanuel. *Earth In Upheaval* (Pocket Books, 1977), p. 43.
[57] Ibid. p. 253.
[58] Allen, D. S. and Delair, J. B. *Cataclysm* (Bear and Company, 1995), p. 68.
[59] Ibid. p. 60.
[60] Hancock, Graham. *Underworld* (Crown Publishing, 2002), p. 522-526.
[61] Ibid. p. 284-285.
[62] Velikovsky, Immanuel. *Earth In Upheaval* (Pocket Books, 1977), p 172-173
[63] James, Peter and Thorpe, Nick. *Ancient Mysteries* (Ballantine Books, 1999), p. 28.

(CONTINUED)

CHAPTER TWO ENDNOTES CONTINUED

[64] Hancock, Graham. *Underworld* (Crown Publishing, 2002). p.595-605.
[65] Dunbavin, Paul. *Atlantis Of The West* (Carroll & Graf Publishers, 2003), p. 84
[66] Ibid.
[67] Ibid., p. 96
[68] *The Search for Atlantis* (History Channel, 2001)
[69] J. W. French. *The Greatest Story Never Told*, p.3-6, Carlton Press, 1969
[70] Ibid., p.3
[71] Velikovsky, Immanuel. *Earth In Upheaval* (Pocket Books, 1977) p 177.
[72] Velikovsky, Immanuel. *Earth In Upheaval* (Pocket Books, 1977) p 177.
[73] Cremo, Michael A. and Thompson, Richard L. *The Hidden History of the Human Race* (Govardan Hill Pub. 1994), p. xvii.
[74] Hancock, Graham. *Underworld* (Crown Publishers, 2002), p. 13.
[75] Ibid. Part 4, p. 309-423.
[76] Hancock, Graham. *Underworld* (Crown Publishers, 2002), p.135.
[77] Hancock, Graham. *Fingerprints Of The Gods* (Crown Trade Paperbacks, 1995), p .135-136.
[78] Cremo, Michael. *Human Devolution* (Torchlight Publishing, 2003), pp. 25-27.
[79] Ibid.
[80] Ibid.
[81] Ibid.
[82] Ibid.
[83] Ibid.

This page provided for reader's notes.

— CHAPTER THREE —

SHIFTING SANDS — SHIFTING POLES

"It is impossible to reflect on the changed state of the North American continent without the deepest astonishment. Formerly, it must have swarmed with great monsters; now we find mere pigmies...since they lived, no very great changes in the form of the land can have taken place. What, then, has exterminated so many species and whole genera? The mind at first is irresistibly hurried into the belief of some great catastrophe; but thus to destroy the animals, both large and small, in Southern Patagonia, in Brazil, on the Cordillera of Peru, in North America, and up to the Bering Straits, we must shake the entire framework of the globe.

No lesser physical event could have brought about this wholesale destruction not only in the Americas but in the entire world...Certainly no fact in the long history of the world is so startling as the wide and repeated extermination of its inhabitants."
                    Charles Darwin, The Voyage of the H.M.S. Beagle[1]

In the second chapter of this volume we looked at the 'historical records' of ancient civilizations and their universally held accounts of great cataclysms repeatedly striking the Earth. We then put all of these ancient accounts together forming a comprehensive picture indicating that a very large 'celestial object' periodically passes our planet—triggering massive 'pole shifts' on a rather recurring basis.

Also, in our second chapter, we looked at the 'forbidden archeological evidence' supporting these ancient accounts of repeated disasters. Thus, as we have seen demonstrated, our planet is in fact littered with the 'shattered' remains of countless destroyed civilizations.

But if our ultimate hypothesis of recurring 'pole shifts' (brought about by the passage of a rogue celestial object) is indeed correct, we need to address the specific geological evidence that Earth's (North and South geophysical poles) really <u>do</u> shift from time-to-time. We must also identify the specific 'celestial object' that theoretically triggers these 'pole shifts.' In the next two chapters we'll answer these two important questions.

Let us now turn to the 'geological evidence' supporting the objective arguments for 'pole shifts' brought about by the passage of a rogue celestial body invading our parent solar system.

Evidence in support of pole shifts

Frozen mammoths

Along the northern latitudes of Earth, in an area known today as the Arctic Circle, recent finds have been unearthed which defy current scientific wisdom and can only be logically explained by a recent shifting of the Earth's geophysical poles.

The Arctic Circle is an area that surrounds the current North Pole. Today this area is shrouded in perpetual darkness for most of the year and temperatures seldom rise above freezing. Because of this extreme cold and relentless darkness, little grows in this region of the world except for a few sparse grasses and various fungi—which are barely able to survive in this ultra-harsh climate.

Despite this harsh, frigid environment however, over the past two hundred years the carcasses of numerous wooly mammoths have been found 'flash-frozen' in areas such as northern Siberia—hundreds of miles within the Arctic Circle. To date, scientists have discovered as many as eighty of these frozen (well-preserved) mammoths within this freezing wilderness.[2]

These giant 'elephant-like' creatures have been found in almost perfect states of preservation, some have even had fresh 'buttercup flowers' and 'ripe seeds' in their mouths, along with other undigested plants in their stomachs—plants which do not, and 'could not' grow in this area today.[3] These mammoths have been so well-preserved in fact, that many early Arctic expeditions feed their sled dogs on the flesh—which is said to have resembled well-frozen beef.[4]

The enigma of these recent mammoths discoveries should be obvious. *How were these giants able to exist in such a harsh/desolate climate? And was the Arctic Circle a much different place before?*

Today, this area of the Arctic Circle is extremely barren and can support very little plant growth, especially the type that would be needed to feed huge animals such as wooly mammoths, which can grow to be over fourteen feet tall and required tons of lush vegetation in order to survive.

Along with the remains of frozen (well-preserved) mammoths, northern Siberia has also yielded the remains of countless rhinoceroses, horses, antelope, bison, lions, hippopotamuses, beavers and a slew of other animals that normally live in warmer climates much further south which could never have survived at this extreme northern latitude. These 'out of place' animal remains have been uncovered in such enormous quantities that early explorers to this area stated:

> *The soil of these desolate (Siberian) islands (are) absolutely packed full of the bones of elephants and rhinoceroses in astonishing numbers.*

> *These islands were full of mammoth bones, and the quantity of tusks and teeth of elephants and rhinoceroses, found in the newly discovered island of New Siberia, was perfectly amazing, and surpassed anything which had as yet been discovered.*

> *Such was the enormous quantity of mammoth remains that it seemed...that the island was actually composed of the bones and tusks of elephants, cemented together by ice-sand.*[5]

Once again we must pause and wonder how this barren 'land of ice' could have supported not only mammoths, but also animals such as horses, rhinoceroses, and even lions?

In the same area of the Arctic Circle, semi-tropical trees and plants have also been found 'flash-frozen' many while they were in full bloom—with green leaves and fruit still on their branches. This vegetation has included figs, water lilies, pines, firs, spruce, cypress, elms, hazels and many others.[6] Today, as in the past, these species of plants could never have grown this far north, certainly nowhere near the present-day Arctic Circle.[7]

Ivan T. Sanderson, a noted biologist and author, commented on this 'out of place' vegetation in a 1969 *Pursuit* magazine science article where he stated:

> *In the New Siberian Islands…whole trees have turned up; and trees of the family that includes the plum; and with their leaves and (ripe) fruit. No such hardwood trees grow today anywhere within two thousand miles of those islands. Therefore the climate must have been very much different when they (were) buried; and, please note, (they could not have been buried in this frozen muck which is rock hard, nor could they have retained their foliage) if they were washed (this) far north by currents from warmer climes. They must have grown thereabouts, and the climate must have been not only warm enough, but have had a long enough growing period of summer sunlight, for them to have leafed and fruited.[8]*

Dr. Immanuel Velikovsky, the renowned author of several popular books on the cataclysmic history of Earth, notes a passage from a nineteenth century book entitled, *Travels in Siberia*, which stated:

> *In New Siberia (island), on the declivities facing the south, lie hills 250 or 300 feet high, formed of driftwood, the ancient origins of which, as well as of the fossil wood in the tundra, anterior to the history of the earth in its present state, strikes at once even the most uneducated hunters…Other hills on the same island, and on Kotelnoi, which lies further to the west, are heaped up to an equal height with skeletons of pachyderms (elephants, rhinoceroses), bison, etc., which are cemented together by frozen sand as well as by strata and veins of ice…[9]*

In his book, *Earth in Upheaval*, Dr Velikovsky asks:

> *What could have caused a sudden change in the temperature of the region? Today the country does not provide food for large quadrupeds, the soil is barren and produces only moss and fungi a few months in the year; at that time the animals fed on plants. And not only mammoths pastured in northern Siberia and on the islands of the Arctic Ocean. On Kotelnoi Island neither trees, nor shrubs, nor bushes, exist…and yet the bones of elephants, rhinoceroses, buffaloes and horses are found in this icy wilderness in numbers that defy all calculation.[10]*

How did all of these animals and plants become frozen in an area in which today, they could never have survived? And how is it that mammoths were killed and then frozen so quickly, that their flesh is still perfectly edible after (many) thousands of years?

The answer is that this geographical area of the globe (Siberia) was at one time in the recent past, located much further south. These animals and the plants they were feeding upon, lived in this area when it was much warmer and subsequently closer to the equator. But when the planet last 'tipped' or 'shifted' on its axis of rotation, this once southern geographic area of Russia was then shifted far to the north, toward the new North Pole—and well within the Arctic Circle of today. The animals and plants that went 'along for the ride' were instantly 'frozen' in their new northern geographic location.

In recent years, Russian archeologists have also uncovered the remains of human civilizations that had previously lived within the Arctic Circle. Today, this area is too far north to be home to such cultures, but thousands of years ago, this same area supported thriving communities.[11]

These 'out of place' animal and human remains, provide clear, unambiguous evidence in support of past 'pole shifts;' evidence, which lucidly indicates that Earth has had a different 'axis of rotation' in its recent geological past.

Further evidence in support of past 'pole shifts' can also be found in the examination of former polar ice caps. Our 21st century science technology now provides us with great new techniques.

Former polar ice caps

Because sunlight strikes the Earth most intensely at the equator and less intensely at the North and South Poles, large accumulations of ice build up at the Polar Regions. This polar ice is collectively known as the northern and southern polar ice caps.

These accumulations of ice (at both polar ice caps), tells us where Earth's geographic poles were located in the near past. In other words, if an area of the Earth was once covered in polar ice, it's a good indication that this geographic area of the planet was at one time situated at one of the planet's geophysical poles.

According to C. Coleman, a noted authority on ice ages:

> *In early times it was supposed (assumed) that during the glacial period a vast ice cap radiated from the North Pole, extending varying distances southward over seas and continents. It was presently found, however, that some northern countries were never covered by ice, and that in reality there were several more or less distinct ice sheets starting from local centers (former poles) and expanding in all directions, north as well as east and west and south.*
>
> *It was found, too, that these ice sheets were distributed in what seemed a capricious (suspicious) manner. Siberia, now some of the coldest parts of the world, was not covered, and the same was true of most of Alaska and the Yukon Territory in Canada; while northern Europe, with its relatively mild climate (today), was buried under ice as far south as London and Berlin; and most of Canada and the United States were covered, the ice reaching as far south as Cincinnati in the Mississippi Valley region.[12]*

The only logical explanation for this contradictory distribution of prior ice caps being located in such geographically different parts of the world is that the Earth's poles have not always been in the same location as they are today. The Earth's poles have tended to move around (via pole shifts), forming new polar ice caps in various geographic locations from time to time.

A few thousand years ago, the northern axis of the Earth's rotation was actually situated over Hudson Bay, in southeastern Canada, not over the Arctic Ocean as it is today. This would explain why glaciers advanced so far into North America during the last ice age but on the other side of the world, in Siberia, it was relatively warm—and large animals thrived.

When the last 'pole shift' took place, the Earth's northern geologic axis of rotation shifted from Hudson Bay, further north, to the Arctic Ocean—thus causing North America to warm and Siberia to cool.

The sudden warmth experienced in North America, (now being much further south due to this shift of the axis to the north), also explains why the former ice cap at the 'old' north pole (Hudson Bay), melted so quickly—causing great flooding in many areas of North America. This flooding has been attributed to the formation of geological features such as St. Anthony's Falls in Minnesota and Niagara Falls in New York.[13]

On the other side of the world in Siberia, however, this once southern 'temperate' climate with semi-tropical trees and animals such as wooly mammoths was transported northward, instantly freezing these life forms within the newly formed Arctic Circle.

The last 'pole shift' moved the North Pole from the Hudson Bay region of Canada to its current position over the Arctic Ocean. But as we will soon discover, many 'pole shifts' have actually taken place on Earth in the distant past.

So where were the poles of the Earth located before the last pole shift? Some of the 'prior' polar locations can be identified in places far removed from the 'current' polar regions of today.

Mr. Louis Agassiz, the famous Swiss naturalist and president of the Swiss Society of Natural Science, went to one of the hottest places on Earth, equatorial Brazil—and found clear evidence of massive polar glaciations in the past. In other words, equatorial Brazil was once covered in polar ice, indicating that it was situated at the Earth's polar regions at one time in the distant past.

Equatorial Africa, Madagascar and India (some of the other hottest places on the planet), have also been covered with ice in the distant past. Not only have massive glaciers covered some of the hottest places on Earth, but also the direction in which these glaciers have flowed has been from south to north, away from the equator of today, the exact opposite of what one would logically expect.[14]

Professor C. O. Dunbar, of Yale University, stated:

> *South America bears evidence of glaciations, in Argentina and southeastern Brazil, even within 10° of the equator. In the northern hemisphere, peninsular India, within 20° of the equator, was the chief scene of glaciation, with the ice flowing north (or from the tropics to higher latitudes). These icecaps covered practically all of southern Africa up to at least 22° south, and also spread to Madagascar.[15]*

So how did some of the hottest places on Earth become covered in deep ice creating new poles?

The answer is that these geographic regions, which today sit close to the equator, were once near (or even at) the former North or South Poles. As our planet has altered its rotational axis over the millennia, these once 'frozen' ice encrusted regions, were 'relocated' to the warmer equatorial regions where they reside today.

As an illustration of this concept, picture a round ball with an X at the top and the bottom. These X's represent the Earth's polar ice caps. Now let the ball roll to the right until the X's are on the sides of the ball. This is exactly what happened to many former polar ice caps. Originally these areas were at the top or bottom of the planet, very close to the Earth's axis of rotation and well within the freezing environment of the arctic, but when the planet rolled over, these former Polar Regions were then 'relocated' to the warm environment of the equator.

Today, because of this prior 'rolling' of the planet, it only looks like there was once ice at the equator, in reality these current equatorial regions were at one time, much closer to the poles.

In addition to studying the tropical regions of the Earth, Agassiz also made an extensive study of Europe. Recent evidence clearly indicates that Europe has also been transported both 'closer to the equator' and 'closer to the poles' at various times in the past.

Agassiz states:

> *The surface of Europe (was) previously adorned with tropical vegetation (having been much closer to the equator) and populated by herds of huge elephants, enormous hippopotami, and gigantic carnivore (all tropical species), then it was suddenly buried under a vast mantle of ice, covering plains, lakes, seas, and plateaus. Upon the life and movement of a vigorous creation fell the absolute silence of death.*[16]

All of this happed as a result of Europe being relocated from the tropics to the polar regions of Earth during a past 'pole shift.' Today, as a result of the planet's last 'pole shift,' Europe now lies between the tropical and Arctic regions of the Earth, in a latitude bearing a milder climate.

Corals in Polar Regions

Spits Bergen is a northern region that sits a thousand miles inside of the Arctic Circle. Today however, large formations of 'warm-water' corals have been uncovered in these frigid waters. These northern waters are currently far too cold to produce these types of tropical corals, but at one time this region was much closer to the equator, and in turn, had warm water that could support tropical coral growth. Warm water corals have also been found in the frigid waters of Alaska, Canada and Greenland, indicating that these northern areas were also at one time, much closer to Earth's Equator.[17]

The plethora of evidence that we have just investigated supporting 'pole shifts,' presents a very convincing argument for these past cataclysmic events. Certainly 'out of place' animal and plant species, former polar ice caps widely distributed in diverse locations throughout the world, and warm water corals within the arctic, present a powerful case for these prior geophysical events.

Simply put, this evidence, which has puzzled many scientists for centuries can only be logically explained by a shifting of Earth's axis of rotation.

As compelling as this evidence is however, some of the most irrefutable evidence supporting prior 'pole shifts' can be found within Earth's numerous lava fields.

Geomagnetic evidence

In essence, the Earth on which we live is a giant magnet—with the poles of the Earth acting as the poles of the magnet.

A compass needle points towards the Earth's poles because the tip of the needle has a small piece of iron in it and this iron tends to 'line up' with the Earth's magnetic field and, in turn, points in the direction of the lines of magnetic force—in other words toward the planet's magnetic poles.

In reality, the Earth has two sets of poles, one set of geological poles (its axis of rotation) and a set of magnetic poles (where the magnetic fields terminate), both are very close to each other geographically, however, and for our purposes here, we may consider them one in the same.

The molten core interior of the Earth is very hot and produces great internal pressure. In fact, the temperature and pressure within the Earth's core is so great, that normal 'solid rock' is liquefied into a 'fluid state' commonly known as lava.

Molten lava, like solid rock, is rich in small iron crystals. When rock is heated to this lava state, the iron crystals are <u>not</u> attracted to the Earth's magnetic fields. But as lava comes to the planet's surface and cools, its iron crystals have a tendency to line up with the Earth's magnetic fields and subsequently point towards its magnetic poles—just like the needle of a compass.

Today, because of this magnetic 'affiliation' of cooling lava, it is possible for geologists to now determine in which direction the Earth's magnetic poles were located when the lava in question cooled. Geologists have spent quite a bit of time examining the Earth's lava fields, both below and above the oceans, and these geologists have conclusively determined that the Earth's poles have indeed shifted many times throughout its history. In fact, geologists have determined that the Earth may have shifted its poles (or axis of rotation) over two hundred and twenty-nine times in the past.[18]

This 'geomagnetic' evidence supporting 'pole shifts' is an important piece of the overall puzzle and further explains a lot of the geologic enigmas found throughout the world. It explains why there are warm water corals in the Arctic Ocean and evidence of massive glaciers in the tropics. And it also explains why there is so many animals buried in the Arctic that could never have actually lived in this area today and why our ancient ancestors claimed that the *"stars came adrift in the sky."* All of the above anomalies are factual consequences of Earth's shifting poles!

Overall, the geological evidence supporting 'pole shifts' is so strong in fact, that many noted scientists through the years have concluded 'pole shifts' may indeed be a reality on Earth.

Austrian meteorologist Julius Hann stated:

> *The simple and obvious explanation of great secular changes in climate, and of former prevalence of higher temperatures in northern circumpolar regions, would be found in the assumption that the earth's axis of rotation has not always been in the same position, but that it may have changed its position as a result of geological processes...*[19]

W. B. Write stated that during recent geological history, there occurred many changes in the position of the Earth's climactic zones that cannot be explained except by a shifting of the planet's axis of rotation or a 'displacement' of the poles from their present position.[20]

British scientist, S. K. Runcorn, from the University of Cambridge, published an article in *Scientific American*, which stated:

> *There seems no doubt that the earth's (magnetic) field is tied up in some way with the rotation of the planet. And this leads to a remarkable finding about the Earth's rotation itself. The Earth's axis of rotation has changed...the planet has rolled about, changing the location of its geographical poles.*[21]

Engineer and long-time 'pole shift' researcher, Hugh A. Brown, authored the groundbreaking book, *Cataclysms of the Earth* and was featured in the *New York Times* and numerous other magazine articles. Mr. Brown firmly believes that the evidence supporting 'pole shifts' is overwhelming and that our planet has obviously undergone numerous 'pole shifts' in the past.

According to Mr. Brown, the same cataclysm that has repeatedly wiped out numerous ancient civilizations and buried mammoths, rhinoceroses and other animals under vast ice sheets—is overdue to happen again. Mr. Brown believes that our planet may undergo these shifts as often as every seven-thousand years or so and when it happens again, *"most of the Earth's population will be destroyed in the same manner as the mammoths of prehistoric times were destroyed."*

Dr. Velikovsky, who we will visit again later in this chapter, states:

> *The finding of warm-climate animals and plants in the polar regions, coral and palms in the Arctic Circle...such changes could not have occurred unless the terrestrial globe veered from its (normal) path...a shift in the astronomical or geographical position of the terrestrial axis...and they must have been sudden.*[22]

Once again, as with most of the other subjects covered in this book, we could continue reviewing the basic evidence supporting 'pole shifts' indefinitely, but in the interest of readability—we will now move on.

Suffice to say that there is more than sufficient scientific evidence to indicate that our planet's poles do in fact 'shift,' it has happened numerous times in the past, and will certainly happen many times in the future. If you are interested in reviewing more detailed case evidence for 'pole shift' theory, please refer to the books listed in our chapter endnotes and bibliography by Hapgood, Velikovsky, White, Dunbavin, Timms and others.

Charles Hapgood

What exactly is a pole shift?

We have referred to this phenomenon as a 'tipping' of the planet in space, or a 'shifting' of the Earth on its axis of rotation. But these statements do not tell us exactly what a 'pole shift' is—only the end result. *When the poles of our planet 'shift,' what exactly happens? What is the mechanism in which these 'pole shifts' actually take place?*

In the third chapter of this Manual, we explored the idea that the Earth's poles have repeatedly changed their location in the past, and as we have seen, numerous ancient cultures possessed knowledge of these periodic alterations in Earth's axis of rotation. The ancient Egyptians, Greeks, Maya, Inca and numerous other cultures, all recorded times in Earth's history when the world 'tipped over' causing the Moon, Sun and stars to change direction in the sky, and the oceans to inundate the land.

Even though it has been widely known for thousands of years that Earth's poles become unstable when the 'terrible comet' passes our planet in space, it wasn't until 1958, that author, professor, lecturer, and acknowledged expert on 'pole shifts,' Charles Hapgood, penned the definitive work on the modern-day geological theory of these periodic planetary disasters.

His seminal book entitled, *Path of the Pole,* has been heralded as a major breakthrough in this field. Hapgood's research into 'pole shift' theory included over ten years of extensive research. Pouring over ancient maps and digging out dozens of research papers from various universities—he painstakingly reconstructed the geological record of Earth. Hapgood concluded that not only have the planet's poles shifted many times in the past, but he also put forth the actual 'mechanism' by which these 'pole shifts' physically take place.

Modern geologists have determined that our planet is composed of several layers. The outermost layer, the surface on which we live, is commonly referred to as the Earth's 'crust.' The more technical name for this outer layer however, is the *lithosphere*. This surface layer is in the neighborhood of 30 to 40 miles thick and is mostly composed of solid crystalline rock. The next layer down is made up of a more fluid-like layer of hot 'molten rock,' and is known as the *'asthenosphere'* or *'mantel.'* [23]

According to Charles Hapgood, what actually takes place during an Earthian 'pole shift' is that the more solid *lithosphere* (crust), slips over the more fluid-like *asthenosphere* (mantel)—a phenomenon known as *'lithospheric displacement'*— (the displacement of Earth's crust).

In other words, Hapgood clearly demonstrated how our planet is constructed like an egg, with the shell of the egg forming the thin 'crust' of the Earth (its lithosphere) and the liquid part of the egg representing the Earth's molten 'mantel' (its asthenosphere). As an eggshell can spin independently over the liquid part of an egg—the Earth's 'crust' can spin independently over its molten 'mantel.' It is this slippage of the Earth's crust over its more 'fluid like' inner layer that is the physical mechanism by which our planet actually shifts its geographic axis of rotation.

In *Path Of The Pole,* Dr. Hapgood discusses the numerous 'pole shifts' in Earth's past, providing convincing evidence and dramatic testimony to support his cataclysmic theories. He not only offers a plethora of solid physical evidence for these past events, but moves on to explore the potential for Earth's 'future' pole shifts.

Hapgood concluded that these periodic 'pole shifts' have caused sudden changes in global climate patterns, inundations of the land by the seas, worldwide volcanic and seismic activities, the formation of new polar ice caps, the emergence of mountain ranges and/or their dislocation, the 'rising' and 'subduction' of global coastlines, the tilting of fresh water lakes, the reversal of river courses, the provenance of tropical animals and plants in polar regions, the extinction of thousands of various animal species, the emergence of brand new species, the reversal of the Earth's magnetic fields and scores of other 'geological phenomena' related to the periodic episodes of destruction and mayhem which repeatedly plague planet Earth.

Even though the vast majority of modern-day geologists tried to completely ignore Hapgood's theories, a few brave and open-minded individuals stepped forward to give Hapgood the credit he truly deserved. One of Hapgood's biggest supporters was none other than the distinguished genius, Albert Einstein, who wrote the inspired foreword to Hapgood's seminal work *Path Of The Pole,* wherein Einstein states:

> *A great many empirical data indicate that at each point on the earth's surface that has been carefully studied, many climactic changes have taken place, apparently quite suddenly. This, according to Hapgood, is explicable if the virtually rigid outer 'crust' of the earth undergoes, from time to time, extensive 'displacements' over the viscous, plastic, possibly fluid inner layers.*
>
> *Such displacements may take place as the consequence of comparatively slight forces exerted on the (earth's) crust..., which in turn will tend to alter the axis of rotation of the earth's crust.*
>
> *I think that this rather astonishing, even fascinating idea deserves the serious attention of anyone who concerns himself with the theory of the earth's development.*[24]

Kirtley F. Mather, professor of Geology, Emeritus, at Harvard University and president of *The American Association for the Advancement of Science*, says about Hapgood's work:

> *The idea that the history of the earth involves the shifting of its thin crust from "time to time" and "place to place" is certain to receive increased attention in the next few years. Knowledge is rapidly accumulating concerning the spatial relations of the "crust" and the underlying "mantel."*
>
> *Information regarding the physical properties of these parts of the stratiform planet is (today) being secured by geologists. Many specific facts are now available concerning local changes of (the) geographic position of (numerous) points on the earth's surface.*

The geographic records of the past are replete with items that suggest significant differences between the latitude and longitude of many places (between) earlier epochs and those of the present time.[25]

Many other scientists have also agreed with the concept of lithosphereic displacement, including geologist K. A. Pauley who concluded:

We are fully justified in concluding that the lithosphere (crust) was displaced during the great Ice Ages, and that the displacements were the direct cause of the alterations in climates during these periods.[26]

UCLA researcher and instructor, Chan Thomas, as well as the late Hugh Auchincloss Brown, engineer and author of *Cataclysms of the Earth*, also believed that 'lithosphereic displacement' was the only theory that explained <u>all</u> of the geological enigmas that have been uncovered.[27]

An important addition to Hapgood's work was provided by Dutch geophysicist, F. A. Vening Meinesz, who stated that certain geological features and planetary changes could only be rationally explained by a shifting of the Earth's crust over the mantle of more than 70°. Meinesz also introduces us to an important geological concept known as 'block faulting' wherein Meinesz stated:

A remarkable correlation to many major topographical features and also to the shearing patterns of large parts of the earth's features (such) as...the North and South Atlantic, the Indian Ocean and the Gulf of Aden, Africa, the Pacific, etc. If the correlation (in these sites) is not fortuitous, and this does not appear probable, we have to suppose that the earth's crust at some moment of its history had indeed shifted with regard to the earth's poles and that the crust has undergone a corresponding block shearing, (also known as block faulting).[28]

The concept of 'block faulting' is very important for us to understand. Not only because it is the direct result of 'lithosphereic displacement' (pole shifts), but because 'block faulting' can help explain so many of the geological changes that have taken place on Earth in the past.

We will now look into a few specific examples of how tectonic plates behave during episodes of lithosphereic displacement.

Block faulting

When the Earth's crust slips around its more fluid-like mantle, the crust does not slip in one neat piece. The Earth's crust is actually made up of a number of individual plates or sections, known scientifically as 'tectonic plates.' It is the movement of these 'tectonic plates' against one another that causes massive earthquakes. When Earth's crust (made up of individual tectonic plates), begins to slip around the fluid-like mantle, the tectonic plates often slide at different rates—some naturally sliding or slipping faster than others.

As these plates begin to slide and push against one another, some are naturally pushed 'upward' by the intense pressure of the plates around them. Other plates are pushed 'downward' by the pressure of the plates above and around them. This tendency for individual tectonic plate movements—the pushing 'upward' and 'downward'—is known today as 'block faulting.'

Let us now look into a few specific examples of 'block faulting' to see how this geologic phenomenon has catastrophically affected Earth in the past.

Examples of upliftment

Throughout the world, geologists have found examples of extreme 'upliftment' of the Earth's crust (lithosphere). Many times these upliftment events have taken place suddenly and with extreme geological force—all in the recent past.

In their book, *Cataclysm*, scientists and authors D. S. Allan and J. B. Delair, discuss an example of extreme upliftment of the Earth's crust that took place in the area of China and radically changed the landscape and climate of this region of the world. Recall from the last chapter when we examined the exploration of the Gobi Desert by Sven Anders Hedin. Remember if you will, how he and four porters uncovered ancient docks, boat keels and buildings on the shores of a once great inland sea that was suddenly and violently transfigured into an inhospitable desert, with sand dunes towering hundreds of feet high.

D. S. Allan and J. B. Delair state:

> *Certainly within human memory a large inland sea, referred to in ancient Chinese records as the 'Great Han Hai,' occupied the Gobi basin. This (inland sea) apparently extended from the Great Khingan Shan in the east toward the Tien Shan and Pamir (mountain) ranges in the west, a distance of some 2,000 miles, and from north to south a distance of some 700 miles. Its volume was accordingly immense.*
>
> *At the time of the sea's existence (several thousand years ago), the entire (Gobi) basin apparently lay from 'two' to 'three' thousand feet lower than it does today, and there is every indication that it was uplifted simultaneously (and suddenly) with the Pamirs and the great ranges of western China and also with the Tibetan plateau immediately to the south. The (sudden) draining away of the water constituting this inland sea must have been a truly devastating event.*[29]

In other words, this enormous inland sea (that once covered the geographic area known today as the Gobi Desert) was thrust 'upwards' in a sudden catastrophic event in the geologically recent past. This upliftment was so powerful and so extreme, that it rose the base of this former inland sea up 'two' to 'three' thousand feet higher in a single devastating event—draining this once magnificent body of water and forming one of the largest/grandest deserts on Earth today. The ancient civilizations that were living on the shores of this once magnificent sea of water was unfortunately and instantly obliterated by drowning in this tragic event.

No wonder indigenous people of China still talk about the lost city of *Takla Makan,* and how it was totally destroyed in a global catastrophe and then swallowed by the sands of the great Gobi.

This area of China is not the only region where geologists have discovered massive and sudden 'upliftments' of the Earth's crust. The *Bayan Kara Shan* mountain range in western China was suddenly 'uplifted' an incredible 6,500 feet during the last episode of lithosphereic displacement.[30] In other areas, the Minya Konka range was 'uplifted' 3,250 feet, the *Yunnan Province* range 6,500 feet, and the *Tibetan Plateau* a whopping 9,750 feet.[31]

This type of massive and sudden 'upliftment' of the Earth's crust has been discovered throughout the world, from the Himalayas to the mountain ranges of South and Central America, from the Orient to the European Alps—massive upliftment has taken place 'suddenly' and 'repeatedly' and 'without warnings' around the globe.

Keep in mind when we say 'suddenly,' we mean just that. Every indication uncovered to date clearly points to these upliftments happening 'instantly,' within a matter of days or ever hours. When the Earth's lithosphere slips, and the tectonic plates buckle and are thrust 'upwards'—the incredible speed and violence of this event is almost incomprehensible.

These recent geological discoveries involving drastic 'upliftment' of the Earth's crust shed new light on just how powerful these episodes of lithosphereic displacement can be. So powerful in fact that they can force areas of individual tectonic plates upwards many thousands of feet—literally creating mountains overnight and transforming the Earth's topography in the mere 'blink of an eye.'

As we have already noted, 'block faulting' causes areas of tectonic plates to 'subside' or be pushed 'downwards' as well as 'upwards.' It is therefore not surprising that we should find clear evidence of tectonic plates that have recently—geologically 'collapsed' around the planet.

Examples of subduction

One of the most dramatic examples of tectonic plate 'collapse' or 'subduction,' can be found around the Azores. As we examined in the last chapter, the Azores are a series of islands sitting atop the Mid-Atlantic Ridge and may have highly enigmatic 'man made' structures submerged under thousands of feet of sea water off their shores. These strange 'out of place' structures have lead many scholars to speculate they might be the remains of the sunken civilization of Atlantis.

As we have mentioned before, whether Atlantis existed or not is beyond the scope of this book. What is important about the sea floor around the Azores however is that this area was, in the not too distant past, high above water!

For many years oceanographers assumed that the sea floor around the Azores was millions of years old and therefore covered in very deep layers of marine sediments. With the advent of modern sonar and other ocean-mapping techniques however, the sediments on the sea floor around the Azores has been found to be extremely thin and in some areas—there is virtually <u>no</u> sediment at all.[32]

The well know oceanographer, Dr. Maurice Ewing, has spent a good deal of time studying the ocean floor around the Azores and summarizes his findings in the following statement:

> *(There is) many thousands of feet of sediment on the foothills of the Mid-Atlantic Ridge. Surprisingly, however, in the great flat plains on either side of the ridge, this sediment appears to lie less that 100 feet thick... Always it has been thought that the sediment must be extremely thick, since it had been accumulating for countless ages...but on the level basins that flank the Mid-Atlantic Ridge our (sonar) signals came back too close together to measure the time between them... They show the sediment in the basins is less than 100 feet thick.[33]*

In addition to thin sediment layers, oceanographers have discovered vast tracts of very young 'beach sand' on the ocean floor around the Azores, indicating that what is now 'ocean floor' was recently an 'above water' beach.[34] In this same area, scientists have also found very young 'lava fields' covering vast areas of this same section of sea floor, indicating that this region of the Mid-Atlantic Ridge was recently subjected to a massive volcanic event.

Because of these current discoveries involving beach sand, thin sediment layers, and young lava field samples, many oceanographers and geologists today believe that the plateau that the Azores sit upon, was at one time in the very recent past, above water. But some type of cataclysmic geological event suddenly 'collapsed' this section of tectonic plate, sinking it 10,500 to 18,440 feet below sea level—all of it *"in a grievous day and night!"*

Even Dr. Maurice Ewing is astonished by the recent findings. Dr. Ewing believes:

> *Either the land must have sunk two or three miles, or the sea must once have been two or three miles lower than now. Either conclusion is startling.[35]*

Recently, other examples of massive tectonic plate 'subduction' have also been discovered. Large areas of the Earth's crust have collapsed into the ocean's depths in the recent past, including a large landmass in the northern Atlantic. The celebrated French geologist, Pierre Termier, spoke of this now vanished Atlantian-like landmass by saying:

> *The conclusion is inevitable: the land which existed about 900km to the north of the Azores...was plunged into the deep, in times so comparatively recent that geologists call it 'the present,' and actually it is as if it all happened—just 'yesterday.' [36]*

Many other examples of extreme crustal 'collapse' can be found throughout the world. Geologists have now determined that the sea floor between Greenland and Norway has recently and suddenly collapsed 9,000 feet.[37] Other massive and sudden 'collapses' of tectonic plates have been found in the Indian Ocean, off the coast of New Zealand and in coastal waters off Alaska.[38]

Subduction of tectonic plates can explain how the ruins of ancient cities end up underwater, as some plates buckle and are thrust 'downward,' below sea level. In the last chapter, we saw an 'extreme' example of subductive 'block faulting' in the underwater ruins sitting 2,200 feet below sea level—off the coast of western Cuba. Block faulting can also explain why there are underwater ruins that lay off the coasts of Alexandria--Egypt, India, Malta, Japan, Cuba, Bimini and many other nations. Subductive 'block faulting' can also explain how an entire island nation like Atlantis could have disappeared beneath the ocean's waves—literally overnight.

It is important to keep in mind that these examples of subduction do not involve small geographic areas, but large sections of 'tectonic plates' often bordering on continental size.

We have described 'block faulting' as the tendency for tectonic plates to be pushed 'upwards' or 'downwards' by the extreme forces exerted on these plates during episodes of lithosphereic displacement. This is however, only a partial explanation of how tectonic plates behave under the phenomenal pressure applied to them when the Earth's crust slips.

When the lithosphere (Earth's crust) begins to slip over the more fluid-like mantel, unimaginable force is placed on these 'tectonic plates' comprising the Earth's surface. This force is so great in fact, that tectonic plates can actually 'shatter' from the enormous pressure exerted upon them.

It is because of this enormous pressure, that the Earth's crust actually has a gigantic 'crack' in it, which travels for over 40,000 miles around the surface of the globe.

Other examples of Earth's 'shattered' crust can be found throughout the world, including such incredible geologic spectacles as the Gangetic Trough (in the Bay of Bengal, India). So extreme is the pressure built up during 'lithosphereic displacement,' that a past episode left this scar on the planet, which is 1,200 miles long, 250 miles in width and incredibly over 6,500 feet deep.[39]

Such massive fracturing of the Earth's crust can be found throughout the world and is a sober testament to the massive force that is generated by the Earth during 'pole shift' events.

Block faulting can also be seen in many other areas of the world. According to researcher, Dr. Immanuel Velikovsky:

> *Much of France was once sea; then it was land, populated by land reptiles; then it became sea again and was populated by marine animals; then it was land again, inhabited by mammals; then it was once more sea, and again land. Each stratum contains the evidence of its ages in the bones and shells of the animals that lived and propagated there at the time, and were entombed in recurrent upheavals.*[40]

Once again, the concept of 'block faulting' can explain how sections of Earth's tectonic plates, (like the one France sits on) can be pushed 'below' sea level for a time—and then subsequently be pushed back 'above' sea level when the crust slides 'up' again.

Block faulting can also conveniently explain the observations of the French naturalist, Georges Dagobert who writes:

> *Every part of the earth, every hemisphere, every continent, exhibits the same phenomenon...the various catastrophes, which have disturbed the strata...have given rise to numerous shifting of the (continental) basin, (tectonic plates). It is of much importance*

> *to (note), that these "repeated" (inundations) and retreats of the sea, have neither been slow nor gradual; on the contrary, most of the catastrophes that (occurred) have been sudden; and this is especially easy to prove with regard to the last of these catastrophes.*
>
> *Our globe has been subjected to a vast and sudden revolution (a pole shift) not further back than five or six thousand years (ago); that this revolution has buried and caused to disappear the countries formerly inhabited by man, and the species of animals now most known; that...it has left the bottom of the former sea, dry, and has formed on it the countries now inhabited; that since the revolution (the pole shift) those few individuals whom it spared have been spread and propagated over the lands newly left dry, and consequently it is only since this epoch that our societies have assumed a progressive march.*
>
> *But the countries now inhabited, and which the last revolution left dry, had been before inhabited, if not by mankind, at least by land animals; consequently, one proceeding revolution (a pole shift), at least, had overwhelmed them with water; and if we may judge by the different order of animals whose remains we find therein, they had perhaps undergone two or three (inundations) of the sea.[41]*

The concept of 'block faulting' (both subduction and upliftment), can clearly explain the varied geological and archeological enigmas uncovered on our planet.

But if pole shifts, caused by the phenomenon of lithosphereic displacement is a reality—what is the actual cause of this lithosphereic displacement? So what type of forces could be powerful enough causing the entire crust of planet Earth to slip over its fluid-like mantel causing a shift?

Kicking and screaming their way into the phenomenon, modern-day sciences first began to answer this question once they finally caught up with the ancient knowledge of the elders. We fail to understand their inability to better interpret Earth's future based upon Earth's obvious past and its history of suffering cyclical patterns of 'pole shift' history and destruction.

Catching up with the past

The understanding that a passing 'celestial object' triggers Earth's periodic 'pole shifts' and the subsequent geophysical upheavals that accompany them is hardly a recent concept. In fact, as we have already discovered, this knowledge dates back thousands of years—to the very beginning of our recorded history. The ancient Sumerians, Egyptians, Greeks, Mayans, Hopis, Aztecs, Toltecs and so many others all possessed 'historical records' detailing how a passing 'celestial object' periodically causes a shift in the Earth's axis of rotation.

This understanding of Earth's great 'cycles of destruction' was common knowledge for many thousands of years. But then, almost two thousand years ago, western civilization slipped into the 'dark ages' and much of this knowledge from the ancient world was forgotten. With the advent of the European renaissance however, western culture began to emerge again from its intellectual slumber—and it is from this 'awakening' that modern science was largely born. As the progress of modern-day science advanced it slowly began to 'rediscover' ancient wisdom.

One of the areas of modern science that blossomed in the European renaissance was the study of astronomy. During the late 1600s and early 1700s scientists began to rediscover the wonders of the universe that surrounds us. It was during this 'renaissance of discovery' that comets (large balls of ice and gas that periodically pass through our solar system) began to be scientifically investigated and rudimentarily understood.

It is from this resurgence of modern science that the English mathematician and physicist, Sir William Whiston, comes into our focus. Whiston was no lightweight in scientific circles. He had the distinction of being none other than Sir Isaac Newton's laboratory assistant, and close friend of astronomer Edmund Halley (after whom the famed Halley's Comet is named).

Whiston was a very educated individual, familiar with all of the latest discoveries in physics, astronomy, geology and mathematics—he was also well versed in ancient history. He studied the ancient cataclysmic accounts of the Sumerians, Egyptians, Greeks and Hebrews, and was extremely well acquainted with the account of Noah's biblical flood. Being familiar with both 'ancient history' and 'modern science,' Whiston began to focus on what could have caused the past cataclysmic events that have repeatedly transpired on planet Earth.

It didn't take Whiston long to put 'two and two' together—for in 1696 and 1717, Whiston published two books detailing Earth's cataclysmic past. Whiston's premise was quite simple— *No internal forces associated with the Earth were capable of generating this type of massive geological upheavals that had obviously taken place in the recent past.*

The obvious cause for these geological upheavals, Whiston concluded, must be 'extraterrestrial' in nature. In other words, only an external, 'celestial catalyst' could account for Earth's violent past—and the culprit, Whiston hypothesized, must be a large 'comet' or other 'celestial body' periodically passing the Earth. Once again the evidence points to Earth's nemesis, *'Wormwood.'*

As we will see in the next chapter, Whiston was as accurate as he could be for his day and age. For the object that causes Earth's 'lithosphereic displacements' certainly behaves like a large periodic comet, but is actually a type of celestial object which was not discovered, or even known about, in Whiston's time.

Whiston's books were very well received in the scientific community and heavily influenced other top scientists of his day. Whiston's findings however, were largely kept within the scientific community—and were, for the most part, not shared with the public.

It took almost another two hundred years for someone to bring these ideas to 'public awareness'—and his name was Dr. Immanuel Velikovsky.

Born 10 June 1895, in Vitebsk, Russia, Immanuel Velikovsky learned several languages as a child and performed exceptionally well in Russian and mathematics. He earned his medical degree from the University of Moscow in 1921, and afterwards moved to Berlin where he met and married Elisheva Kramer, a young and very talented violinist. Little would everyone know that one day Velikovsky would revolutionize how modern-day scientific studies of the Earth and its properties would be conducted and written about?

While in Berlin, Dr. Velikovsky became the editor of the Journal, *Scripta Universitatis,* which contained articles by Jewish scholars and eventually gave rise to the Hebrew University at Jerusalem. The esteemed physicist, Albert Einstein, also prepared the mathematical/physical sections for this historic publication. If you'll recall, Albert Einstein also wrote the forward to Charles Hapgood's, *Path Of The Pole.*

Then in 1923, Velikovsky moved to Palestine and began a lucrative medical practice in *Tel Aviv.*

But medicine would only hold Dr. Velikovsky's interest for so long. In 1940, Velikovsky became fascinated with the subject of Earth's cataclysmic past and subsequently spent a decade studying the vast reservoir of relevant scientific evidence available. In 1950, Dr. Velikovsky published his first book entitled, *Worlds In Collision.* In 1952, he went on to publish, *Ages in Chaos* and then in 1955, *Earth in Upheaval.* Finally, the true facts were beginning to emerge.

Dr. Velikovsky's three books, which detailed the geological evidence of Earth's catastrophic history, were all met with astounding praise from the general public—and all became 50s 'best sellers,'—it seems as if the public simply—*'got it.'*

Since Whiston's books were published however, the scientific community had changed quite dramatically. Throughout the late 1800s and early 1900s, Whiston's work was largely forgotten, ignored, or intentionally suppressed by subsequent scientists—causing Whiston's brand of 'catastrophic geology' to fall out of vogue. In addition, very few scientists of the 1950's were intimately familiar with the ancient cataclysmic history of the Earth and subsequently had a hard time appreciating Velikovsky's grasp of the 'bigger picture.' As a result, Velikovsky's work was met with an almost violent reaction from the <u>scientific community</u>—even though many of his concepts were already scientifically established or have since been proven to be correct.

Like Solon, Copernicus, Galileo, Newton, Nostradamus, Edgar Casey and many other scientific geniuses whose ideas were presented well 'before their time,' Dr. Velikovsky was academically 'crucified' by a <u>scientific community</u> that no longer wanted to 'publicly' deal with the reality of Velikovsky's groundbreaking rediscoveries.

In his book, *Pole Shift,* author John White, comments on this scientific reaction to Velikovsky's work. White states:

> *In one breath, it seemed, an unknown outsider (Dr. Velikovsky) had profaned the most sacred doctrines of celestial cause and effect—doctrines jealously guarded by the "high priests" of technological society—"scientists." Because of that cosmological heresy, Velikovsky would not be allowed a (fair) hearing.*

> *In the name of (modern) science…his data would be denounced, and, even worse—maliciously distorted; his views would be peremptorily blocked from presentation on the podium and in professional journals, his books would be boycotted and scurrilously reviewed, his supporters summarily fired from positions they had held responsibly for many years, his integrity impugned, his reputation blackened, (and) his very name made anathema, (to be shunned).*

Savage verbal attacks would be made against both the man and the work by people who bragged, in the same breath, that they had not read his books. And all because he had challenged a (scientific) dogma. [42]

Why was the scientific community so brutally critical of Velikovsky—what were they afraid of?

Those answers stem from several reasons, but certainly one of the main ones is 'deliberate suppression.' Velikovsky had simply struck a nerve! His concepts and elevated perception was a little 'too accurate' for the comfort level of the 'powers that be.' Velikovsky was therefore the focus of an intentional (international) campaign to 'shut him up' and 'discredit' his work.

Recall from the last chapter how many governments and scientific organizations throughout the world have continuously suppressed, buried or destroyed specific/forbidden archeological evidence pertaining to Earth's catastrophic past. As we concluded, these governments and other institutions engage in this type of suppressive and destructive behavior to 'hide' the truth of Earth's cataclysmic history, keeping their 'great cycles of destruction' from public awareness— therefore preventing panic and further social, financial and religious instability.

In the last chapter we also looked at a phenomenon known as the *'knowledge filter'* in which modern scientists tend to dismiss, or in this case, ruthlessly attack evidence that does not fit into their concept of 'the way things were or should be.' Dr. Velikovsky was also the unfortunate recipient of this type of blind and deliberate prejudice—shameful in these modern times!

Will these negative factions also attack this book, its authors and our conclusions? We pray not!

After studying the vast historical, archeological and geological evidence, Velikovsky only arrived at the same conclusion that many others have—that a passing 'celestial object' has caused the slippage of the Earth's crust around its more liquid mantel numerous times in the past.

These 'lithosphere displacement' events did not happen slowly or smoothly however, and when they took place, there were violent global 'earthquakes' and 'inundations' of the land by the ocean. These 'lithosphere displacements' also caused massive 'folding,' 'tearing' and 'block faulting' of the Earth's crust—thus forming great mountain ranges, giant geologic chasms and 'decimating' most animal or human populations around at the time.

Velikovsky believed that through these 'pole shift' events, complete species had ceased to exist and mankind had been repeatedly wiped out—thus leaving only a small remnant left who found themselves struggling to survive in the difficult atmospheric and physical conditions that always follow these episodes of periodic 'lithosphereic displacement' events.

According to Velikovsky, planetary 'pole shifts' must have occurred and repeatedly so, under the impact of specific external (extraterrestrial) forces. Velikovsky's work goes on to establish that many worldwide cataclysmic events and physical phenomena (for each of which the principal cause was most often vainly sought), but was easily explainable (scientifically) by a single devastating event—the arrival of a periodic extraterrestrial visitor of 'cosmic' origin into our solar system. *["And the name of the star was Wormwood...Revelations - Chapter 8, Verse 11."]* Dr. Velikovsky states:

> *The displacement of the shell (crust) alone requires forces not in existence on the earth itself: and the turning of the earth's axis in a new direction requires more powerful forces still.... We cannot imagine any causes or agent for this, unless it is an exogenous agent, an "extraterrestrial" cause. For the removal of the poles from their places, or the shifting of the (planet's) axis, also, only an external agent could have been responsible.*[43]

As we have alluded to, when the Earth's crust slips around its fluid-like mantle, violent forces tear the outer surface of the crust—virtually to pieces. These episodes of 'lithosphereic displacement' set off a vast litany of geologic catastrophes. After an entire lifetime of research, Dr. Velikovsky summarizes some of these upheavals in his final conclusions:

> *Let us assume, as a working hypothesis, that under the impact of an (external) force or the influence of an agent, (rogue celestial object)... the axis of the earth shifted or tilted. At that moment an earthquake would make the globe shudder. Air and water would continue to move through inertia; hurricanes would sweep the earth, and seas would rush over continents, carrying gravel, sand and marine animals, and casting them on the land.*

> *Heat would be developed (within the earth), rocks would melt, volcanoes would erupt, and lava would flow from fissures in the ruptured ground and cover vast areas. Mountains would spring up from the plains and would travel, and climb on the shoulders of other mountains, causing faults and rifts (to develop). Lakes would be tilted and emptied, rivers would change their beds; (and) large land areas with all their inhabitants, would slip under the sea. Forests would burn, and the hurricanes and wild seas would wrest them from the ground on which they grew and pile them, branch and root, in huge heaps. Seas would turn into deserts, their waters rolling away.*

> *And if a change in the velocity of the diurnal (24 hour) rotation—slowing it down— should accompany the shifting of the axis, the water confined to the equatorial oceans by centrifugal force would retreat to the poles, and high tides...would rush from pole to pole...moving from the equator up to the mountain ridges of the Himalayas and down the African jungles; and crumbled rocks torn from splintering mountains would be scattered over large distances; and herds of animals would be washed from the plains of Siberia.*

> *The shifting of the axis would change the climate of every place, leaving corals in Newfoundland and elephants in Alaska, fig trees in northern Greenland and luxuriant forests in Antarctica. In the event of a rapid shift of the axis, many species and genera of animals on land and in the sea would be destroyed, and civilizations, if any, would be reduced to ruins.*[44]

Dr. Velikovsky is not the only modern researcher to conclude that an extraterrestrial object is the ultimate cause for the slippage of the Earth's crust.

In their book, *Cataclysm*, authors D. S. Allan and J. B. Delair, arrive at the same conclusion regarding the ultimate cause for Earth's 'pole shifts' saying:

> *Only some closely-approaching 'cosmic object' of considerable size could activate the titanic forces which, through part and parcel of a wider, more profound, universal uniformitarianism, only become naturally unleashed during such confrontations, and would be necessary to produce such gargantuan topographical and biological changes so rapidly and extensively on Earth.*[45]

We believe the research contained in this book easily confirms Velikovsky's conclusions, et al. Author and researcher, Peter Warlow, who received honors in mathematics and physics at Keele University in England, worked independently of Dr. Velikovsky and others—but came to the exact same conclusions!

According to Warlow, there is more than ample evidence to suggest that the Earth's crust slips over its fluid-like mantle. And, like Dr. Velikovsky, Warlow also believes that the passage of a large 'celestial object' is the ultimate culprit for these periodic pole shifts.

According to Warlow:

> *A feature of many of these recent investigations (into pole shifts) is the rapidity of change. Many (researchers) are forced to conclude that sedimentation, glaciations, climate, water temperature, polar wanderings, and outbursts of volcanism occurred or changed suddenly, and often such events occurred on a worldwide scale.*
>
> *The theory proposed here could account for all of the above data and observations...I propose a (polar) geographic reversal. Not only can this explain the above data, but it also brings into perspective many otherwise enigmatic archaeological, astronomical, historical and other data.*[46]

Warlow then goes on to state that a passing 'cosmic body' is unequivocally the ultimate cause of these geographic reversals (pole shifts).

But if a celestial object is the actual cause of Earth's pole shifts, how large would such an object have to be in order to cause this catastrophic event? In other words, how massive would an object have to be (to have a large enough gravitational effect on Earth) to cause our poles to shift? And what is the likelihood of such an object existing in the space around us and then passing our planet?[47]

Through Warlow's research, he calculated the minimum mass needed by this passing 'celestial object' to actually cause Earth's lithosphere to slip over its more fluid-like mantle. Warlow states:

> *We may reasonably use the Moon, that at its present distance from the Earth and at a declination of 12°, as a datum for the comparison of torques. The postulated body passing near the Earth is very likely to pass through a declination angle of 45°, and from*

that position the torque necessary to bring about an inversion of the Earth (pole shift)
would be obtained from, for example, a body of ten times the mass of the moon at a
(center-to-center) distance of about 3.3 x 10-4 km, or for a body of Earth mass at a
distance of about 6.6 x 10-4 km.[48]

In other words, an object only ten times the size of our own moon, at the right distance and
angle, could place enough gravitational torque on the Earth to cause our planet's crust to slip
over its mantel. As we shall see in the next chapter, there are plenty of objects wandering around
the Milky Way galaxy to account for such an encounter. Once again, we believe that if Planet-X
were to invade our solar system—its immense size and mass would certainly trigger a pole shift.

We must also keep in mind that when we mention pole shifts—even slight alterations in Earth's
rotational angle can cause enormous geologic changes to occur. In his book, *Atlantis Of The
West*, author Paul Dunbavin, does an excellent job describing the geology of pole shifts. Mr.
Dunbavin lucidly points out that pole shifts <u>do not</u> necessarily have to entail 'major' alterations
in Earth's axis of rotation in order to have dramatic and catastrophic effects.

According to Mr. Dunbavin:

For a shift of just a single degree of latitude…(causing an equatorial change of)…say,
45° to 46° would imply a change in sea level of about 373 meters (approximately 1000
feet). Even a pole shift of just a fraction of a degree would be enough to cause noticeable
effects around world coastlines, especially at temperate latitudes.[49]

Simply put, even relatively small objects having only minor effects on our planet's rotational
angle—can cause phenomenally destructive geologic events to occur.

John White

John White is an internationally known researcher/author of the popular book, *Pole Shift*. White
holds degrees from Dartmouth College and Yale University, and has taught both English and
Journalism at the college level. He's also held positions such as Director of Education for the
Institute of Noetic Sciences (a research organization founded by Apollo 14 astronaut Edgar D.
Mitchell, to study human potential and planetary problems.)

As a lecturer and seminar leader, White has appeared at colleges and universities and before
public and professional organizations throughout the U.S. and Canada. He's also made
numerous radio and television appearances across the nation speaking about his 'pole shift'
theories, research, and the substance of his *New York Times* best selling book, *Pole Shift*.

After studying the scientific evidence of 'pole shifts' for many years, Mr. White has concluded
what physical effects can be expected during the next event and how these effects will impact the
society in which we live. In fact, Dr. Jeffrey Goodman, author of the best selling book, *We Are
The Earthquake Generation,* stated: "*too many coincidences and warning signs are being discovered by scientists for us to ignore White's important work.*"[50]

Exactly what will happen during the next major pole shift and will it be an apocalyptic event for planet Earth in modern-day times?

According to White, this 'ultimate planetary disaster' won't be a pretty one and will bring Earth to a complete standstill! According to White:

> *Enormous tidal waves would roll across the continents as the oceans became displaced from their basins. Electrical storms with hurricane (force) winds of hundreds of miles per hour would sweep the planet. Tremendous earthquakes and lava flows would wrack the land. Poisonous gases and ash would fill the skies.*
>
> *Geography would be altered as seabed's rose and landmasses submerged. Climates would change instantly. And if the (pole) shift were less than a full end-over-end roll, the polar ice caps…would melt rapidly… while new icecaps would begin to build at the new polar locations.*
>
> *Last of all, huge numbers of organisms, would be destroyed, including people, with signs of their existence hidden under thick layers of debris, (muddy) sediments and ice—or at the bottom of newly established seas.* [51]

This description may certainly be disturbing, but at the same time, must be taken seriously in light of recent evidence supporting Earth's periodic 'pole shifts'—tragic geologic events that may end up causing the death of our present-day human civilization—again.

In summary

The modern 'geological evidence' that we have looked at in this chapter should convince any rational thinking adult that 'pole shifts' are a planetary reality.

Evidence such as 'out of place' animal and plant remains found in northern geographic areas where they could never have existed today; evidence of former polar 'ice caps' located all over the world including some of the hottest places on Earth; evidence of warm water corals found in the frigid waters of the Arctic; and geomagnetic evidence from lava fields that conclusively indicate that Earth has undergone hundreds of 'pole shift' events in the past.

We have also briefly looked at the brilliant work of Charles Hapgood and none other than the great Albert Einstein to see how these and other brilliant pioneers of modern science are in agreement regarding 'pole shifts' and the physical mechanism of 'lithosphereic displacement,' which shifts the Earth's crust over its fluid-like mantle—distorting and buckling our planet's tectonic plates in the process.

The buckling of Earth's tectonic plates causes some sections of the lithosphere to be thrust upwards (upliftment) and other sections to be thrust downwards (subduction) through a process referred to as 'block faulting.' Block faulting can explain how mountain ranges can be suddenly thrust upwards in a single devastating event, or how ancient civilizations can suddenly end up at the bottom of the ocean—all of 'it' as a direct result of Earth's buckling crust.

In addition, researchers like Dr. Immanuel Velikovsky and many others, have firmly concluded that these 'pole shifts' are ultimately caused by the passage of a large 'celestial object.' This passing object has a strong 'gravitational' effect on the Earth, so strong in fact, that its passage places enough force on Earth's crust to cause it to slip/sliding over its liquid mantel.

With all of the compelling evidence supporting periodic 'pole shifts' brought about by the passage of a large celestial object, why aren't we (as a species) more 'in tune' with what has actually taken place on this planet in the past—and what is likely to happen again in the very near future? More specifically—will the upcoming 2006-hurricane season continue to escalate in both number and intensity producing killer tropical storms in both the Atlantic and Pacific?

In going a step further—let's state these same key questions in yet another way:

1) If our ancient ancestors had left us so many 'historic accounts' of a 'terrible comet' wreaking havoc across our globe setting our geographic poles in motion on a recurring basis, and 2) if the physical/archeological evidence uncovered around the planet strongly supports those 'ancient historical' accounts of past calamities, and 3) if this 'geological evidence' also clearly indicates that our planet's geophysical poles have shifted many times in the past—(with a passing 'celestial object' actually triggering the real cause of these shifts), then why aren't we, as a species, paying more attention to this recurring 'cycle of destruction' in which we are currently caught up (like in New Orleans)? And what could be more important to America than its continued existence during this time of ongoing planetary weather instability and the constant threat of global terrorism taking advantage of the planet's global weather-related misfortunes?

In conclusion

It was Dr. Immanuel Velikovsky who wrote:

> *As important as the 'world catastrophes' conclusion is, it grows in significance for almost every branch of science when, to the ensuing question, "Of <u>old</u> or of <u>recent time</u>?" The answer is given, "Of <u>old</u> and of <u>recent</u>."*
>
> *There were global catastrophes in pre-human times, in pre-historic times, and during modern historical periods. We are descendants of survivors, themselves descendants of earlier survivors, who were also survivors... and the liturgy goes on and on...* [52]

As a species—we have known about the 'usual inundation' for thousands of years, and for these same 'thousands' of years we have been peering out into the blackness of space, hoping to be able to anticipate the return of Earth's next 'destructive cycle.'

And yet today, 'modern science' looks incredulously at these ancient 'historic accounts' and the efforts our ancestors made in order to both warn us—and to try and save themselves. Our scientific 'priests' arrogantly dismiss this ancient information as being foolish 'fairy tales' and

the 'anxious' behavior of our ancestors as the actions of 'ignorant savages'—completely missing their message and unfortunately, completely missing their 'obvious warnings' for the future.
As a species—we have known about 'destroyed civilizations' for thousands of years and our ancestors put together vast libraries of ancient knowledge to help us avoid following in their fatal footsteps.

And yet, we've burned/destroyed all of these repositories of ancient knowledge to the ground and blatantly disregarded the loss of this knowledge as meaningless and unimportant. Besides, was the cry—*What could these ancient primitives have taught us anyway?*

Modern science turns its back on these ancient ruins and dismisses the stories they're tying to tell us, or 'they' simply pretend that these ruins don't exist altogether. Our leaders exacerbate our ignorance and bury these ancient sites under tons of dirt and concrete, so as to not 'alarm the public' by informing them of a catastrophic history they have no business knowing about in the first place! *Question: Does the term 'international scientific cover-up' apply here?*

As a species—we've known about the tendency of our fragile home planet to periodically 'shift' on its axis of rotation for thousands of years, and we've known that this recurring phenomenon has been repeatedly triggered by the passage of the mystical *'terrible red comet—Wormwood.'*

And yet, *modern science* has 'academically crucified' any honest attempts to understand this geological and astronomical phenomena. As a modern-day scientist, if you would like your career to be 'instantly over,' just start investigating 'pole shifts,' or rogue 'celestial objects'—and security will be escorting you 'out of the building' faster than you can say 'what cover-up.'

Our *species* is at a crossroads! We can either decide to deal with the cataclysmic evidence that is all around us and thus urgently direct our attention to the next rapidly approaching 'cycle of destruction,' or we can continue to ignore, hide and attack the obvious—in which case this 'current chapter' of human history will not be around much longer—and we, too, are going to find ourselves "*starting over again as children.*" If we keep refusing to learn from our past—we are surely going to repeat it!

In 1889, well over a hundred years ago, a little known work by Marshall Wheeler entitled, *The Earth—Its Third Motion*, summed up the situation we are currently in rather nicely. In fact, Wheeler's insight sums up this book rather nicely! Referring to the next 'pole shift'—Wheeler stated:

> *The earth will come to rest at 90° from its starting point, reversing the present position of the poles and the equator...The whole world should be informed of this fact, and means taken to forever perpetuate that knowledge so that, when the dread event transpires, mankind should not lapse "again" into prehistoric barbarism, but, instead, the rhythm of man's existence be raised to a higher plane of action.*[53]

Well put, Mr. Wheeler—well put!

CHAPTER THREE ENDNOTES

[1] Darwin, Charles, *Voyage Of The H.M.S. Beagle.*

[2] White, John, *Pole Shift* (A.R.E. Press, 1998), p. 19.

[3] Ibid., p.19.

[4] Ibid., p.28.

[5] Velikovsky, Immanuel, *Earth In Upheaval* (Pocket Books, 1977), pp. 4-5.

[6] Ibid., p. 40.

[7] White, John, *Pole Shift* (A.R.E. Press, 1998), p. 30.

[8] Ibid., pp. 30-31.

[9] Ibid., p. 125.

[10] Ibid., p. 124.

[11] Velikovsky, Immanuel, *Worlds In Collision* (Dell Publishing, 1970), pp. 330-331.

[12] Hapgood, Charles, *Path Of The Pole* (Adventures Unlimited Press, 1999), p. 47.

[13] White, John, *Pole Shift* (A.R.E. Press, 1998), p. 75.

[14] Velikovsky, Immanuel, *Earth In Upheaval* (Pocket Books, 1977), p. 37.

[15] Ibid., p. 37.

[16] Ibid., p. 33.

[17] Ibid., p. 41.

[18] Hapgood, Charles, *Path Of The Pole* (Adventures Unlimited Press, 1999), pp. 4-11.

[19] White, John, *Pole Shift* (A.R.E. Press, 1998), p. 58.

[20] Ibid., p. 59.

[21] Ibid., p. 61.

[22] Velikovsky, Immanuel, *Earth In Upheaval* (Pocket Books, 1977), p. 54.

[23] Hapgood, Charles, *Path Of The Pole* (Adventures Unlimited Press, 1999), p. 18.

[24] Ibid., pp. xiv-xv.

[25] Ibid., p xii.

[26] White, John, *Pole Shift* (A.R.E. Press, 1998), p. 59.

[27] Timms, Moira, *Beyond Prophecies and Predictions* (Ballantine Books, 1994), p. 85.

[28] White, John, *Pole Shift* (A.R.E. Press, 1998), p. 59.

[29] Allan, D. S., and Delair, J. B., *Cataclysm* (Bear and Company, 1997), p. 26.

[30] Ibid., p. 26.

[31] Ibid., p. 26.

[32] Ibid., p. 31.

[33] Ibid., p. 32.

[34] Ibid., p. 32.

[35] Ibid., p. 32.

[36] Ibid., p. 32.

[37] Ibid., p. 33.

[38] Ibid., p. 34.

[39] Ibid., p. 37.

[40] Velikovsky, Immanuel, *Earth In Upheaval* (Pocket Books, 1977), p. 13.

[41] White, John, *Pole Shift* (A.R.E. Press, 1998), pp. 54-55.

[42] Ibid., pp. 110-111.

[43] Velikovsky, Immanuel, *Earth In Upheaval* (Pocket Books, 1977), p. 121.

[44] White, John, *Pole Shift* (A.R.E. Press, 1998), pp. 125-126.

[45] Allan, D. S., and Delair, J. B., *Cataclysm* (Bear and Company, 1997), p. 68.

[46] White, John, *Pole Shift* (A.R.E. Press, 1998), p. 135.

[47] Ibid., p. 136.

[48] Ibid., p. 141.

[49] Dunbavin, Paul, *Atlantis Of The West* (Carroll & Graf Publishers, 2003), p. 41.

[50] Goodman, Jeffery, *The Earthquake Generation* (Doubleday Publishing, 1998), p. 121.

[51] White, John, *Pole Shift* (A.R.E. Press, 1998), p. 53..

[52] White, John, *Pole Shift* (A.R.E. Press, 1998), p. 53..

[53] Dunbavin, Paul, *Atlantis Of The West* (Carroll & Graf Publishers, 2003), p. 79.

— CHAPTER FOUR —

PHANTOM ASTRONOMY

> *"One day Phaethon, son of the God Zeus, began to have daunts about his divine origin. In order to prove his divinity, he demanded permission to drive the chariot of the Sun across the sky for one day. The impetuous Phaethon took hold of the reins of the Sun, but the horses, no longer restrained by the firm hand of their usual driver, sensed Phaethon's inexperience and rushed wildly through space—and Phaethon was not able to regain control.*
>
> *The chariot of the Sun veered from its normal course and came too close to the Earth. Rivers dried up, soil began to burn and the Mother Earth was cracked and set ablaze. An appeal was made to the god Jupiter that if the Earth's poles, already smoking from the heat of the vagrant chariot, were to burn through, the entire Earth and even the celestial palace of Jupiter would tumble."* *...Ancient Greek Mythology...*

Archeoastronomy is the study of the efforts made by ancient civilizations in order to understand the cosmological universe around them. In other words, it's the study of ancient astronomy. As we alluded to in chapter two, almost every ancient civilization seems to have had an obsessive 'obsession' with charting/studying/understanding movements of the Sun/Moon/planets and stars.

From ancient Europe, Africa, South America and the Orient, our ancient ancestors built elaborate observatories, sacred astronomical temples and other massive, yet intricate structures in order to keep track of even the slightest changes in the celestial canopy. In the event of any change, the appearance of a comet for example, these ancient cultures would often display a 'doomsday anxiety' regarding these events believing in that: *"their 'dreaded cycle' of doomsday was about to revisit planet Earth—another time—following the last time!"*

Recall from the second chapter, when we asked ourselves: "What could have happened to these ancient cultures that had put them so 'on edge,' and made them so 'anxious' regarding any new celestial changes in the heavens?"

Since asking ourselves these questions, we have seen the 'physical evidence' of the past catastrophic events that have transpired on this planet, and this clear-cut evidence should put into proper perspective why these ancient people were so shaken up! (Pardon the pun).

Many modern-day scientists have dismissed this 'astronomical obsession' of ancient cultures as merely primitive superstition, or their elementary efforts to help determine when to plant crops or hold certain religious ceremonies or set up their annual cultural calendars.

These modern explanations for the ancient's fascination with the heavens may be partially true—but there is much more to their story than present-day scientists are willing to admit. According to the ancients themselves, they were about largely keeping track of the motion of the heavens in order to calculate or 'foretell' the coming of the next great 'cycle of destruction' that almost every ancient civilization believed revisited this planet on a regular/recurring basis.

As we have seen in former chapters, these recurring catastrophes clearly involve a shifting of the Earth's poles, which is brought about by the passages of a large celestial object. This scenario (tracking the timing of this celestial object's passage and in turn, the great 'cycles of destruction' that follow), would more realistically explain why the ancients had an 'astronomical obsession' and a 'doomsday anxiety' over the motion of the heavens. By studying the movement of various planets and stellar constellations, they could not only count off the long periods of time in between passages of this object (and in turn pole shifts) —but as the time for this object's arrival drew nearer, they would 'head for the hills' at the appropriate time.

The idea of their planting crops or simply knowing when to hold yearly celebrations was the ultimate cause for this watchfulness of the heavens, and for the building of such elaborate ancient observatories, is extremely belittling towards these ancient civilizations. For these everyday or even yearly events, the ancients had shadow clocks and sundials in use, which are more than sufficient for most yearly 'calendar' purposes.[1] The ancient cultures of this planet did not have to build elaborate and complicated observatories for mundane reasons; they built these extremely precise structures in order to count down long periods of time and to anticipate the next destruct-tion cycle of their world as they knew it to be.

For example, the ancient monument known as Stonehenge, built thousands of years ago on the southern plains of Britain, has been referred to as a carefully planned astronomical observatory—and an instrument to measure the passage of time.[2] According to astronomer and mathematician, Sir Fred Hoyle, *"Stonehenge is a 'predictor,' an instrument for foretelling celestial events and a (sophisticated) facility for noting them on predetermined dates."* [3]

According to noted author, researcher and historian, Zecharia Sitchin:

> *The more we know about Stonehenge…the more incredible Stonehenge becomes. Indeed, were it not for the visible evidence of the megaliths (themselves)…the whole tale of (this monument) that could compute time…and foretell eclipses and determine the movements of the Sun and the Moon would have sounded so implausible (coming from) Stone Age Britain, that it would have been considered (as) just a myth.[4]*

According to Kristen Lippincott's book, *Astronomy*:

> *Even though the precise significance of the standing stones at Stonehenge remain the subject of debate, it is clear from the arrangement of the stones that it was erected by prehistoric people specifically to record certain key celestial events, such as the summer and winter solstices and the spring and autumnal equinoxes. Although Stonehenge is the best known of the ancient megalithic monuments, the sheer number of 'similar sites' throughout the world underlines how many prehistoric peoples placed an enormous importance on recording the motions of the Sun and Moon.[5]*

On the other side of the world, high atop the 10,000-foot Andes Mountains, sits the ancient Incan city of Machu Picchu. Like Stonehenge, Machu Picchu has also been described as a *"complex solar-lunar stone computer to serve as a calendar (for the great cycles of destruction)."* [6] The Inca, as well as their descendants, made it quite clear that Machu Picchu was used as both an observatory for determining solstices in order to keep track of long periods of time, and as a ritual location to ensure the Sun would keep moving in the sky and not alter its course—and thereby not bringing destruction to the world once again.[7]

Dozens of other ancient astronomical structures dot the globe. These structures, all built many thousands of years ago, often show a sophistication and knowledge of celestial mechanics that has stunned modern-day scholars and astronomers alike.

If the ancients were so obsessed with astronomy and the regular movements of the heavens over long periods of time, shouldn't we 'tune into' why? Could these ancient civilizations have known about the periodic passage of a rogue celestial object? And could this object pass our planet on a fixed timetable, triggering massive cataclysms and occasionally a shifting of the Earth on its axis of rotation? Could this same object be once again approaching us from space? And could our own near future hold a catastrophic 'rude awakening' that is almost upon us?

Like our ancient ancestors, let us now look into the heavens in order to see what they might tell us about our own planetary destiny!

The grand universe in which we live

Most people today take the workings of the universe completely for granted. Why the Sun rises in the east and sets in the west, what celestial mechanics produce the Earth's seasons or why we have 24-hours in a day, are often not part of the average persons daily concerns. To prove this point, in a recent 2002 survey conducted with the American public, the majority of people surveyed, about 60%, did not know that Earth traveled around the Sun one time—in one year.

For our purposes here, however, such a 'lack of understanding' about the cosmos around us will not suffice. If we are to understand what has transpired on this planet in the 'far distant' past and what may be about to happen again in our very 'near' future, we must have at least a basic understanding of the celestial environment that surrounds us.

We will therefore begin our journey through the known universe right in our own backyard—with our own solar system.

At the center of our solar system sits our very own Sun, an average G2-type star that is composed primarily of 75% hydrogen and 25% helium. Within the very center of the Sun sits its fiery core. So extreme is the pressure and temperature of the Sun's core, that its hydrogen nuclei are compressed and fused into helium—the same process that takes place in a hydrogen bomb.

Through this process of continuous nuclear fusion the Sun converts 240 million tons of its matter into energy every minute.[8] The sun's mean distance from Earth is about 93 million miles (150 million km) and its diameter is about 864,000 miles, with a mass 330,000 times that of Earth's.

Compared to the rest of the planets in our solar system the Sun is enormous, containing more mass than all of the nine planets put together. As a matter of fact, our Sun contains 99.8% of all the mass in our entire solar system. Needless to say, the Sun, because of its huge magnitude, has an enormous gravitational influence that extends far out into space for billions of miles.

The Sun not only has a strong gravitational influence on the solar system, but an enormous magnetic influence as well. Powerful magnetic fields cause the Sun's outer surface, known as the corona, to eject huge amounts of charged gasses into space in dramatic events called CME's (coronal mass ejections). The magnetic fields of the Sun are so powerful, that they also disturb the transfer of heat radiating out from the Sun's core. These differences in heat transference cause areas of the Sun's fiery surface to be cooler than others and these darker 'cooler' areas are known as sunspots.

Today, it is believed by many solar scientists that the greater the magnetic disturbances on the Sun, the greater the disruption of heat transference from its core, and in turn, the greater the number of sunspots on the solar surface.

Even though the Sun is approximately 93 million miles away, solar activity can have a strong effect on the Earth. Both CME's and sunspots can have dramatic effects on the Earth's weather, (and in turn) on the proper workings of man-made devices such as satellites and electrical power grids. CME's for example, can fry the electrical components of satellites and overload the capacity of electrical power grids on Earth, thus shutting down these critical systems leaving our society in the dark and without the benefit of modern communication systems.

The Sun also produces what is commonly known as the 'solar wind.' The pressure and heat from the solar wind is what causes passing comets to 'off-gas' their gaseous materials, forming the classic streaming 'tail' that is seen as most comets near the Sun. Because the solar wind is responsible for the out-gassing of comets, the tail always points away from the Sun.

As we move out into space, away from the Sun, the first planet of our solar system we encounter is Mercury. Mercury is only slightly larger than our own Moon, but has a mass (weight) about four time that of the Moon. This fact is believed to be the result of a large iron core that takes up a quarter of its radius.[9]

Even though Mercury is the closest planet to our Sun, and is relentlessly baked by this solar inferno, it is still over 35 million miles away from the Sun's explosive surface. Mercury is a hot, lifeless planet whose surface features eerily resemble that of our own moon.

As we continue to move away from the Sun, the next planet we encounter is Venus. Venus is the sixth largest planet in the solar system and sits over 67 million miles from the Sun. Sometimes referred to as Earth's sister planet, having 80% of the mass (weight) of the Earth and 95% of the diameter. Venus is Earth's sister planet however, in name only. The atmosphere of Venus is composed of a thick cloud of carbon dioxide and sulfuric acid. This thick, noxious cloud-cover produces an intense 'greenhouse effect' driving Venus's surface temperature up to 900° F.[10] Venus is the most brilliant planet, second in order from the Sun and easily seen by the naked eye.

The third planet from the Sun is Earth, the fifth largest in our solar system and the only planet in our system known to support life. Earth sits approximately 93 million miles from the Sun and unlike many other planets in our solar system has only one moon, which travels around the Earth every 29.5 days. The Earth itself spins on its axis of rotation once, in one sidereal day (23.56 hours) and travels entirely around the Sun once every year. Earth spins on its axis of rotation a little over 365 times while traveling once around the Sun.

Our planet contains a gaseous atmosphere made up of approximately 20% oxygen and 80% nitrogen. As we have already seen, the surface of Earth, also know as the 'crust,' is composed of a series of segments know as tectonic plates. These plates float over an inner layer of molten rock known as the mantel. It's the tension between these tectonic plates, caused by their motion over the 'fluid-like' mantel, which gives rise to global earthquakes and volcanic activity.

The fourth planet from the Sun is Mars, the seventh largest planet located 141 million miles from the Sun. Also known as the red planet, Mars is believed to have had liquid water seas on its surface very similar to that of Earth and may have even supported life in the distant past.

But something extremely terrible and violent happened to Mars, distorting the planet's shape and stripping away most of its atmosphere. Some astronomers actually believe that a large comet (or possibly a planet) collided with Mars in the past. Today, Mars exists as a cold, lifeless, inhospitable remnant of what it once seemed to have been.

Just outside of Mars lies the asteroid belt. It is believed that this massive band of rubble encircling the inner solar system, was at one time a planet, but a massive collision with an unknown object smashed this former planet into countless pieces—which today make up this asteroid belt.

Outside of the asteroid belt lie the giant gas planets of Jupiter, Saturn, Uranus and Neptune. Like the Sun, these planets are mostly composed of hydrogen and helium, but are not massive enough to ignite and burn like the Sun. They are therefore large, but not large enough to become full-fledge stars.

Jupiter for instance, located over 482 million miles from the Sun, is large by planet standards. It is twice the size of all the other planets in our solar system put together and is 318 times the size of Earth. The size of Jupiter is so great; that its gaseous hydrogen atmosphere is compressed into liquid hydrogen as one moves towards its center. At its very core, the pressure is so great, that liquid hydrogen is literally compressed into its metallic form. Jupiter also stands out among the planets as having a gigantic 'red spot' that is actually a continuous cyclonic storm that constantly circles the planet.

If Jupiter had been even more massive than it is, its own weight would have caused such enormous pressure to internally build up—its core of hydrogen would have started the process of nuclear fusion (combining hydrogen molecules into helium), thus igniting this gaseous giant and giving birth to another star

If Jupiter had not been massive enough to form a star, but several times more massive than it is, it would have been too big to be considered a planet and would have been classified as an object known as a 'dwarf star.' A dwarf star is an object that is too big to be considered a planet, but not quite big enough to sustain the nuclear 'fusion' of hydrogen in its core to become a real star. Dwarf stars, also called 'brown dwarf stars,' just 'smolder' under the weight of their own mass-iveness—but never fully ignite. We will come back to these 'celestial objects' know as 'brown dwarfs' later in this chapter.

As we move out further away from the Sun, the next planet we encounter is Saturn. Saturn is the second largest planet in the solar system and has a chemical composition very similar to that of Jupiter—but far smaller in size. Saturn is best known for its stunning series of outer 'rings' composed of different-sized ice particles encircling this majestic planet. Saturn is located 886 million miles from the Sun.

Uranus is four times larger than the Earth, making it the third largest planet in the solar system. Uranus sits a whopping one billion, 780 million miles from the Sun. The rotational axis of Uranus is so tilted (about 98° from the plane of its orbit), that Uranus is literally spinning on it side. This odd axis of rotation is believed by many astronomers to be the result of a massive collision with an unknown space object.

This is a good point to pause in our exploration of the solar system to point out an interesting but alarming fact.

As we first stated in our Introductory Overview, we live in a universe which is both beautiful yet catastrophic in its nature. Everywhere that we look throughout the cosmos we find signs of past cataclysmic events—events so significant that they can't be adequately described!

Uranus is certainly not alone in showing signs of a past disruptive encounter. We have already mentioned that both Mars and the asteroid belt—also exhibit the same end result of cataclysmic collisions. The truth of the matter is that every planet in our solar system, including the Earth, can be shown to exhibit irregularities in their orbits or rotational speed that can be directly traced back to destructive celestial encounters in the past.

According to the book *Cataclysm,* written by D. S. Allan and J. B. Delair:

> *The overall picture presented by the solar system shows that its principal members comprise a basic orderly assemblage of rotating and orbiting objects that have (all) apparently experienced various derangements resulting in many kinds of aberrant and anomalous motions which...have apparently been caused by one or more unknown influences in the past...the history of the solar system could justifiably be said to be recurrently catastrophic.[11]*

As we shall soon see, there is a very good reason that our entire solar system demonstrates signs of suffering past cataclysmic 'celestial' encounters.

Continuing on our journey through space, Neptune is the fourth largest planet located 2 billion, 792 million miles from the Sun, and like Jupiter, sports a giant 'dark spot' in its atmosphere that is as large as planet Earth.

At the distant edge of our known solar system lies Pluto. Pluto is so small that many astronomers think it should not be classified as a true planet, but instead, should be considered as a large asteroid, or even a comet that was wandering by and became captured by the gravitational influence of our Sun. Pluto is a mere 1,409 miles in diameter and sits well over 3 billion miles from the Sun.

Even though our solar system has nine 'official planets,' it is still mostly empty space. All of the planets in our solar system have vast distances between them. Like the Earth, all of the planets in our system are traveling (or orbiting around the Sun), while they are spinning on their own axis of rotation. In addition to the nine 'official planets,' thousands of orbiting comets and asteroids also travel around the Sun, forming a huge 'merry-go-round' effect of space debris, with the Sun acting as the central 'axis of rotation.'

Comets (believed to be made of mostly interstellar dust/ice/gas) as well as asteroids (believed to be made of mostly rock and iron), can continuously circle the Sun while staying within the solar system (similar to the way most planets do), or they can travel around the Sun and then head off into deep space, outside the limits of our solar system. Sometimes these circulating objects leave the solar system and do not return, while other times, they travel in and out of the solar system repeatedly—suggesting that *Planet-X* may be one of these cosmic anomalies.

The reason that objects like comets can leave our solar system and then return again, is due to the fact that our Sun is probably part of a binary system, meaning that the Sun may have a dark 'sister star' sitting out in deep space (waiting to be officially discovered)? Astronomers have not actually seen this other star, but many scientists have now hypothesized its virtual existence.

It is believed by many astronomers that these 'cyclic' objects leave our solar system on highly elliptical orbits, traveling out into deep space where they eventually travel around Earth's 'sister star,' and are then sent back into our inner solar system and eventually back out towards the Sun. Objects may travel around these two stars over and over again in an almost endless loop.

Picture a racecar traveling around an elliptical racetrack. The car travels around one turn (our sister star) and is sent back toward the opposite turn (our primary Sun). And so it goes, round and round and round through cosmic time.

Not all eccentrically orbiting objects (such as comets) travel around our sister star. A good example of a periodic visitor to our solar system (that stays much closer to home) is the famed Haley's Comet. Once every 76 years this object travels through our solar system, around our Sun, and then out of our system and back into deep space, but then returns again only 76 years later. Haley's comet, because of its quick return, probably doesn't travel very far away from our solar system before being sent back towards the Sun—certainly not as far as our sister star.

Today astronomers think there may be many other celestial objects that have this same 'cyclic' passage through our solar system, but their orbits may involve much longer periods of time. Some comets for example (possibly around 40) have orbital periods of between 100 to 1,000 years. But the vast majority of comets, maybe as many as 100,000 of them (and the ones that probably go all the way around our sister star), may have orbital periods of thousands of years—possibly as long as 40,000 years to complete a single orbit.[12]

Asteroids are generally considered small objects by cosmic comparison, with most being less than 625 miles in diameter and the majority being under a few feet in diameter. Comets on the other hand can be enormous. In fact, some astronomers today have hypothesized that the planet Jupiter, the largest planet in our solar system, many have at one time been a comet that was captured by the gravity of the Sun becoming our largest planet. Most comets are not this large, but potentially can be.

As if our own solar system and its celestial mechanics were not impressive and vast enough, our Sun is only one star in more than 100 billion stars that make up what is known as the Milky Way galaxy. The Milky Way system is so large in fact, that a single beam of light, traveling at a mind boggling 186,000 miles per second, would take over 100,000 years to travel from one side of the Milky Way to the other.

The Milky Way, however, is only one of hundreds-of-billions of other galaxies that make up the known universe—the dimensions of which truly strain the mind and imagination in trying to comprehend its cosmic majesty as demonstrated in chapter one.

This is, of course, a somewhat 'over-simplified' version of the universe and solar system in which we live, and there is a lot more to the cosmos than the basic description we have presented here. Today, even for modern astronomers, there are more things about the universe that we <u>do not</u> know—than that in which <u>we do</u>.

Take the simple classification of space objects for example. *At what size is an object no longer considered a rocky asteroid and starts being classified as a small planet? At what point does an object stop being classified as a large planet and starts being considered a dwarf star? Do we classify a large gaseous object several times the size of Jupiter as a planet, or because of its elongated orbit around our Sun—should we consider it to be a massive comet?*

Modern-day astronomers simply don't know enough about the universe to have very precise answers to these questions and there is much controversy about how to classify certain celestial objects. Somehow if an asteroid becomes large enough—it is arbitrarily placed into the planet category. If a planet becomes large enough—it is placed into the 'dwarf star' category, and if a dwarf star becomes large enough—it will ignite and then be considered a full-fledged star.

Keep in mind that all of these classifications are relative however. Take the planet Jupiter for example; today it has a fairly circular orbit around our Sun—and so we classify it as a planet. But if Jupiter were to have a highly elliptic orbit around the Sun and it were to come close enough to the Sun's solar wind to off-gas some of its gaseous planetary material (forming the classic tail that is seen with most comets), we would in turn classify Jupiter as a giant comet.

In a sense, we could say that an object is classified as a comet, due more to its orbital behavior than its composition or even its size. The line between our classification schemes, however, is fuzzy and there is often no 'clear-cut' <u>classification</u> or <u>division</u> that exists. Simply put, a specific object may be called by <u>different names</u>, at <u>different times</u>, by <u>different people</u>, for <u>different reasons</u>, and/or <u>different motives</u>.

Earlier in this chapter, we mentioned that the ancient civilizations of Earth were 'obsessed' with watching the heavens and counting down the long 'cycles of time' between passages of the large celestial object that periodically causes great geologic damage to Earth.

But how are we to ever know what this object really is? If we are looking for a specific object (the one that passes our planet and occasionally causes our poles to shift), how can we ever identify it in such a vast and complicated universe? And even if we could identify this object, how would we know how to classify it with such arbitrary terms for different celestial objects?

As we will soon see, determining what this object is, and how to classify it, might not be as difficult as it at first appears.

By many names—but one object

It has long been suspected that there is more going on within our own solar system than the majority of modern humans realize. The ancient cultures of the world firmly believed that our solar system included additional planets that many modern-day astronomers, at least publicly, are reluctant to acknowledge or research.

The ancient Sumerians for example (who lived over six thousand years ago), stunned modern astronomers with the breadth/accuracy of their astronomical knowledge believing that our parent solar system actually consisted of 'ten' planets—not the 'nine' that we 'officially' acknowledge today. In the second chapter of this book, we briefly mentioned that according to the ancient Sumerians this 10th planet was called *'Nibiru,'* which means: *"Planet of The Crossing."*

The ancient Sumerians believed that this *"Planet of The Crossing"* mostly travels in deep space, beyond the edges of our known solar system. But once every thirty-six hundred years or so, this *"Planet of The Crossing"* travels back through our solar system—passing around our sun like a giant periodical comet—then traveling off into deep space again, only to return approximately 3,600 - 4,000 years later to terrorize planet Earth.

The ancient Sumerians also believed this *"Planet of The Crossing"* caused great geologic damage to Earth, which includes massive earthquakes, floods and even on occasion—a slippage of the Earth's crust—a process we now know as 'lithospheric displacement.'

The cyclic timing of this so-called *"Planet of The Crossing"* is important, because if you'll also recall from chapter two, the ancient cultures of India, the Orient, Mesopotamia and the Americas, also believed that the Earth's 'cycles of destruction' take place about 3,600 - 4,000 years apart.

Could there be a large celestial object attached to our solar system that is as massive as a planet or even a dwarf star, but behaves like a comet? Could this be why so many ancient cultures were 'terrified' of comets and why so many of these cultures, even today, still retain a 'doomsday anxiety' regarding these celestial visitors?

We find this *"Planet-X"* hysteria has seemingly spread to global Internet interests—'big time.'

Could this "Planet of The Crossing," called 'Nibiru' by the ancient Sumerians, be the actual culprit for Earth's pole shifts? Could the timing of this object's passage be why so many ancient cultures believed that the Earth underwent cyclic destruction every 3,600 - 4,000 years?

Could this "Planet of The Crossing" called "Nibiru" by the ancient Sumerians, be the very same 'object' that the ancient Egyptians called "the terrible comet," the people of South and Central America called "the sky serpent," and the Hopi called it "Saquasohah," and the Babylonians "Marduk," and the Chinese calling it "the red dragon?"

Could this be the same object that has been called the "dark star," Earth's "nemesis," and "the destroyer of civilizations?"

The logical conclusion to all of these questions is obviously —yes!

Just like the ancient cultures of the Earth were experiencing the same global cataclysm but recording them in 'different ways,' these same civilizations were also observing the same celestial object—but simply calling it by 'different names.'

We must also conclude that this rogue 'celestial object' has a fairly predictable orbit (possibly around thirty-six hundred years) and it was the attempt to keep track of this object's periodic passages that made the Sumerians, Maya, Inca, Egyptians and so many of their ancient counter-parts build and maintain very sophisticated and accurate observatories—all in a gallant effort to keep track of this object's 'cycle of destruction' which it reaps upon the Earth.

The ancient Sumerians may have called this *"Planet of The Crossing," "Nibiru,"* but modern-day astronomers have now labeled it *Planet-X*.

The search for Planet-X

Today, the science of astronomy is in its infancy; we still know little about our own solar system and even less about the universe at large. Even the little that we do know (or at least think we know) about our solar system—has only recently been discovered.

For instance, the planet Uranus was completely unknown to western scientists until very high-powered telescopes could be produced in 1781. Neptune was only pinpointed by astronomers (guided by mathematical calculations) in 1846, and it wasn't until the 1930s that Pluto was actually discovered.

Today, astronomers are still struggling to identify all of the objects in our own solar system. It wasn't until 1999 that Prospero, Setebos and Stephano, three of Uranus's moons were discovered. In January of 2003, astronomers announced that they had just discovered three new moons of the planet Neptune. These types of discoveries are happening all the time, almost on a daily basis. We are however, still in the beginning stages of our astronomical knowledge and there is a lot about own solar system that we still don't know or understand.

For example: After Pluto was discovered in the 1930's, it became evident that this was not the last of our solar system's planets that needed to be accounted for. For several decades after the discovery of Pluto, astronomers watched as the outer planets of our solar system displayed strange 'wobbles,' and seemed to behave as if they were being 'pulled' out of their normal orbits by something from deep space—something quite massive existing outside of our solar system.

Astronomers soon concluded that indeed, something else was out there, something extremely massive with an incredibly strong gravitational signature—perturbing the outer planets of our known solar system. Astronomers labeled this unknown and mysterious object *"Planet-X."* *(X simply stands for unknown, so Planet-X is a designation for an unknown planet.)*

In 1972, the *Institute of Theoretical Astronomy* in Leningrad used the perturbations in the orbit of known comets to help calculate the existence of *Planet-X*. In that same year, astronomers at the *Livermore Radiation Laboratory* in California used the perturbations in the orbits of Halley's comet and two other (unspecified) objects to also mathematically demonstrate the existence of this massive and mysterious object traveling outside of our visible solar system.[13]

By the late 1970's, most astronomers had enough theoretical and mathematical evidence to be convinced that our solar system was in fact composed of more than the nine 'known' planets. Just like the ancient Sumerians stated in their historical records, our solar system had a '10th Planet,' which seemed to be traveling in deep space out beyond the normal boundaries of the solar system. The only thing left to do at this point was to identify this dark, mysterious object traveling somewhere outside the orbit of Pluto and to determine its exact 'orbital track' around our Sun. In other words, <u>where</u> exactly was this object, and more importantly—<u>where</u> was it going and <u>when</u>!

Then, in the early 1980's, the search for the mysterious 10th Planet *(Planet-X)* strangely escalated in intensity as NASA and other governmental institutions suddenly became 'very interested' in this astronomical enigma. In December of 1981, *Astronomy Magazine* carried an article stating:

> *Astronomers are readying (visible light) telescopes to probe the outer reaches of our solar system for an elusive planet much larger than the Earth. Its existence would explain a 160-year-old mystery. The pull exerted by its gravity would account for a wobble in Uranus' orbit that was first detected in 1821 by the French astronomer, Alexis Bouvard.*
>
> *Dr. Tom Van Flandern of the U.S. Navel Observatory thinks this "tenth" planet may have between two and five Earth masses...his team also presumes that, like Pluto, the plane of the undiscovered body's orbit is tilted with respect to that of most other planets, and that its path around the sun is <u>highly elliptical</u> (like that of a comet).[14]*

Could it be that modern astronomy was just catching up to the ancient Sumerian's knowledge of our solar system? Could this massive object (perturbing the outer planets) be the same object the ancients called 'Nibiru'—"The Planet of The Crossing?"

And shouldn't we assume that the ancients (including the Sumerians) 'got it right' the <u>first time</u>?

The above article makes <u>two</u> important points that should be noted at this time. First, this story mentions this sought after object has a highly 'elliptical' orbit around our Sun. This means that its orbital course takes it through our inner solar system as it travels around our Sun, and then back out into deep space—just like a comet. It's this object's passage through our inner solar system (where the Earth is also located)—that causes all of the geologic upheavals to our planet.

The second important point the above article mentions is that this huge celestial object, many time larger than Earth, has an orbital plane which is 'tilted' to the normal orbital plane of our solar system. In other words, picture a large dinner plate sitting on a table. If our Sun was hypothetically located in the middle of this plate, all of the known planets would be traveling around the Sun while remaining on, or close to, the plate itself—this is what's known as the orbital plane of the solar system. The nine known planets in our solar system orbit around the Sun in a semi-flat plane of travel.

But this sought after 10th Planet does not follow this normal orbital trajectory. It travels around the Sun by coming up from 'under' or 'below' the plate, and then travels away from the Sun 'above' the plane of the plate. This 'abnormal' orbital path may be another reason why it is so difficult to visually locate this object approaching our inner solar system from <u>behind</u> the Sun.

In other words, if this object travels around the Sun by coming up from under the Earth's normal orbital plane—it may only be possible to see this object approaching from the southern most part of our planet—the South Pole. Note: In recent years it has been rumored that there is an unusual amount of astronomical equipment and scientists stationed at the South Pole (Antarctic), thus leading some to speculate that these scientists (from many countries) may all be watching for this 10th Planet's 'southern' approach.

Throughout the early 1980's, however, astronomers searched for this elusive 10th planet without success. Even though NASA could theoretically determine <u>where</u> this planet <u>should be</u> located, and then point their powerful light gathering telescopes in <u>that direction</u>, this object did not seem to be emitting any 'visible' light signature—and NASA was then forced to try and find another means of actually observing this massive 'dark' object approaching us from deep space.

And so it was on 19 June 1982 that the *New York Times* reported:

> *A pair of American spacecraft may help scientists detect what could be a 10th planet...the National Aeronautics and Space Administration (NASA) said Thursday. Scientists at the space agency's Ames Research Center said the two spacecraft, Pioneer 10 and 11... might add to (the) knowledge of a mysterious object believed to be beyond the solar system's outermost known planets. The space agency (NASA) said that persistent irregularities in the orbits of Uranus and Neptune suggest some kind of mystery object is really (out) there.[15]*

On 28 June 1982, *Newsweek Magazine* also reported:

> *When scientists noticed that Uranus wasn't following its predicted orbit for example, they didn't question their theories. Instead they blamed the anomalies on an as yet unseen*

planet and, sure enough, Neptune was discovered in 1846. Now astronomers are using the same strategy to explain quirks in the orbits of Uranus and Neptune.

Thomas Van Flandern of the U.S. Naval Observatory…admits a tenth planet is possible, but argues that it would have to be…big…at least the size of Uranus (or larger).

To resolve this question, NASA is staying tuned to Pioneer 10 and 11, the planetary probes that are flying through the dim reaches of the solar system on opposite sides of the Sun.[16]

Both of these articles from June 1982 are also important because they both mention that NASA was using the Pioneer 10 and 11 spacecraft in an attempt to positively identify *Planet-X*. The reason this is important is because both of these spacecraft are equipped with 'infrared detectors.' Remember, NASA was not having any luck finding this object with 'visible light' telescopes, so they had to try something new—and 'infrared' detection equipment was the next logical step.

The search for the 10th planet stayed in the news throughout 1982 and into 1983. According to another *New York Times* article dated 30 January 1983:

Something out there beyond the farthest reaches of the known solar system seems to be tugging at Uranus and Neptune. Some giant gravitational force keeps perturbing the two giant planets, causing irregularities in their orbits. The force suggests a presence that's far away and unseen, a large 'celestial object' that may be the long-sought Planet-X.[17]

QUESTION: Why all the sudden interest in Planet-X? With budget restraints being what they are, why was NASA, JPL, The U.S. Naval Observatory and the Ames Research Center (utilizing both the Pioneer 10 and Pioneer 11 spacecrafts and a host of other powerful observatories from around the world) all of a sudden becoming so 'interested' in 'Planet –X' in the early 1980's — and not so much now?

Did NASA and other government institutions begin to figure out and accept the true cataclysmic history of planet Earth? Did it all of a sudden dawn on someone (in the government) that "Nibiru" might be on its way back into the solar system? And, therefore, was it time to start looking for this object (again) like so many ancient civilizations in the past did?

Then, later in 1983, NASA struck pay dirt! NASA's newly launched IRAS (Infrared Astronomical Satellite) actually spotted a large, dark, mysterious object coming towards us from the depths of space. Their discovery was first mentioned in a 1983 *Washington Post* interview with the chief IRAS scientist from JPL in California, Dr. Gerry Neugebauer.

The *Washington Post* article stated the following:

A heavenly body possibly as large as the giant Jupiter and possibly so close to Earth that it would be part of this solar system <u>has been found</u> in the direction of the constellation, Orion, by an orbiting telescope (IRAS)… So mysterious is this object that astronomers do *not know if it is a planet, a giant comet, or a nearby proto-star (dwarf star) that never got hot enough (or big enough) to become a star.*

"All I can tell you is that we don't know what it is," said *Gerry Neugebauer, chief IRAS scientist.*

The most fascinating explanation of this mystery body, which…casts no (visible) light and has never been seen (before) by optical telescopes on the Earth or in space, is that it is a giant gaseous planet, as large (or larger) than Jupiter. (Keep in mind that Jupiter is 318 times the size of Earth).

"If it is really that close, it would be a part of our solar system," said *Dr. James Houck, of Cornell University's Center for Radio Physics. "If it is that close, I don't know how the world's planetary scientists would even begin to classify it."*

The object (has been spotted) on the western edge of the constellation of Orion…and there has been some speculation that it might be moving toward Earth! [18]

As we shall soon see, the fact that this object casts no 'visible' light and was finally spotted by an 'infrared' telescope, is a very important piece of evidence in identifying what this object actually is.

And then on 10 September 1984, *US News & World Report* published an article entitled: *"Planet X—Is it really out there?"* According to this article, astronomers were studying this newly discovered object, which had now been verified several times, but still were not sure exactly what it was. The article mentioned that the pioneer 10 and 11 space probes were going to help further investigate this mysterious object, which was suspected to be the legendary 10th Planet.

The reason that scientists from NASA were having a difficult time identifying *Planet-X,* and in turn classifying it, was that these modern-day astronomers had never actually encountered this type of celestial object before. *(Even though our ancient ancestors apparently did with success!)*

Then, all of a sudden, any further 'confirmation' or 'public discussion' of this object from any 'official source'—immediately stopped. Scientists at NASA, JPL and many other government institutions studying the location of *Planet-X,* were mysteriously and officially 'silenced' and 'would not' or 'could not' discuss this subject any further. *Shouldn't we be asking them why??*

Any further investigation of this mysterious object was also at this point, 'compartmentalized.' Compartmentalizing is a process of breaking a project into so many small, isolated parts, that the people working on the project have no idea of what the full project entails or is made up of. A good example of this is the designing and building of new secret military aircraft. Different teams of people work on different components of the plane, some work on a wing, others on the landing gear, still others on the electronic systems, and so on. Very few people, however, know what their individual systems are ultimately being designed for—and only a few people at the very top of the project know the airplane's overall design, components and military designation.

As we will see, suppressing a scientific finding like the discovery of the 10th Planet, and then compartmentalizing any future research of this object, is extremely effective. Today most astronomers, even within NASA itself, have no idea this object has been discovered and is probably headed toward planet Earth.

As the 1980's moved along, it was rumored that both the Pioneer 10 and 11 space probes were continuing to monitor this newly discovered celestial object, triangulating its exact location and calculating its trajectory and speed, but NASA (who now had the topic of *Planet-X* sealed under a lid of national security)—would not 'officially' confirm any of this information.

This sudden 'wall of silence' is certainly understandable in light of what we have already investigated in this book. *If the Earth has been repeatedly visited in the past by this now 'inbound' object, and if this object's massive gravity were responsible for destructive geophysical upheavals of the past (and the total destruction of many ancient civilizations), the last thing any 'government officials' would want to do is start alerting the general public to this predicament?* It is likely that once NASA and other government institutions began to realize the full magnitude of the situation we are currently facing, the lid of national security was tightly placed over any further discussion of *Planet-X*, and subsequently, any further release of information regarding the details of this object was strictly prohibited and continues to this day.

But secrets such as this are hard to maintain and soon Dr. John Anderson, a celestial mechanics investigator with NASA's Pioneer spacecraft project, confirmed to reporters that he believed a large 'celestial object' was orbiting our Sun—even though recent analysis of the trajectories of the Pioneer 10 and 11 spacecraft have shown no indication of the gravitational effects of this celestial object.[19] Oops! *Could it be that the rumors about the Pioneer 10 and 11 spacecrafts (being sent out to track this celestial object) were more accurate than the public was being told?*

Dr. Anderson also went on to tell reporters that this object in question (the 10th Planet) probably traveled in an elongated 'ellipse' around our Sun—nearly at right angles to the plane of the orbits of the 'nine' planets in our system as it approaches Earth <u>from behind</u> (the light) of the Sun.

Once again, picture all of the planets in our solar system traveling around a dinner plate and this tenth planet (acting like a rogue comet)—coming up from <u>under</u> the plate and crossing through the plane of our solar system at a right angle—then heading back out into deep space again <u>above</u> the plane of the plate.

Could this tendency for Planet-X to 'cross' the orbital plane of the other planets in our solar system be why the ancient Sumerians referred to this object as the "Planet of The Crossing?"

NASA and other government research institutions continued to maintain a tight grip on the release of any further information regarding *Planet-X* over the next several years, but then a public relations nightmare suddenly struck NASA.

In the 1987 edition of the *New Science and Innovation Encyclopedia,* a diagram was accidentally published within an article discussing the purpose of the Pioneer 10 and 11 space probes. This diagram clearly showed both space probes triangulating a fix on what was labeled the "Tenth Planet." [20] Needless to say, both NASA and the *New Science and Innovation Encyclopedia* had some serious explaining to do! —Oops again!! *Or was this 'Oops again' a planned leak?*

We can only assume that this information was accidentally leaked and was never supposed to be published or released into the public domain. The article was immediately retracted and once again any further information regarding the 10th Planet was tightly suppressed—but persistent rumors still circulated regarding NASA's clandestine observations (via its two satellites).

Note: As of 2001, NASA scientists have publicly admitted that both the Pioneer 10 and 11 spacecrafts are 'suddenly' and 'mysteriously' being pulled out of their (normal) trajectories by some 'unknown' gravitational force. *(You can bet that someone at NASA knows 'exactly' <u>why</u> these two spacecraft are being pulled off course—because they know it's the gravitational effects of the approaching Planet-X.)*

What exactly is Planet-X?

It is clear by NASA's own admission that they were hunting for *Planet-X* in the early 1980's, and also by their own admission they found it within a few years of looking for it. Even after NASA placed a 'gag order' on the public release of any new info regarding *Planet-X*, it was clear that NASA was still interested in this object, and occasional leaks confirmed that NASA was indeed continuing their clandestine observation and tracking of this mysterious, enigmatic object.

But if NASA was not going to publicly release any more information regarding Planet-X which should, in and of itself, tell us of the impending problems this approaching object is suspected to cause how can we, the uninformed public, know anything more about this object and especially what this mysterious object actually is?

The universe has billions of objects flying around in space, and as we have already seen, the line between the classifications of celestial objects can be fuzzy at best.

So, if Planet-X is currently approaching us from deep space, and this object is the famed "Planet of The Crossing," and the ultimate cause for Earth's pole shifts—what exactly is Planet-X? An asteroid? A planet? A dwarf star? A comet?

In a way, *Planet-X* could be described as any of these types of objects; it circles the solar system like an elliptic asteroid, behaves like a comet when near the Sun, is called a planet by ancient and modern astronomers, and as we shall see, is prophesied to be a star. Even though there is a lot of 'crossover' between these categories however, there must be a way to identify exactly what this object is—and in turn what we can expect from it upon its next passage through our system.

We can start by acknowledging that the 'celestial object' in question possesses certain characteristics, and that these characteristics can logically lead us directly to a reasonably accurate classification of this 10th planet.

First, the object must be massive enough, and have a large enough gravitational effect to cause the Earth's crust to slip around its fluid-like mantel as it passes us in space—thereby causing a shifting of our planet's geologic axis of rotation. Therefore, we can rule out objects normally classified as asteroids and comets, for they do not possess the 'mass' needed for the proper gravitational effects.

Secondly, the object in question is seldom mentioned slowly approaching the Earth by any ancient civilizations. In other words, many ancient cultures mention a 'terrible comet' in the sky, as its reaping havoc on the Earth, but few if any mention it being sighted long ahead of time and then slowly becoming larger and more pronounced in the sky as time goes on. It seems to simply appear out of nowhere and before anyone knows it—all manner of Earthly tempest is released. Not being able to visually see this object (until it is directly upon us) is a very important clue into what this object actually is.

Recall from the fourth chapter when the ancient Sumerian *"Book of Enki"* stated that for 'days' before the groaning and shaking of the Earth began, *'Nibiru'* was seen in the sky. They didn't say weeks, or months, or years, just days. Keep in mind that the ancient Sumerians were expert astronomers for their time. They kept a close watch on the heavens and if this *"Planet of The Crossing"* (the arrival of which they were surely anticipating), snuck up on them and was only visible 'days' before its gravitational affects were ripping their world apart, therefore, we must assume *Nibiru* must be extremely difficult to see with the naked eye.

In their book *Cataclysm*, authors D. S. Allan and J. B. Delair, give an example of an ancient Hindu text describing the approach of the 'celestial object' responsible for triggering the great flood. Their account states that the ancient Hindu god Brahma and his attendants observed the arrival of a 'celestial object' (that within the space of an hour) was of the largest size. It remained in the sky and (subsequently) triggered a worldwide flood.[21]

These are extremely important pieces of our puzzle, because from everything that is known about this object, we can safely say it 'sneaks' up on the Earth and is therefore not illuminated under normal conditions. Remember that in the early 1980's NASA started looking for this 10th planet using large 'visible light' telescopes, but had no success. It wasn't until they started using 'infrared' telescopes that they found what they were looking for—and even these had to be launched into space, outside of Earth's atmosphere, in order to be able to see this object. As already mentioned, the Pioneer 10 and 11 spacecrafts are both equipped with infrared detectors, which is why these space vehicles were selected to help in monitoring and tracking *Planet-X*.

This lack of visible luminescence (until the object is physically in the Sun's solar wind and actually out-gassing its atmospheric material) rules out normal rocky planets and illuminated stars and leaves only one category of celestial objects—brown dwarfs!

Brown dwarfs are too small and cool to be considered true stars and too massive to be classified as planets. A brown dwarf, sometimes known as a failed star, is essentially a rogue celestial object that tried to become a star, but never quite made it. Scientists believe they form the same way real stars do, but never accumulate quite enough critical mass to sustain nuclear fusion at their cores. In other words, this particular type of celestial object just becomes a gigantic, dark, dense mass of smoldering space debris that never quite makes it to genuine 'star status.'

Is the entire concept of a giant 'brown dwarf' star cruising the solar system still unthinkable?

These objects are so massive, however, that if one were to pass through our inner solar system (even if it remained millions of miles from Earth), its massive gravitational influence would be more than ample to violently rip the Earth's crust around its molten core. A brown dwarf star is the perfect candidate to sneak up on Earth and cause 'lithosphereic displacement'—thus triggering the massive floods, earthquakes and violent winds, with which we are now so familiar.

Brown dwarfs are also known as the 'dim bulbs' of the universe, which means that they are often very hard to see. They tend to emit light almost exclusively in the 'infrared' spectrum (which is why the initial sighting of *Planet-X* was made using an infrared telescope). In other words—they emit very little 'visible light' and are almost impossible to see without infrared equipment. This is also why many ancient cultures referred to our solar system's brown dwarf as the *'dark star.'*

Although the existence of brown dwarf stars was theoretically debated for many years, astronomers could never actually see them because, as we have just mentioned, they emit almost no 'visible light.' In 1983, when astronomers discovered the (so called) 10th Planet approaching our solar system, they had never seen this type of object before and subsequently weren't sure of how to classify it—or even what to call it. This fact exists because there was no known scientific information on brown dwarfs at that time.

It wasn't until 1995 that astronomers working with Mt. Palomar observatory (in southern California) caught up with NASA's earlier discovery and then released the first 'public' confirmation of their brown dwarf discovery. Remember that NASA and other government agencies had found a much closer brown dwarf, *Planet-X*, in 1983, but since this discovery had been officially buried, the astronomers at Mt. Palomar apparently had no idea that they were not (in reality) the first scientists to prove the existence of these mysterious celestial objects.

Anyway, according to an Internet press release from 1995 entitled: *Astronomers Announce First Clear Evidence of a Brown Dwarf:*

> *The brown dwarf, called Gliese 229B…is a small companion to the cool red star Gliese 229, located 19 light-years from Earth in the constellation Lepus. Estimated to be 20 to 50 times the mass of Jupiter, Gl 229B (the brown dwarf) is too massive and hot to be classified as a planet as we know it, but too small and cool to shine like a star. At least 100,000 times dimmer than Earth's Sun, the brown dwarf is the faintest object ever seen orbiting another star.*

> *"It looks like Jupiter, but that's what you'd expect for a brown dwarf." The <u>infrared</u> spectroscopic observations of GL229B, made with the 200-inch Hale telescope at Palomar; show that the dwarf has the spectral fingerprint (similar chemical components) of the planet Jupiter—an abundance of <u>methane</u>! Methane is not seen in ordinary stars, but it is present in Jupiter and other giant gaseous planets in our solar system.* [22]

Once again, this 1995 'public' discovery of a new brown dwarf had to be made using NASA's 'infrared' telescopes, just like the 1983 discovery of the brown dwarf that is eccentrically orbiting our own Sun—Earth's eternal nemesis—*Wormwood*. We find it hard to understand why our government finds it so 'difficult' to level with the American People! The 'truth' is the 'truth!'

This article also mentions another very important point. This discovered brown dwarf is rich in the flammable gas, <u>methane</u>. Recall how many ancient civilizations recorded that the passage of the 'terrible comet,' rained 'fire from the sky,' setting the world ablaze and melting stone structures. Also recall how we proposed that the 'celestial object' in question forms a flammable hydrocarbon (methane) tail that sweeps across the Earth as it passes between our planet and the Sun—thus forming a flammable 'blowtorch' in Earth's atmosphere. This high concentration of 'methane' is exactly what we would expect from the 'terrible comet' based on the historical and archeological evidence that we've uncovered during our research.

And this same press release goes on to say:

> *Brown dwarfs are a mysterious class of long-sought objects that form the same way stars do, that is, by condensing out of a cloud of hydrogen gas. However, they (the brown dwarfs) do not accumulate enough mass to generate the high temperatures needed to sustain nuclear fusion at their core, which is the mechanism by which stars shin.*

> *If (this) dwarf formed as a binary companion (to the star it is orbiting), its orbit probably would be far more elliptical (like that of a comet) as seen on most binary stars.*[23]

Remember that our own solar system is a suspected binary system (the Sun and our dark sister star). Because our own Sun may be part of a binary system, the brown dwarf associated with our solar system has a highly elliptical orbit (like a comet) between the two stars.

In recent years numerous brown dwarfs have been scientifically detected circling other solar systems especially those solar systems that have a central Sun that is part of a binary system like our own. On 7 January 2002, *ABC News* released a story by Paul Recer, an *Associated Press (AP)* science writer wherein his article stated:

> *WASHINGTON (AP)—Astronomers have captured a direct image of a massive, planet-like object called a brown dwarf in close orbit of a distant star very much like the Sun.*

> *Michael Liu, a University of Hawaii astronomer, …said the parent star of (this) brown dwarf is "basically the same as our Sun. It's like a clone of our Sun, a solar twin."*

> *According to Michael Liu, "This discovery implies that brown dwarfs <u>frequently</u> companion to average, Sun-like stars similar to our own."* [24]

What does astronomer Michael Liu mean by 'frequently' companion to Sun-like stars like ours?

So, just how common are these rogue 'celestial objects' known as brown dwarfs? If brown dwarf stars have been found to act as large, periodic comets around other stars, what is the likelihood that our own solar system could have its own brown dwarf star associated with it?

In recent years it has been determined that brown dwarf stars may in fact be as numerous as visible stars. The universe at large may not discriminate between the alleged formation of full-fledged illuminated stars and smoldering brown dwarfs. If there is enough gas in a certain area of space to condense into a large enough object to sustain the nuclear fusion of hydrogen at its core, then a genuine star is born. If there is not quite enough gaseous matter to cause the intense pressure needed for nuclear fusion, then the object just smolders thus becoming a brown dwarf.

Both NASA and JPL have confirmed the preponderance of brown dwarfs in 1999. Dr. Davy Kirkpatrick, a senior staff scientist with JPL said: *"Because our (infrared) telescopes can only see the closest examples (of brown dwarf stars) this means the Milky Way galaxy must be brimming with objects (just) like these."* [25]

Other recent surveys have concluded that brown dwarfs are so common, that our galaxy probably contains at least one hundred 'billion' of them! In the year 2000, the University of Pittsburgh announced that brown dwarfs were so numerous—more than 50 of the so-called extra-solar planets (that were discovered orbiting other stars in recent years) were in fact, brown dwarfs.

Brown dwarfs have also been found 'wandering' around in space. In June of 2001, *Space.Com* released an article stating that the Hubble Space Telescope had found six Saturn-size objects 'wandering' just outside of our own solar system. According to this article, the objects, which have not yet been officially classified, *"do not shine like stars or orbit like (normal) planets."*

Kailash Sahu, one of the scientists that made the discoveries said that: *"By all known definitions these newly discovered objects were large planets, albeit lost and wandering."* [26] These massive 'wandering' objects may eventually become affiliated with the gravitational influence of a far-distant solar system and eventually play the part of destructive—rogue comets.

These same scientists went on to say that the objects, because of their relatively small size in relation to actual stars, should be labeled sub-brown dwarf stars.

So if brown dwarf stars are so numerous throughout the galaxy—and if these celestial objects often attach themselves to solar systems like our own (acting as giant periodic comets), would it not be considered <u>unusual</u> if our Sun <u>did not have</u> a brown dwarf associated with it?

In fact, according to a 1999 *ABC News* article, a Professor of Physics at the University of Louisiana, Dr. John J. Matese, working with astronomers from the U.S. and the U.K., stated that based on the latest research into the perturbations of long period comets, they now believe there is strong evidence of our own solar system having a brown dwarf star gravitationally bound to it. This brown dwarf has since been labeled our 'doomsday twin.' [27]

There is still further evidence however, that our solar system is periodically visited by a brown dwarf star.

Recall from the last chapter when numerous ancient cultures reported that as the 'terrible comet' passes our planet, it has a 'bloody-red' appearance. These same cultures also witnessed a rain of 'red dust' and 'hailstones of iron' falling to Earth, turning the waters of rivers, lakes and oceans a blood-red color. It should be noted that these same exact descriptions (the bloody-red effects), seem to be observed on a global basis culture to culture—over and over again through antiquity.

In June of 2002, astronomers working with UCLA reported:

> *Astronomers have seen evidence for what they think are the largest planet-like storms known, colossal (meteorological) structures similar to hurricanes occurring on obscure, poorly understood objects called brown dwarfs. Embedded in the hot storms are squalls of 'iron rain'...over time, brown dwarfs cool. Eventually, the iron and other gases condense into liquid drops, just as water condenses in the Earth's atmosphere...Once thought to be rare, brown dwarfs...(which harbor 'iron' in both the gas and liquid phase) are now considered to be as common as stars, and perhaps even more so.*[28]

On 24 January 2003, *The Christian Science Monitor* magazine ran an interesting story entitled: *"Brown Dwarfs: Stillborn Stars With Molten Iron Rain."* Excerpts from this article state:

> *Brown dwarf atmospheres are very hot...(and) at extreme temperatures like that, lots of chemicals would be vaporized and swirling, even stuff like iron and silicon. Over time, as the brown dwarf cools off, there has to be a transition period when the vapors in the atmosphere condense, much like steam condensing back into water droplets as it cools. This condensation phase would fill vast cloud layers with liquid metals...creating a downpour of molten iron rain.*[29]

In addition to iron being present in both the liquid and gaseous states within the atmospheres of brown dwarfs, some astronomers believe these iron tempests also contain this metal in a 'dust' or 'powder' form.[30] All of this iron liquid and powder would oxidize in the swirling and complex 'chemical soup' of a brown dwarf—in other words—all of this iron would 'rust.'

As the brown dwarf star passes our planet, the solar wind from our Sun would cause the off-gassing of this iron in its atmosphere. As its red 'iron dust' tail neared the Earth, dust from the passing object would cause a 'rain of rust' over the entire globe. This 'rain of rust' is the reason so many ancient cultures testified to the Moon and stars turning a bloody 'red' color. This iron rust would also fall out of the Earth's atmosphere making the land, rivers and oceans appear as if they too, were turning to blood. *Remember Moses turning the rivers blood red with his staff in Egypt?* We believe that *'Wormwood's* last return may have coincided with the Exodus in Egypt.

The oxidized iron in the atmosphere of the brown dwarf is what also gives this object its bloody-red appearance in the sky, and why such ancient cultures as those of China (and the Orient) called this same object—the 'red dragon.'

Modern-day geology has confirmed this 'rain' of oxidized iron hitting Earth in the past within sediment samples taken from around the world. For well over one hundred years, geologists have been finding massive 'deposits' or 'layers' of oxidized ferric iron particles which are tinted a rusty red color and are commonly referred to being like a 'red clay.' The most recent of these layers of oxidized iron was put into place within the past few thousand years and is so extensive, that according to D.S. Allan and J.B. Delair in their book, *Cataclysm*:

> *To account for the enormously high tonnage (of the oxidized iron) here, we must imagine either a veritable meteor blizzard continuously pounding the Earth for weeks on end, or*

> *the Earth passing through, or being passed by, a vast cloud of metalliferous debris which enveloped more or less every part of the planet's surface almost simultaneously.*[31]

Aside from this passing brown dwarf having a 'bloody-red' appearance and raining 'blood' upon the Earth (all due to its iron oxide content), many ancient cultures referred to this passing celestial object as twisting like a fierce serpent in the sky—leading them to refer to this object as the 'cosmic serpent,' 'sky serpent' or 'cloud serpent.' Other ancient cultures describe this object as developing great 'horns' like a demon or 'wings' like a giant terrible bat.

In 2002 and 2003, astronomers observed a brown dwarf with massive flares erupting from its atmosphere as it neared a distant star similar to our own Sun. Astronomers have since concluded that the atmospheres of brown dwarf's can erupt with powerful flares if the magnetic fields encircling them are disturbed by another strong gravitational force. If a brown dwarf passes close to another large object, like a planet or a star, the brown dwarf's magnetic fields will then become disturbed and highly twisted, producing an electrical discharge of its own outer atmosphere thus causing enormous 'flares' spinning off into space.

This electrical 'discharge,' or 'flaring' from the atmospheres of these objects, is what made our ancient ancestors describe the brown dwarf that passes our planet as 'twisting like a serpent' in the sky, or producing the 'horns of a demon,' or the 'wings of a bat'—all the result of gravitational and magnetic disturbances occurring within our inner solar system.

As with most of the chapters in this book, we could go on and on stating additional examples and giving further references pertaining to the subject matter at hand, but in the continued interest of developing an 'overview' of the big picture—we will now move on.

In conclusion

The ancient civilizations of our planet demonstrated time and again to have been brilliant astronomers, possessing knowledge of celestial mechanics that has continued to perplex their modern-day counterparts. These same ancient cultures also displayed a strong 'doomsday anxiety' over the steady motion of the heavens, believing that certain 'changes' in the celestial canopy would signal the beginnings of another 'pole shift' and the end of their civilization—again. These same cultures believed a large celestial 'comet' or 'planet' passed Earth on a periodic basis, triggering these 'pole shifts' and the litany of geophysical upheavals that always accompany them.

This passing object, too large to be an asteroid or a normal comet, is at the same time difficult to visually see as it approaches the Earth and has a tendency to 'sneak up' on us—as our ancient ancestors unfortunately discovered. Often this object was seen only '<u>days</u>' or merely '<u>hours</u>' before it unleashed a litany of dreaded/deadly geophysical events upon the world.

This lack of visibility, coupled with the fact that this object displays a whopping gravitational influence on our planet as it passes, has lead us to conclude this object must be in a class of 'celestial wanderers' known to modern-day science as 'brown dwarf' stars. The particular brown dwarf in question more than likely orbits around our Sun and our sister star in a large 'elliptical' orbit that may take a little over thirty-six hundred years to complete its passage.

Since brown dwarfs are so common throughout the cosmos, and since astronomers have witnessed them 'elliptically' orbiting other solar systems similar to our own, the idea that our solar system should have a brown dwarf associated with it—should now come as no surprise.

In fact, modern-day scientists have been speculating about this object's existence and current whereabouts for hundreds of years, and by the early 1980s, started urgently looking for it using powerful 'light-gathering' telescopes. These proved unsuccessful however, and NASA quickly switched to using infrared telescopes in order to find what they already suspected was out there.

NASA soon found the object they were looking for, but since modern astronomers had never seen this type of celestial body before (brown dwarfs), they were not sure of exactly what to call it, how to classify it, or even what it was. A blanket of national security was then quickly placed over this discovery as NASA realized the potential planetary destruction this massive object's eventual arrival will likely cause planet Earth.

The brown dwarf that orbits our solar system (like a large periodic comet) has been called by many names throughout the millennia. It has been referred to as the 10th Planet, *Planet-X,* the terrible comet, the bloody comet, the red dragon, the feathered serpent, the cloud serpent, Typon, *Nibiru*, Earth's nemesis, and countless other names throughout history. Whatever name we choose to call it however, its passage often brings 'doom' and 'destruction' to mankind. Forcing those ancient civilizations to "*start civilization over again as children,*" wiping out most of their recorded history and causing 'post modern humans' to have become a species with an 'historic amnesia.' We, (as a modern-day species), do not remember our past because most of it has been violently and instantly obliterated!

In addition, we have reviewed the modern scientific evidence that brown dwarfs contain methane, a flammable hydrocarbon gas. As the brown dwarf enters our inner solar system, the solar wind from our Sun causes this methane to start 'off-gassing' into a long flammable tail directed away from the Sun and eventually towards the Earth. As long as this flammable tail stays in the emptiness of space, it poses no threat, but as the tail of this brown dwarf hits Earth's atmosphere, a literal blowtorch is produced, setting the Earth ablaze and burning everything it encounters including stone columns, temples—even the planet itself. *(Remember the many examples of the 'vitrified' ruins of ancient cultures?)*

This does not mean that the entire Earth is always set on fire every time this object passes us. This brown dwarf passes Earth fairly quickly and its tail may only glance off part of our atmosphere or even occasionally miss our planet altogether (depending on its trajectory). This 'tail of fire' however, possesses the potential for great damage if it hits our planet in just the right way, as it apparently has done many times in the past.

The passing brown dwarf also develops a twisting 'bloody-red' appearance in the sky. This twisting is due to the flaring of its gaseous atmosphere in response to magnetic disturbances caused by the Earth and Sun. The 'bloody-red' color is due to chemical reactions that take place in the atmosphere of the brown dwarf, reactions that oxidize its iron into 'iron oxide' or 'rust.' These red 'oxidized iron' compounds can enter the Earth's atmosphere, turning rivers into blood, and causing the Moon and stars to turn a bloody-red color.

Could NASA and other scientific agencies have spotted an approaching brown dwarf star on its way into our solar system? And are we seeing a scientific cover-up from NASA, knowing about an approaching brown dwarf star, but not wanting to openly release this information for fear of panicking the public? And therefore what will be the end effect on planet Earth the next time this brown dwarf passes us in space?

As we will see in the next chapter, the evidence that a large brown dwarf star is approaching our solar system may be manifesting itself all around us—offering us a hint as to what we can expect in the near future (2009-2012). All we need to do is carefully read the cosmic signs of what we believe are approaching our world, analyze this knowledge—then prepare ourselves accordingly.

In watching the rash of severe weather patterns and specific disaster events happening across America this spring, one thing becomes quite obvious. Almost every newscast—regardless of the TV channel or hour—appears to be reporting on one local weather disaster after another—from the west coast to the east coast and from the Canadian border down to Mexico. 'Something' is radically wrong with Mother Nature—be it *'global warming'* or *'Planet-X'* or both together!

CHAPTER FOUR ENDNOTES

[1] Sitchin, Zecharia, *When Time Began* (Avon Books, 1993), pp. 120-121.
[2] Ibid., p. 33 and 42.
[3] Ibid., p. 48.
[4] Ibid., p. 51.
[5] Lippincott, Kristen, *Astronomy* (Dorling Kindersly Publishing, 2000), p. 8.
[6] Sitchin, Zecharia, *When Time Began* (Avon Books, 1993), p. 234.
[7] Ibid., p. 29.
[8] Lippincott, Kristen, *Astronomy* (Dorling Kindersly Publishing, 2000), p.38.
[9] Ibid., p. 45.
[10] Ibid., p. 47.
[11] Allan, D. S. and Delair, J. B., *Cataclysm* (Bear and Company, 1997), p. 205.
[12] Ibid., p. 199.
[13] *Incredible Stories* (Barnes and Noble Books, 1992), p. 14.
[14] Astronomy, *"Search for the Tenth Planet,"* December 1981.
[15] *New York Times*, 19 June 1982.
[16] *Newsweek, "Does The Sun Have A Dark Companion,"* 28 June 1982.
[17] *New York Times*, 30 January 1983.
[18] O'Toole, Thomas, *Mystery Heavenly Body Discovered* (Washington Post, 31 December 1983)
[19] UPI, *Scientist Thinks 10th Planet May Exist*
[20] *New Science and Innovation Encyclopedia* (H. S. Stuttman, 1997, Westport, Connecticut).
[21] Allan, D. S. and Delair, J. B., *Cataclysm* (Bear and Company, 1997), p. 211.
[22] Http://www.crawford2000.co.uk/brown.html.
[23] Ibid.
[24] Recer, Paul, *ABC News .com, Astronomers Find Brown Dwarf Orbit*, 7 January 2002.
[25] Media Relations Office, JPL, 1 June 1999.
[26] Sparks, Heather, *Space.com, Hubble Finds Mysterious Saturn-Sized Object,* 28 June 2001.
[27] http://www.planetxvideo.com/planetxvideo2.html.
[28] Britt, Robert Roy, *Space.com, Iron Rain Found In Greatest Planet-Like Storms Known*, 3 June 2002.
[29] Thaller, Michelle, *Christian Science Monitor, Brown Dwarfs: Stillborn Stars With Molten Iron Rain*, 24 Jan 2003
[30] Luttke, M.,Helling, Ch., John, M., Jeong, K. S., Woitke, P., *Dust Formation In Brown Dwarfs*, Astronomische Gesellscaft Abstract Series, Vol. 17, 2000
[31] Allan, D. S. and Delair, J. B., *Cataclysm* (Bear and Company, 1997), p. 298.

— CHAPTER FIVE —

SIGNS OF THE APPROACH

In the second chapter of this book, we investigated the 'historical accounts' of a massive celestial object triggering 'pole shifts' on a recurring basis. Then in the third chapter, we looked into the 'archeological evidence' supporting the fact that these ancient cultures were recording events that actually transpired. And in the fourth chapter, we explored 'geological evidence' that our planet repeatedly undergoes pole shifts and that these pole shifts take place through a slippage of the Earth's crust around its fluid-like mantle in a process known as lithosphereic displacement.

In chapter four, we also journeyed through the cosmos and determined that the actual celestial object that triggers these episodes of 'lithospheric displacement' is known as a 'brown dwarf' star. These massive celestial objects form the same way in which stars do, but never fully develop the internal pressure at their cores needed to sustain the process of nuclear fusion. These massive celestial objects subsequently remain dark—producing very little 'visible' light.

Regrettably, brown dwarf stars often act (in large part) as huge periodic comets throughout the universe, with massive 'gravitational' and 'destructive' effects on the planetary bodies that are unfortunate enough to be in their orbital pathways.

We also briefly mentioned how NASA found an approaching brown dwarf star in 1983, but 'covered-up' this discovery with a blanket of secrecy. We can only speculate as to why this discovery was so quickly concealed by NASA, but it's a safe assumption that they knew about the periodic destructive influence this object has on our planet and did not want to 'panic' the public over the catastrophic events that are rapidly approaching planet Earth. Later in this book we will come back to the government's ongoing involvement in this unfolding situation.

All four of these previous chapters however, have simply laid down a solid 'foundation' for our understanding the situation in which we presently find ourselves. The preceding chapters have, out of necessity, largely dealt with the 'past.' But if we are to fully understand the seriousness of our current predicament, we must deal with more than what has happened in ancient times—we must try to understand our current situation (now) and how it will affect us in the near future. The following chapters will therefore exclusively deal with 'present' and 'future' events as they begin to manifest themselves all around the world.

For many years scientists have theorized that if a large celestial object (such as a brown dwarf star) was approaching Earth, we would or should begin to see physical 'signs' of its approach decades before we would see the actual 'object' itself.

In other words, as this large object approaches our solar system from the depths of space, its tremendous mass and gravitational influence will start to have a noticeable physical effect on our planet and its nearest celestial neighbors. Even though we may not be able to visually see this approaching object with our naked eyes (which can only see {it} in the 'visible light' spectrum), we should be able to anticipate its approach by analyzing the 'physical affects' that this object's massive gravitational field is producing on our planet.

As we will soon discover, a litany of geological and meteorological phenomena are currently manifesting on Earth, already giving us strong scientific evidence that something is starting to go terribly wrong/haywire with the geophysics of this fragile blue world.

Let us now investigate some of these physical changes currently taking place around us and see if our investigation may shed new light on what may be headed our way!

The Earth's slowing rotation and magnetic collapse

One of the marvels of our modern-day society has been the development of atomic clocks that are extremely accurate time-keeping devices—precise enough to be within 'one second' of time every billion years.

As accurate as these atomic clocks are however, in recent years they have needed adjusting on numerous occasions due to the fact that Earth's physical rotation is apparently 'slowing down.'

This slowing has not gone unnoticed by the media. As early as 1984, the *Washington Post* reported that, *"The Earth has experienced an unexpected slowdown in its rotation."* [1] In July of 1988, the *Wall Street Journal* also reported that scientists at the U.S. Naval Observatory and the Jet Propulsion Laboratory discovered that the Earth is 'slowing down' and developing strange 'wobbles' in its normal 'axis of rotation.' [2]

In July 1990, *Omni Magazine* reported that between 24 January and 3 February 1990, the Earth's rotation had suddenly and unexpectedly 'slowed down' again.[3] On 9 August 1991, even the *New York Times* reported that the Earth's rotation is mysteriously 'slowing down.' [4]

This 'slowing' in our planet's rotation appeared gradual at first, but has rapidly continued to 'decelerate' throughout the 1990s. Reports of this phenomena have continued over the years and, to the dismay of many geodynamic scientists, Earth's slowing rotation only 'seems' to be getting more dramatic as time passes.

On 30 December 1998, the *BBC* reported that the last minute of 1998 would actually have 61 seconds in it. The 'extra second' being added to compensate the atomic clocks because Earth's rotation is now 'slowing down.' [5] In 1999, the *BBC* again reported that the National Physical Laboratory was planning to kick-off the year 2000—by adding an extra second as well.

Scientists have found this 'slow down' in Earth's rotation—albeit unnerving, and have attempted to concoct all types of explanations to justify why this phenomenon is taking place. To date however, all of these theories have been woefully inadequate and the truth of the matter is that most scientists have no idea why this time deceleration is happening. *And don't you find it also unnerving that these scientists have 'no clue' as why this time-loss phenomenon is happening?*

Another important consequence of Earth's rotational deceleration is the effect it's having on our planet's magnetic fields. Most geologists today believe that Earth's magnetic fields are produced deep within the interior of our planet by the cyclonic flow of molten magma. This magma is rich in iron and its 'circulation' or 'movement' (inside the planet's molten core) subsequently generates powerful magnetic fields that are then strengthened by the rotation mass of the Earth. These generated magnetic fields surround our planet with a magnetic atmosphere known as the magnetosphere, (the outer-region of the Earth's ionosphere) where the planet's magnetic field controls the motion of charged particles, as in the Van Allen belts.

These magnetic fields surrounding Earth form magnetic poles on opposite ends of our planet; and these magnetic poles, consisting of a north and south 'dipole,' are normally closely aligned with Earth's geophysical axis of rotation.

Even though the movement of internal magma generates Earth's magnetic poles, it is believed that Earth's rotation affects the strength of these poles. This inter-connection means that the faster Earth rotates, the greater the strength of the magnetic dipole and the slower it rotates, the weaker its dipole.

Because of this connection between Earths's 'rotational speed' and the strength of its magnetic fields, as our planet decelerates—its magnetic fields have subsequently weakened. As the Earth's magnetic fields continue to decrease in strength (due to Earth's slowing rotation) the two magnetic poles of our planet (the dipole), are becoming more and more unstable in their geographic positioning and are now starting to radically drift from their former positions.

In 2002, journalist, Nicola Jones, of the *New Scientist* reported:

> *The Earth's magnetic poles might be starting to flip say researchers who have seen strange anomalies in our planet's magnetic field.*
>
> *The magnetic field is created by the flow of molten iron inside the Earth's core. These circulation patterns are (then) affected by the planet's rotation, so the field normally aligns with the Earth's axis—forming the north and south (magnetic) poles (the dipole).*
>
> *But the way minerals are aligned in ancient rock shows that the planet's magnetic dipole (opposite magnetic poles) occasionally disappear altogether...When the dipole comes back into force, the north and south poles can swap places.*
>
> *Now Gauthier Hulot from the Institute of Earth Sciences in Paris and his colleagues think they have spotted early signs of another reversal.*
>
> *They have (recently) used data from the Orsted satellite to study strange variations in the Earth's magnetic field. In particular, one large patch under South Africa is pointing in the opposite direction from the rest of the Earth's field and has been growing...*
>
> *The anomalies have already reduced the overall strength of the planet's magnetic field by about 10 per cent, (a very conservative estimate—the actual 'per cent' loss may be much*

greater.) If they continue to (decrease) at the same rate, the Earth's dipole will disappear…

"We can't really tell what will happen (next)," says Hulot. "But we speculate that we're in an <u>unusual situation</u> that might be related to a (forthcoming) reversal." [6]

This is a very important article, not only because it points out that Earth's magnetic fields are decreasing in strength, but that the 'flipping' or 'shifting' of our magnetic poles has already begun. These 'magnetic' pole shifts have happened many times in the past and may act as a precursor to Earth's many catastrophic 'geological' pole shifts.

In fact, the 'magnetic' poles of Earth have become so geographically unstable, that according to Larry Newitt, from the *Geological Survey of Canada*:

The North Magnetic pole could soon abandon Canada, migrate north of Alaska and eventually wind up in Russia. This magnetic pole, which has been steadily drifting, has picked up its pace in recent years and could exit Canadian territory as soon as 2004. [7]

So as Earth 'slows down' in its rotation, the magnetic fields surrounding our planet are rapidly weakening, and the 'magnetic poles' are rapidly drifting from their normal positions at Earth's geographic axis of rotation.

What's causing this unexplained slowing in our planet's rotation and the magnetic anomalies that are accompanying this slowing process?

The answer is, we believe—the approaching brown dwarf, *(aka—The Planet Of The Crossing)*.

As this brown dwarf star approaches our planet from the depths of space, its massive gravitational influence is 'pulling' on the Earth, slowing its normal rotational speed. In other words, the gravitational attraction of this approaching brown dwarf is placing additional 'drag' on the Earth's rotation, similar to gently placing a finger on a spinning top—thus the top begins to decelerate rapidly slowing down.

As the Earth's rotational speed slows, its magnetic fields decrease in strength and its dipole starts to drift—these factors may soon lead to a 'magnetic' pole shift. A magnetic pole shift (a reversal of the Earth's dipole) may unfortunately be a precursor for a more catastrophic 'geologic' pole shift.

Eventually, if the brown dwarf gets close enough, its gravitational influence will become so strong it will completely overpower Earth's normal rotation, causing a slippage of our planet's crust over its molten mantle—producing a geologic pole shift, also known as 'lithosphereic displacement.' Keep in mind that it could be a drastic shift—or one that is less severe in its impact.

After the brown dwarf passes Earth it will move away from us, back out into deep space. Our planet's rotation will then return to normal, albeit with a different geological axis of rotation. All life forms here will slowly readjust—including mankind—but 'it' won't be easy or enjoyable!

Admittedly, modern science understands little about the workings of gravity and the magnetic environment of our planet. Because of this lack of core understanding, we cannot be absolutely sure that the brown dwarf's gravity is the <u>only real reason</u> for Earth's slowing rotation and our collapsing/wandering magnetic poles, but in light of everything else we've examined this theory makes the most sense.

Increased earthquakes

Gravity is largely an attractive force. The larger the mass of an object in space, the greater its gravitational pull upon all other objects around it. Like our Sun (which is very large and has an enormous gravitational attraction), the incoming brown dwarf star also has a strong gravitational attraction to all of the objects around 'it' in space.

As the brown dwarf nears our inner solar system, it has an ever-increasing gravitational 'effect' or 'attraction' on our planet. As we've discovered in the previous section of this chapter this increasing gravitational effect is currently causing our planet to apparently 'slow down' in its rotational speed in orbit.

As the brown dwarf continues its approach, it increasingly competes (gravitationally speaking) with our Sun's gravitational attraction on our planet. In other words, Earth is slowly being placed in a 'tug-of-war' between the gravitational attraction of our Sun and the approaching brown dwarf star.

As these competing 'gravitational effects' continue to manifest themselves on our planet, greater physical strain is placed on Earth's crust and in turn greater physical pressure on the individual 'tectonic plates' making up this crust. These elevated physical pressures exerted on Earth's tectonic plates causes greater slippage between these plates therefore producing more earthquakes.

As tectonic plates <u>slip</u> or <u>slide</u> past each other, energy is released in the form of seismic waves. Modern instruments called seismographs record this energy and represent it on a logarithmic scale, known as the Richter scale. The higher an earthquake ranks on this scale, the more energy was released and therefore the greater the quake's magnitude/intensity — (a 7.8 / 8.5 / 9.0).

When tectonic plates slip against one another and a small amount of energy is released, earthquakes in the 1.0 to 2.0-magnitude range are produced. These small quakes can barely be felt by someone standing close to the exact area of slippage (known as 'its' epicenter). If more energy is released by plate slippage, earthquakes will be produced that are strong enough to be readily perceived by anyone close to the epicenter, these often register in the 3.0-3.5-magnitude range.

Earthquakes that measure in the 4.0 to 7.0-magnitude ranges are powerful enough to cause significant damage to structures and can result in massive loss of life. Truly great quakes, (like those in the 7.5 to 9.0+ range or larger), will not only demolish modern structures and whole communities, but can also significantly change the topographical layout of the land as well. Having lived through the nasty 6.8 Northridge, CA, quake on 01/17/04—I swear that during the 2 minutes, 21 seconds of horrific pounding that destroyed my apt. building, I truly believed I was about to die.

If a large celestial object is in fact approaching Earth from deep space, placing greater physical pressure on our planet's tectonic plates, the question we must ask ourselves is: *"Are more Earthquakes currently taking place across our planet and what are the real reasons?"*

According to the U. S. and other global governments at this time—*"Absolutely not!"*

In fact, the U. S. Government (through their agency the U.S. Geological Service, aka, the USGS) has spent a lot of time, energy and money over the past decade trying to convince the general public that there is <u>NO</u> definitive increase in earthquake activity whatsoever—and anyone who says otherwise—is flat-out wrong and a 'fear monger!"

Over the past several years, the USGS, through press releases, articles and scientific conferences, has urgently stepped up their efforts to persuade the public that everything is normal in regards to earthquake numbers and there is no real need for public 'panic' or 'concern.'

So determined is the USGS in convincing the public that earthquakes are <u>not</u> increasing, they have recently been accused of deliberately 'downgrading' earthquake magnitudes and 'under-reporting' earthquake numbers in a concerted effort to make seismic data appear less alarming—showing the public that nothing is 'out of the ordinary' in regards to planetary seismic activity.

Whether the USGS has been 'cooking' its earthquake books however, is not the main issue here. What is important for us to address is that while the USGS has been insisting that earthquakes are <u>not</u> on the rise (and has been offering a plethora of excuses to justify this claim), the number of planetary quakes has, in reality, been steadily and alarmingly increasing!

A cursory look into the USGS's own Website reveals quite a different/provocative story from what this agency has been telling the public.

In 1990, earthquakes of magnitude 4.0 to 4.9 were numbering around <u>4,493</u> worldwide, but have steadily increased ever since, and in 2002 numbered <u>8,650</u>—indicating that over this twelve year period of time, earthquakes of this magnitude almost doubled.[8]

In 1990, earthquakes in the 3.0 to 3.9-magnitude range numbered <u>2,457</u> throughout the world, but have also steadily increased and in 2002, numbered <u>6,999</u>—more than doubling in number. Earthquakes in the 2.0 to 2.9-magnitude range also dramatically increased from <u>2,364</u> in 1990 to <u>5,642</u> by 2002—also more than doubling in number for this same twelve-year period.[9]

These earthquake figures listed for 2002, do not represent an unusual or exceptional year, or some type of 'numbers manipulation,' or even better reporting of seismic data, but the end result of a steady 'yearly increase' in reported worldwide quake patterns.

To further illustrate this point, in 1990, <u>16,612</u> total earthquakes were recorded worldwide. By 1995, the total number had steadily risen to <u>21,007</u> and by 2002 reached a staggering <u>27,459</u>.[10]

We can also see this 'alarming' trend in seismic activity by isolating and then examining just the worldwide earthquakes of magnitude 3.0 or greater. Going all the way back to 1970, the number of earthquakes 3.0 or greater was averaging about 3,500 per year throughout the world. But by 1980, this number had risen to over 6,000. By 1990, this number had raised again to 8,000, and by 1998 the total number of 3.0 or greater quakes had reached a staggering 17,000—an increase of over 480%.[11] The increased quake numbers for years 1999-2006 are truly staggering—and with no apparent end in sight.

This 'increasing trend' can also be seen in the number of earthquakes posted on any given month over this same period of time. In 1970, the greatest number of quakes posted for any given month of this year more than likely represented the long-term average and numbered a little over 400. By 1980 however, this number had dramatically climbed to over 800. By 1993 the most earthquakes posted for a single month was over 1,200 and by 1997, the highest monthly total broached a whopping 1,700.[12] We find monthly totals rising dramatically for years 1998-2006.

Once again the increased numbers for all-sized quakes during years 1998-2006 are off the wall with the stats filling nearly a quarter page. For example major quakes above the 3.5 - 4.0 range: on **5/27/98** a 6.2 in Adana, Turkey; on **8/17/99** a 7.4 in Izmit, Turkey and a 5.0 in Bollinas, CA; on **8/20/99** a 6.7 in Costa Rica and a 5.0 in Montana; on **9/21/99** a 7.6 in Taiwan; on **10/16/99** a 7.1 in Hector Mine, CA; on **11/12/99** a 7.2 in Duzce, Turkey; on **1/10/2000** a 4.3/4.3/4.2 in Cloverdale, CA; on **8/03/2000** a 5.2 in Yountville, CA; on **12/20/2000** a 4.6/4.3 in Burney, CA; on **1/13/01** a 7.7 in El Salvador; on **1/26/01** a 7.7 in Gujarat, India; on **2/28/01** a 6.8 in Puget Sound; on **11/03/02** a 7.9 in Denali Fault, AK; on **1/22/03** a 7.6 in Colima, Mexico; on **9/25/03** a 8.3 in Hokkaido, Japan; on **12/22/03** a 6.5 in San Simeon, CA; on **12/26/03** a 6.0 in Parkfield, CA; on **10/23/04** a 6.6 in Niigata, Honshu, Japan; on **12/26/04** a 9.0 (plus subse-quent tsunamis) in Northern Sumatra, S.E. Asia; on **1/01/05** a 7.1 in Celebes Sea; on **3/02/05** a 7.1 in the Banda Sea, located between Sulawesi (Celebes) and New Guinea, and an 8.7 in Northern Sumatra; on **3/28/05** a 7.8 again in Northern Sumatra; on **5/13/05** a 7.8 in Tarapaca, Chile; then between **6/15-19/05** a 7.2 / 6.7 / 5.0 off the northern coast of CA; on **9/9/05** a 7.7 in New Ireland Region, P.N.G.; on **10/08/05** a powerful 7.6 shook Pakistan, Afghanistan and India; on **12/12/05** a 6.7 hit remote Hindu Kush regions of northern Afghanistan; on **1/07/06** a 7.6 in the Banda Sea, located between Sulawesi (Celebes) and New Guinea; then on **2/22/06** a 7.0 in Mozambique, Africa; and lastly on **2/26/06**, we had a 6.4 hit south of the Fiji Islands. And as of this writing date on **4/6/06** there were –0– major quakes recorded on a global scale over the 6.5 magnitude range.[13]

With all of the above dates clearly listed—why the USGS is still publicly insisting that global earthquakes are not increasing in <u>frequency</u> and <u>severity</u> remains a stone-ground mystery? And one can only imagine that <u>this</u> government agency is somehow looking at seismic figures 'other' than those posted on their 'own' Website. (That's a little humor.)

In actuality, the USGS is claiming that the increase in quake numbers throughout the world is simply the result of better monitoring, a by-product of the recent placement of more seismographs in more remote locations around the world. At first, arguments like this seem reasonable and provide a sufficient explanation for an uncritical and naively accepting public.

But if this USGS explanation is indeed true, why are the number of earthquakes in the U.S. (which has been heavily monitored now for several decades), also showing this same alarming increase in their frequency and intensity?

It should be noted that every year over 50,000 detectable quakes are felt and recorded in California alone, and they are still waiting for the 'really big one' to strike at any moment along the San Andreas fault system. Experts say this fault may be about to unleash an epic earthquake in the Coachella Valley—one of the nation's primary fruit and vegetable (breadbasket) providers.

According to Dough Yule, a geologist at California State University at Northridge, (which itself was badly damaged by the 17 January 1994 disaster striking the LA region at exactly 4:20 AM): *"The primary fault in California—the big dog—is the San Andreas, and it's important for people to remember that."* As the principal generator of the feared 'big one,' the San Andreas once dominated the quake-worries of most Californians. *"The San Andreas will (eventually) produce the largest earthquakes,"* Yule told *LA Times-Washington Post Service* writer, Paul Pringle. [14]

In the U.S., earthquakes of magnitude 4.0 to 4.9 numbered <u>283</u> in 1990, but steadily increased to <u>540</u> by 2002—almost doubling. Earthquakes of magnitude 3.0 to 3.9 numbered <u>621</u> in 1990, but also steadily increased to <u>1,523</u> in 2002—more that doubling. In the 2.0 to 2.9 range they went from <u>411</u> in 1990 to <u>1,234</u> in 2002, more than tripling. The overall number of earthquakes in the U. S. for this same twelve-year period went from <u>2,268</u> in 1990, to <u>2,725</u> in 1995, then dramatically upwards to <u>3,878</u> in 2002. [15]

The dramatic rise in yearly earthquakes that we tracked from 1990–2002 is staggering in both numbers and intensity. Beginning with 2003, a total of 67 major quakes (ranging from 4.0 to 8.3) were recorded with 70% of them over the 6.0 range; in 2004 a total of 48 major quakes (ranging from 3.0 to 9.0) were recorded with 83% of them over the 6.5 range; in 2005 a total of 46 major quakes (ranging from 4.1 to 8.7) were recorded with 75% of them over the 6.7 range; and in 2006 (to date) a total of 6 major quakes (ranging from 3.0 to 7.6) were recorded with 65% of them over the 6.4 range in Richter Scale intensity. [16] The above 'figures' have spoken…

No matter how best we try and tinker with our *Planet-X* (2009/2012) equation—the answer always come back the same: *"Nothing, I'm afraid, can change the shape of things to come, nothing…"*   — *And the name of the star was 'Wormwood…'*

Real time date: 03/07/2006

These alarming increases are more than minor fluctuations in earthquake cycles. They represent a clear 'signal' that something is happening very quickly with the geophysics balance of this planet—something significant, which the USGS will not be able to 'cover-up' or 'explain' much longer to the American public and world.

Our escalating earthquake trends/patterns do not stop here, however. The frequency of so-called 'great quakes,' those over 8.0 in magnitude, is also becoming more prevalent. In 1920, the average 'annual frequency' of these 'monster earthquakes' was around 0.1 or 10% for any given year. Meaning that over a ten-year period it was probable that a 'great quake' (8.0) would happen somewhere in the world, one time. [17]

Isn't it interesting that as 'time flies by' on Earth—'things' here only seem to be getting worse?

This 'annual frequency' of great quakes remained virtually unchanged throughout most of the 20th century. In the 1990s however, this 'annual frequency' rate started to increase dramatically and by 2001, the average annual frequency of 'great quakes' had risen to 1.0 or 100% per year. This means that instead of a 'great quake' happening once every ten years—they are now likely to happen once each year.[18] This is an alarming increase of 1000% frequency and still climbing.

Actually, in the 1990s, there have been as many as 'three' of these 'great quakes' in a single year, leading some researchers to state there has been a thirty-fold or 3000% increase in 'great quakes.' *[Remember that the 26 December 2004 quake in SE Asia was a 9.0 magnitude event.]*

Not only has the frequency and severity of earthquakes raised dramatically around the world—but the depth deep within the Earth's crust (from which these 'monster quakes' are originating) is also on the rise.

'Deep quakes' are earthquakes that originate from a depth of up to 500 kilometers beneath the surface of the Earth (a kilometer is a little less than a mile). These 'deep quakes' offer seismologists an indication of how much pressure is building up between the tectonic plates of Earth's crust. The theory holds that the more pressure being placed on these tectonic plates—the deeper the epicenter of the resulting earthquakes.

In 1970, the average number of 'deep quakes' being recorded around the world each year was about 100. By 1980, this average number had risen to 200 and by 1998 the number of 'deep quakes' being recorded had risen to an alarming 600![19] Clearly something is causing a dramatic increase in the pressure on the Earth's crust, which is in turn producing more 'deep quakes.'

This alarming increase in earthquakes and the escalating destruction they are causing has not escaped the attention of the media. On 22 January 1999, *ABC NEWS* reported that in 1998, 9,000 people were killed throughout the world by earthquakes, a number which represented a 300% increase from the year before (1997) and a staggering twenty-fold increase since 1996.[20]

As bad as this devastating earthquake trend was, on 17 January 2000, *ABC NEWS* again reported that 1999 was an above average year for the number of earthquakes and more than 22,000 people were killed.[21] This trend of massive casualties has unfortunately continued and in 2001—21,436 people were killed in major global seismic events.

This alarming increase in earthquake casualties has also not gone unnoticed by elected officials of the U.S. government. On 30 April 1999, *CNN* reported that the U.S. House of Representatives passed a bill that would allocate more than 200 million dollars for the fiscal year 2000, designated for new computer projects to monitor and analyze this 'alarming up-tick trend' in global earthquake activity.

Is this the reason most major American cities are conducting earthquake retrofitting projects?

Once again, despite all of the evidence to the contrary, the USGS continues to 'sell' the public that nothing is 'out of the ordinary' here, and that everything 'appears to be normal' in regard to our planetary seismic trends/activity/performances shooting upwards to record highs.

So why is the USGS 'down-playing' the reality of increasing earthquake numbers and why would they mislead the public regarding this alarming increase in seismic activity? Would they allegedly 'lie' or possibly even 'distort' specific seismic data in order to convince the public that 'nothing' is wrong? What type of agenda could be driving the USGS' unofficial actions/policies?

The answers lie in the fact that some of the 'largest' and most 'populated' cities, not only in the U.S., but also around the world, are sitting atop seismic time bombs! And these time bombs are unfortunately set to go off (we believe) in the very near future. This is best demonstrated by the events of 26 December 2004 at precisely 7:00 AM in SE Asia. *Can we ever forget seeing the devastation in the hundreds of home videos taken as giant tsunami waves swept the region dead?*

This was a mega-powerful 9.0 magnitude undersea earthquake that exploded six miles deep along a 620-mile-long tectonic subduction plate beneath the Indian Ocean (off the coast of North Sumatra near Malaysia)—and was this century's most devastating global earthquake event.

It created a series of 50-75 foot (7 story) killer tsunami waves traveling at speeds of 500 mph stalking most of SE Asia with its dozen island nations and killing more than 285,000 people across thousands of miles of tropical beaches, island resorts, seaports and crowded SE Asian cities; a mega-disaster that is only a small hint of what's coming soon to visit planet Earth.

The United States earthquake focus

When most people think of seismically active areas of this country they immediately think of California, Seattle/the NW, Alaska and Hawaii. But the truth is—most of our major U.S. cities are built <u>over</u> or <u>quite near</u> major faults lines (faults are the 'seams' between tectonic plates).

Many of these faults are capable of producing 'sizable' or even 'catastrophic' earthquakes at any moment. Most of these faults found throughout Earth's crust are normally not as active as the famous San Andreas (beginning in the ocean off San Francisco, then running inland and south-ward toward Palm Springs and the Salton Sea) in the western U.S. *But if the current trends in these seismic activities continue—wouldn't these normally inactive faults suddenly begin to trigger monster quakes now in unprecedented numbers and violence?*

For example, geologists have recently discovered clusters of seismic faults running from Salt Lake City, Utah, south to Las Vegas, Nevada, and north into Idaho.[22] These faults are capable of producing powerful earthquakes that could potentially change the topography of the western U.S. if they suddenly became active and started to slip against one another in dramatic fashion.

Another area of potentially giant seismic problems has recently been identified and labeled as the New Madrid Seismic Zone, running through most of the mid-western U.S. (and down the full length of the Mississippi River) that could ultimately affect states such as: Arkansas, Illinois, Oklahoma, Iowa, Indiana, Missouri, Tennessee, Mississippi, Louisiana, Ohio, Florida and others. Major cities like Memphis, St. Louis, New Orleans, Moline and Cape Girardeau are vulnerable!

This vast 'seismic area' consisting of numerous individual 'faults' is, for the most part, not very active, although it has occasionally produced powerful earthquakes in the past. The last series of large quakes happened there over a hundred and fifty years ago. This flurry of powerful earthquakes is ironically believed to have been triggered by, of all things, a passing comet. *Hummm! Now where have we heard that story before?*

As we already know, the notion that passing celestial objects can trigger disasters is not a new idea. But in 1811, 'theory' became 'reality' when a relatively small but bright comet passed close to Earth and actually triggered a cascade of powerful earthquakes along several parts of the New Madrid Fault Zone. The *Pittsburgh Gazette* ran a series of articles commenting on this passing comet's gravitational affects stating:

> *The extent of the territory which has been shaken (by the comet), nearly at the same time, is astonishing—reaching on the Atlantic coast from Connecticut to Georgia and from the shores of the (Atlantic) ocean inland to the State of Ohio...In North Carolina (near Asheville) a volcano has appeared, and...in an eruption a few days since, a flood of lava poured out which ran to the distance of three quarter of a mile. The affects (of this passing comet) are portentous and alarming.*[23]

These earthquakes (produced by this passing comet) were not minor tremors, but powerful seismic events that were felt over thousands of square miles and were of such magnitude they had actually changed the course of the mighty Mississippi River—and for a short time even caused it to flow backwards. It's been estimated that three of these earthquakes along this 'hot' zone fault measured 8.6 / 8.4 / 8.7 and are ranked as some of the most powerful earthquakes ever recorded.

Today seismologists are very concerned that at any moment this same seismic zone is capable of once again producing 'catastrophic' earthquakes throughout central/SE portions of the U.S. Keep in mind that this passing comet of 1811 was a relative 'baby' in 'cosmic terms.' And, if this 'small object' could produce these sudden and powerful seismic/volcanic events along the entire East Coast of the U.S., imagine what destruction a passing brown dwarf star would cause!

If the individual faults in the New Madrid Seismic Zone were affected by a large gravitational force and started to suddenly release all their built up tension (like they would during the passage of the brown dwarf)—it would produce a catastrophic disaster unknown to modern-day man.

In the eastern U.S., the story remains virtually the same. Recent geologic studies indicate that a series of fault lines running from Canada in the north—to Florida in the south (with most major east coast cities located near, or even on fault lines) poses a serious threat. If any of those faults were to suddenly slip, the seismic energy released would produce an unthinkable disaster.

One of the most worrisome examples of a potential seismic catastrophe lurks right under New York City itself. This particular fault in question runs directly under Manhattan, Central Park and Greenwich Village. Geologists currently believe that this fault line system has been building up tension for hundreds, if not thousands of years, and if this tension were suddenly released (like it would during a pole shift), New York City would be totally demolished![24]

The remainder of the eastern seaboard is in the same predicament, from Massachusetts, New England, the Carolinas, Georgia and so on—a seismic apocalypse is simply waiting to transpire.

Once again, because most of these faults running throughout the U.S. have been appreciably inactive for centuries, maybe even millennia, the general public is totally unaware of how potentially disastrous these particular areas between tectonic plates can be. The general public simply has no idea of the international calamity that would be unleashed if these faults started to slip, releasing their built-up physical tensions—producing monstrous seismic waves (earthquakes) that would literally shatter modern civilization not only in the U.S.—but across the globe.

Keep in mind that we are using the U.S. merely as an isolated example. The fact is—the entire crust of our planet is permeated with these hidden and largely inactive faults. Inactive for now that is—and with no future guarantee they won't later collapse!

At this point, the precise answer as to 'why' the USGS is deliberately misleading the public regarding the ever-increasing number of earthquakes—should now be obvious. *Are the motives of the USGS simply misguided by official policy and not meant to actually deceive the public?*

Someone at the USGS knows that an increasing amount of stress is being placed on Earth's tectonic plates (by the approach of the brown dwarf), and this stress will only become greater as this object continues its approach. As this stress increases, so will the number of earthquakes until, eventually, a series of catastrophic seismic events will be unleashed on some of the most populated cities in the U.S. and throughout the world.

Is the USGS downplaying the increasing seismic trend, because telling the public the truth of what is transpiring would cause an unprecedented level of panic? The question just raised is to 'enlighten' our readers—not 'panic' them!

Would the USGS telling the public <u>the truth</u> of what's coming actually empty the cities and/or panic the public? And, if so, to where would you evacuate all these millions of people?

The last thing any government 'wants' or 'needs' is to create a widespread panic. To inform the general public of the coming seismic calamity would result in a mass migration out of the major popu-lation centers producing a logistical and relocation nightmare—(shades of New Orleans). Additionally, since the entire surface of planet Earth is permeated with fault lines, theoretically no geographic area will totally escape massive earthquakes when this brown dwarf star gets close enough. This inevitable reality will be especially true when our planet's entire lithosphere begins to slide over its molten mantle.

For a government simply trying to maintain control over society, informing the public of the ever-increasing stress being placed on Earth's crust is admittedly an inherently bad idea! The current governmental policy can <u>only</u> realistically be one of <u>stay put</u>, <u>hope for the best</u> and then <u>ride it out</u>. Therefore, expect the USGS to maintain its current 'policy of denial' for as long as possible—maybe even longer.

As if all this current seismic information were not bad enough, in recent years the gravitational effects of the approaching brown dwarf has started to become so strong that it is now actually deforming the shape of the Earth itself. Only since the advent of space travel in the 60s was it possible to view the precise shape of Earth and view its physical characteristics in greater detail.

On 7 August 2002, John Roach, writing for *National Geographic News*, released a story entitled: *"Why Is Earth's girth bulging?"*

It seems that the gravitational 'attraction' or 'pull' of the approaching brown dwarf is so strong that it's causing planet Earth to 'bulge' at her equator and 'flatten-out' at her poles—deforming the Earth's crust and further producing changes in the gravitational/magnetic fields of our planet.

According to Roach's article:

> *This is heavy. Something massive is...causing the planet's (shape) to get wider around the equator and flatter at the poles, according to a pair of scientists studying the (Earth) with sensitive satellite instruments.*
>
> *The scientists are uncertain as to the reasons for this phenomenon, which was just the opposite for several decades prior to 1997..."the world, that was getting rounder, started getting more oblate [flattened at the poles]," said Christopher Cox, a research scientist at the Space Geodesy Branch of NASA's Goddard Space Flight Center in Greenbelt, Maryland.*
>
> *"It (the change in Earth's shape) has finally gotten so big, that we can't explain it with any known mechanism," said Cox, who co-authored a paper in the August 2nd issue of The Journal Science, (on this change in the Earth's shape.)*[25]

According to the remainder of Roach's article, scientists have been speculating that the current reduction in our polar ice caps (which we shall investigate shortly) has removed so much weight from both Polar Regions of Earth, that our planet's shape <u>was</u> becoming rounder ('thinner' at the equator and 'taller' at the poles). But now this 'rounding' trend has mysteriously and suddenly reversed itself, and the poles are getting 'flatter' while the equator is getting 'wider.' This change in Earth's shape is happening suddenly and dramatically and has scientists (that don't know or recognize the fact of the approaching brown dwarf)—completely baffled.

This phenomenon is exactly what we would expect, however, if a large celestial object were gravitationally 'pulling' on the Earth from space—the equator would 'bulge' as the poles would begin to 'flatten.'

Recall from the second chapter when the ancient Sumerians recorded that in a prior passage of the brown dwarf *(Nibiru—"The Planet Of The Crossing" to the Sumerians),* the gravitational effects on the Earth were so strong; that it pulled (at least part of) the polar ice caps right off and into the sea!

We can now see the beginnings of this powerful gravitational effect in the deformation of the Earth's crust. *Will this cosmic phenomenon eventually be announced by the 'powers that be?"*

Since the entire crust of the Earth is being deformed by the increasing gravitational attraction of the approaching brown dwarf, it should also come as no surprise that a new 'seismic phenomena' has recently started to develop—'global earthquakes.'

As Earth's crust is 'stretched' at the equator and 'flattened' at the poles, low intensity seismic waves have been traveling throughout the entire lithosphere of Earth, simultaneously setting off seismographs from Antarctica to Europe. These so-called 'global quakes' are another symptom of what is manifesting under our feet at any given second—even at this very moment.

As the gravitational 'pull' of the brown dwarf becomes even greater, these worldwide seismic events will only increase dramatically. Eventually the gravitational strain on our planet will become so great—that Earth's lithosphere could/may slip—producing a 180 degree 'pole shift.'

Clearly, earthquakes and other geologic anomalies are on the rise, and although most scientists today are 'officially' at a loss to explain this increase, we can be fairly certain that the cause is increased stress being placed on Earth's crust by the ever-increasing gravitational influence of what we believe is this approaching brown dwarf—'*Wormwood.*'

Unfortunately, by the time most scientists become convinced or truly realize, accept or 'publicly' acknowledge what is actually happening to our planet—it will be far too late for most individuals to do anything about it. —They will ultimately be unable to save themselves or their families! (More on this point later.)

Increased volcanic and geothermal activity

It is logical to assume that as a large celestial object (such as a brown dwarf star) approaches Earth, an ever-increasing gravitational 'strain' would be placed on our planet's body—slowing down its rotation, eventually collapsing its magnetic fields, then deforming its crust and increaseing the number of ever-larger earthquakes recorded each year as we approach 2009/2012.

If in fact this situation is happening, and Earth is being gravitationally affected by the approach of this massive space object, wouldn't we also see a dramatic increase in the planet's volcanic activity around the globe? Aren't volcanoes the driving forces that create continent building?

Volcanoes are formed when molten rock from Earth's interior flows upwards forcibly breaking through to the planet's surface. Most of the volcanic activity that takes place on Earth however, actually happens deep down on the floor of the oceans—this type of volcano is called a submarine volcano. Scientist are not exactly sure just how many of these submarine volcanoes are erupting at the bottom of the sea at any given time, but the number is believed to be significant and growing every year.

Could submarine volcanoes lead to global warming?

One of our working theories in trying to more accurately pinpoint the physical dynamics of 'Global Warming' —centers around the idea that these sometimes monstrous (thousands of feet high and miles in diameter) submarine volcanoes are releasing intense heat, steam and minerals into the cold sea resulting in a gradual warming cycle now affecting the Atlantic/Pacific/other planetary seas. If we are right—this process is obviously having it effect on the past several hurricane seasons highlighted by past and present hurricanes: *Carla, Donna, George, Andrew, Camille, David*, and most recently—*Bonnie, Charlie, Frances, Ivan, Jeanne, Wilma, Katrina* and of course, *Rita*. On June 1 the hurricane cycle begins anew and 2006 promises to be challenging.

Even though many scientists believe that the number of 'submarine' volcanoes have been drastically increasing over the past several years, getting an accurate count of them is difficult at best and today these researchers are not sure of the exact number currently erupting worldwide. We will therefore limit our primary discussions of volcanic activity to 'terrestrial' volcanoes—those that erupt on the planet's dry surface.

Terrestrial volcanoes

The usual type of volcanoes that most people are familiar with are called 'terrestrial' volcanoes—those that erupt above the oceans on dry land throughout the planet.

A quick look at the number of 'terrestrial' volcanoes erupting each year also paints a gloomy picture and may unfortunately herald more of what's in store for us in our immediate future.

In 1995 there were <u>4</u> major volcanoes actively erupting. In 1996 there were <u>9</u>, in 1997 the number had risen to <u>12</u>, in 1998-<u>13</u>, in 1999-<u>18</u>, in 2000-<u>22</u> and in 2001, there were an estimated <u>35</u> major volcanoes erupting around the world.[26] We can't obtain valid stats for years 2002-2006.

This dramatic increase in volcanism is still further evidence that something profound is currently happening to the geology of this planet. Many scientists today believe that this increasing trend also applies to 'submarine' volcanoes as well—but again, because these volcanoes erupt below the oceans' surface they are very difficult to accurately count.

Like the increase in earthquake activity, most of this escalating volcanic activity is currently being 'downplayed' by the USGS—presumably to avoid concern and ultimately 'panic' on the part of the public. Instead of being notified of this increasing trend in volcanic activity, most of Earth's population doesn't even realize it's taking place, and therefore, subsequently doesn't give this escalating volcanic trend a second thought. In fact, in recent decades, we have (as a society) ignored volcanic danger—building large towns and even major cities precariously close to areas prone to potential volcanic eruptions—especially in the northwestern U.S.

Part of the reason for this modern-day 'volcanic apathy' stems from the fact that our species has been fortunate because there have <u>not been</u> any 'large' volcanic eruptions over the past several thousand years. Many people remember the Mt. St. Helens eruption in May 1980, but this event was small in comparison to truly large volcanic events.

Since we have not experienced any 'monster' eruptions for millennia, we have become largely unaware of just how powerful and devastating these events can be. It is a grave mistake however, to underestimate the destructive power of volcanoes and their aftermath!

When large volcanoes erupt, they send incredible amounts of scalding ash and rock into the atmosphere—raining down over vast areas of our planet. This volcanic ash and rock can collapse buildings, cover roads, suffocate animals and humans alike, ruin crops and cause massive conflagrations (fires). In addition to spewing out scalding ash and rock, volcanoes can produce enormous amounts of poisonous gasses such as carbon monoxide and sulfur dioxide, which threaten any animals/plants unlucky enough to be downwind of this noxious deadly cloud.

Our modern-day society has never really experienced a true 'monster' volcano erupting. One of the largest volcanic eruptions that has taken place in 'modern' times (even though it was relatively small in comparison to those from ancient times) occurred when the Indonesian volcano, Krakatau, erupted in 1883.

So powerful was this volcanic event that its initial blast generated a giant tsunami (tidal wave) estimated at 115-200 feet high, which decimated the coastal regions of Java and Sumatra, destroying numerous cities and killing tens of thousands of people. So loud and powerful was the Krakatoa eruption that it was heard over three thousand miles away.[27]

As powerful as Krakatoa was however, it was relatively small in comparison to the volcano that ravaged the Indonesian island of Tambora in 1815. This eruption was so large and sent so much volcanic ash into Earth's atmosphere, that it plummeted global temperatures (by blocking out natural sunlight) for the better part of a year, causing massive crop failures and widespread famines around the world. On the opposite side of the world in the United States, temperatures were so dramatically affected, that 1815 was know as 'the year without a summer.'[28]

But as powerful as these volcanic events were, they pale in comparison to the volcanoes that decimated our ancient ancestors. In order to encounter really big volcanoes, we must travel back in time thousands of years, to the last passage of the brown dwarf. It is from this period in ancient history that the Minoan civilization was obliterated by a volcanic eruption that literally destroyed 90 percent of the Mediterranean island of Thera (Santorini).

This eruption was so large that it ejected seven 'cubic miles' of molten magma in its blast zone sending volcanic ash high up into Earth's stratosphere—which subsequently blanketed thousands of square miles of the eastern Mediterranean and extending into many parts of Asia.

To put the Thera volcano into proper perspective we turn to the book, *Doomsday*, written by *New York Times* best-selling author, Richard Moran. In his book, Moran comments on the Thera eruption, the destruction of the Minoan civilization, and what a similar volcanic eruption would mean to our modern-day society. Mr. Moran states:

> *To put the destruction of the advanced Minoan civilization into modern perspective, picture a volcanic eruption in the northern hemisphere huge enough to wipe out the major cites of the United States, Europe, and Asia; laying waste to crops and killing off tens of millions of meat producing animals; destroying regional commerce and transportation systems by making it impossible to ship goods or travel via ash-covered roads, railways, and airports; and causing a hemisphere-wide communications blackout as fiery debris knocked out land lines and clouds of ash so saturated the atmosphere that wireless transmissions were severely disrupted.*

The end result would be the total collapse of most, if not all, societies in the northern hemisphere. We would be returned to—at best—Medieval times.

With the breakdown in supply, distribution, and transportation of foodstuffs, super-markets would be abandoned, and people would be forced to resort to the barter system to obtain ever-shrinking food and fuel supplies. Wars would erupt between the rich and the poor, looting would become rampant, and law and order would surely break down into uncontrollable social chaos.[29]

Unfortunately for us, we may be headed towards this same type of volcanic apocalypse in the very near future assuming that we're right about *Wormwood's* ominous threat in 2009/2012.

On 4 August 2003, *ECTV* released an article entitled: *"Volcanoes In California, Idaho and Pacific Northwest Building Towards Catastrophic Eruptions."* [30]

To summarize this article, geologists believe that a series of 'catastrophic' volcanic eruptions are about to unfold in the western part of North America. These potential eruptions would likely include volcanoes such as Mt. Baker (WA), Mt. Rainier (WA), Mt. St. Helens (WA), Mt. Hood (OR), Three Sisters (OR), Mt. Shasta (CA), Cinder Cone (CA), and Chaos Crags (CA), to name just a few. In total, there are more than twenty-seven potential volcanic peaks that could erupt at any moment in the western regions of North America i.e., —Mt. Saint Helens in Washington.

Many of these volcanoes have been inactive for centuries, but now some mysterious geological process within the Earth is producing enormous pressure on all of these western U.S. volcanic sites. This sudden increase in internal volcanic pressure is rapidly forming lava domes/calderas/swarms of earthquakes around these awakening 'volcanic monsters' and their surrounding cities.

The above article goes on to say that if this dramatic and sudden increase in internal magma pressure continues, it could produce a catastrophic series of volcanic eruptions that would be greater than any recorded in (modern) human history—all within the very near future (meaning a few months to a few years as 2009-2012 approaches).

This alarming increase in volcanic and geothermal activity also has geologists around Yellow-stone State Park in a drastic state of both concern and optimism for tourists.

On 29 July 2003, *MSNBC* released a fascinating article entitled: *"Norris Geyser Basin Closed Due to Geothermal Activity."* This article goes on to state:

At Norris Geyser Basin, new steam vents and mud pots are popping up, some geysers are draining themselves and Pork Chop Geyser has erupted for the first time (in years).

All that, and the ground temperature has risen to 200 degrees Fahrenheit...hot enough to boil water...cook eggs...not to mention kill trees and other plants.[31]

A summer vacation to Yellowstone State Park this year is doable but with caution and alertness! But the sad fact remains that it would be impossible to escape the area should an eruption occur.

In a related 4 August 2003 cover story, *Unknown Country* ran a compelling article entitled: *"Yellowstone Geothermal Activity Has Scientist Concerned."*

This article stated:

> *U. S. Geological Survey geologist, Lisa Morgan, reports that there is a 100-foot high bulge in the bottom of Yellowstone Lake that has appeared in the past year. Scientists believe that this bulge could result in a (catastrophic) hydrothermal explosion…the bulge is in Mary's Bay at the north end of the lake, a site that has experienced hydrothermal explosions in the past.*
>
> *Morgan and her team are studying the lake (in great detail now) and plan to prepare a danger assessment in the fall.*[32]

For the record, Yellowstone has had these hydrothermal explosions in the past and when they take place, they are powerful enough to rain debris over hundreds-of-thousands of square miles —essentially blanketing the continental U.S. under several feet of volcanic ash. When Yellowstone does blow up again, and it will eventually blow, this event could be catastrophic enough to essentially put an end to the United States, as we know it—no 'exaggeration' or 'fiction' here!

In fact, one of the largest 'mass extinctions' that has ever taken place on Earth (and there have been many) is called "The Great Dying" by many scientists. Today, this massive extermination is believed to have been caused by volcanic eruptions that were so powerful, they killed off 95% of all life on our planet—essentially putting an end to the Permian period in Earth's history.[33]

Today, scientists are concerned because they are not sure what is causing this dramatic increase in geothermal activities and volcanoes, not only in the U.S., but also throughout the world! Around our entire planet, once 'dormant' volcanoes are suddenly being 'reactivated' and now becoming potential killers. To date, geologists have identified over 500 potential volcanoes that could erupt at any moment and every year this number is dramatically climbing. If only a small number of these volcanoes were to erupt—the result could be a catastrophic volcanic nightmare.

As bad as the current volcanic situation seems to be however, it may be about to get a lot worse! On 19 April 2002, *ECTV* reported that scientists have recently discovered two 'super plumes' rising towards our planet's surface from its molten lava/magma interior.

Essentially these 'super plumes' are massive pockets of molten rock (magma), which are rapidly moving towards the surface of our planet. Once these 'super plumes' of rising magma reach Earth's outer crust, they will violently break through causing an untold volcanic apocalypse!

According to this *ECTV* article:

> *Two super plumes of molten rock appear to be powering through the boundary between the Earth's upper and lower mantle, perhaps feeding volcanoes and affecting the movement of the planet's crust.*

> *New evidence of the super plumes located beneath the south central Pacific Ocean and southern Africa comes from studies of seismic waves conducted by scientists at the University of California at Berkeley and reported in Friday's issue of the Journal Science.*[34]

These 'super plumes' of rising magma are already starting to noticeably affect the surface of the Earth located directly above these rising plumes. *Strangely, not another word from scientific circles about these phenomena has made the press recently—so naturally we wonder—why not?*

This article goes on to say that the plateaus of southern and eastern Africa (sitting directly above this rising magma) have been pushed 1,600 feet higher than the surrounding areas around them. In addition to this large portion of Earth's crust being pushed upwards, massive amounts of heat are radiating from these large upwelling pockets of molten rock and ash.

It the next section of this chapter we shall see how heat radiation from these, and many other sources, is affecting our entire planet—giving rise to the troubling 'global warming' theory.

Once again, a large increase in geothermal and volcanic activity is exactly what would be expected if a massive celestial object (such as a brown dwarf star) were approaching the Earth, placing an ever-increasing strain on our planet's crust and causing a greater upwelling of molten magma from Earth's interior.

Will this strain on Earth's crust continue to increase with the approach of this object—ultimately becoming so great that it will surely cause a slippage of the planet's entire crystal surface, thus resulting in a massive planetary pole shift? Will this upcoming pole shift be accompanied by massive volcanic activity, covering the world's cities in volcanic ash and blocking out sunlight—plummeting global temperatures and potentially causing the start of another ice age?

El Niño / La Niña and global warming

Our planet is essentially a large 'electric motor' floating through the vastness of space. Molten magma within Earth's interior acts as an electromagnetic dynamo, generating electrical currents that flow around our planet between her positive and negative magnetic poles (the dipole).

If a large celestial object such as a brown dwarf star were approaching Earth, it would cause significant disturbances in these magnetic fields. These disturbances would cause 'interference' in Earth's magnetic currents, and in turn, would produce heat (similar to an electric wire heating up when it has a short). This heat would then radiate outward from Earth's interior warming our entire planet from within (thus greatly affecting the temperature of the planet's oceans).

In 1997, a number of key scientists who studied the phenomenon known as *El Niño* and *La Niña*, proposed a controversial but logical theory. They postulated that *El Niño*, a phenomenon that heats global ocean temperatures much higher than normal was in fact being caused by excessive heat 'radiating' out of Earth's molten magma interior.

In other words, as the interior of our planet heats up, this heat radiates upwards into the oceans, causing an increase in normal water temperatures—creating the condition known as *El Niño*. It's just like heating up a large pot of water on a stove—the increased heat from the Earth's interior heats up the planet's many oceans.

This heat radiating up from Earth's interior not only heats the planet's oceans, but also has a profound effect on both the Polar Regions and primary glaciers on our planet. *Are the scientific reports of huge glacial melts at both the Arctic and Antarctic regions connected to this El Niño effect? And if they are—is there any way to mitigate the effects of El Niño and global warming?*

Not only has *El Niño* become a huge problem in recent years, but also the massive ice sheets on both the Arctic and Antarctic continents have been rapidly thawing/breaking up. In a recent *World-watch News Brief*, science writer Lisa Mastny pointed out that: PAST, NOT NOW !

> *The Earth's ice cover is melting in more places and at higher rates than at any time since record keeping began. Reports from around the world compiled by the World Watch Institute show that global ice melting accelerated during the 1990s—which was also the warmest decade on record (for the planet).*[35]

In actuality, the Polar Regions of our planet are currently melting with alarming speed and today most climatologists are extremely concerned. *Remember the movie, The Day After Tomorrow?*

BOGUS.

On 25 November 2002, *CBS Network News* reported that the ice sheets in the Arctic Sea (North Pole) is "*melting faster that previously thought*" and could entirely "*disappear in a few more decades.*"[36] *(Or maybe even sooner?)* NOT TRUE AT THIS-POINT.

NOT TRUE! The Earth's South Pole, also known as the Antarctic, has also been experiencing this alarming rate of melting ice. In fact, the Antarctic is deteriorating so fast, that enormous segments of its ice sheets are breaking off into the ocean and melting every year. This melting is taking place so fast in fact, that many scientists have recently stated that the Antarctic ice sheets are literally 'deteriorating' before our very eyes.

On 19 March 2002, *ECTV* released an *Associated Press* article reporting that a gigantic segment of Antarctica known as the Ross Ice Shelf had just lost an enormous section that simply broke off and was adrift at sea. This segment of the Ross Ice Shelf was so large that it measured 40 miles wide and 53 miles long—covering more square miles than the state of Delaware.

In the winter of 2002, the University of Colorado's *National Snow and Ice Data Center* reported that an enormous section of the Antarctic known as the Larsen Ice Shelf had just lost another large segment measuring more than 3,250 square kilometers in size and was larger than the entire state of Rhode Island. ANTARCTIC ICE IS ACTUALLY INCREASING, SPREADING OUT + BREAKING OFF ICE ALONG THE OUTER EDGES.

This type of massive 'fracturing' or 'breaking-up' of the planet's polar ice sheets has become almost commonplace in recent years. And further—numerous news reports are now rolling in almost every week regarding this rapid melting of both Polar Regions. NO LONGER TRUE.

Unfortunately, the rapid melting of the Ross and Larsen Ice Shelves could have much greater consequences for planet Earth than most people realize. These ice shelves currently act as massive 'frozen' dams preventing the entire Antarctic ice mass from sliding into the ocean and melting—ultimately causing global flooding of biblical proportions (just like in Noah's time).

If the Ross and Larsen Ice Shelves continue breaking up, soon nothing will be left holding the entire Antarctic ice cap in place and it will slide into the ocean. If this were to happen, even by conservative estimates, planetary sea levels would rise more than 200-feet. At first this may not sound like an overwhelming disaster—but think again. *Aren't most major port cities (by nature of their locations) already sitting at sea level or merely a few feet above their high-tide marks?*

If a 200-foot increase in sea level were to take place, most of the world's major port cities such as Tokyo, Hong Kong, Shanghai, Rio de Janeiro, London, Stockholm, Rotterdam, San Francisco, Portland, Los Angeles, San Diego, New York, Miami, Jacksonville, Tampa, New Orleans and many others—would be largely underwater by perhaps a 100-feet or more. *How long did it take for greater New Orleans to flood—some have said less than two hours?*

The elimination of these global seaports would bring the world's economies to a grinding halt. Further, oil could not be shipped out of the Middle East bringing automobile, train and airplane transportation to a major global standstill. Commercial and consumer products such as cars, televisions, computers, textiles and countless other goods would pile up in factories throughout the orient. Bananas, coffee and sugar could not be transported out of South America. Wheat, corn and other critical food supplies could not be shipped out of the U.S., thus bringing mass starvation to billions of people around the world.

If a 200-foot rise in sea level were to take place, not only would the planet's economy essentially collapse, but also the property damage and loss of life would be unparalleled in modern-day times. We must keep in mind that over half the world's population now lives and works within twenty-feet of sea level. The loss of these residential and commercial structures would also cause a planet-wide refugee problem—and that between disease, starvation and social/governmental chaos—it would kill more millions of people.

This increase in sea level would also wipe out huge tracts of agricultural land and almost the entire fishing industry—causing a planetary famine that could, in and of itself, kill billions more.

The melting of the polar ice caps is not the only way in which Earth is currently thawing out, however. Glaciers throughout the world have been rapidly retreating and subterranean permafrost has been melting turning the normally frozen Siberian tundra into rotting swampy marshes.

Many scientists today blame this massive thawing and increase in ocean temperatures on a phenomenon known as 'global warming'. In recent years this term has been used so frequently it's now crept into our vocabulary becoming a proverbial 21st century 'household word.'

The concept of global warming is fairly simple to understand, at least on the surface. According to climatologists, global warming is the result of increased greenhouse gasses that have accumulated in our atmosphere. These gases, which are produced from a wide range of sources including industry, agriculture, transportation and nature itself, trap heat within Earth's atmosphere—thus preventing it from radiating back out into space. Greenhouse gases like carbon dioxide,

THIS THEORY IS UNPROVEN AND HAS BEEN LARGELY DISCREDITED! CAN YOU SAY 'CLIMATEGATE'?

methane and even excess water vapor, act like a large insulating blanket—surrounding the Earth and locking in atmospheric heat.

Like most scientific theories, especially those concerning Earth's complex atmosphere, global warming is extremely controversial. Exactly what effect these greenhouse gases are having on our atmosphere is uncertain and today scientists are lined up on both sides of this politically charged issue. The U.S. is still a holdout in not signing the global Kyoto Accord Agreements.

So, are these greenhouse gases and the resulting phenomenon of global warming responsible for Earth's increased temperatures? The answer is yes—in part.* There is no doubt that modern-day man with his 21st century technologies plays a dangerous and continuing game with mom nature.

★ VERY SMALL, IF ANY!   *NO LONGER TRUE!*

Global warming is most likely 'taking effect,' as every year Earth is getting warmer and warmer. But global warming is not the ultimate or absolute single cause of Earth's heating. Global warming cannot fully explain *El Niño,* or the rapid melting of our polar ice caps and arctic permafrost (tundra)—only massive amounts of heat radiating from Earth's interior could be responsible for such widespread geothermal effects planet-wide as our oceans begin their warming trends.

Global warming is however, exacerbating the problem, making an already bad situation even worse. Global warming is not ultimately causing the massive thawing and heating of Earth, but the trapped greenhouse gases are certainly helping to accelerate the process whatever it is!

If Earth is heating up from the magnetic and gravitational effects of an approaching celestial object, then the other planets in our solar system should also be experiencing similar effects? After all, if Earth is being gravitationally and magnetically affected by the approaching brown dwarf, then all of the other planets in our solar system should also be experiencing these same dynamic changes as well.

Unfortunately, numerous reports <u>have surfaced</u> over the past several years describing the apparent heating-up of other planets throughout our solar system. One of the most dramatic examples of this has been attributed to the melting of the ice caps on the planet Mars. In November 2001, the *BBC* reported that the polar ice caps on Mars were 'suddenly' and 'mysteriously' melting away. Indicating that this planet is also experiencing the same cosmic effects as on Earth. *RIGHT, NOT MANMADE!*

But this warming trend has not been limited to only Mars. As far back as 25 June 1998, the *BBC* was reporting that Neptune's largest moon, Triton, is noticeably 'getting warmer.' [37] In a similar story, astronomers have recently found that the planet Saturn is getting significantly brighter—a clear indication that this planet may also be warming up.

On 23 August 2002, *CNN* reported that even the outermost planet, Pluto, located 3,674 billion miles from the sun—*may be undergoing a global warming.*" [38]

In fact, all of the planets in our solar system appear to be undergoing this same type of interior heating—both solid and gaseous alike—in one form or another.

Hopefully, NASA has been spending its money wisely on dozens of space probes over the years.

Could Venus, Mars, Saturn, Triton, Pluto, Earth, and the rest of the solar system all be heating up as a result of electromagnetic and gravitational effects of the approaching brown dwarf star? Could this approaching object be ultimately responsible for the heat radiating out of Earth's interior, heating up our planet's oceans and be melting both polar ice caps? YES !

Once again, like many of the topics discussed in this chapter, we cannot be absolutely sure this is the only reason for the increased temperatures throughout the solar system, but in light of everything else going on, it certainly fits into the overall picture. Here's a big difference example!

Climate fluctuates naturally between warm and cool periods. But the past 20th century has seen the greatest warming in at least a thousand years, and natural forces can't account for all of it. The rise of CO_2 and other greenhouse gasses are expected to continue rising = 'global warming.'

OLD, LARGELY DISCREDITED INFO.

The Sun

As we mentioned in chapter five, our Sun is an enormous ball of burning hydrogen gas that is so large, more than one million Earths could fit inside its interior. The outer-surface of the Sun is known as its *photosphere*—and is relatively thin in comparison to the rest of the Sun's mass.

Within the interior of this solar inferno, hot circulating gasses continuously produce strong magnetic fields, similar to the way in which the Earth's internal magma circulates and forms our own planet's magnetic fields. And like the magnetic fields of Earth, our sun's magnetic fields form 'magnetic' poles located on opposite sides of the Sun at the Sun's axis of rotation and these opposite magnetic poles are scientifically known as the 'solar dipole.'

We've already investigated how the approaching brown dwarf's heavy gravitation is affecting Earth's magnetic 'fields' and 'dipole.' If the Earth's magnetic environment is being affected by this object's approach, however, we could safely speculate (or best hypothesize) that the Sun's magnetic 'fields' and 'dipole' are also being affected by this object's massive gravitational force.

In fact, our sun is currently being affected by the gravity of this approaching object and this gravitational disturbance is having a dramatic influence on the solar environment causing the Sun to ultimately behave erratically—(i.e., sunspots, solar flares and coronal mass ejections—(CME's).

On 9 January 2001, *ECTV* reported that solar scientists have now said "*absolutely*" and "*without reservation*," that we have recently been witnessing an unprecedented display of 'strange' solar activity/energy during the past 20 years to present.

As our Sun's magnetic fields are distorted (similar to the way in which the Earth's fields are also being distorted), it's causing a host of erratic solar problems including increased solar flares, appreciable magnetic anomalies and a deviation away from the Sun's normal 11-year solar cycle.

It was actually the famous pioneer of modern science, Galileo, who first observed dark spots on the solar surface. These dark areas are today known as sunspots. In the mid-nineteenth century (about a hundred and fifty years ago), other astronomers also started recording cyclical patterns in the number of sunspot that were present on the solar surface at any given time.

As these astronomers recorded the number of sunspots on the solar surface, they quickly realized there were times when sunspot numbers were at their maximum. These periodic peaks in sunspot numbers were separated from each other by about 11 years. There were also times when sunspot numbers seemed to almost disappear altogether. These periods of diminished sunspot numbers were also separated from each other by about 11 years. —*Is there a real linkage here?*

This 11-year cycle of increasing and decreasing sunspot numbers then became known as the 'solar sunspot cycle.' Sunspots gradually build up in number reaching a maximum—and then decrease again in numbers reaching their minimum, only to build back up again to their maximum numbers—and all within a single 11-year period.

These dark areas that form on the Sun's surface are caused by strong magnetic fields that lock solar gas in a specific place, causing this gas to slightly cool. These cooler areas on the solar surface appear dark in contrast to the rest of the Sun—these darker, 'cooler' areas are what we call sunspots.

The number of sunspots on the solar surface at any given time is important for us to examine, because sunspots are a direct indication of the Sun's solar 'magnetic' environment. Simply put, sunspots are a direct indication of the Sun's magnetic activity. We find that the greater the number of sunspots—the more magnetic disturbances are taking place on the Sun's surface, thusly—the fewer the number of sunspots— the less magnetic disturbances are occurring.

According to NOAA (the National Oceanic and Atmospheric Administration), we are currently in solar sunspot cycle number 23, and as of January 2002, should have had a maximum of around 75 sunspots on the solar surface. But the actual number of sunspots as of January 2002 has reached over 150 —further indicating that something is disturbing our Sun's magnetic fields more than expected at this time.

In fact, according to NASA, solar cycle 23 should have reached its peak in January of 2001, with a maximum sunspot count somewhere in the neighborhood of 150. But as late as April 2002, the sunspot count had climbed to a staggering 300 to 450—too high of a number—and far too late in solar cycle 23[39] now greatly affecting terrestrial magnetism and certain other related phenomena.

This increase in the number of sunspots may not seem like a major concern, but the fact that 'three times' the predicted number of sunspots has recently been recorded—is a direct indication of radical magnetic disturbances in the Sun's magnetic fields. *And it's not getting better??*

This is an important additional piece of evidence indicating that the approaching brown dwarf is having an effect on our Sun's normal activity and the primary cycles of its fueling operations.

The radio-flux measurements of the Sun are also an indication of magnetic activity. According to NOAA, as of January 2002, the radio-flux emissions from the Sun should be at a maximum of 135. However, as of this date, our Sun is continuing its erratic behavior and the actual radio-flux transmissions have reached a staggering 235.[40] *This large increase in the radio-flux emissions is still another indication that something is very wrong with our Sun's normal pattern of behavior?*

Although not a hot-topic of scientific discussion—irregularities in the Sun's behavior (over the past two decades) <u>has caused</u> a 'silent alarm' to be called in most major countries' governments. In addition to increased sunspots and radio-flux, our Sun, like the planets in our solar system—is apparently heating up. A recent NASA article reported by *Unknown Country* entitled: *"Sun May Be One Reason It's Getting Hotter"* stated:

> *One reason for global warming could be that the Sun's radiation has increased by .05% per decade since the late 1970s."* The article went on to say *"This trend is important because, if sustained over many decades, it could cause significant climate change."* [41]

Clearly something is affecting our Sun! Something beyond our comprehension is causing the solar sunspot cycle to radically deviate from its normal path, producing heightened radio-flux emissions generating increased solar activity in the form of additional heat. But one of the most startling aspects of what is currently happening to our Sun is also affecting its magnetic poles.

Recall how earlier in this chapter we examined the Earth's magnetic fields and learned that as our planet slows in its rotational speed, its magnetic fields are decreasing in strength. This decrease in Earth's magnetic fields is currently causing our planet's magnetic poles to radically wander away from their normal positions and may eventually lead to a 'magnetic' pole shift in Earth's near future.

On 22 April 2003, NASA released an article admitting that these same types of magnetic anomalies are currently taking place within our Sun's magnetic field environment.

So according to NASA:

> *Three years ago, something <u>weird</u> happened to the Sun. Normally our star, like the Earth itself, has a north and a south magnetic pole (the solar dipole). But for nearly a month beginning in March 2000, the Sun's south magnetic pole faded, and a north pole emerged to take its place. The Sun had <u>two</u> north poles.*
>
> *"It sounds impossible, but it's true,"* says space physicist, Pete Riley, of Science Applications International Corporation (SAIC), in San Diego.[42]

This NASA article then goes on to say the usual 'things' found in these types of news releases—*"That everything is 'normal' and there's nothing for the 'public' to be concerned about."* But then this same article kind of drops a real 'bombshell' on their usual 'modus operandi'!

According to the remainder of NASA's article:

> *In 2001 the solar magnetic field completely flipped; the south and north poles swapped positions, which is how/where they remain now.*[43]

Wow! Apparently our Sun has already undergone its 'magnetic' pole shift. This magnetic pole shift is big news—which, in and of itself, could eventually have cataclysmic effects on Earth! Remember that the Sun controls every aspect of what happens on Earth—good or bad, everyday.

Why is it that our global media sources are essentially ignoring these important solar events and what could be the ultimate cause of these recent magnetic disturbances occurring on the Sun?

Once again we must turn our attention to the gravitational effects of the approaching brown dwarf. This object's intense gravity has not only started to force Earth's magnetic poles to shift, but has already caused a 'total' and seemingly 'permanent' magnetic 'pole shift' to our Sun!

Aside from causing a 'magnetic' pole shift, increased sunspots, and other magnetic anomalies, the approaching brown dwarf is causing a dramatic increase in magnetic storms raging on the Sun's surface. These storms cause enormous portions of the Sun's outer atmosphere known as the corona, to be blown away from the Sun's surface in violent eruptions known as coronal mass ejections— (CMEs). Now it's starting to get personal as these violent CME's lash out at Earth.

These CMEs can overload Earth's power grids causing massive blackouts, frying the sensitive electronics of satellites causing massive disruptions in communications, and interfering with radio transmissions hampering the abilities of emergency workers to perform critical jobs.

As the gravitational effects of the approaching brown dwarf dramatically increases, the current problems taking place on the Sun are only going to get worse year after year.

A hint of what may lie in store for us was revealed in a *Washington Post* article dated 18 August 2003 wherein this article stated:

> *Emergency departments across the country—including some in the District of Columbia, Maryland and Virginia—report unsettling stories of officers who can't call for backup, dispatchers who can't relay suspect descriptions, and firefighters who can't request ambulances because of experiencing (a growing number of) radio 'dead spots.'*

> *"Just by the grace of God or good luck, we've been able to avoid a major problem," said Gary Manougian, a police officer in Portland, OR. "But I don't think we can go on like this indefinitely."*

> *Dozens of agencies large and small—from New York City to Androscoggin County, Maine—have registered complaints, and one public safety coalition estimates that (radio) interference is (now) a major growing problem in at least 27 states.*[44]

Even though this article alludes to 'cell phone' interference as being the ultimate cause of these disruptions in emergency radio communications, the reality is—that the investigators are not sure just what is responsible for these disruptions. The truth of the matter is, authorities have no idea what's causing these radio/cell/telephone interference problems or why they're escalating.

Apparently these officials have not been watching the recent activity on the Sun. The above *Washington Post* article only points out a growing problem—a single example in a much larger pattern of problems involving radio, television, cell phone and other communication interference scenarios—all being caused by massive explosions on the Sun that are hurtling charged particles (CMEs) at Earth—knocking out our 21st century wireless communications in mere seconds.

But our problems with the Sun do not stop here, however. On 19 June 2003, *Rumor Mill News* released an article entitled: *"NASA Worried Over Sun's Activity."* According to this article:

> *The rumors suggest NASA has been handed a gag order issued by the DOD (Department of Defense). The reason for this order is directed at our spy satellites. It is suggested that in the name of national security (NASA) can no longer confirm or deny recent and current solar activity (as being) at dangerous levels.*
>
> *Over the past week a reported 65 C-Class flares, 16 M-Class flares, and 2 X-Class flares have occurred. In just the week prior, another 2 X-Class flares and 4 M-Class flares erupted. In addition to solar flares, perhaps as many as 45 CME's (coronal mass ejections) emerged. Another area of concern is our 'power grids.' If Earth experiences a direct hit from any one of these M-Class or X-Class flares, it could in fact cripple our (global) infrastructure (in a serious way).[45]*

Reports such as this have become commonplace over the past few years as NASA and other governmental agencies are becoming increasingly concerned over the Sun's recent erratic behavior and changes in its magnetically-charged energy fields.

This bizarre behavior from our Sun has continued and in October and November of 2003, a series of solar flares were produced—one of them being the largest eruption ever recorded by modern-day solar science. —Thankfully this flare was directed away from the earth.

Between the Sun's recent magnetic disturbances including large numbers of sunspots, massive CME's and a complete reversal of its magnetic fields—it would clearly appear as if our Sun is also being adversely affected by the approach of this rogue celestial object—'Wormwood.' As this object continues to advance closer and closer to the Sun, its monster gravity is only going to increasingly affect the way in which our own solar body (the Sun) continues to function.

Increased space debris

Asteroids are essentially large rocks hurtling through space at incredible speeds. Although rare—asteroids occasionally strike our planet causing massive damage. It is thought that just such an asteroid wiped out the dinosaurs 65 million years ago—and other such asteroids may have played a significant part in obliterating life on Earth at least nineteen other times in the past.

It has been proposed that if a large celestial body such as a brown dwarf star were approaching Earth, a debris field of huge asteroids, dirty comets and dust (caught up in this object's massive gravitational field), would accompany and surround 'it' in space. As this object approaches our inner solar system—we would begin to encounter the leading edge of its debris field as a prelude to the object's actual arrival. In other words, a few years before this object actually passes Earth, we could be increasingly hit by space debris at the leading edge of this object's trajectory.

Although asteroids only occasionally strike our planet, the past several years have seen a gradual increase in both the number of smaller asteroids actually 'hitting' our planet and the number of 'near misses' of even larger asteroids that threaten us.

Why is it that NASA and other government agencies tend to keep a tight lid on this information?

As of January 2002, however, this parade of near misses from large asteroids suddenly becomes alarming! *But certainly not alarming enough to alert or inform the general public?*

As a small example, on Tuesday, 8 January 2002, the *Associated Press* announced that a large asteroid dubbed 2001 YB5 had just missed hitting planet Earth the day before. This *Associated Press* article went on to say that another large asteroid, known as 2001 UU92, was also going to barely miss us on Friday, 11 January 2002.

This same *Associated Press* article went on to say that if either of these objects had hit the Earth, it would have obliterated a medium size country the size of France and would have been the *"Worst disaster in recorded human history."*

Then the very next week, on Wednesday, 16 January 2002, *Reuter's News Agency* reported that another two asteroids had once again just missed planet Earth. These asteroids, designated 734-1991, and 2002-AO11, had nearly collided with the Earth earlier that day. The article went on to say that if either of these asteroids were to have directly hit our planet—they would have caused a major "global climactic catastrophe" in these modern-day times.

As if these near misses weren't scary enough, this same *Reuters* article went on to say that: *"Five more large asteroids were expected to barely miss the Earth in the latter part of January 2002."*

These articles represent small, isolated examples of the recent 'near misses' that only seem to be increasing by the day.

Keep in mind that these are just the known asteroids that NASA is 'spotting' and then 'reporting' to the public. And there might be many other 'large' asteroids barely missing us each day that NASA, or other dedicated astronomers—just never see coming at us.

NASA also recently released a 'strange' but revealing statement saying, *"We may, or may not, release information regarding upcoming near-earth objects to the public. We will take each of these near misses on a case by case basis."* —*Don't you find this a curious, troubling matter?*

In other words—don't plan on being informed by NASA if anything 'important' or 'serious' is going to take place! If this increasing debris field continues to approach Earth, and it looks as if we are going to be struck by a piece of the brown dwarf's debris field, one thing is for sure—the public will probably not be forewarned by the very authorities responsible for protecting us!

Not only has a parade of large cosmic debris been flying past us in space, but also the smaller and more numerous space debris particles have been entering our atmosphere, even hitting our planet—with increased frequency. —*Aren't the smaller pieces often called 'shooting stars??*

On any given night (if you're lucky enough to be out in an empty desert or a place far enough away from the city), looking up into the nighttime sky provides a cosmic light show of 'shooting stars' that will astound you. Big ones, little ones, long ones and skinny ones all perform for free.

On 23 July 2001, *Reuters*, *Space.com*, and the *Associated Press* all carried a story stating:

> *Reports of a possible meteor shower flooded police and government telephone lines along the U.S. East Coast on Monday, authorities said. The sightings of what some described as a fast-moving meteor prompted evening rush-hour motorists to pull off suburban highways west of Philadelphia.*

> *Airline pilots in flight issued reports of similar sightings to federal aviation officials in Pennsylvania, Delaware and Maryland. Authorities said eyewitness accounts came from upstate New York to Virginia.*

> *A Reuter's reporter saw a tapered object shaped like a trumpet bell falling diagonally through the western sky near Westchester, Pennsylvania. The objects(s) emitted a lustrous rainbow of colors…and finally 'rust-colored red.'*

> *People living near Montoursville, Pennsylvania, a rural community 130 miles northwest of Philadelphia, reported hearing a loud explosion after seeing the unidentified (Arial) object. A state police dispatcher said one woman reported that the blast broke windows in her home. There were also unconfirmed reports of people finding (strange) debris on the ground.*

> *"It was a ball of fire," Mark Barbour of Syracuse, New York, told CNN. "It looked like something you would see from the movies."* [46]

On 19 December 2001, the *Denver Post* reported that a blazing fireball had exploded 15 miles over the Earth above La Garita, in Saguache County.[47] On 27 April 2001, *ECTV* reported that a loud Aerial explosion had just rocked eastern Australia.[48]

On 4 December 2003, Reporter Neil McMahon wrote an article entitled: *"The Night Sydney Went Bang, and Nobody Knew Why."* According to this fascinating news item:

> *Buildings shook, windows rattled and terrified residents thought their homes were crashing around them—but nobody has any idea what caused a mysterious explosion that shook Sydney's north and west late last night.*

> *Police began receiving phone calls about 10:20 (PM) of an enormous explosion, with reports coming from an area stretching from Wiseman's Ferry to the lower Blue Mountains. In about 20 minutes, River stone police station alone received more than 100 calls from worried residents.*

> *Police stations at St Mary's, Richmond and Mount Druitt were among others swamped by calls. One officer said she had heard and felt the explosion. "The windows moved and the ground shook," she said. "I thought it had happened right where I was, in the building I was in. Everyone who felt it said it felt like his or her house was going to implode. We had so many calls it was ridiculous."* [49]

These types of reports involving cosmic debris hitting our atmosphere, causing loud explosions, flashes of light in the sky, even sometimes hitting Earth itself, are becoming more and more common place over the past few years—strongly suggesting that our planet is encountering an ever-increasing debris field associated with the approaching brown dwarf.

In fact, there have been so many recent reports involving space debris hitting Earth, that to list all of the reports here would be impossible. Suffice to say that the frequency with which our planet is being pelted is dramatic and only seems to be increasing by the day.

Another recent cosmic discovery that has scientists extremely concerned is the approach of space debris no larger than grains of sand.

In August 2003, a number of news agencies including the *New Scientist* and *ECTV* reported that an enormous cosmic 'dust storm' has entered our solar system and is headed towards Earth. The article goes on to say that the ultimate effect this approaching dust storm will have on Earth is 'unknown' but scientists have speculated it could be catastrophic.[50]

On 1 November 2002, *Space.Com* reported that dust clouds and other space debris (now within our inner solar system) are so thick, they are reflecting sunlight back towards Earth—producing 'false dawns' in the nighttime sky.

Could we be entering the thin leading edge of this debris field of an approaching brown dwarf star? Could this field of 'space junk' wreak havoc on our planet long before we even see this brown dwarf star coming at us?

As this ever-present field of space debris has moved closer and closer to Earth, it has also left an indelible mark on the outer planets of our solar system. In recent years dozens of news articles have surfaced mentioning how the outer planets of our solar system have been repeatedly struck by large pieces of space debris. Some of these impacts have been so powerful, they have produced explosions larger than Earth itself violently 'shaking' planets many times more massive than ours. *Remember pictures taken of Jupiter being bombarded by giant meteors in 2003?*

We have been very fortunate not to have been hit by any large pieces of this approaching debris field—but our luck here on Earth isn't going to last forever!

Global weather

We have saved the subject of Earth's weather as the last topic presented in this chapter because more that any other physical phenomena presented so far, our planet's weather is the end result of everything we have investigated to date.

Our planet's weather systems are influenced by a litany of other factors. Earth's climate is the end result of a complicated amalgamation of factors that meteorologists are still struggling to understand today. Earth's weather is affected by magnetic and solar disturbances like CME's from the Sun, planetary magnetic and rotational factors, increased volcanic activity, cosmic dust and debris, seismic disturbances and global warming—even the <u>weather itself</u> over enough time.

Since all of these diverse factors affect Earth's weather and all of these factors are currently undergoing dramatic and rapid changes, it should come as no surprise that our planet's weather is also undergoing great change—dramatic changes that can't be covered-up or ignored forever.

Every passing year more and more weather records are broken around the world. Record high and low temperatures, record droughts and floods, record rain and snow fall, record numbers of hurricanes, typhoons and tornados are all happening on a yearly, if not a weekly, or even daily basis.

On 4 July 2003, *CNN* released an article entitled: *"Extreme Weather on the Rise."*

According to this article:

> *Anecdotal evidence that the world's weather is getting wilder now has a solid scientific basis in fact following a dramatic global assessment from the World Meteorological Organization (WMO).*
>
> *A study released Wednesday by the WMO—(a specialized climate science agency of the United Nations)—says: "The world is experiencing record numbers of extreme weather events, such as droughts and tornadoes."*
>
> *Citing numerous examples of strange weather, the WMO said: "When viewed together they represented a 'clear' and 'alarming' trend towards wilder weather patterns."* [51]

In fact, over the past several years, more and more climatologists have bravely come forward by noting that Earth's weather is becoming increasingly erratic and even more unpredictable.

Recently, the U.S. *National Academy of Sciences* has also warned that based on their research, we can expect 'sudden' and 'widespread' climate changes in the immediate future.[52]

In July of 2003, numerous climatologists publicly stated that Earth's weather has gone *"haywire"* and according to Rajendra Pachauri, the head of the United Nations' main panel on climate change, *"Something (strange) is disrupting the entire global climate system."* [53]

Once again, it is important to state that Earth's weather is not becoming more erratic due to any one given factor, but instead is the end result of many factors all playing a curious and certain 'role' and/or 'part' in the overall climate picture for the planet.

Today, we do not fully understand all of the factors that cause Earth's weather patterns. But it is safe to say that if our planet's magnetic, rotational, solar, seismic, volcanic and other systems are all currently undergoing 'dramatic' and 'sudden' changes, and if Earth's weather is affected by all of these other related planetary systems—then it should be obvious as to 'why' our planet's normal weather patterns are going 'haywire.' Our world's climate patterns are simply responding to the approach of the 'terrible comet'—'*Wormwood.*'

If present weather conditions on Earth are valid indications of the future—we're in big trouble!!

In conclusion

Our investigation of the physical changes presently taking place on our planet has once again merely scratched the surface of this subject. Even a partial review of the geophysical and meteorological phenomena currently taking place could easily fill an entire book all by itself.

Even the partial evidence that we've examined in this chapter however, should make it clear that something is going terribly wrong with not only our planet, but most of the other solar system planets surrounding us in space as well.

We believe the 'cosmic handwriting' is clearly 'on the wall' and that the scientific evidence is plain to see for anyone willing and brave enough to look/analyze/think/act. And it's time we stop using mundane and provincial excuses to explain away what is happening to our world. We must quickly realize that changes in Earth's rotation, her magnetic fields, earthquake and volcanic activities, her climate, weather problems and a host of other conditions (both here on Earth and throughout the solar system), are not isolated or unrelated events—but individual pieces of the same cosmic puzzle!

It's time we face the music and the potential disaster of a brown dwarf approaching us from space! 2009/2012 is only a heartbeat away—the time for thoughtful preparation is now!

As this celestial object nears, (in theory) its enormous gravitational attraction is causing our planet to radiate more heat out of its interior thus warming the oceans, melting the polar ice caps, thawing out the arctic permafrost and causing havoc with the world's weather patterns.

Could this phenomena become part of the current 'global warming' equation? And is former Vice President Al Gore's movie, <u>An Inconvenient Truth</u>, closer to the 'truth' than anyone understands at this time in our planet's history? NOPE.

(Note: Be sure to check out the special 'global warming' commentary in the Exhibit section of this book for an in depth look into this timely issue.)

Planet-X's gravitational 'pull' may be causing our planet to bulge at its equator and the increased physical pressure being placed on its crust may be translating into an ever-greater number of earthquakes and active volcanoes. Our sun appears to be going berserk, our weather systems gone haywire, our planet's rotation is slowing, our magnetic fields are collapsing and our dipole rapidly wandering. All this is occurring as an ever-increasing number of comets, asteroids and cosmic dust particles parade past Earth—some small—others much larger.

No other 'commentary' or 'parade of scientific facts' is necessary at this point! The evidence that you've just read simply speaks for itself.

The passage of this 'terrible comet' has taken place numerous times in the past, with disastrous consequences for our ancient ancestors. The stage is currently being set for the next 'big act' in this ongoing 'cosmic drama' and present-day mankind are going to be the unfortunate players!

Two key questions in this scene are, 1) your role in this drama and 2) are you ready to play it?

I'M RAPTURE READY!

CHAPTER FIVE ENDNOTES

[1] www.Troubledtimes.com
[2] Ibid.
[3] Ibid.
[4] Ibid.
[5] http://news.bbc.co.uk/low/english/sci/tech/mewssid_244000/244293.stm.
[6] http://www.newscientist.com/news/print.jsp?id=ns99992152
[7] http://www.earthchangestv.com/secure/breaking_news/may20.../may20.../0509series.html
[8] USGS Website, http://neic.usgs.gov/neis/eqiists/eqstats.html.
[9] Ibid.
[10] Ibid.
[11] http://www.Troubledtimes.com
[12] http://www.phoenixpages.com/cilwa/metaphysics/earthquakes.htm.
[13] "http://www.infoplease.com/ipa/A0197840.html" and http:/quake.usgs.gov/recent/recent.html
[14] The Oregonian, Portland, Oregon, 15 December 2005, Science Section, see Quake, p. A13-14
[15] USGS Website,"http://neic.usgs.gov/neis/eqiists/eqstats.html" .
[16] USGS Website, http://earthquake.usgs.gov/eqinthenews/2003/2004/2005/2006
[17] www.Troubledtimes.com
[18] Ibid.
[19] Ibid.
[20] http://more.abcnews.go.com/sections/scitech/dailynews/earthquakes990122.html.
[21] http://abcnews.go.com/sections/science/dailynews/earthquakes000107.html.
[22] Hutton, William, *Coming Earth Changes* (A.R.E. Press 1996), pp. 83-89.
[23] Kay, Tom, *When The Comet Runs* (Hampton Roads Publishing, 1997), p. 44.
[24] Ibid., p. 100.
[25] Http://news.nationalgeographic.com/news/2002/080807_020807_earthrirth.html.
[26] www.Troubledtimes.com
[27] Moran, Richard, *Doomsday* (Alpha Publishing, 2003), p. 50.
[28] Ibid., p. 50.
[29] Ibid., p. 43.
[30] http://www.earthchangestv.com/secure/2003_articles/0803
[31] http://www.msnbc.com/local/pnboz/norrisgeyserbas.asp
[32] http://www.unknowncountry.com/img/email/cmast.gif.
[33] Moran, Richard, *Doomsday* (Alpha Publishing, 2003), p. 39.
[34] http://www.earthchangestv.com/secure/Breaking_News.../0419superplumes.html.
[35] Ibid., p. 70.
[36] http://www.cbsnews.com/stories/2002/11/25/tech/printable530762.shtml.
[37] http://www.yowusa.com/archive/september2002/xkb06/xkb06.htm.
[38] Ibid.
[39] Battros, Mitch, *The Challenge Of A Shifting Scientific Paradigm* (ECTV, 8/4/03) www.ectv.com
[40] http://sec.noaa.gov/SolarCycle/
[41] http://www.unknowncountry.com/news/print.phtml?id:2600.
[42] http://science.nasa.gov/headlines/y2003/22apr.currentsheet.htm?friend
[43] Ibid.
[44] http://www.washintonpost.com/ac2/wp_dyn/a7270_2003aug17?lanquage=printer.
[45] http://www.rumormillnews.com/cgi-bin/forum.cgi?read=33180
[46] http://dailynews.yahoo.com/htx/nm/20010723/sc/life_sightings_dc_3.html.
[47] Schrader, Ann, *Colorado Sleuths Track August Fireball* (The Denver Post, 19 December 2001)
[48] http://www.earthchangestv.com/breaking/april_part2_2001.../0427aystrailia.html
[49] http://www.smh.com.au/articales/2003/12/04/1070351666682.html.
[50] http://www.earthchangestv.com/secure/2003_articles/0803_/articles/0803_articals/printerfriendly/10duststorm.html.
[51] http://www.earthchangestv.com/secure/2003_articles/0703_1articals/printerfriendly/04extreme.html.
[52] http://www.csmonitor.com/2001/1214/p2s2-usgn.html.
[53] Battros, Mitch, *Is July's Weather a Precursor to August Prophecy?* (ECTV, 7-25-03) http://www.ectv.com

This page provided for reader's notes.

— CHAPTER SIX —

THE ANCIENT SCIENCE OF PROPHECY

Prophecy—the ability to foretell future events before they actually happen. This mysterious human ability has been the source of fascination and controversy for thousands of years. Pharaohs have sought the advice of prophets, emperors have been astounded by their abilities, and kings have put them to death over unpopular predictions. Many modern-day church denominations also include prophecy in their teaching doctrines now—while others totally distain it.[1]

The popularity of modern-day prophecy has been reflected in numerous surveys/polls conducted over the years. In many of these polls, upwards of 86% of (mixed gender) adults said that they believed in the validity of prophecy. In fact, according to the University of Chicago's National Opinion Research Council, 67% of all adult Americans actually believe they, themselves, have experienced a precognitive event at least one time in their lives.

Even though many people firmly believe in psychic abilities and modern science has positively confirmed the reality of this arcane phenomenon, as in the past, prophecy still remains a controversial and heated subject—especially in religious circles.

Many people are uncomfortable with the idea of 'psychic phenomena' because we really don't understand (or control) how these 'prophetic abilities' operate. In other words, many prophets apparently see clear 'glimpses' into the future—but we still don't understand exactly how or why these 'gifted ones' are able to accomplish their psychic feats. It's simply human nature to 'ridicule' or become 'suspicious' about mystical or spiritual things we fail to fully understand.

Regardless of your personal take on 'prophecy' and 'clairvoyance' the fact remains, however, that certain people (from time-to-time) are able to psychically perceive selected events that will take place in the future or have in the past. Sometimes these people have the unique ability to visually 'witness' (mentally seeing through the newer science of 'Remote Viewing'—a mental discipline using power(s) of the human mind to incredibly 'perceive/see') certain events taking place 'outside' of the normal confines of linear 'space' and 'time'—both forward and backward.

As a side note to our fascinating subject on 'Remote Viewing,' physicist Harold (Hal) Puthoff, Ph.D. (a fellow researcher and good friend), is Director of *The Institute For Advanced Studies* in Austin, Texas. Hal's been following my progress in writing this book over the past several years.

We've kicked around the idea of assembling a crack team of professional 'Remote Viewers' to determine 'if' and 'when' we could research the following 'X' criteria: 1) if there's a real-time *Planet-X* lurking around out there? 2) And if there is, where's it headed (either into or out of our solar system)? 3) If 'X' is real and actually coming at us approximately when should we expect 'X's' arrival? And 4) does 'X' really look like what most of our predictions/prophecies/ancient accounts describe it to be; i.e., the 'Red Dragon'/fireball in the heavens/dark star/cosmic serpent/terrible comet/Typhon/the great destroyer/Saquasohah/Planet of the Crossing and *'Wormwood?'*

Dr. Puthoff, one of the original pioneers of 'Remote Viewing' science and two of his colleagues, Russell Targ of SRI International (formerly the Stanford Research Institute) in Menlo Park, California, and a self-tutored student of parapsychology named Ingo Swann—set out in the early '70s to put the controversial subject of 'Remote Viewing' on the scientific map. Running a successful series of psychic experiments they tested a number of qualified individuals using their unique mental powers to establish a number of pre-established 'viewing' objectives—some of them non-military related while others primarily supported in-depth Pentagon-related projects.[2]

Let's hope the success of this book paves the way for Hal and his institute associates to launch a new 'Remote Viewing' effort 'looking into' the actuality that 'X' may be heading our way in 2009-2012. On 4 April 2005, I received a proud letter from Dr. Puthoff wherein he wrote me:

> *"This (your Planet-X book) is so exciting, I can hardly believe it! Thanks for sharing it with me and I apologize for the delay in returning it—I'll really not ever do that again. I got bogged down in my 'day job.'*

> *"If you find any way for me to help or contribute, let me know. —A truly riveting 'tour de force!' Cheers, Hal."* - END -

I treasure my relationship with Dr. Puthoff and look forward to the opportunity of working with him in the near future. Thanks, Hal, you've been a great research associate and a true inspiration.

In addition to 'Remote Viewing' techniques, most psychic individuals often perceive these future events by different 'means.' Many are visited by angelic entities showing them images of events that will come to pass. Others view future events while in a 'dream-like' or 'trance state,' or during 'deep meditation.' Still others mysteriously lose consciousness and suddenly find themselves confronted by graphic images of the future. The infamous prophet Nostradamus, for example, would witness vivid images of the future while the 'seer' would remain visually transfixed staring into a small glass-like pool of water.

Like many of the subjects within this book, this chapter is not intended to prove or disprove the reality of psychic phenomena. But knowing what we already know regarding this approaching brown dwarf star and the geologic phenomena of Earth's lithosphereic displacement (pole shift), when clairvoyant individuals do witness these events coming to pass in prophetic visions of the future —we should definitely take a moment, keep an open mind and then hear them out.

The fact is that numerous prophets throughout the centuries have foreseen great changes taking place on planet Earth in our near future. Often these visions involve a shifting of our planet's axis of rotation, which triggers enormous geologic upheavals and a dramatic alteration of Earth's topography. At other times prophets have had visions of a terrifying 'celestial object' that will appear in our sky, reaping havoc and destruction across the world.

These prophetic individuals often believe they've witnessed these future events in order to warn mankind, hoping their prophetic visions will educate receptive individuals to prepare themselves before these dreaded events come to pass again. We can, of course, choose to ignore these dire warnings but we'll be doing so at our own peril—like viewing the forest without seeing the trees.

[handwritten marginal note: QUESTIONABLE STUFF!]

186

Our best course of action is to keep an open mind regarding the reality and accuracy of psychic abilities. We should listen to their messages seeing if 'they' fit into what we already suspect the future may hold for us. Even though we may not always like the messages that prophets foretell, they've proven a long history of being right about future events. —And it would be unwise to dismiss their prophetic warnings without careful witness and consideration.

Let us now investigate some of the prophetic warnings from some of the better-known/well-renowned visionaries—some from the past and some from the present. Let's investigate if their messages will further illuminate our understanding of what may be headed our way!

The Holy Bible (King James Version)

THE TRUE AUTHORITY.

Today, when we talk of upcoming *Earth Changes*, we have the luxury of an extensive scientific vocabulary at our disposal in order to communicate these ideas. We banter around terms such as *pole shift*, *lithosphereic displacement*, *block faulting* and *brown dwarf star* because our modern-day advancements in science offers us a new dictionary of rich terms to effectively communicate specific *Earth Changes* concepts/terminology.

Thousands of years ago however, the writers of the Holy Bible had no such linguistic arsenal at their disposal. These gifted individuals had to convey their prophetic visions saddled with the limited terminology of their day.

As we know, pole shifts are periodic in nature and have happened hundreds of times in the past. The writers of the Bible were familiar with this cyclic nature of Earth's pole shifts and eluded to these events both in the 'past' and in the 'future.'

Instead of using our modern terminology however, the writers of the Bible describe these pole shifts by the 'physical effects' that take place in their wake. In other words, the Bible describes pole shifts as times when the stars, Moon and Sun move strangely in the sky, or when vast amounts of volcanic ash block out sunlight, causing the Sun and Moon to 'go dark' or 'withdraw' their light. They also described pole shifts as times when the entire Earth trembles and becomes inclined—causing great floods to envelope the land.

In addition, the writers of the Bible also described the passage of the brown dwarf by the 'physical effects' this object has on the Earth as well. They often described the passage by phenomena such as the Sun, Moon or land turning into blood as 'red' iron oxide dust is blown from the brown dwarf's atmosphere and covers the Earth, or as an eagle with a <u>red tail</u> screaming across the sky.

The writers of the Bible described these future pole shifts and brown dwarf passages, taking place at a time of great destruction. They often referred to these events as "*The Last Judgment*" or "*The Day of the Lord*" or "*Armageddon*" or "*The Chastisement.*"

An example of this type of 'symptomatic' description of geophysical events can be seen in the book of Joel. When the Old Testament was assembled it was written less modern-day verbiage and scientific bias. They essentially wrote about what they saw, understood and believed in.

> *(Joel 2:10) The earth shall quake before them; the heavens shall tremble; the sun and the moon shall be dark, and the stars shall withdraw their shining.*

> *(Joel 2:30-31) And I will shew wonders in the heavens and the earth, blood and fire, and pillars of smoke. The sun shall be turned into darkness, and the moon into blood, before the great and terrible day of the Lord come.*

The biblical prophet Joel is clearly using the limited terminology of his day to describe some of the physical manifestations that will take place when the brown dwarf passes Earth in the future and our planet's poles shift. The prophet Amos also describes some of the same physical effects of a future pole shift when he states:

> *(Amos 8:9) And it shall come to pass in that day, saith the Lord God, that I will cause the sun to go down at noon, and I will darken the earth in the clear day.*

In the New Testament of the Bible, the theme of an upcoming pole shift remains the same.

> *(Matthew 24:29) Immediately after the distress of those days (the passing brown dwarf), the sun will be darkened, and the moon will not give its light; the stars will fall from the sky, and the heavenly bodies will be shaken...*

> *(Mark 13:24-25) But in those days, after that distress (the passage), the sun will be darkened, the moon will not give her light; the stars will come falling from the sky, the celestial powers will be shaken.*

> *(Luke 21:9-11) Nation will rise against nation, and kingdom against kingdom. There will be great earthquakes, famines and pestilence in various places, and fearful events and great signs from heaven. There will be signs in the sun, moon and stars. On the earth, nations will be in anguish and perplexity at the roaring and tossing of the sea (due to gravitational influences). <u>Men will faint from terro</u>r, apprehensive of what is coming on the world, for the heavenly bodies will be shaken.*

The last sentence of (Luke 21:9-11) relating to *"men fainting from terror,"* points out the importance of being forewarned and prepared for these coming events. If you're aware that these events have taken place in the past and are simply a part of Earth 'great cycles' that <u>don't</u> spell the end of the world, you will be much more likely to deal with the passage of the brown dwarf rationally and calmly. If you're aware that these events are once again coming, you can prepare yourself spiritually, physically and mentally to better deal with your tasks at hand— simply surviving. *In this case being forewarned is truly being forearmed!* And there is no need to psychologically 'freak out' when things around you start falling apart, simply hold it together.

As revealing as these prophetic messages are, however, some of the most detailed Biblical warnings of what our future holds can be found in the last book of the Bible, known as the Book of Revelation. This apocalyptic book was written 1,900 years ago by St. John the Divine and has fueled controversy throughout the centuries due to its enigmatic language. Revelation is probably the most confusing book in the New Testament and the Catholic Church doesn't teach it.

Armed with the understanding by reading previous chapters of this book—the encrypted messages of Revelation should be easier for you to decipher—so let's begin by taking some notes.

One of the most revealing descriptions of future events contained within the Book of Revelation is a vivid account of the next passage of this failed brown dwarf star—which 'it' refers to as—*WORMWOOD*. This account of the brown dwarf's next passage is so detailed in fact, it describes this object's 'bloody-red' tail as it flies through the heavens and the 'red' iron oxide fallout that poisons the waters of Earth while darkening the Sun, Moon and stars.

> *(Revelation 8:10-13) And the third angel sounded, and there fell a star from heaven, burning as though it were a lamp, and it fell upon the third part of the rivers and upon the fountains of waters; and the name of the star is called <u>Wormwood</u>; and the third part of the waters became (poisoned by) Wormwood; and many men died of the waters, because they were made bitter (toxic from the iron oxide). And the fourth angel sounded, and the third part of the sun was eclipsed and the third part of the moon and the third part of the stars, so that the third part of them was darkened, and the day was darkened for a third part of it, and the night likewise. And I beheld, and heard an eagle, <u>having a tail red as it were blood</u>, flying through the mists of heaven, saying with a loud voice, Woe, woe, woe to those who dwell on the Earth, by reason of the other sounds of the trumpets of the three angels which are yet to sound!   -END -*

The last sentence of this chapter which mentions <u>an eagle flying through heaven with a red tail saying</u>, *"Woe, woe, woe to those who dwell on the Earth, by reason of the other sounds of the trumpets of the three angels which are yet to sound!"* —is important to keep in mind. Remember the passage of the brown dwarf is <u>not the end</u> of the physical calamites—it's <u>just the beginning</u>.

The Book of Revelation also goes on to vividly describe the physical damage this object's deadly passage will cause, saying:

> *(Revelation 6:12-14) And I looked when he had opened the sixth seal, and behold, there was a great Earthquake; and the sun became black as sackcloth of hair, and the moon became as blood; and the stars of Heaven fell to the Earth, even as a fig tree casts it green figs when it is shaken by a mighty wind. And the heavens separated as a scroll when it is rolled separately; and every mountain and island shifted from its resting place.*

As *Wormwood's* tremendous gravitational effect takes hold of Earth, enormous physical pressure is placed on our planet's crust causing a *"great earthquake."* Volcanic ash subsequently turns the Sun *"black as sackcloth"* and 'red' iron oxide dust blown off the surface of the brown dwarf by the solar wind makes the moon *"become as blood."*

As the solid lithosphere of our planet begins to slide, the gigantic tectonic plates comprising the Earth's continental make up commences to buckle and move. Block faulting begins to happen, and as a result, *"every mountain and island shifted from its resting place."*

This section of Revelation also gives us a glimpse of the 'sheer chaos' and 'societal breakdown' this next passage of *Wormwood* is going to cause when it says:

> *(Revelation 6: 15-17) And the kings of the Earth and the great men and the commanders of thousands and the rich and the mighty men and every bondman and every freeman hide themselves in caves and in clefts of the mountain, and said to the mountains and the rocks, fall on us, and hide us from the face of Him who sits on the throne and from the wrath of the Lamb; for the great day of His wrath is come, and who shall be able to stand? - END -*

Clearly the *"kings of the Earth"* and the *"commanders of thousands"* (government and military leaders) will have a hard enough time trying to save themselves and preserve the continuity of government—much less assisting the hapless populace. You (the reader) would be wise to keep this point in mind as you continue reading this book. Simply stated, if you're going to survive these upcoming global cataclysms, you're going to have to save <u>yourself</u> first—don't be expecting help from anyone outside <u>yourself</u>—especially the government or military who'll soon be overwhelmed/preoccupied by the severity of what's coming! More on this in later chapters.

TRUST IN THE LORD. ACTS 21: 36

As frightening as the Book of Revelation is, however, it also brings us an ultimate message of hope/optimism. For this final book of the Bible clearly states that after the trials of the upcoming *Earth Changes* subside, 'peace and prosperity' will return to our planet as 'the Good Shepard' brings a 1,000 year 'golden age' of 'spiritual enlightenment' manifesting here on planet Earth.

AMEN!

The 'Our Lady Of Fatima Prophesies'

One of the most famous and provocative accounts of *Earth Changes* prophecy comes to us from the past—a miraculous Christian melodrama called the Fatima Prophecies.

At exactly noon on Sunday, 13 May 1917 and precisely on the Feast of the Ascension, Lucia, Francisco and Jacinta, three small innocent children ranging in age from seven to ten, were busy tending their sheep together in a natural depression called *Cova da Iria,* near the herding village of Fatima, located about 80 miles north of Lisbon, Portugal.

On the stroke of 12:00-pm that day, a brilliant flash of light appeared out of a clear blue sky suddenly startling the three children. Then a second blinding flash drew their attention to a small tree, in front of which suddenly appeared (like in a holographic image), a beautiful lady wearing a sparkling rosary around her neck. She told the three children not to be afraid—that she had come from heaven to speak with them and to give them a warning about the future of Earth.

After asking them to return to this same spot (at precisely the same time) on the thirtieth day of each of the next six months, the Lady mysteriously rose into the sky and disappeared.

So closely following her directions the three children returned to *Cova da Iria* exactly one month later accompanied by several incredulous villagers. Once again at precisely noon, this time a small white light floated down from the sky hovering above the same tree. Right on time, the Lady appeared again to begin speaking to the children about events that were going to happen in their future. A short time later the Lady again departed, and as she did, all the villagers present heard a great sound (like that of a loud rocket)—as she instantly vanished high up into the sky.

News of the shining Lady's appearances rapidly spread throughout this staunchly Catholic community and bulging crowds soon gathered around the children as they attended subsequent visitations. For her next appearance one month later (and subsequent visitations thereafter), the mysterious Lady of Fatima conveyed a series of 'three' specific prophecies to the small children regarding future events here on Earth.

Upon receiving these three prophesies, the children reported what the lady had told them to the Catholic Church. The Church in turn released the following information regarding the first 'two' of these 'three' prophecies to the public. This information can be summarized as follows:

1) WW I would soon end (which it did one year later) and...
2) There would be an even more terrible war (WW II) that would break out during the reign of Pope Pius XI and would be 'heralded' by an unknown light in the nighttime sky.

So it was no surprise when this weird illumination of the sky actually happened on 25 January 1938, when the skies over the northern hemisphere suddenly came aglow with a spectacular crimson light looking much like *"a reflection of the fires of hell,"* as soon reported by the *New York Times* who had devoted nearly a full page reporting this strange celestial occurrence. And true to her word—WW II did break out in 1939 when Hitler invaded Poland—forever plunging Europe and the world (including the U.S.) into the heat of prolonged global conflict.

The Lady of Fatima added that another major war would be averted if Russia converted back to Christianity (it did in 1989) as the old Soviet Union collapsed under President Gorbachov's perestroika leadership and President Reagan's persistent mission—*"Mr. G. —tear down that wall."*

3) Strangely, the third Fatima prophecy given to the children by the heavenly Lady has, to this day, never been fully revealed to the world. And those who are familiar with this third prophecy loudly proclaim that it's simply too 'horrible' to be discussed and therefore—should become known as the 'third secret' of Fatima—kept a hush, hush subject.

It seems that in 1917 (after this third message was delivered to the church by the three children), it was not read, but instead sealed in an envelope with specific instructions from the Lady not to open it until the year 1960. That envelope was then entrusted to the care of the Vatican.

It's reported that upon opening this sealed 'third secret' prophecy in 1960, Pope John XXIII began to tremble with fear and is said to have almost fainted from the shear horror of what the message foretold. Even though the Lady of Fatima had given specific instructions for the 'third prophecy' to be opened and then revealed to the public at that time (back in 1960), Pope John resealed the envelope vowing that its apocalyptic message would never be released to the world.

What could be so 'horrible' / 'terrifying' about this' third secret' message given at Fatima? And why would Rome's Catholic Church attempt to suppress this important Christian information?

Exactly what this 'third secret' prophecy of Fatima contains is still open to hot debate, but it's largely agreed that part of it's message deals with the future demise of the Catholic Church that 'it' says will happen during an upcoming period of great planetary cataclysm and human travail.

Unfortunately, many of the key details of this important prophecy have not yet been 'officially' released to the public and the Church in Rome continues to desperately keep the specifics of this <u>last</u> and <u>final</u> message given to the children at Fatima—a closely guarded Vatican secret.

But because the Lady of Fatima had specifically instructed that this third prophecy be released to the public in 1960, and upon opening the message the Pope adamantly refused to deliver it to the world, conflict began to brew within the Church itself over following the Lady's instructions. Apparently, not agreeing with Pope John XXIII's difficult decision to conceal this 'third secret' prophecy, close Vatican insiders decided to 'leak' at least 'part of it' to the Italian press.

So on 15 October 1963, the newspaper, *Nues Europa,* printed what they claimed to be (at least) part of the third Fatima prophecy that they'd received from informants inside the Vatican who believed that message needed to be released. The leaked segment of the 'third' prophecy stated:

> *For the Church, too, (at the end-times), the time of its greatest trial will come. Cardinals will oppose cardinals and bishops against bishops. Satan will march in their midst and there will be great changes at Rome. What is rotten will fall, never to rise again. The church will be darkened and the world will shake with terror (as the poles shift). The time will come when no king, emperor, cardinal, or bishop will await Him who will, however, come, but in order to punish according to the designs of my Father.*

No wonder the exact content of the Lady's third prophecy is still being suppressed, hidden by a fearful Vatican even today—despite the heavenly Lady's instructions that it 'could' and 'should,' be fully revealed to the public in 1960.

Rampant speculation continued to swirl around the exact contents of this 'third secret' throughout the 1960s and 70s. Then in 1980, Pope John Paul II made a startling statement to a small group of Catholic parishioners who privately asked him why the 'third secret' had not yet been fully revealed by the church. The good Pope's philosophical comments where later printed in a German magazine called *Stimme des Glaubens.* Pope John Paul II's confusing and vague answer to the parishioners stated the following commentary:

> *It should be sufficient for all Christians to know this much: a message in which it is said that the oceans will flood entire sections of the Earth; that, from one moment to the other, millions of people will perish...there is no longer any point in really wanting to publish this secret message. Many want to know merely out of curiosity, or because of their taste for sensationalism, but they forget that 'to know' implies for them, a 'responsibility.' It is dangerous to want to satisfy one's curiosity only, if one is convinced that we can do nothing against the catastrophe that has been predicted.[3]*

This partial release of the third Fatima message is only the proverbial tip of the iceberg however. Vatican insider, Father Malachi Martin, furnished an even more revealing glimpse into the actual 'root cause' of this upcoming catastrophe contained within the third prophecy of Fatima.

Father Martin was a former Jesuit priest and a full professor at the Vatican's Pontifical Biblical Institute. He held doctorates in history, archeology, and Semitic languages. A brilliant scholar, he served in Rome (at the prestigious Vatican Observatory) from 1958 to 1964, where he was the associate of Cardinal Augustine Bea and none other than the Pontiff himself, who had opened the third prophecy of Fatima, Pope John XXIII.

Father Martin was privy to the entire third prophecy of Fatima (which was communicated to him directly by the Pope), and although he would not break his vow to keep secret the exact context of the 'third secret' prophecy, he did inadvertently release the main theme of the prophecy in a nationally syndicated radio interview with 'metaphysical space guru,' Art Bell on 5 April 1997.

Father Martin indicated that a large celestial object, possibly a comet, was approaching the Earth and its affects were going to be disastrous! The end result of this comet's passage was in fact, going to be worse than anything that could be imagined on Earth causing a global cataclysm on a scale unknown to modern-day humanity.

The object's passage would also lead to massive conflicts within the leadership of the Catholic Church and ultimately its absolute destruction. According to this interview, Father Martin mentioned this planetary cataclysm possibly taking place in the very near future—quite possibly within 10-12 years. *(Note: 1997 – 2009 = 12 years)*

Unfortunately, Father Martin died shortly after Art's show aired under very 'mysterious' circumstances and it's been suggested that he 'may have said a little too much' in his 1997 radio interview on the Art Bell show. This isn't the first time that a mysterious death has occurred over '*X.*'

Shortly after Father Martin's death, a close associate of his named, Kathleen Keating, released a bombshell book entitled: *Earth, The Final Warning.* Keating's book indicated a celestial event, possibly a passing comet, would soon usher in a period of great planetary destruction. People needed to heed this warning preparing themselves and their loved ones for this upcoming event.

As an interesting side note, the Vatican recently built several 'state-of-the-art' solar observatories around the world. Suspiciously, all the doors of these expensive/high-tech observatories are sealed to the public. And further, the Vatican subsequently refuses to discuss the real purpose of these observatories or what their telescopes are currently searching for. *Now why would the Vatican, a religious institution, be so interested in what's going on in outer space? And why would they need several exotic observatories strategically located at key points around the planet?*

Could these observatories all be busy gazing at the same incredible incoming celestial object—a brown dwarf star called 'Wormwood' as found in the New Testament's Book of Revelation?

And will the appearance of this massive and terrifying celestial visitor trigger a pole shift that will bring down the Vatican in a swift and sudden event long-predicted—but never publicly admitted to—by past Popes and the Catholic Church hierarchy currently running the Vatican?

It's important to note these Fatima prophecies weren't given to us just to invoke fear, but are a prophetic warning. Their true intention: to motivate us spiritually, mentally, physically and emotionally preparing ourselves, so we'll be able to face these upcoming *Earth Changes,* ultimately surviving them—then take part in the dawn of a new 'millennium chapter' that awaits our planet.

If we accept the reality of these heavenly visitations (whether one's Catholic or not), we must then evaluate the consequences of 'what' the Blessed Lady said to the three children and 'why'?

Veronica Lueken

In 1988, just as NASA and others were working overtime to conceal the discovery of the approaching brown dwarf, a gifted Catholic visionary named Veronica Lueken experienced an interesting series of visitations from the Blessed Virgin Mary in the town of Bayside, New York. Part of the Blessed Virgin's message to Veronica stated:

> *Look up and see what lies beyond your windows; a ball that is fast hurtling towards the earth (the brown dwarf)...For even the scientists have failed to recognize the speed of this ball.[4]*

Could NASA, through its clandestine observations, have underestimated the speed by which this celestial object is approaching? And could this object arrive much sooner than NASA originally calculated? Since NASA still knows very little about brown dwarfs and especially how they behave in the stellar regions of space, the idea that they've miscalculated its speed and possibly other critical details of its approach seems reasonable—*although strange considering?*

In another visitation the Blessed Virgin goes on to tell Veronica:

> *I repeat again, the earthquakes will increase in volume. California shall be struck. New York shall be struck. As I told you once before, there will be earthquakes in places that have never known a quake.*

> *It will startle them (the people of the Earth) and frighten them, but will they come to their knees? Few will, my child, because I can tell you this; they will not have the time to make amends; that is the sad part, my child.[5]*

We have already documented in the previous chapter of this book that earthquakes are rapidly on the rise as the mighty gravitational effects of the approaching brown dwarf places an ever-greater physical strain on our planet's crust. According to the Blessed Lady's words in the above paragraph we can expect this mounting earthquake trend to continue—especially years 2006 - 2012.

In addition to increased earthquakes, the above paragraph gives us another example of just how fast this object is traveling and how suddenly it will visually appear in our sky. For the Blessed Virgin states that these events will happen so fast—that *"they (the people of the world) will not have time to make amends."* When this event transpires it's going to be fast, furious and final!

The Blessed Virgin then shows Veronica an image of this approaching 'ball of fire' and how it will effect our Sun before triggering Earth's pole shift—which will involve great earthquakes. Veronica describes one of her visions stating:

> *I see a huge ball and the sun; it's a ball of fire. And this is another ball of fire (the brown dwarf). And a piece is now broken off, and it's hitting into the sun. And there—Oh! Oh!*

It's an explosion. Oh, I can't look. Oh! Everything seems so still and I see people now holding onto the chairs in their houses. Everything is rocking.[6]

This would seem to be a vivid description of *'Wormwood'* approaching the Earth and briefly appearing as a 'second' Sun in our sky. A piece of the brown dwarf (or a large piece of its fore-ward debris field) crashes into the Sun, triggering an enormous solar flare. As our planet's crust begins slipping around its molten core, the entire planet shudders as frightened people cling to any thing solid in their homes. Apparently, the entire planet is literally rocking!

The Blessed Virgin continues her message referring to the approaching brown dwarf as the *"Ball of Redemption."* She mentions its flammable (reddish) hydrocarbon tail and the great loss of life that will ensue upon this object's fiery passage.

She also mentions that scientists and ordinary men alike will have no explanation for this object's sudden appearance. Keep in mind that NASA has kept this upcoming event so secret that when it does takes place—most scientists and especially the general public will be in for one hell of a really big surprise!

The Blessed Virgin continued:

> *…Many will die, yes; this Earth will be cleansed with a baptism of fire! Many will die in the great flame of the Ball of Redemption. (Keep in mind that the brown dwarf's flammable hydrocarbon tail has set the Earth ablaze in the past).*
>
> *They (people) will be eating and drinking and marrying, and then comes the Ball. Their flesh shall burn and dry up and blow off their bones as though it never existed. All those who have defamed their bodies, the temples of the Holy Spirit within them, these bodies will burn.*
>
> *…Scientists will look with fright as will the ordinary man. Know, my child that no scientist will know an explanation for its appearance, the Ball of Redemption nears, and many will die in the great flame of the Ball of Redemption.*[7]

In concluding her message to Veronica, the Blessed Virgin says:

> *Now you are bargaining with the final count, my children. For as night will turn into day, and day will fall into darkness, that day will come when you will cry out for mercy, and it will be too late. The Ball of redemption shall take from your Earth three-quarters of mankind. Your country, America the beautiful, has not witnessed (such) a massive scale of destruction and death (as you will soon see).*[8]

This same alarmingly high casualty rate is unfortunately reflected within most other prophecies!

As we've seen demonstrated by the number of similar reference to these *Earth Changing* events cited throughout this book—the end conclusion becomes a constant—planet Earth will be facing several years of catastrophic events quite possibly ending in 2012 with a devastating polar shift.

Saint Hildegard of Bingen

Born in Bockelheim, Germany in 1098, Hildegard of Bingen was educated at the Benedictine Convent of Disenberg and eventually became its Mother Superior in 1136. She was renowned for being a prolific writer and composer and was very influential throughout Europe for her sharp mind and keen wit. She's best known today for her apocalyptic visions of the future carefully noted in her many convent writings.

She recorded these visions between 1141 and 1155 A.D., and subsequently placed then into a collection of writings entitled: *Scivias*, which is Latin for *"You will know."* Interestingly, her writings often mention a 'great nation' across the ocean, which is remarkable because this 'great nation,' presumably the U.S. —was unknown at the time of her writings in the 12ᵗʰ century.

According to the prophetic visions of St. Hildegard:

> *After the Great Comet (passes), a great nation across the ocean (the U. S.) will be devastated by earthquakes and storms with great waves of water. There will be want (starvation) and plagues; the ocean will flood the others (presumably other countries). The entire coast will live in fear; many will be destroyed.*[9]

St. Hidegard would seem to be in agreement with so many other prophets throughout history that have sacrificed so much in order to send us these dire warnings about our future. Make no mistake—this cosmic object is coming and it's going to power-shift our planet's poles!

In fact, so prevalent is this idea of an approaching celestial object within the field of prophecy, that many researchers over the past several hundred years have become quite convinced of the reality of this pending event—their research, books and many writings all saying the same thing.

A recent example can be seen in Rev. R. Gerald Culleton's book, *The Prophets and Our Times*.

In 1941 during the war, and after carefully studying all of the religious prophesies from the past, Rev. Culleton became absolutely convinced that a large celestial object was on its way towards Earth and was going to cause a significant amount of damage as it passes us. He subsequently wrote, *"The Comet by its tremendous pressure (gravitational pull) will force much (water) out of the oceans flooding many countries..."* [10]

Padre Pio

A Capuchin monk, who lived from 1887 to 1968, was one of the few priests in recent times to genuinely bare the stigmata of Christ's crucifixion (meaning that Father Pio would sympathetically bleed from his hands as if he, too, had been crucified by nails).

Born, Francesco Forgione, in the tiny village of Pietrelcina on 25 May 1887, he is said to have displayed unusual intuitive abilities as a child. At the young age of 15 he entered the Catholic monastery there and was thereafter known as Padre (father) Pio.

Over the course of several years, Father Pio received a series of prophetic warnings regarding the future while in deep prayer. According to the incredible visions of Father Pio, the heavens will become 'disturbed' and begin to drift as the brown dwarf passes our planet. A rain of flammable hydrocarbons will envelop the Earth (the hurricane of fire). The Earth's poles will then shift, causing massive earthquakes, extreme weather conditions and many volcanic eruptions that eject massive amounts of smoking ash and fire—all of which blacken the skis across the world.

Here are a few excerpts from these divine communications and they, too, reveal bad news:

> *Watch the sun and moon and the stars of the Heavens. When they appear to be unduly disturbed and restless, know that the day is not far away...Pray that these days will be shortened.*

> *The day of revenge is near—nearer than you can imagine! And the world is sleeping in false security! Keep your windows well covered. Do not look out. Light a blessed candle and pray. Do not go outside the house. Provide yourself with sufficient food. The powers of nature shall be moved and a rain of fire shall make people tremble with fear, Have courage! I am in the midst of you.*

> *Hurricanes of fire will pour forth from the clouds (the hydrocarbon tail) and spread over the entire earth. Storms, bad weather, thunderbolts, and earthquakes will cover the earth for two days. An uninterrupted rain of fire will take place (as the brown dwarf passes)!*

> *How unconcerned men are regarding these things. Which shall so soon come upon them, contrary to all expectations (that things are currently normal). How indifferent they are in preparing themselves for these unheard of events, through which they will have to pass so shortly!*

> *This catastrophe shall come upon the earth like a flash of lightning (suddenly). At which moment the light of the morning sun shall be replaced by black darkness! No one shall leave the house or look out a window from that moment on.*

> *There shall be great confusion because of this utter darkness in which the entire earth shall be enveloped, and many, many shall die from fear and despair.*[11]

Ultimately, the good Father's message is simple. Don't be complacent—become informed as to what is approaching the planet. Prepare yourself spiritually, physically, mentally and emotionally for when the dreaded events happen—then we take cover, pray, think clearly and ride it out.

Although this Italian monk's apocalyptic message has fueled controversy for many decades, the good padre obviously struck a sensitive nerve within the Catholic Church—because in July of 2002, the Pope bestowed the highest honor possible on Padre Pio by canonizing him—thereby making Pio a saint of the faith and Holy Church in Rome.

The newly canonized Saint Pio's visions not only resonated with the Catholic Church hierarchy (which should tell us something of the catastrophic events they obviously now believe are approaching), but with loving parishioners throughout the world. Today, Saint Pio's shrine in the village of San Giovanni Rotondo is visited by over eight million pilgrims every year and is second only to the shrine of Our Lady of Guadeloupe in Mexico, a cathedral in Mexico's Capital.

Then on 2 December 2003, a life-size bronze statue of Saint Pio located in the town of Branca-leone (in southern Italy), started weeping blood—leading many of his followers to believe that his apocalyptic visions of the future might now be closer at hand!

A similar dire warning about the future can also be found in the works of Marie-Julie Jahenny, the 19th century cleric who astounded parishioners with his prophetic insights. Father Jahenny stated:

> *The crisis will explode suddenly...No one outside a shelter will survive...red clouds like blood will move across the sky (the passing brown dwarf). The crash of thunder will shake the earth and sinister lighting will streak the heavens out of season (electrical discharges between the brown dwarf and Earth). The earth will be shaken to its foundations (pole shift). The sea will rise; its roaring waves will spread over the continent. The bodies of the wicked and the just will cover the ground. Three-quarters of the population of the globe will disappear. Half the population of France will be destroyed.[12]*

Once again, this crisis will explode 'suddenly' because the brown dwarf is very difficult to see until it's right upon us. The object's passage will trigger a momentous pole shift and Earth will be left with a massive casualty count and a century of clean up.

As we have already stated, all of these prophecies are given to us as a warning in order for us to be proactive taking steps to help our families and ourselves to survive what's approaching. The high casualty count doesn't have to happen. The coming events are survivable with a little foresight, preparation and courage. Stay informed, inform others, prepare, persevere and pray!

Brigham Young

In the 1800s, a religious man named Joseph Smith received a series of visitations from an angelic being. Joseph was told to copy the text of a series of copper plates and the Book of Mormon came into existence subsequently forming the Mormon religion headquartered in Salt Lake City.

This church is also known as the Church of the Latter Day Saints (emphasis on Latter-Day). Many people do not realize that this denomination of Christianity has a very apocalyptic message attached to it. One of the church's early leaders, Brigham Young, made a statement that reflects the severity of the upcoming *Earth Changing* events this religion is expecting, thus offering us an additional glimpse into what many others in the world also believe is headed our way.

From Brigham Young's Journal of Discourses we read:

> *You will hear of magnificent cities now idealized by people sinking into the earth entombing the inhabitants. The sea will heave beyond its bounds engulfing many*

countries. Famine will spread over the nation…The time will come that gold will hold no comparison in value to a bushel of wheat.[13]

The Mormons are expecting a massive planetary cataclysm in the very near future. This cataclysm will involve great changes to the topography of Earth and an ensuing global famine could ravage our American society. Today, the Mormon religion is well known for encouraging its followers to keep a one-year supply of food, water and living necessities on hand. Their religion also maintains canning and food storage co-ops for its members. Obviously Mr. Young had some divine insight as to what's expected in our collective future.

David Jevons

In the 1970s, a young man from Great Britain named David Jevons began to give a series of prophetic readings on a wide variety of subjects. These readings became known as the *Ramala Prophecies,* and have been translated into a number of best selling books that have astounded readers with the spiritual depth and insight of this intuitive's remarkable message.

In the late 1970s, a group of people asked Mr. Jevons what he thought of the predicted upcoming *Earth Changes*, to which Jevons replied:

> *I will begin by making a simple statement…It is a cosmic fact that all forms of life, no matter what the level of evolution, are born, die, and are born again, in an endless cycle of evolution. The earth has done this many times (in the past)….*
>
> *I believe that the major Earth Changes will be initiated by what I will call the "Fiery Messenger." There is even now a star of great power (the brown dwarf) proceeding towards our Solar Body (the Sun). The star, at this moment, is invisible to the human, or even telescopic eye, but is set on a path, which will bring it into conjunction with our Planetary System. As it passes by it will affect the motions of all the planets of our System, therefore, will bring about changes on the surface of the planets themselves. The effect of the passage will be to set in motion the Earth Changes that are prophesied (pole shifts). Various lands will sink; others will rise (all resulting from block faulting).*[14]

David Jevons was then asked, *"The star that was spoken of, has it passed through this Solar System before?"* And to which Mr. Jevons replied, *"Yes."* He was then asked, *"Is it Halley's Comet?"* To which Jevons responded, *"No. It is far Bigger than that."* [15]

The Grail Message

Shortly before the massive devastation inflicted by World War II, an important message was given to our planet, which has since been referred to as the *Grail Message*. Not a whole lot is known about the origin or the deeper implications of why this communication was offered—but its message is unmistakable. Once again the impact of what it says begs us to consider the future consequences if we ignore the warning signs contained in this prophetic warning that states:

> *For years now, 'knowing ones' have been speaking of the coming of this especially significant STAR...Its power sucks the waters up high (gravitational pull), brings weather catastrophes and still more. When encircled by its rays (gravity) the earth quakes.*
>
> *Since the event in Bethlehem (the birth of Christ) there has been nothing like it... Unerringly and unswervingly the COMET pursues its course, and will appear on the scene at the right hour, as already ordained thousands of years ago (when it last left our solar system but was destined to return in 3,600-4,000 years).*
>
> *It will take years to come to this point, and years before the COMET again releases the Earth from its influence.[16]*

Enter Edgar Cayce

Edgar Cayce, the 'Sleeping Prophet,' was born near Hopkinsville, Kentucky on 18 March 1877. As a child, he displayed unusual powers of intuition and often astounded his parents by telling them things that would happen long before they actually did. *Was this ability a gift or problem?*

At the age of 21, he developed a mysterious paralysis in his throat muscles losing his voice (a very common occurrence among people with prophetic abilities). A close friend suggested that Cayce be placed into a hypnotic sleep to see if this would help his stricken voice. He agreed, and once placed into this altered state of consciousness, Cayce received several telepathic suggestions from a spiritual source promising 'it' would help prevent him from losing his voice again. Upon following this spiritual advice—Edgar Cayce's voice was permanently restored to normal.

It wasn't long before Cayce reentered this altered 'state of consciousness' asking for spiritual guidance in order to help other people with their medical conditions. Edgar started receiving this spiritual guidance and soon found himself working with several local area doctors around the Hopkinsville and Bowling Green areas of Kentucky. His psychic medical insight was used to help these physicians diagnose their patient's medical conditions. Cayce's powers of intuition quickly astounded these physicians as Edgar was rapidly acquiring a large number of such medical success stories to his strange and prophetic diagnosing skills.

The medical doctors that Cayce worked with eventually submitted a formal report to the Clinical Research Society in Boston, Massachusetts. The member clinicians and researchers in this society were amazed by the results of Cayce's psychic medical abilities and word spread quickly in the medical community regarding his incredible diagnostic talents and success rates.

People suddenly began to contact Cayce from all over the world asking him for assistance with their more difficult medical problems. On 9 October 1910, *The New York Times* ran a feature story covering Cayce's remarkable abilities with two full pages of headlines and pictures. From that point on, he became known throughout the world as the great 'sleeping prophet,' all because he'd received his clairvoyant medical messages while in an unconscious 'sleeplike' state.

When Cayce came out of his 'sleeping trance,' he'd have no idea of what he'd said during the sessions while his wife (or secretary) wrote down his verbal communications as dictated to them.

Edger Cayce was a very devoted husband and father, a Sunday school teacher, a professional photographer and yet he's best remembered today for his incredible psychic insights. By the time Cayce died on 3 January 1945, giving over 14,000 psychic readings for more than 6,000 people worldwide—he'd become one of the most famous clairvoyants in American history.

Although most of Cayce's readings dealt with medical diagnosis and treatment, he occasionally mentioned other subjects—especially when asked a specific question during his trancelike states.

On 19 January 1934, while conducting a random reading for a client, Edgar Cayce suddenly made a statement sounding very similar to a New Testament biblical passage Luke wrote saying:

> *...As to the material changes that are to be as an omen, and as a sign to those that this is shortly to come to pass—as has been given of old, the sun will be darkened and the earth shall be broken up in divers places...[17]*

Startled by this 'enigmatic' and 'out of character' religious statement, Cayce was then asked to further clarify what he was referring to. He then replied with one of the most infamous prophecies ever made during his incredible life as Cayce went on:

> *As to the changes physical again: The earth will be broken up in the western portion of America. The greater portion of Japan must go into the sea. The upper portion of Europe will be changed as in the twinkling of an eye. Land will appear off the east coast of America. There will be the upheavals in the Arctic and in the Antarctic that will make for the eruption of volcanoes in the Torrid areas (the area between the Tropic of Cancer and the Tropic of Capricorn), <u>and there will be shifting then of the poles</u>—so that where there has been those (areas) of a frigid or the semitropical (these) will become the more tropical, and moss and fern will grow.[18]*

Cayce clearly seems to be forecasting a future time when the geographic poles of our planet will shift, triggering massive geologic changes and causing a drastic alteration in Earth's climate patterns. These are, of course, changes to which we are now quite familiar.

Although Cayce did not dwell on the subject of *Earth Changes*, he was asked to further elaborate on these upcoming cataclysms during a later session to which he replied:

> *The earth will be broken up in many places. The early portion will see a change in the physical aspects of the west coast of America. There will be open waters in the northern portions of Greenland. There will be new lands seen off the Caribbean Sea, and dry land will appear. There will be the falling away in India of much of the material suffering that has been brought on a troubled people...South America shall be shaken from the uppermost portion to the end, and in the Antarctic off of Tierra Del Fuego land, and a strait with rushing waters.[19]*

Once again, Edger Cayce talks about the great geologic upheavals that will take place as a result of the coming pole shift. His prophecy is logical and seems to clearly reflect the end results of 'block faulting,' pushing tectonic plates both <u>upwards</u> and <u>downwards</u> as the crust of the Earth slips over its fluid-like center.

In several later prophecies he also mentions a shifting of the poles, which cause extreme geological changes, adverse weather patterns and massive food shortages. And in other readings, Cayce encourages people to learn to 'live off the land' —to spiritually, physically, mentally, and philosophically prepare themselves for the hardships afflicting our planet in the near future.

The exact cause for the upcoming pole shift was only briefly addresses during Cayce's life. When asked what would cause the upcoming cataclysms, he said:

"...cosmic activity or influence of other planetary forces and stars..." [20]

This would certainly seem to indicate that Cayce's readings also point to a 'cosmic trigger' for the upcoming pole shift and that 'planetary forces' and 'stars' (brown dwarfs) will act as the ultimate cause for these approaching geologic catastrophes to occur.

Numerous researchers have studied Cayce's prophecies throughout the years and many books have been written about his life and important warnings to the world. What has impressed so many people about his prophetic foresight is that his readings make perfect geological sense. Cayce somehow knew about fault lines and geologic tendencies years before those facts were discovered by modern science. When one considers that Edgar Cayce only had a seventh grade education, his life's work becomes all the more incredible and important for us to understand.

Ramatis

Over 30 years ago, the famous Brazilian spiritualist, Ramatis, predicted an enormous 'celestial object' from deep space would pass our planet, in the near future. According to Ramatis, this object's powerful gravity would draw the Earth's axis into a different position (pole shift), which would produce a series of devastating geological effects on mother Earth. [21]

Native American Prophecy

Native American prophecy reflects a vast and rich cultural heritage that is as profound as it is ancient. Even though different Native American tribes saw the subject of prophecy somewhat differently, we now present an 'overview' or 'summary' of their impressive body of work.

The prophecies of Native Americans often talk of this important day of 'Great Purification,' which will eliminate the <u>old world</u> giving birth to the <u>new</u>. These *Earth Changing* events take place at the hands of a passing cosmic visitor that triggers a realignment of our planet's rotation and a series of subsequent geophysical upheavals across the globe.

The Native Americans believe that we are rapidly approaching this day of 'Great Purification' and when this event takes place, this current world will be no more than a memory. And the new world that emerges will be one of spiritual harmony, where people will live with the natural laws of nature and humanity—something our modern-day world has yet to accept or understand.

The Hopi

The Hopi are one of the Native American tribes residing in the Southwestern U.S, primarily in the 'Four Corners' area—where Utah, Colorado, Arizona and New Mexico all share a common boundary point. They are a peaceful, fun-loving people that have preserved their culture, history and prophecies for longer than the recorded history of the U.S. has been in existence.

In December of 1992, Hopi Nation elders personally appealed to a general assembly of the United Nations in an attempt to get the U.N. to take appropriate actions helping to prepare the world's populations for what's approaching. Part of the Hopi elder's address to the U.N. stated:

> *Today you see increasing floods, more damaging hurricanes, hail storms, climate changes and earthquakes as our prophesies said would come. Why do animals act like they know about the Earth's problems and most humans act like they know nothing? If we humans do not wake up to these warnings, the great 'day of purification' will come to destroy this world just as the previous worlds were destroyed.[22]*

According to the Hopi:

> *When the Blue Star Kacchina (the brown dwarf) makes its appearance in the heavens, the 'Fifth World' will emerge (and our current 'fourth world' will be destroyed).[23]*

Author, Tom Kay, comments on this prophecy of the Hopi in his book, *When The Comet Runs*, wherein Mr. Kay writes:

> *The Hopi Indians believe that we are living in the "fourth Age," an age they also believe is fast drawing to an end. Their ancient legends claim that, as Earth rotates around its axis, it is held in place by two enormous celestial angels, and that the destruction of the three previous ages were caused when these two angels abandoned their posts.*
>
> *They predict that <u>soon</u>, the angels will <u>again</u> abandon their posts, and that this will happen when a "blue star" that is fast approaching will enter our solar system.[24]*

Hopi prophecy clearly indicates that Earth will soon undergo the passage of the brown dwarf and this passage will trigger a shifting of our planet's poles.

Note: The Hopi Elders have recently released a public statement to the world warning people to prepare for this upcoming event. They advised everyone to have extra food and water on hand. According to the Hopi, people should also make peace with their friends, family, themselves and with the Great Spirit (God). These preparations should be made immediately before it's too late to do so—or before conditions on the planet become impossible for us to survive.

Mary Summer Rain

Once the brown dwarf passes and our planet's poles shift, great geophysical changes will take place on our world's surface. The prophecies of Mary Summer Rain, and her spiritual mentor and teacher, No-Eyes, give us a glimpse into the pure and total destruction that will happen upon the next celestial fly-by of *'Wormwood.'*

Mary Summer Rain is a Native American clairvoyant who has written several popular books entitled *Phoenix Rising, Spirit Song,* and *Dream Walker.* She's also been featured on the *NBC* television special, *Ancient Prophecies*, which reviewed some of her more recent visions concerning the upcoming pole shift, as well as thoughts of her mentor, No-Eyes. Together, they managed to create some of the most provocative/startling prophecies affecting us in the 21st century.

No-Eyes is a Shoshoni tribesman who was born without the use of his physical eyes; but what he lacked in normal eyesight, he more than made up for with his powerful extrasensory vision. Mary Summer Rain studied under No-Eyes for many years until she, herself, also developed this remarkable ability to see into the future.

In one of her visions, Mary Summer Rain clearly sees the upcoming pole shift caused by the brown dwarf's passage wherein Mary states:

> *...the Great Lakes were flooding down through the Mississippi River <u>as the earth tilted into its new axis position</u>...and the Mississippi River will stretch its present shorelines to an incredible new width to accommodate the in-rushing waters of the Great Lakes.*[25]

In her book *Spirit Song*, Mary gives a detailed description of a vision she received which conveys the widespread geologic damage and social chaos that will be present in the aftermath of the upcoming pole shift. Because of the Earth's displaced lithosphere, her vision shows the continents in a different orientation in relation to the planet's rotation. As she views the damage caused by the shift—she runs a commentary over the events she is witnessing. Mary states:

> *We surveyed the entire continent of North America. The familiar geographic shape was changing its format at a rapid rate (the result of block faulting). We watched the movements as though we were viewing it through a child's ever-changing kaleidoscope. Yet, this was no game. The earth was no toy. This was real. Everything had tilted down to the right (as a result of the pole shift). Alaska was now the tip of North America. Mexico wasn't south anymore, but rather west. New York was only partially visible.*

> *On closer inspection, we found that all of North America's east and west coasts were gone. Florida appeared to be ripped entirely off the continent. The major fault lines had cracked. The San Andreas (on the west coast) ripped through the land like some great mean giant tearing a piece of paper. The torn shred drifted out into the churning ocean.*

> *The waters of the world literally swished back in one huge movement, paused, and came surging back to seek a new level of balance (as the poles shifted). The great movement (of water) washed over hundreds of islands. Hawaii was gone completely. Borneo, Sumatra, Philippines, Japan, Cuba, United Kingdom—all vanished within a blink of an eye.*

> *We closed in on the United States. It wasn't as wide anymore due to the lessening of the coastal areas. The Mitten State, Michigan, was covered with angry rushing waters.*

Upper Michigan had been torn away with the force of Lake Superior's emergency exit. All the Great Lake waters were forging downwards, following the Mississippi River. Massive land areas on either side of the Mississippi River were flooded out of view. A great trench was being dug by the powerful force of the rushing waters. The land area below Michigan was drowned. Water was everywhere.

There was no land under an imaginary line from Houston to somewhere around Raleigh, North Carolina. Most of New York, Pennsylvania, and Ohio were under water. All of Michigan and Indiana were. The United States was now divided completely. The eastern portion was an island.

...When the time came for these changes, it would be a long time before the survivors were able to get a true and accurate picture of the extent of the damage. I looked far to my left and saw that all of the coastal lands west of the Sierra Nevada were gone.

A large portion of the Appalachian Range split and spread out. The Great Divide (the Rocky Mountains) appeared to be fairly untouched. Volcanoes spewed in much of the western section of the land...

The view of the earth (then) grew large as if we were watching it through a telescope lens. We descended directly above Omaha, Nebraska. I felt as if I was watching some horror movie conceived in the mind of evil. Horrible scenes were graphically played out in vivid detail. The city was in ruin. The tall buildings were left in their nakedness of iron skeletons. Concrete and glass lay scattered about in huge piles of rubble. People ran amok screaming in hysterics. Gore was everywhere. Crushed and mutilated bodies lay in agony over the dead. Fires burned like torches from the gas lines. Hot electrical wires lay sparking. It was total chaos.

We drifted out to the suburbs. The scenes here were less massive in destruction, but they were typical of the larger city. The low buildings were leveled and the ones still standing were being attacked by hoards of mindless people. They stormed in every store that had any kind of food. They trampled each other, caring little for the injuries they inflicted upon the humans underneath their feet. I couldn't believe that civilized mankind could so quickly be reduced to such animal instincts of survival. They were down to the basest of actions. They were shooting one another. They were in throngs; some just roaming about, some storming private homes in an effort to get whatever they could find. The owners were shooting into the crowds. They were desperately trying to defend their domain.

Animals ran wild. The zoo had been affected by the quake and cages were twisted, loosening wires and gates. The wild creatures were confused with their sudden freedom. Lions and cougars mauled screaming people. Elephants stampeded in herd, trying to remain together. Reptiles roamed the streets. I felt sick.[26]

It's remarkable that nearly each and every one of these prophecies bears the exact description of the physical damage to Earth that's expected should we suffer the anticipated shift in 2012.

The above description of Mary Summer Rain paints a horrible picture of the massive damage that will be inflicted on the world when the brown dwarf passes and our planet shifts on its axis of rotation. It will not be the end of the world—but for a period of time it will seem like it.

One of the most important aspects of Mary Summer Rain's description is that of the 'social breakdown' and chaos that will occur after the shift. There will be small groups of people that will cooperate and band together for their common good. These cooperative groups will have a much better chance of surviving these future *Earth Changes*.

But in general, society will deteriorate into total anarchy when the next flyby takes place! When grocery stores lay in ruins, roads are collapsed and basic services like water, electricity and gas supplies are completely shattered or eliminated—most people are going to 'freak out' big time, and unfortunately—we'll witness the worst side of human behavior on a larger than life scale.

Wormwood's next passage will usher in a rebirth, however, as a new way of life and a new paradigm emerges from the ashes of this battered world. A hint of this new social mentality/way of life is mentioned by Native American prophets such as Sun Bear, a special mentor to me whom I met in Landers, California, in 1979 at the site of the Integratron. I was visiting the widow of the late George W. VanTassel, one of the early pioneers of the 50s/60s UFO movement. We'd spent several days together at Giant Rock Airport, the site of numerous UFO desert gatherings.

(NOTE: The Integratron is located 175 miles NE of LA near the small Mojave Desert town of Landers. This machine is a non-metallic dome-shaped structure that stands 38 feet high measuring 158 feet in diameter. The dome itself is an electrostatic, magnetic generator with an armature four times larger than any other in existence. The dome does not contain any nails, bolts or other metal assembly, yet the dome is six times stronger than commercial building codes require and is held together much like a Chinese jig-puzzle. From early March to October 1983, I lived on the Integratron property site helping George's widow, Dorris to repair/recover from a devastating seasonal monsoon flood that consumed the area shortly after I arrived from South Miami, FL.

According to VanTassel, in 1947 he received specific instructions (to build the Integratron) from an ET visitor who landed one night wanting to talk with George sleeping out in the desert at Giant Rock—the largest free standing stone in the world covering 5,800 square feet and is seven stories high estimated to weigh 13,300 pounds. The exact purpose of building this Integratron machine was never fully understood. We'll be covering it in a new book presently under writing entitled, *The Reality Engineer*. (See B&W Giant Rock pictures/news article in Exhibits section.)

Sun Bear

Like many of the prophetic messages coming to us from around the world, Sun Bear told me that Native American prophecies foretell of a great 'golden age,' a period immediately following the upcoming pole shift which will be dictated by social harmony, cooperation and love by mankind.

Sun Bear was the medicine chief and founder of the *Bear Tribe Medicine Society* and one of the most influential Native American visionaries of this century. He lived between 1929 and 1992 and during his lifetime displayed amazing abilities of clairvoyance and spiritual wisdom.

I still have a special 'clay shard,' a gift given me by Sun Bear dealing with future Earth events. According to a dream Sun Bear once had, a 'new age' will begin shortly after the great shift and will begin a time of spiritual enlightenment and harmony on Earth because in Sun Bear's vision:

> *After the period of the cleansing, we'll be going into the 'fifth world.' The people moving into this world will be from all over the globe, but they will share the same level of consciousness, (but) found in their own individual ways.*

> *I've had dreams in which I'm at a place, and a small group of people comes over a hill. We all embrace and say, "Brother, Sister, you survived." In this world, there aren't any "isms." We don't ask, "Well, what church do you belong to?" or "What this or that do you belong to?" None of that really matters (any more).*

> *After the cleansing, we will see only people who know how to reach out and learn. We'll see people who are always seeking spiritual knowledge. People will know that their survival came about because they had made a good effort to live in love and harmony.*[27]

The prophecies of the Hopi, Mary Summer Rain and Sun Bear are but a small sample of the rich and insightful body of Native American Prophecies that have been given to the world. As a whole, these prophecies predict a horrifying 'celestial flyby' in the near future followed by a shifting of the Earth's poles. But as bad as this event will be, however, it will also usher in a new spiritual world that will be far superior to this old one—the one in which we currently live.

But how will this next world become so different from the ones before it? If mankind has been through these pole shifts repeatedly in the past, and each new rebuilt society is basically no better than the previous ones, how is this next world going to be any better than the civilizations before it? And what miraculous change is going to take place that will suddenly override the negative aspects of human nature to create a 'golden age' largely free from the normal problems that humankind has brought upon themselves over the millennia?

The answers lie in an enigmatic phenomenon that's been quietly affecting our world, a subtle/ mysterious 'cosmic interaction' that's been transpiring right under our noses. A recent 2005 Gallup Poll indicated that a whopping 89% of Americans believe in the actuality of UFOs/ ETs, that they also accept the fact of an imminent extraterrestrial landing taking place in the near future, and that our government's been conducting a TOP-SECRET UFO/ET cover-up since 1947.

As a 'bona-fide' UFO/ET researcher, I represented the U.S. at *The First World UFO Congress* in Tucson, AZ; the evidence presented there in 1991 was overwhelmingly in favor of the above.

Inside The UFO/ET Enigma 2007 through 2012

This is as good a place as any to discuss one of the most controversial subjects of our time— UFOs and extraterrestrial life visiting planet Earth. People have very strong opinions on this subject—both for and against. We'll not argue the merits of this subject here and we certainly can't investigate the extensive body of evidence supporting this mystical phenomenon within the limited framework of this book. All that we can do is simply mention these other worldly beings and note how they are 'apparently' connected to Earth's upcoming pole shift and the subsequent rebirth of a better society in its aftermath; and if true they'll fulfill the covenant made by them to come to our assistance at the time of the pole shift via mankind's worst nightmare from space.

The fact is that millions of credible people throughout the world have testified that they have experienced 'visitations' or 'abduction scenarios' with 'beings' that are not of this world. These people are not whackos, drug addicts, crackpots or schizoid personalities crackpots—but rather they're all professional doctors, police officers, airline pilots, corporate CEO's, Presidents, husbands/wives/kids—a vast cross-section of everyday Americans. Collectively, these individuals are known as 'contactees'/'abductees' coming from all walks of life and from all over the planet.

Enter James J. Hurtak, Ph.D.

NEW AGE/FALSE TEACHINGS!

One such noted extraterrestrial contactee is James J. Hurtak, Ph.D., the president and founder of *The Academy For Future Science* headquartered in Los Gatos, California. This Academy is a non-profit educational organization with special emphasis on language, cultural history and the advanced technologies involved in Third World Cultures, an international endeavor showing a basis of positive futures through popular acceptance of science and education in the 21st century.

J.J. Hurtak is a well-respected and noted social scientist, researcher, author, lecturer and a world-renowned authority on extraterrestrial intelligence. Dr. Hurtak and his wife, Desiree, travel the world devoting their time and energy to international problem solving on a masterful level. On several occasions, J.J. has addressed the United Nations lecturing/consulting/solving a number of critical issues in his field. Proudly—Dr. Jim and Desiree are both close friends and mentors, too.

Dr. Hurtak has also authored numerous books including *The Book Of Knowledge: The Keys of Enoch*, 612 pages of higher spiritual teachings given on seven levels of awareness designed to be read/visualized/accepted in preparation for the arrival of *The Brotherhood of Light (ETs)* to be delivered for the quickening of *The People Of Light. (See their Website: http://ref@affs.org)*

Now Entering The Keys of Enoch

In January of 1973, while teaching in southern California, Dr. Hurtak had a series of profound contacts with *'higher beings of light.'* The account is recorded in his book entitled, *The Book Of Knowledge: The Keys of Enoch* which was written on the basis of his mystical experiences with two 'angelic messengers,' or in modern-day metaphysical language, *'Whole Light Beings.'*

These messengers called Enoch and Metatron, took him into various 'higher dimensions' or 'levels of experience.' In ancient times, this was called a *'Merkabah experience.'* During his brief sojourn into the experience of 'higher universes,' Enoch encoded sixty-four Keys of Knowledge to Professor Hurtak—in order that all of this precise knowledge be retained in his memory for recording and publication. Much of this coded mystical information has already come to pass in terms of fulfilling 21st century prophecy.

One has a profound sense while reading *The Keys of Enoch* that it's a code book that requires, in addition to a good metaphysical/kabalistic background, a deep sense of humility and devotion to the existence of a 'Divine Plan' at work behind the material ordering of 'universal creation.'

Dr. Hurtak's experience can be described as '*A Cosmic Voyage through the Many Planes of Life*' underscoring a unified history/mixture of science and scripture. Although he was trained as a Social Scientist and a Specialist in Oriental studies of Tibet and China, the good Doctor was always interested in bigger questions: *What is the nature of the universe and scientific discovery? What truth does science hold in terms of the bigger picture of Life? How do religious claims to truth differ from scientific claims? The Keys* have come, in their own right, to be a great catalyst for propelling many modern thinkers to see a higher side to science and how we (as a planet) are taking a quantum jump forward.

It is important to mention that since *The Book Of Knowledge: The Keys of Enoch* was first published in 1973, many of its forecasts in the field based in science, anthropology and archaeology have now come true. Here are a few examples among those in Hurtak's book that have already been proven as credible by other Specialists and Scientists in his field:

Key 105 and *Key 108 (1973)* state that the direct connection between the star shafts of the Great Pyramid in Egypt and the three major stars in the belt of Orion as being one of the important places of evolutionary programming. This teaching was later made popular through Robert Bauval and Adrian Gilbert who proved this celestial relationship in 1992.

For example it says in *Key 108:11: During previous geomagnetic cycles the North star shaft of the Great Pyramid originally pointed towards the circumpolar star of Alpha Draconis and the south star shaft pointed towards the Taurus-Orion constellations.*

Key 105 (1973) also states that: '*tremendous solar flares*' will trigger '*cataclysmic imbalances*' with the Earth's geophysical condition. In 2004 and 2005 the greatest solar flares ever measured by NASA authorities were recorded. Many scientists argue these measurements are important for understanding and studying super-storms and other global catastrophic environmental changes taking place at this time.

Key 110 (1973) states the coming of an extraterrestrial intelligence known as Semjaze to Earth. In 1975 the Swiss farmer, "Billy" Meier and Col. Wendell Stevens (Retired US Air Force)—(he's another good friend), confirmed on film and in transcript reports (in a series of books) the reality of a Semjase intelligence that had landed in several mountainous regions of Switzerland.

What significance does this have for our future? The Keys are important because it also has two maps. One in *Key 215 (1973)* gives a description of twelve "earlier areas of human evolution" and most of these areas have shown signs that previous civilizations once existed in these places.

One demarcation given is at exactly 121 degrees, 27 minutes Longitude East, bisecting the island of Flores in Indonesia where a new branch of miniature human beings were found called *Homo floresiensis* in 2003. This finding was reported in the prestigious journal, *Nature,* in 2004. *Is it a strange coincidence or isn't that the exact location (or near it) for the 12/26/04--9.0 mega-quake and giant tsunami that tore through Indonesia killing hundreds of thousands in a heart beat?*

And these same text lines also offer the exact coordinates for the finding of ancient underwater monuments (temples and pyramid-type structures) off the coast of Yonaguni, China, and Taiwan.

In 1997 Prof. M. Kimura of Okinawa invited Hurtak to join him in the underwater exploration of the Japanese underwater temples that were later the subject of all major Japanese news agencies and the film documentary, *The Temple of Mu,* that was shown on Fox television (Australia) in 1999. And now, *Key 215* was also showing us that there have been previous cycles of human civilization that have been completely obliterated from the face of mother Earth.

Perhaps the most famous map in the book is found in *Key 105* entitled, *The Return of the Dove.* Dr. Hurtak believes that should a devastating pole shift event occur, there are still safe areas on the North American continent, which are outlined on this map. He considers the Midwest part of the heartland best suited for survival, although it's interesting to note there are certain cities like 'New Orleans' that he has placed completely 'outside' the (safety zone area) of the Dove's body.

The Keys of Enoch also contain an impressive list of scientific prophecies already fulfilled with many more to come. Although Hurtak does not mention that there will be changes due to collisions of other planetary bodies, he does see the need for our preparation. Most importantly for Dr. Hurtak is the need for mankind's spiritual preparation, since he believes that there are both *'higher angelic/celestial life forms,'* as well as *'extraterrestrial life forms'* who are aware of these future *Earth Changes,* and who are personally watching us to assist those who are truly asking for their helpful intervention—possibly an ET rapture-like scenario.

We read in *Key 309:23: At this time the biosatellites working with the Brotherhood of Light in the F8 to K2 spectral range are being prepared to deliver man from his own path of destruction and from the negative commands that are issuing from independent intelligences not serving the Office of the Christ as these future events unfold.*

Dr. Hurtak acknowledges that we all have to become consciously aware of what is taking place on the planet (what we've previously referred to as the 'bigger picture' out there), and to listen to that small voice within us that guides us to where we need to be—and what we need to accomplish—now in the moment. *THE KEYS TEACH: "GOD'S PLAN HAS NO END. IT IS LIFE IN THE HOUSE OF MANY MANSIONS."*

We sincerely thank Jim and Desiree Hurtak for their kind thoughts, words and service. We believe that the mystical messages contained in *The Keys* is 'must reading' for every serious researcher, metaphysician and reader interested in the future destiny of planet Earth.

Many times contactees/abductees have been shown images of great cataclysms striking Earth in the near future. These individuals have also been shown images of Earth tipping on its axis of rotation and yes, some have even been told that a brown dwarf star is approaching our planet. According to these ET's, as many as 75% of humanity may be eliminated by this next passage of the brown dwarf. This massive decrease in human population will mean that humans, (as a species), will be largely non-viable immediately following the pole shift—should one occur.

Aside from being shown images of impending global cataclysms, many of these contactees have also testified that 'some' ET groups have taken genetic material from them, and that these ET's then used this fertile material to developed a race of hybrid beings, <u>part human</u> and <u>part alien</u>.

For the most part, these contactees/abductees are treated very well while in contact with these other worldly beings. These pre-selected people are not harmed and these ETs seem to come from a civilization that's highly advanced spiritually, technically and socially. These ETs often communicate to their human contactees the still primitive nature of our planet's principal species (mankind), and how the universe is filled with intelligent life that one day (when Earth's populations evolve to a higher consciousness level), will be able to <u>openly</u> land/interact/talk with us.

So, here's the big question! *If all of these credible people have reported contact with ETs and these people have been shown images of an upcoming pole shift and the massive destruction and loss of life this shift is going to cause, what do you suppose the hybrids are for?*

If you said: <u>our planet's replacement population</u> you'd probably be right and you're not psychic!

It would seem from the available evidence that a race of aliens has been monitoring the 'cyclic' destructions of our planet for some time. They have largely, up until now, had a hands-off approach and have let nature and planetary evolution take its course here as in the past.

But now they've decided to take a more assertive role in the evolution of this planet. They will let the 'pole shift' happen and those people now listening to their warnings by taking appropriate action will largely survive. Immediately after the shift happens these ETs will land to help those individuals left standing when the dust clears. They will then repopulate Earth with these more advance hybrid species—thus ending the ignorant reign that humans have had here for so long.

This new 'golden age' becomes a reality because humans will not be solely responsible for creating it. Our species will not end/our bloodlines won't die/humans will exist in a 'minority' capacity as Earth essentially changes hands becoming a new home for a homo-hybrid species!

Present-day mankind can either accept their future or reject it! Enough said, so let's move on!

Nostradamus

SOMEWHAT INTERESTING BUT NOT A PROPHET OF GOD.

Few prophets through the ages have captured the imagination and interest of our world as that of Nostradamus. In fact, out of all the books ever published since 1555—only the works of Nostradamus and the Holy Bible have been in continuous print.

Born Michel De Notredame in Saint-Remy, France, in 1503, he's more popularly know by the Latinized version of his name, Nostradamus. He was born/cast into a family of Jewish descent that had been forcibly converted to Catholicism by the Catholic Church of its day.

During his lifetime, Nostradamus proved himself to be a gifted physician, mathematician and astrologer—but what he's best known for are his series of startling predictions about the future.

Nostradamus had to walk a very 'fine line' reality regarding his visions of the future, for if the Catholic Church found out about his prophetic powers, they would have likely prosecuted him for being a sorcerer, burning him at the stake. In the days of Nostradamus, charges of witchcraft were widespread and serious. It's been estimated that from the 11th to the 18th centuries that as many as nine million people were executed in Europe on charges of conspiring with the devil and practicing witchcraft. The Catholic Church of its time was fraught with various paranoia

In order to avoid being accused of such charges, Nostradamus concealed his prophecies in 942 rhyming verses call 'quatrains.' He then took these 942 'mini-poems' and arranged them into groups of 100, which are referred to as 'centuries.'

To further conceal his visions for the future Nostradamus used clever play-word applications by spelling certain words backwards and then using allegorical 'astrological' language to throw off any snooping Church officials from his scent as a writer of these allegorical 'centuries.'

An overall study of Nostradamus prophecies paints a truly fascinating and remarkable picture. Many scholars who have studied his work believe that over half of his predictions have already come true. He has been credited with predicting the deaths of popes and kings, including the exact dates of their demise and the strange circumstances in which they died. And he also prophesized the French Revolution, the rise of Napoleon, the rise of Hitler, the Second World War, the rise of Mussolini, the Kennedy assassination and dozens of other historic events.

He foretold of future technologies that were to come including fleets of ships that would travel underwater (submarines) and machines that would wage war in the clouds (airplanes). He foresaw the atomic bomb, the Persian Gulf War and to the dismay of many, the collapse of the Catholic Church during a period of planetary upheavals.

As fascinating as this gifted prophet's visions were, however, we are most interested in the prophesies of Nostradamus that have to do with the upcoming passage of the brown dwarf and the geologic changes that will take place in its wake.

Nostradamus saw great changes taking place on Earth around the time of the new millennium. As the 1900s gave way to the 2000s, this gifted clairvoyant indicated that a great 'king of terror' would appear in the skies reaping havoc throughout the land. This celestial object's appearance would trigger wars, famine, earthquakes, floods, and ultimately—a shifting of our planet's poles.

In Quatrain X-72 Nostradamus writes:

> *(Around the new millennia), seventh month, <u>from heaven will come a great King of Terror</u>: to bring back to life the great King of Angolmois. Before and after Mars to reign by good luck.*[28]

Although certainly open to broad interpretation, it's now widely believed that this great 'King of Terror' is none other than the incoming brown dwarf—'*Wormwood.*' And in the pandemonium caused by this object's approach, an individual that was presumed dead (possibly Saddam or Osama?) briefly reemerges back onto the public arena. As far as the timing of this event goes, it would seem as if the planet Mars is prominent right before the 'King of Terror' appears again in the sky and (it) may still be significantly visible immediately following the event.

Remembering back in time, it appears the ancients were obsessed with all 'things' astronomical!

In August of 2003, the planet Mars made its closest pass to Earth in 60,000 years and is conspicuously visible as the brightest object (other than the moon) in the nighttime sky. One could also say that Mars 'reigns' in the sky for all to see. *Did this close approach of Mars signal the opening of the time window for the brown dwarf's coming approach in 2007-2009?*

He continues the prophecy in quatrain II-41:

> *The great star will burn for seven days; the swarm will cause two suns to appear. The big mastiff will howl all night when the great pontiff will change country.*[29]

The brown dwarf (great star) will be visible in our sky for seven days. The 'swarm' of gas, dust and other debris will cause this object's 'complex' to appear as a blazing 'second sun' in our sky. As the brown dwarf approaches, animals will become very uneasy, the big mastiff (the Pope's dog) will howl all night, as the great pontiff (the Pope) flees Rome to a safer location in another country.

Quatrain II-43 states:

> *During the appearance of the bearded star the three great princes will be made enemies. Struck from the sky, peace, and earth quaking. Po, Tiber overflowing; serpent placed on the shore.*[30]

When the bearded star (the brown dwarf) suddenly appears, panic is going to break out all over the world. In this sudden confusion, conflicts can erupt almost instantly. War will break out between three great princes (most likely between Russia, China and the U.S.). Massive global earthquakes will quickly follow this sudden escalating conflict. The Po and Tiber Rivers will then overflow causing massive flooding throughout Europe and the Middle East. The last sentence involving a *"serpent placed on the shore"* may involve a nuclear weapon being used on a coastal country, possibly Israel or the U.S.—but it's exact meaning is unknown at this time.

In quatrain I-46, Nostradamus continues:

> *Very near Auch, Lectoure, and Mirande great fire will fall from the sky for three nights. A most stupendous and astonishing event will occur. Very soon afterwards the earth will tremble.*[31]

As we've already examined, the passing brown dwarf rains fire on the Earth due to its passing flammable tail composed primarily of methane. It is therefore logical that Nostradamus would see this 'rain of fire' lasting for three days/nights as the dwarf passes. He also mentions that soon after the 'rain of fire' arrives great 'earthquakes' will 'tremble' the Earth directly resulting from this object's powerful gravitational forces and the great stresses placed on the Earth's crust.

Nostradamus also sees the alteration in Earth's rotation and may have even seen the pole shift caused by the brown dwarf's passage. In a frightening prophecy from his writings entitled, *"Epistle to King Henry II of France,"* Nostradamus writes:

> *…A great movement of the globe will happen, and it will be such that one will think the gravity of the earth has lost its natural balance, and that it will be plunged into the abyss and perpetual blackness of space. There will be portents and signs in the spring, extreme changes, nations overthrown, and mighty earthquakes.[32]*

This passage would clearly indicate/suggest a strange 'movement' in the Earth's rotation causing it to momentarily spin out of control—making it seem as if 'gravity' had lost its natural balance.

In still other quatrains, Nostradamus goes on to describe how the 'great star' will rain blood, iron, and false dust on the Earth, all indicative of the red 'iron oxide' fallout from this passing object's fiery tail. He also predicts that this object's passage will cause great famine, plagues and warfare to envelop the Earth—resulting in a social 'breakdown' of what's left of society.

In her award-winning book, *The Man Who Saw Tomorrow*, Erika Cheetham summarizes some of Nostradamus eloquent 'quatrains' regarding this upcoming passage wherein she writes:

> *After great misery for mankind an even greater approaches (from space) when the great cycle of the centuries is renewed (thought to be around, or slightly after the year 2000). It will rain blood (iron oxide), milk (volcanic ash), war and disease (will envelop the land).*

> *In the sky will be seen a (ball of) fire, dragging a trail of sparks. <u>Mabus</u> (a word play on Saddam spelt backwards?) will then soon die and there will come a dreadful destruction of people and animals. Suddenly vengeance will be revealed, a hundred hands, thirst and hunger, when the Comet will pass.[33]*

As one studies the prophecies of Nostradamus, and especially his predictions regarding the approaching 'great star,' it becomes apparent that he is describing the same upcoming incident with this celestial object as so many other visionaries. His terminology may differ slightly, but his overall message is the same. *Can all of these prophets, with such similar visions of the future—be merely a coincidence? Or are these gifted clairvoyants witnessing the same event with their marvelous gifts of second sight?*

Mother Shipton   INTERESTING, BUT NOT A PROPHET OF GOD.

As was the case with Nostradamus in France, sixteenth century England was also a dangerous place to be a prophet, especially for women who would readily be accused of practicing witch-craft if any of their prophecies came true. It was from this perilous time for prophets and seers that the enigmatic and brave Mother Shipton foresaw the world that was to come.

Although we know very little about her life, it is believed she lived between the years 1488 and 1561. Born Ursula Sonthiel in Norfolk, England, she is said to have exhibited powerful psychic abilities from an early age. When she was 24, she married Toby Shipton and was thereafter known as Mother Shipton.

During her lifetime she foresaw a wide range of future events, many of which dealt with circumstances and technology that would not exist for hundreds of years after her death. Because her strange prophesies largely dealt with technological advancements that didn't exist in her day, her visions invoked both fear and fascination from people throughout Europe for many centuries to follow.

Needless to say, the authorities of her time were quite threatened by her future insights and while she was alive, she was warned to 'shut up' or face charges of witchcraft and subsequently be charged—then burned alive at the stake. It is believed that this is unfortunately what happened to her, but before she was executed she wrote her psychic visions into a series of *stanzas* or *rhymes* which where only discovered after her death.

The original copy of her prophecies is believed to have been found shortly after her demise, but was essentially ignored and then forgotten about. In fact, this original copy of her prophecies wasn't brought into public awareness until almost 80 years after her execution.

Although lost for five generations, in 1641 a small seven page booklet was finally published having the cumbersome title: *The Prophesies of Mother Shipton In the Reign of King Henry the Eighth, Foretelling the Death of Cardinal Wolsey, the Lord Percy and Others, and Also What Should Happen in Ensuing Times.* (Try saying that fast ten times in a row.)

This original book containing the prophecies of Mother Shipton soon captivated the people of Europe with its strange, seemingly magical forecast into the future and much was written about this enigmatic seer throughout the better part of two centuries. But just as the technology mentioned in her visions began to manifest throughout society, her popularity largely ran its course, and by the late 1880s—her work quietly fell out of the public's interest.

Fascination with her incredible abilities was renewed, however, when the well-respected magazine of Australia, *Nexus,* received a copy of her prophesies in February 1995. Nexus magazine ran an article discussing how they obtained this copy, saying:

> *This rare collection of Mother Shipton's prophecies was sent to us by a Nexus reader who told us that, thirty years ago, she painstakingly transcribed them and managed to smuggle them out of the Mitchell Library, in Sidney, Australia, (now the State Library of New South Wales).*

> *The originals were kept in a locked room, along with other volumes of prophetic writings deemed unsuitable for viewing by the general public.*

> *To our knowledge, this particular translation has never been made available to the public before appearing (here) in Nexus.*[34]

At first, Nexus magazine's editor, Duncan Roads, was suspicious of the prophetic treasure that had suddenly fallen into his lap, but after several interviews with the lady who copied this rare text and some further investigation of her story, the magazine staff became convinced of the legitimacy of her account.

Apparently, this lady had copied the prophecies from several scrolls that had been stored in two old jars for well over a hundred years. Why these prophetic manuscripts were locked away from public viewing and how they came to Australia in the first place still remains a mystery. Either way, the story of Mother Shipton that has emerged in recent years is as follows.

Apparently, convinced of her impending execution for being a witch, Mother Shipton wrote down her prophecies in *stanzas,* similar to the writing style of Nostradamus, and sealed them away from the prying eyes of her executioners. They would be found by an illiterate dairymaid and held in secret by her family for almost 100 years before being published in 1641. Within her writings, Shipton comments on how her works would be found and eventually published using a printing press (which did not exist in Mother Shipton's day), and then hopefully read by a more understanding and enlightened society that would be capable of appreciating and deriving some benefit from her insights and wisdom.

Mother Shipton's work starts out with:

I know I go, I know I'm Free
I know that this will come to be.
Secreted this, for this will be
Found by later dynasty.

A dairymaid, a bonny lass
Shall kick this tome as she does pass
And five generations she shall breed
Before one male child learns to read.

This is then held year by year
Till an iron monster trembling fear
Eats parchment, words and quill and ink
And mankind is given time to think

And only when this comes to be
Will mankind read this prophecy
But one man's sweet's another's bane
So I shall not have burned in vain
—Mother Shipton[35]

At the time these prophecies were first published in 1641, society had still not advanced enough to fully understand the full meaning of her insightful messages. Although the people reading her works in the 17th century were astonished that some of her prophecies accurately predicted the *Great Fire of London*, the *Civil War of England* and the *Great Plague of 1665*, most of her prophetic visions talked of strange vehicles and events that the people of that day simply could not possibly relate to, or fully comprehend. In the 1600s—her amazing prophecies were more of a 'novelty' or 'strange' curiosity—than her 'insightful glimpses' into the world's future.

Isn't it amazing how certain individuals through 'time' become so vitally important in the future!

It wasn't until the recent 'rediscovery' of her writings in Australia that we (the people of the 21st century)—have developed enough technology to understand what she was trying to tell us. It took hundreds of years for us to 'catch up' to her insight. She was simply way ahead of her time and the people of medieval England had no real concept of the unique ideas of which she wrote.

Her prophecies seem to be directed more towards our time to us in this day and age. Her visions simply contained much of the cultural development and progress that we now enjoy because her ultimate predictions apply to today's society. In other words, Mother Shipton mentions the example of an automobile when she writes: "*A carriage without horse will go,*" and her prophesies contain so many other examples of modern technology because it was not until this technology existed that the bulk of her prophecies were to be pertinent—thus becoming relevant.

Once modern industrial society had fully developed, Mother Shipton's prophecies all fall into place instantly. For example, she foresaw modern 'wireless' communications, hydroelectric power, municipal water systems, and/or steam boilers, when she says:

> *Around the world men's 'thoughts' will fly*
> *Quick as the twinkling of an eye.*
> *And water shall great wonders do*
> *How strange. And yet it shall come true.*[36]

She then describes what seem to be modern transportation tunnels, submarines and uniformed military or commercial pilots as she writes:

> *Through towering hills proud men shall ride*
> *No horse or ass move by his side.*
> *Beneath the water, men shall walk*
> *Shall ride, shall sleep, shall even talk*
> *And in the air men shall be seen*
> *In white and black and even green.*[37]

Some of her prophetic visions describe modern iron ships and what many believe to be the California gold rush:

> *In water, iron then shall float*
> *As easy as a wooden boat.*
> *Gold shall be seen in stream and stone*
> *In land that is yet unknown.*[38]

At the time of her writings in 1560—California was yet unknown.

She also describes modern agricultural harvesters, airplanes and today's machine-driven agricultural practices:

> *And roaring monsters with man atop*
> *Does seem to eat the verdant crop*

> *And men shall fly as birds do now*
> *And give away the horse and plough.*[39]

Mother Shipton even describes the woman's liberation movement (a phenomenon occurring in the later part of the 20th century), with the last two lines being open to interpretation:

> *For in those wondrous far-off days*
> *The women shall adopt a craze*
> *To dress like men, and trousers wear*
> *To cut off their locks of hair.*
> *They'll ride astride with brazen brow*
> *As witches do on broomsticks now.* [40]

She indicates that when modern humans have developed motion pictures, submarines and aircraft 'only then' will a great majority of mankind die.

> *When pictures look alive with movements free*
> *When ships like fishes swim beneath the sea*
> *When men like birds shall scour the sky*
> *Then half the world, deep drenched in blood shall die...*[41]

The above prophesies of Mother Shipton are truly impressive and clearly indicate that she was witnessing (as a prophetess) actual images of the times in which we now live. No wonder she was so misunderstood by the people of her own time when she further stated that mankind needed time to 'develop' or 'think' before they would be able to understand her messages and her warnings to the world.

Mother Shipton certainly had a clear image of the times in which we live, but what is even more astounding is what she has to say about <u>our</u> immediate future. This gifted clairvoyant from sixteenth century England actually foresaw our coming destruction at the hands of the approaching brown dwarf. Her prophesies were largely not for the people of her time, but instead have been sent down to us, with our submarines and airplanes as a dire warning—and a call to prepare!

The first message that she leaves us concerning the brown dwarf's passage is the approximate timing of the upcoming cataclysmic event when Shipton writes:

> *A fiery Dragon (Halley's comet) will cross the sky*
> <u>*Six times*</u> *before this earth shall die.*
> *Mankind will tremble and frightened be*
> *For the sixth (passage) heralds in this prophecy.*[42]

Based on the work of numerous scholars, it is strongly believed that the 'Fiery Dragon' Mother Shipton is referring to in this *stanza* is none other than Halley's comet. In sixteenth century England, comets were often depicted as dragons and it was just after the writing of her prophecies that the famed Halley's comet was named and made one of its historic passes.

Halley's comet passes our planet once every 76 years and it would seem as if Mother Shipton used this comet's periodic passage as a sort of 'cosmic clock' in order to warn us of the time frame of her ensuing predictions.

Counting forward from the time period in which her prophecies were written, Halley's comet passed our planet in the years 1607, 1682, 1759, 1835, 1910 and 1986. This means that 1986 marked the 'sixth' passage of this 'Fiery Dragon' and the start of the 76-year window that Mother Shipton's cataclysmic prophecies are believed to take place in. According to Mother Shipton's cosmic clock, the brown dwarf will pass our planet sometime between 1986 and 2062.

Although a 72-year window may not seem to be a great help, keep in mind that the total or entire prophecy of Mother Shipton (regarding the 'Fiery Dragon—"Wormwood') actually spans a number of years, from the time of the objects passage, to the years immediately after the pole shift. Therefore the object's passage is likely to be much closer to 1986 than 2062 (we believe between 2009-2012). She also states this prophecy would be unleashed once the 'sixth' flyby of Halley's comet takes place, she did not say just before the seventh passage in 2062. Her prophecy for the passage states as follows:

> *For seven days and seven nights*
> *Man will watch this awesome sight.*
> *(The passage of the Brown Dwarf)*
>
> *The tides will rise beyond their ken*
> *To bite away the shores, and then*
> *The mountains will begin to roar*
> *And earthquakes split the plain and shore.*[43]

As we have already examined, the brown dwarf's passage creates tremendous gravitational effects on the Earth, rising global oceanic tides to unprecedented levels and triggering massive earthquakes and volcanic eruption changes in our planet's surface topography.

Mother Shipton's prophecy then continues describing a fleeing/panicked/frightened public with their 'social/political/religious breakdown' of spirit that transpires. This society then crumbles with humans killing each other in their hysterical effort to secure the now dwindling resources that accompany this truly world changing event. And she continues:

> *And flooding waters, rushing in*
> *Will flood the lands with such a din*
> *That mankind cowers in muddy fen*
> *And snarls about his fellow men*
>
> *Man flees in terror from the floods*
> *And kills, and rapes and lies in blood*
> *And spilling blood by mankind's hand*
> *Will stain and bitter many lands.*

He bares his teeth and fights and kills
And secrets food in secret hills
And ugly in his fear, he lies
To kill marauders, thieves and spies.[44]

As we've already mentioned, this object's passage will not spell the end of the world, just a major change in life as we know it. The brown dwarf's passage will cause massive geologic and sociologic upheavals however, and in the immediate aftermath of these events—humans will display both selfless sacrifices and unbridled cruelty. But the human race will go on (at least for a while) and one way or another, society will be rebuilt upon the ashes of the old.

Mother Shipton next addresses life on Earth once this social and geologic chaos dies down:

Who survives (unreadable text) and then
Begin the human race again.
But not on land already there
But on ocean beds, stark, dry and bare.[45]

As previously examined, clairvoyants such as Edger Cayce and others mention not only the 'sinking' of current landmasses into the sea, but also the 'rising' up of the land that is presently underwater. As we know, this phenomenon takes place through the process of 'block faulting,' as some plates are pushed <u>upwards</u> above sea level and others are thrust <u>downwards</u> below sea level. This new 'dry land' mass that is thrust upwards from the ocean floor will be free of the rotting refuse of the old world and will provide great benefits to the rebuilding of a new society.

And Mother Shipton also talks about the benefits for humans of this newly 'raised' land, the lasting fear that this object provokes on the survivors, and how easily (we as a species) forget about the periodic passage of this dreaded celestial object.

Not every soul on Earth will die
As the Dragon's tail goes sweeping by.
Not every land on earth will sink
But these will wallow in stench and stink
Of rotting bodies of beast and man
Of vegetation crisped on land.

But the land that rises from the sea
Will be dry and clean and soft and free
Of mankind's dirt and therefore be
The source of man's new dynasty.

And those that live will ever fear
The Dragon's tail for many years
<u>But time erases memory</u>
You think it strange. But it will be.[46]

Mother Shipton again mentions the cyclical return of this mysterious object and mankind's continuing forgetfulness when she writes:

> *And when the Dragon's tail is gone*
> *Man forgets, and smiles, and carries on*
> *To apply himself too late, too late*
> *For mankind has earned deserved fate.*
> *(Because of his forgetfulness)*
>
> *His masked smile, his fate grandeur*
> *Will serve the Gods their anger stir.*
> *And they send the Dragon back*
> *To light the sky—his tail will crack*
> *Upon the planet and rend the earth*
> *And man shall flee, king, lord, and serf.*[47]

As startling/shocking as these prophecies about the dwarf's coming passage are, Mother Shipton sent us even more remarkable insights about Earth's future. We've already mentioned the impact significance of our growing modern-day UFO/ET enigma and how a careful study of this phenomenon reveals the reality of alien contacts. But Shipton also covers the metaphysical/arcane roles these beings play in planning for our race's new future (by introducing their homo-hybrids into society after the pole shift event.) And the good Mother Shipton has something to say about this incredibly complex issue too:

> *And before the race (humans) has built anew*
> *A silver serpent (space craft) comes to view*
> *And spew out men of like unknown (hybrids)*
> *To mingle with the earth now grown*
>
> *Cold from its heat, and these men can*
> *Enlighten the minds of future man*
> *To intermingle and show them how*
> *To live and love and thus endow*
>
> *The children with the second sight.*
> *A natural thing so that they might*
> *Grow graceful, humble, and when they do*
> *The 'Golden Age' will start anew.*[48]

It's obvious from our current <u>action/reaction</u> global behavior patterns (re: the subject of UFOs/ ETs), and the historical track record that we (the human race) display—being completely 'out of touch/truth' with what's repeatedly happening to our world. *Will Earth enter into a new 'golden age' because we'll be delivered by an alien civilization? Will warfare, disease, ignorance and social strife disappear (after the shift) because the alien/human hybrids won't allow the prevailing insanity on this planet to continue unchecked? Will Homo sapiens be phased out, eventually replaced in favor of Homo hybrids—just like early humanoids replaced the Neanderthals?*

In closing our lengthy discussion of Mother Shipton's prophecies, she sends us a final warning, part of which is written on her tomb stone at her grave site in the town of Knaresborough, not far from Essex, England: The final message on her headstone reads:

> *Here lies she who never ly'd,*
> *Whose skill often has been tried,*
> *Her prophecies shall still survive*
> *And even keep her name alive.*[49]
>
> *The Dragon's tail is but a sign,*
> *For mankind's fall and man's decline.*
> *And before this prophecy is done,*
> *I shall be burned at the stake, at one,*
>
> *My body singed and my soul set free*
> *You think I utter blasphemy,*
> *You're wrong; these things have come to me,*
> *The prophecy will come to be.*[50]

The universal time line

Ask any person who's had a prophetic vision about 'when' the events they've just witnessed are going to actually take place and they will likely pause pondering the question. Clairvoyants often say that 'timelines' are the most difficult aspect of their visions in which to gauge these events. Often prophets can clearly see the events in question taking place, but only have a general idea or 'feeling' about when—not if— these events will occur.

This difficulty in determining the exact timeframe of a prophetic vision's actual manifestation is likely due to the fact that psychic perception seems to take place outside of the normal confines of time and space. Psychics can clearly perceive these events happening, but correlating these visions within our perception of real-time can challenge even the most gifted visionary.

Despite the timeline challenge, most prophets have placed the upcoming passage of the brown dwarf (and the resulting pole shift) in our current timeframe or loosely around the turn of the millennia (when the Piscean Age shifts into the Age of Aquarius). *But can we be more specific as to the timing of this event? If we're to prepare ourselves for these upcoming events is it possible to know the exact point in time when they will transpire?* The answer is—MAYBE!

According to his compelling book, *When the Comet Runs*, Tom Kay believes:

> *Many sources discuss the "comet/star," and almost every single one claims that the phenomenon is a recurring event. The only difference seems to be in the interval of time (between passages); however the majority are in the 3,000 to 4,000 year time frame, which could place its most recent (last) appearance during the time of the Exodus as described in the Old Testament, and Noah before that.*[51]

The fact that the last passage of the brown dwarf may have played a part in the Exodus drama of the Jewish people from Egypt is not a new or improbable idea. This connection has been repeatedly made and talked about by many authors such as Yves Dupont. In the book, *Catholic Prophecy, The Coming Chastisement*, Yves Dupont states:

> *Let us recall briefly the situation which afflicted the Egyptians, the crossing dry-shod of the Red Sea and the prolonged duration of the day. In Mexico, on the other hand, a prolonged night was recorded as evidenced by archaeological discoveries. The passage of the Comet (brown dwarf) at that time was recorded, not only in the Book of Exodus, but also in other documents: the Egyptian papyrus, a Mexican manuscript, a Finnish narration, and, many others....*

> *Will the comet to come be the same as that of Exodus? It is not impossible when we consider the description of the plagues as given in Exodus and those described in our Christian prophecies.*

> *When the tail of the Exodus comet crossed the path of the earth, a red dust (iron oxide), impalpable, like fine flour, began to fall. It was too fine to be seen...but it colored everything red and the water of the Egyptians was changed into blood...After the fine rusty pigment fell over Egypt, there followed a coarser dust "like ash," this is recorded in Exodus, for then it was visible...*

> *The narrative of the Book of Exodus confirms this and is in turn corroborated by various documents found in Mexico, Finland, Siberia, and India. It is therefore certain that a comet crossed the path of the earth more than 3000 years ago, causing widespread destruction.*

> *This is the kind of phenomenon (if the prophecies are accurate), which is soon to strike the earth again.*[52]

Modern-day Biblical archeologists have continued to study the records of Exodus and have subsequently zeroed in on an exact time frame for this event. Many scholars today believe the exodus of the Jewish people form Egypt took place approximately 3600 years ago.

As previously mentioned in this book, the ancient Sumerians believed Nibiru, *(The Planet of The Crossing)*, made its passage through our solar system every 3600 years. If the Biblical account of Exodus actually took place approximately 3600 years ago (as many Biblical scholars now believe), and if the ancient Sumerians were correct in recording that '*Nibiru*' has a 3600-year orbital period—we had all better buckle down into our seat belts! Fact is by all accounts at hand, we're now getting very close to the brown dwarf's next passage and we're all in for one hell of a roller coaster ride! *But when—exactly—will 'Wormwood's' make its next passage?*

The Maya, who followed Earth's great 'cycles of destruction' with almost fanatic fervency, seem to have indicated that the pole shift would happen on 24 December 2012, but this 'may' or 'may not' be the case—as some Mayan scholars have disputed this date, claiming that the actual event will happen either <u>right before</u> or <u>right after</u> the 2012 date.

In any event—2012 appears to be the right date we should be addressing in this dilemma!

In his book, *Comet of Nostradamus*, author R. W. Welch interprets Nostradamus' astrological 'hint' or his time 'clue' in trying to determine what the most 'likely' date for the terrible comet's passage is—he thinks August of 2004. Again, this date was based on certain astrological hints, which 'may' or 'may not' have been correctly deciphered. In other words, Nostradamus' exact timeframe is open to some logical debate.

Other prophets like Edger Cayce have simply stated that the 1980s and 1990s would be a time of increasingly geologic change (which it's been) and these increasing *Earth Changes* would eventually culminate in a pole shift some time soon after the year 2000. Obviously this date proved incorrect; nothing major happened! So once again this only offers us a vague window of opportunity in which to look for this pole shift event to occur.

Mother Shipton indicated that the brown dwarf would pass our planet within a 72-year window sometime after 1986. On the other hand—Father Malachi Martin also mentions its passage 10-12 years of 1997, which would place this event sometime <u>before</u> or <u>at</u> the year 2009.

The visions of these prophets can be so similar in their specific details but differ so greatly in the timing of these foreseen events due to the distorting nature of cosmic time, thus being able to clearly see the events, but only sensing a general time frame for their physical manifestation.

To compound this problem of pinning down an exact date for the brown dwarf's next passage, the timing of the object's cycle may itself vary. Today, modern astronomers know that certain cyclical comets can vary in the timing of their orbits. These variations can sometimes involve hundreds of years or possibly even longer in certain cases. The brown dwarf star that passes through our solar system (acting like a large periodic comet) may vary in the timing of its passage based on cosmic factors we know nothing about. The timings of its passage could deviate by days, weeks, years, decades, or even hundreds of years based upon different passages and upon certain unknown criteria.

Therefore, the best that we can hope for is only a general idea of when to expect this object's next passage and the resulting pole shift. This may not be what we'd like to hear, but it's the reality of our current situation. Even the government's top astronomers (whom we believe are studying this incoming object in secret along with the Vatican), may not fully understand its speed, trajectory or other important celestial factors—and therefore themselves—may only have a general idea of when this object will again pass us in space.

Conclusion

No single prophet, regardless of how gifted they may be, has a monopoly on the whole story of what is to come. Each prophet is simply given a 'glimpse' into the future so we must listen to all their prophetic messages if we're going to fully grasp the magnitude of what's approaching us. Each prophet provides us a <u>small piece</u> of the <u>giant puzzle</u> and we must patiently/persistently assemble these <u>smaller pieces</u> in order to see the <u>whole picture</u>. In placing all of the prophecies that we have examined side-by-side—a clearer picture of what's to come slowly emerges.

A large celestial object that looks like a comet (but acts more like a star) will suddenly appear in the sky. '*X*' will be visible for only seven days before it releases its unholy destruction upon the Earth. A rain of fire (methane) and blood (iron oxide) will then envelop the globe.

As the brown dwarf passes Earth, its enormous gravity field causes earthquakes, violent weather, volcanoes and floods that crescendo in a shifting of the Earth's axis-of-rotation. This pole shift then causes even greater and more extreme earthquakes, volcanoes, violent weather and flooding. The shifting of the poles subsequently causes Earth's tectonic plates to buckle, pushing some continental plates above sea level and others below it.

As Earth's lithospheric displacements begin, enormous quantities of seawater will spill out of their oceanic basins inundating the land sending massive (tsunamis) walls of water far inland.

But the messages of 'doom' put forth by most prophets is also tempered with an array of healthy redemptive 'hope.' For out of the ashes of the post 'pole shift' world—our traumatized planet will be rebuilt with a renewed 1,000-year-long 'golden age' of peace, prosperity, and enlightenment that will eventually rule throughout the land.

This new spiritual 'golden age' may not however, be the result of only our own (the human race's) doing. It would seem as if our species has been given its 'big' chance on this planet, and now—following '*X's*' devastating passage and our collective global mismanagement behavior—a far more advanced homo-hybrid race is going to 'beam in' as 'Star Trek's Scotty' would say—to help us clean up our mess here.

We may have a new species living next door to us, side by side as our neighbors—homo-hybrids—half man/half alien—as once again mankind starts his culture over as 'children.'

Remembering Mother Shipton's final message…*"What a strange world it shall come to be, you think not, but you will see!"*

The entire topic of 'prophecy' has always been a controversial subject, not only in the earlier centuries of mankind's evolution—but even now in the 21st century.

When speaking of prophecies in general, most people immediately think of the Bible. According to Cyrus H. Gordon a noted scholar: *PHAHF iht,* is an ancient word taken from the Greek, where it means *one who proclaims*. The Biblical prophets spoke out most about the evils of their own time. But Biblical prophecy also described what would happen if people did or did not do certain things, and what the prophets hoped for in their people's futures. The great age of Hebrew prophecy began in the 700's B.C., with the so-called "writing" prophets, Amos, Micah, Hosea, and Isaiah. Hebrew prophecy is distinctive in its lofty poetry and its plea for social justice. [53]

Modern-day prophecies take many forms and formats—but the overriding message is still the same especially when it comes to the subject of *Planet-X*: once again these prophecies describe *'what will happen if people did or did not do certain things, and what the prophets hoped for in their people's futures.'* The old adage that states—*"the handwriting's on the wall"* is probably right on the money and begs the eternal question of the age—*is anybody out there listening?*

CHAPTER SIX ENDNOTES

[1] www.themystic.com/mystical/articles/e/esp.extrasensory.perception.html

[2] Smith, Paul H., Excerpts from: *Reading The Enemy's Mind* (Reader's Digest, March 2006), p 175-176

[3] http://www.whatdoesitmean.com

[4] Keating, Kathleen, *The Final Warning* (Picasso Publishing, 2000), p. 4.

[5] Ibid., pp. 112-113.

[6] Ibid., p. 38.

[7] Ibid., p. 120.

[8] Ibid., p. 122.

[9] Hefley, Lee, *Prophecies of the Ages* (Goodman Media Group, 1999), p. 23.

[10] Cullerton, Gerald, R., *The Prophets and Our Times* (Media Publishing, 2005), p. 127.

[11] Ibid., pp. 26-27.

[12] Ibid., p. 26.

[13] Kay, Tom, *When The Comet Runs* (Hampton Roads Publishing, 1997), p. 78.

[14] Ibid., pp. 25-27.

[15] Ibid., pp. 29-30.

[16] Ibid., pp. 33-34.

[17] Auken, John Van, *The End Times* (Signet Books, 2001), p. 76.

[18] Ibid., p. 78.

[19] Ibid., p. 82.

[20] Kay, Tom, *When The Comet Runs* (Hampton Roads Publishing, 1997), p. 48.

[21] Ibid., p. 35.

[22] http://www.samsara2003.com/

[23] Kay, Tom, *When The Comet Runs* (Hampton Roads Publishing, 1997), p. 42.

[24] Ibid., p. 38.

[25] Ibid., p. 61.

[26] Ibid., pp. 76-78.

[27] Ibid., p. 219.

[28] Welch, R.W., *Comet of Nostradamus* (Llewellyn Publications, 2000), p. 2.

[29] Ibid., p. 5.

[30] Ibid., p. 5.

[31] Ibid., p. 3.

[32] Kay, Tom, *When The Comet Runs* (Hampton Roads Publishing, 1997), pp. 38-39.

[33] Ibid., p. 33.

[34] Ibid., p. 133.

[35] Ibid., p. 134.

[36] Ibid., p. 135.

[37] Ibid., p. 135.

[38] Ibid., p. 135.

[39] Ibid., p. 137.

[40] Ibid., p. 137.

[41] Ibid., p. 137.

[42] Ibid., p. 138.

[43] Ibid., p. 144.

[44] Ibid., p. 144.

[45] Ibid., p. 155.

[46] Ibid., p. 146.

[47] Ibid., p. 142.

[48] Ibid., p. 147.

[49] Ibid., p. 137.

[50] Ibid., p. 154.

[51] Ibid., pp. 36-37.

[52] Gordon, Cyrus, H., *The World Book Encyclopedia, (Prophecy)*, p. 729.

— CHAPTER SEVEN —

ORDER OUT OF CHAOS

For many thousands of years our ancient ancestors recorded and preserved historical accounts of a terrible comet that periodically passes our planet, triggering unparalleled geologic upheavals with its tremendous gravitational force.

By the 1600s even modern-day scientists began to realize that episodes of great global cataclysms are clearly preserved in the geologic record of Earth. These same scientists also started to recognize that a periodic cosmic visitor, possibly a large comet, was the responsible culprit for these repeated planetary catastrophes.

By the late 1880s, modern astronomers started looking for this destructive 'extra solar' object and began to mathematically calculate its location based on the effects that its enormous gravitational attraction was having on the outer planets of our solar system.

Then by the late 1970s, the U. S. Government realized the serious situation that our planet was in and assigned a host of scientific and military agencies to help locate and track this mysterious celestial object which was lurking somewhere beyond the boundaries of the known solar system.

In the late 1970s and early 1980s, these space agencies started searching for this object using powerful light-gathering telescopes, but as we know, these proved unsuccessful because this sought after object emits almost no visible light.

It wasn't until 1983 that the U.S. Naval Observatory using orbiting high-tech infrared telescopes discovered what they were looking for—a brown dwarf star approaching our solar system. In reality, it took until 1984 before these same astronomers could be absolutely sure of what they had theoretically discovered in space.

Of course at the time of this discovery, astronomers had never seen a brown dwarf star before, so when this one was eventually located, scientists had no idea of what this object was, how to categorize it—or even what to call it.

Arbitrarily, they referred to this newfound space object as *Planet-X* because of its enormous 'planetary' size. This object however, was not behaving like a normal planet and astronomers soon realized that this object's orbit was more like that of a periodic comet—traveling in a highly elliptical path around our Sun.

After this initial discovery was heralded in a multitude of articles appearing in such reputable publications as *The Washington Post* and the *New York Times*, the lid of national secrecy was quickly placed over this discovery and the release of any further information regarding this enigmatic object was tightly restricted.

Apparently the exuberance of this discovery rapidly wore off as the implications for future global disasters sobered the government's initial mood of elation. In other words, once this object was discovered, it didn't take long for the U.S. Government (and many others) to put 'two and two' together realizing the potential destruction this approaching object could eventually cause Earth.

But now that the U.S. Government knew of this approaching object and the potential for a future planetary catastrophe, there were some difficult questions that needed to be answered! *Namely, how much damage is this passing object going to cause and what is the government going to do about this impending situation?*

The answers to those questions are not simple ones and at this time we must clarify an important point. Up until this chapter we've treated the dwarf's passage in a very 'black and white' manner. Simply stating that the brown dwarf's visit is severe enough to cause pole shifts to occur. But the truth is—the brown dwarf doesn't <u>always produce</u> enormous damage on Earth every time it passes through our solar system.

As we know, our solar system is mostly empty space and there is plenty of room between the planets for the passage of this brown dwarf star. The Earth is also orbiting around the Sun and is therefore in a somewhat different position in relation to the brown dwarf's passage on each subsequent fly-by event.

In other words, if the timing of this object's passage is just right, and it happens to pass 'directly' between the Earth and Sun (as the Earth orbits around it) the gravitational effects of the dwarf are extreme enough to cause lithosphereic displacement of the Earth's crust to occur, causing what is commonly referred to as a pole shift. These pole shifts have, of course, happened hundreds of times in the past but they <u>do not</u> take place <u>every time</u> the brown dwarf passes through our solar system.

In reality, pole shifts may take place only 20% of the time this object passes through our solar system. What is far more likely to occur (about 60% of the time) is that the brown dwarf passes just in front of, or behind our planet as it orbits around the Sun. In this case the dwarf's gravitational effects are greatly reduced—and even though problematic—are far less damaging than a partial or complete geologic pole shift.

If however the dwarf passes through our inner solar system when the Earth is on the opposite side of the Sun (about 20% of the time) there would likely be no geologic damage at all! In fact, if the timing of this object's passage was just right—we might not even realize the passage had taken place at all.

If pole shifts (slippages of the Earth's crust) take place only 20% of the time, and the brown dwarf's orbital period is approximately every 3,600 - 4,000 years, then pole shifts may only take place on average once every 20,000 years. Also keep in mind that pole shifts can be massive, involving large changes in Earth's crustal placement or, at times can be minor, involving very slight changes in Earth's crustal positions. If large upheavals in Earth's crust take place the geophysical effects can be much greater than if only small changes occur. Large or small—any and all *Earth Changing* movements are going to prove dangerous and difficult to those involved.

When the brown dwarf was discovered in the early 1980s, all of these considerations must have been discussed behind NASA's closed doors with some astronomers calculating massive damage being inflicted on the Earth while others calculated no damage whatsoever.

Don't forget, we still know very little about how these celestial objects behave in space and even less about how their enormous gravity fields may affect planet Earth. In such a climate of uncertainty, dissenting scientific opinions are sure to be the 'rule' rather than the exception. Today, it's likely that NASA and other scientific government agencies are still uncertain about exactly how much damage '*X's*' anticipated passage is going to cause.

So what, then, was the U. S. Government going to do? Is the upcoming passage going to spell complete destruction via a pole shift—possibly a 20 % chance? Or, is the approaching object going to produce geologic upheavals on a far lesser scale—producing smaller disasters that are bad—but still manageable—maybe a 60% chance? Maybe we'll get really lucky and the brown dwarf's passage will not affect Earth at all—also a 20% chance?

Whatever is going to happen however, the U.S. Government was going to have to decide what it was going to do—and quickly! Unfortunately, they were faced with a dilemma. If the government underestimated the amount of damage that's going to be inflicted on the Earth, it wouldn't be ready for the anticipated passage; preparations would be inadequate and the government would fall far short of being able to effectively deal with what's coming.

If on the other hand the government over-estimated the damage that will result, then valuable resources/time/manpower would be wasted in preparing for something that never manifested.

After listening to all the conflicting viewpoints from the government's assembled scientists, the administration hierarchy more than likely decided to bet on the 'best' odds. In other words, it's a safe assumption the government decided the next passage was going to cause significant damage to Earth, but not to the extent that couldn't be effectively dealt with. The government more than likely decided on the 60% damage scenario. The brown dwarf's next passage would cause big damage (coastal flooding, earthquakes, a few volcanoes etc.), but nothing on the scale of total planetary destruction that usually results from a pole shift. WE KNOW WHAT THE BIBLE PREDICTS, HOWEVER!

Keep in mind that even if the brown dwarf does not pass directly between the Earth and Sun (and it might not), massive damage is still likely to be inflicted upon the planet. Although a full-blown pole shift might not take place, the massive gravitational influence of the brown dwarf is still going to cause severe damage to our world.

Even without a full pole shift, the object's intense gravity could cause sea levels to dramatically rise, flooding coastal regions for many hundreds of miles inland. One or two massive volcanic eruptions could also blanket entire continents under several feet of hot ash and plummet global temperatures causing the destruction of agriculture—starving millions (if not billions) of people to death worldwide. Massive global earthquakes would totally collapse roads and bridges making transportation impossible and rupture public utilities—eliminating water, heat and electricity to billions of needy people. Even if we don't have a full-blown pole shift, the effect of the passing brown dwarf is unimaginably destructive, notwithstanding the threat of terrorism!

Since the federal government made the decision it could handle whatever this passing object is going to throw our way, the start of 'disaster preparations' was going to have to begin in earnest.

The problem was how to prepare for an event like this without 'informing' and 'panicking' the general population. The government decided they could <u>never inform</u> the public of what they knew was coming, for to do so, would trigger a chain of social and political upheavals that might end up causing more internal damage and civil chaos than the actual object itself.

So the government decided to take the only logical course of action it could. Preparations for the upcoming event would take place 'covertly'—using multiple 'cover stories' as excuses for any 'official" preparation efforts that had to be made.

In other words, the government would 'secretly' get ready for the approaching cataclysm while trying to appear as if there were <u>no preparations</u> taking place at all. Everything would continue to appear relatively normal to the public while any disaster preparations that had to be accomplished would be done for an alleged 'different' reason.

Keep in mind that when we say *The Government* —we're talking about only the very 'upper levels' of government. Your local DMV office/city council/police department would have no idea of the incoming brown dwarf or the disaster preparations being made for its arrival. If need be, they would only be told the official 'cover stories' to justify and elicit their participation.

Once the U.S. Government knew about the approaching brown dwarf and the necessity to prepare for its approach, one other important decision had to be made: *who should be informed about this approaching situation?* The U.S. Government could not logically go it alone, and preparation activities were going to have to involve a multi-national effort at every level.

Official Government cover-up policies?

It wasn't long after the Government realized the potential severity of our current situation, that then president, Ronald Reagan, went before an assembled body of the United Nations and made a very enigmatic statement, wherein the President said:

> *In our obsession with antagonisms of the moment, we often forget how much unites all the members of humanity. Perhaps we need some outside, universal threat to make us recognize this common bond. I occasionally think how quickly our differences worldwide would vanish if we were facing an alien (cosmic) threat from outside this world.*[1]

Needless to say, at the time this globally important statement was made, it produced quite a few 'puzzled' facial expressions from the news media covering the President's speech. *What the heck was President Reagan talking about—possibly an alien threat from outside this world?*

In hindsight, what Reagan was doing was selectively bringing the United Nations on board in preparation for the upcoming global catastrophe—should it occur. The Government had the wisdom and foresight to realize that the coming attractions would be a 'global event' and the best organization to ultimately coordinate those preparation efforts is the U.N. body—should it act.

But Reagan informing the hierarchy of the U.N. was just the first step, the U.S. Government, and now those of a few other countries—still had to figure out how they were going to actually prepare for the brown dwarf's passage without 'tipping off' the public regarding what's approaching us from space.

As we have already mentioned, all disaster preparations were going to have to take place 'under the table' or 'covertly' in order to prevent 'panicking' the public.

So the decision was made to utilize actual situations that were current problems at hand using these as 'valid reasons' to prepare for the upcoming passage. In a sense, this idea would kill two birds with one stone. The governments of the world could address obvious problems that needed attention in the first place—and at the same time 'conceal' their disaster preparation activities while addressing these initial homegrown 'domestic' problems.

These cloaked disaster preparations would also have to be implemented gradually over the course of many years in order to further conceal these clandestine preparations from the public.

Question: *Was Y2K, the infamous computer meltdown that was supposed to take place at the beginning of the year 2000, a 'real' or 'imagined' problem? And could this situation have been 'hyped' and 'over-sold' to the public in order to allow the government to place all sorts of disaster preparations in place? Isn't it strange that such a 'big deal' was made over this event, and that so many disaster preparations were implemented—but nothing significant happened?*

But Y2K was only a single opportunity to push disaster plans forward. If the governments of the world were going to adequately prepare for the magnitude of what was coming, they were going to need much more extensive and involved 'cover stories' than this single Y2K opportunity.

The decision was then made to use two primary problems that needed to be addressed; these are 'drug use' and 'terrorism.' While the governments of the world invested resources to wage their 'wars against drugs' and 'terrorism,' they could easily address both these important issues, while also 'covertly' make the preparations necessary to deal with the upcoming global cataclysm.

Both the 'war on drugs' and 'war on terrorism' make fantastic 'cover stories' allowing a meaningful world government to engage in all types of preparatory behavior that would otherwise raise way too much suspicion from the public. Simply put another way, if a government wants to achieve some sort of a preparation objective (lets say beefing-up the National Guard for example)—all it has to do is tell the public that its being done for the 'war on drugs,' and/or the 'war on terrorism' (or both) —and the general public easily buys it!

Let us take a moment and emphatically state that drugs and terrorism are both totally 'real' and 'dire' problems throughout the world! And these problems must be immediately and responsibly dealt with. We are not belittling the seriousness of these problems when we say they are being used as 'cover stories!' And it is the belief of this author that we (the U.S.) or any other country, could be struck with a catastrophic terrorist attack at any moment—possibly using nuclear or biological weapons. It's just that in the act of addressing these horrific problems, the world's governments can also engage in all sorts of 'preparatory behaviors' that would otherwise raise unwanted suspicion thus tipping off the public to those specific preparations congruently being made for the approaching brown dwarf.

Of course, what makes a good cover story in the first place is a certain element of truth (either 'real' or simply 'perceived'. <u>Cover stories</u> must be <u>believable</u>. If you tell the public that you are doing something for a certain reason, there has to be a reasonable amount of logic behind these actions. In other words, you need a good 'excuse' to accomplish the 'end objective.'

Realizing that the governments of the world are preparing for upcoming global catastrophes—let's take a look at their recent actions. Let us peer beyond the facade of what the public is 'officially' being told and let's read between the lines of the 'cover stories' to catch a glimpse of what's really going on; all the while remembering the wise old adage, *"Where there's smoke—there's probably fire."*

Martial law GOD FORBID!

In actuality, there is nothing the governments of the world can realistically do to prevent the gravitational damage the brown dwarf may inflict on our planet as it passes. All they can do is to 'batten down the hatches' and 'clean up the mess' when it's all over.

Before we look into the specific preparations taking place for the brown dwarf's passage, we must keep a very important guiding principal in mind—the economy! In the U.S. today, consumer spending drives two-thirds of our economy—one of the most powerful and richest economic systems in the world. That means that the lifeblood of our entire financial system depends on the exchange of 'consumer' goods and services—both domestic and foreign.

What drives our economy is everyone spending money at Wal-Mart/Costco/Sam's Club/Target/MacDonalds/Walgreens/local/regional grocery chains and gas station mini-marts. The corporate infra-structure that allows you to buy gasoline, grocery shop, go out to lunch, wash your car, and a host of other consumer related activities—is what keeps America's economy going.

Those infrastructures that support these economically vital activities are, for the most part, extremely fragile—and must be protected if the U.S. is going to survive and then rebuild after the upcoming catastrophic events.

Once the approaching brown dwarf becomes visible in the sky the general public is going to panic! In this climate of panic, if the government allows 'law and order' to break down, spilling anarchy into the streets, unruly crowds will severely damage the vital economic infrastructure by which the U.S. and all other western economies are so dependent. If uncontrolled rioting and mayhem spill out of local neighborhoods and into the business districts of society (burning, looting and ultimately destroying the businesses that drive this, and other global economies), we're going to have a very difficult time recovering from the upcoming disaster.

Using New Orleans as a clear cut example—the National Guard should have been deployed there the moment it became evident *Katrina* (a CAT-3) was going to ravage the city and its residents.

Therefore, as the brown dwarf nears our planet, martial law will have to be declared! The government must take immediate steps to 'lock down' society—with an iron fist if necessary, if we as a nation are going to have any hope of recovering from the *Wormwood's* passage.

Martial law is essentially a complete governmental/military take-over of everything. The Constitution and Bill of Rights are suspended, stripping the public of their normal rights and privileges, while people are ordered to stay in their homes and wait official instructions. If you leave your home and dare venture out into the streets—you will be arrested and placed in a detention/relocation center—or even worse—shot! (More on this later).

In other words, as the approaching brown dwarf starts to become obvious to the general public, the military will be called out, martial law will be declared/enacted and people will be required to stay in their homes.

The realization that martial law is being prepared for has not gone unnoticed by the media. On 27 July 2002, investigative journalist, Ritt Goldstein, wrote an article entitled: *"Foundations Are In Place For Martial Law In The U.S."* This timely article, which was picked up by a number of press services stated:

> *Recent pronouncements from the Bush Administration, and national security initiatives put in place in the Reagan era, could see <u>internment camps</u> and <u>martial law</u> in the United States...*
>
> *Recent pronouncements by President George Bush's domestic security chief, Tom Ridge, and an official with the U.S. Civil Rights Commission, should fire concerns that these powers (of martial law) could be employed or a 'de facto' drift into their deployment could occur.*
>
> *FEMA (the Federal Emergency Management Agency), whose main role is disaster response, is also responsible for handling U.S. domestic unrest (rioting and looting).*
>
> *From 1982-84 Colonel Oliver North assisted FEMA in drafting its civil defense preparations. Details of these plans emerged during the 1987 Iran-Contra scandal.*
>
> *They include ...providing for the suspension of the constitution, the imposition of martial law, internment camps, and the turning over of the government to the President and FEMA.*
>
> *Today Mr. Brinkerhoff (the former deputy of FEMA) is with the highly influential Anser Institute for Homeland Security. Following a request by the Pentagon in January (that the U.S. Military be allowed the option of deploying troops on American streets), the institute in February published a paper by Mr. Brinkerhoff arguing the legality of this.[2]*

This article is merely an isolated example of numerous articles that have been published over the past several years—all indicating that the U.S. Government (as well as other governments around the world), are currently laying plans for the implementation of martial law policies.

As we've already stated, a number of 'current problems' in society can be used as 'cover stories' in order to hide or conceal preparations for the incoming brown dwarf. Today, we are all too familiar with the color-coded 'alert system' used for terrorism. In reality this color-coded system is perfect for other types of national emergencies including the approach of *Planet-X!*

The planning for martial law and its relationship to the color-coded terrorist alert system can be reviewed in an article from the *New Jersey State Bureau* entitled: *"Red Alert? Stay Home, Await Word."* This revealing article states:

> *If the nation escalates to 'red alert,' which is the highest in the color-coded readiness (listing) against terror (or other national emergencies), you will be assumed by authorities to be the enemy if you so much as venture outside your home…*

> *"This state is on top of it," said Sid Caspersen, New Jersey's director of the office of counter-terrorism.*

> *Caspersen, a former FBI agent, was briefing reporters, along side Gov. James E. McGreevey, on Thursday, when for the first time he disclosed the realities of how a red alert would shut the state (and the rest of the country) down.*

> *A red alert would also tear away virtually all personal freedoms to move about and associate.*

> *"Red means all noncritical functions cease," Caspersen said. "Noncritical would be almost all businesses, except health-related."*

> *A red alert means there is a severe risk of a terrorist attack (or other national emergency), according to federal guidelines from the Department of Homeland Security.*

> *"The state will restrict (all forms of) transportation and access to critical locations," says the state's new brochure on dealing with terrorism.*

> *"You (the public) must adhere to the restrictions announced by authorities and prepare to evacuate, if instructed (especially from low lying costal areas that could flood). Stay alert for emergency messages."*

> *Caspersen went further than the brochure. "The government agencies would run at a low threshold," he said. " The state, local police, emergency management people (and Military), would take control over the highways."*

> *"You literally are staying home, is what happens, unless you are required to be out. No different than if you had a state of emergency with a snowstorm."* [3]

Even though this article is directed to the state of New Jersey, these emergency plans involving the 'lock down' of society are federally directed, and apply to all states equally across the country. This color-coded terrorist alert system provides a convenient vehicle for the declaration of 'martial law,' whether the reason is 'terrorism' or some other 'national emergency.' Recently several prominent members of Congress have all but dismissed this color-coded system—*why?*

Once again, when the public sees what's coming and realizes the predicament they're in—they will panic. The government will simply declare a 'red alert' and lock down society. A plethora of emergency measures and actions will immediately go into effect and people will be told to stay in their homes and not venture out into the street under threat of becoming 'the enemy.'

This declaration of martial law will be vital to preserving the infrastructure of society. If the general public were allowed to run wild in the streets in the days preceding the dwarf's passage or even immediately afterwards—they would rip the vital economic infrastructure of this country to pieces in a matter of hours. *(Remember what happened in New Orleans following Katrina?)*

In order to provide an additional level of protection, economically vital businesses such as large grocery store chains, the Wal-Mart's, Targets, Sam's Clubs and others, have placed massive banks of cameras and other security-related devices around their buildings and parking lots.

These cameras will help provide additional 'security and crowd control' measures once desperate mobs start forming in their parking lots—trying to obtain any last minute supplies they can get their hands on. Simply put, these companies are placing so many security devices on their buildings because they're going to need them!

At this point we should also mention the 'unsavory' or even the 'unthinkable' situation—but one that would be naive of us not to at least consider. The governments of the world may not wait until the brown dwarf is visible before instituting martial law. It is possible, although hard for some to believe, that an event (possibly a terrorist attack using a weapon of mass destruction, (a WMD), could be preemptively 'staged' in order to declare a societal 'lock down,' thus instituting a 'militarized' form of government before the dwarf ever becomes visible.

General Tommy Franks may have inadvertently alluded to these plans in a 21 November 2003 interview. An article by *NewsMax* entitled: *"Gen. Franks Doubts Constitution Will Survive WMD Attack"* stated:

> *Gen. Tommy Franks says that if the United States is hit with a weapon of mass destruction that inflicts casualties, the Constitution will likely be discarded in favor of a military form of government (martial law).*
>
> *Franks, who successfully led the U.S. military operation to liberate Iraq (and)...the former commander of the military's Central Command, warned that if terrorists succeeded in using a weapon of mass destruction (WMD) against the U.S. <u>or one of our allies</u>, it would likely have catastrophic consequences for our cherished republican form of government.*[4]

General Franks would not have made this statement unless plans were already in place to suspend the U.S. Constitution and then declare martial law. *Is it possible that a government would deliberately 'stage' a terrorist attack in order to institute martial law, thus putting prearranged plans into place and making final disaster preparations days, weeks or possibly years before the actual passage of the brown dwarf?* The possibility is there—and we should not ignore or dismiss this reality as being conspiratorial in its nature or intent.

The institution of 'martial law' however, is not an easy achievement in a society with so many people and guns—and especially people that at least 'consider' themselves to be free men and not usually told what to do by the authorities. Once martial law is declared and the people are ordered to stay in their homes, it's likely there will be a certain/fair amount of public defiance. Therefore, in order to accomplish this 'lock down' of an open society, a long chain of events must take place—the first starting with an Executive Order issued by the President.

Executive Orders already in place — GOD HAVE MERCY ON US!

Unbeknownst to most Americans, in November 1994, then President William J. Clinton passed Executive Order #12938. The details of this and other 'national security' related Executive Orders (and their constitutionality) are far too extensive to cover in this book. However, a brief mention of this one particular Executive Order is important for us to review at this time.

What Executive Order #12938 did was to consolidate a number of pre-existing Executive Orders and place the United States under a perpetual State of National Emergency—a condition that has never 'officially' been lifted. Since we are 'currently' living under this 'State of Emergency,' the President and all other departments of the Executive Branch of government have almost unlimited federal powers to act in the best interests of our national security and global military deployment (should they decide to do so.) *Is this fact necessarily a bad reality state for the U.S.?*

YES, IT'S BAD!

Although these 'emergency powers' for the most part, have not been publicly exercised, at least not yet, they would not have been created if there were no need for their use in the first place.

Since we are currently living in a State of National Emergency, the President and the Executive Branch of government have the federal power to mandate the following:

* Institute a complete/instant martial law edict upon our society in the U.S. and its territories
* Seize all forms of communications, including radio, television and global Internet service
* Restrict all forms of travel both local/regional/foreign (at every level in every state)
* Seize/control all means of media/communications/transportation including air/ground/rail
* Regulate all forms of private enterprise (taking over corporate and private businesses)
* Seize all forms of agriculture, farming, livestock and fishery businesses
* Call up reserve military forces amounting to 2.5 million troops (if necessary)
* Assign/recall/deploy our troops from foreign soil for all U.S. military forces as necessary
* Organize and control the means of national production, including utilities, power and gasoline
* Seize any and all personal property including cars, homes, firearms/ammo, goods and clothing
* Seize any and all personal commodities such as food, water, money, and heating fuels, etc.
* Draft ordinary citizens to perform labor under government command (when/where needed)
* Regulate the flow of all national currency/banking operations both domestic and foreign
* Open and close our national borders as/where/when necessary
* And many other ways to control/manage every aspect of our society and the lives of its citizens

Executive Order #12938 essentially gives the government the ability to not only declare martial law, but also suspend all remnants of our constitutional form of government. Whether these actions are right/wrong/good/bad is not the real issue here. *The basic issues are: why have these measures been put into place and why does Executive Order #12938 remain open on the books?*

The excuse that was presented to the public justifying President Clinton declaring a State of National Emergency and signing Executive Order #12938 was of course, the threat of 'terrorism' theoretically being used against the U.S. At first this may seem reasonable, but stop and think about these implications for a minute.

Declaring that the United States is in a current State of National Emergency is a very extreme declaration and the actions this declaration allows the Government to take are even more radical.

What type of suicide bomber with a truckload of fertilizer in Oklahoma City would justify declaring martial law, or drafting ordinary citizens to perform labor, or moving throughout the nation seizing the personal property and weapons of ordinary civilians from all walks of life?

Think about it! Not even the horrific events of September 11ᵗʰ, Pearl Harbor, or even World War II itself, were severe enough to justify these extreme measures.

What type of horrific event could be approaching us that would lead the government to believe that it is fighting for its very existence and that almost any action imaginable is now justified? What up-coming event has our government making such radical preparations and what would such an event mean to you and your family?

President Clinton's executive order with all of its ramifications has already been enacted. *But is the reason for this enactment the truth, or could it be a clever 'cover story' for something even more ominous looming in our future?*

A Federal State of National Emergency and the suspension of our entire form of constitutional government certainly seems a little extreme for almost any terrorist attack imaginable, but not for a massive cataclysm caused by the passage of a brown dwarf.

If massive areas of our nation were underwater or covered by volcanic ash, if food was scarce and millions were starving, if large portions of our country were reduced to rubble or if our nation had no electrical power, water or gas services, extreme measures would certainly be warranted in order to salvage what's left of our 21ˢᵗ century society.

If civilization as we know it was dealt a severe blow and the government was truly fighting for the continued survival of our nation, then the drafting of ordinary citizens starts to make a lot more sense. If the shattered remnants of our population were starving to death, seizing the personal property of others or forcibly taking over various forms of private enterprise starts to make better sense. You can read these executive orders at: www.disastercenter.com/laworder.

We need to look at the bigger picture and do something that the general public seldom does, stop blindly accepting policies/facts/things at face value. So read between the lines and THINK.

Military operations

Having disaster plans for the implementation of martial law and making the necessary legal adjustments to validate its declaration, does not necessarily mean that you can effectively enact it. The government must also have the physical ability to order/maintain its martial law edict over an 'unwilling' or an 'uncooperative' public. In other words, the government can have all of the martial law plans it wants already put into place, but if it doesn't have the real-time ability to physically 'enforce' these plans—it mean nothing and is purely an academic exercise.

In 1878, the Posse Comitatus Act was passed forbidding the U.S. military from engaging in any domestic (within our U.S. borders) law enforcement duties. But in recent years this act has been deliberately eroded and chipped away, clearing the path for the military to engage in full-scale law enforcement (martial law enforcement) activities on our streets.

In 2001, the *Christian Science Monitor* reported:

> *After decades of projecting force overseas, the Pentagon for the first time has placed the continental United States under an American military command….*
>
> *In what senior US officials call the most important change of its kind since World War II, the Pentagon created a new unified command (The Northern Command) granting a four-star general responsibility for land, aerospace and sea defenses of the United States.*
>
> *The entity Northern Command), "will command U.S. forces that operate in the U.S. in support of civil authorities in case of natural disasters, terrorist attacks on U.S. soil, or other civil difficulties," said Defense Secretary Donald Rumsfeld yesterday.*
>
> *The overhauled structure also placed previously unassigned parts of the globe— including Russia, Canada, Mexico, and Antarctica—under U.S. Military command for the first time. And as a result, the entire world is divvied up among American commands (also) for the first time.*[5]

This is a very interesting/important article for a number of reasons. First, it not only states that this military restructuring is being put into place to support civil authorities (martial law), but that these preparations are directed toward 'natural disasters' and other 'civil difficulties.' The last section of this article is also puzzling when it states that Russia, Canada, Mexico and even Antarctica, are now under U.S. Military command. *Why would Russia, Canada, Mexico and even Antarctica be currently placed under a U.S. military command structure? (Note: We'll come back to the exchange of foreign troops between different countries shortly).*

What type of 'natural disasters' and 'civil difficulties' would warrant restructuring our entire military's overall command? What type of 'natural disaster' or 'civil difficulties' would not only affect the U.S. but all of these other countries as well—including Antarctica? (Keep in mind that Antarctica may be the primary observation post for the monitoring of this incoming object). If Katrina/Rita and the other hurricanes weren't enough in 2005—what should we expect in the up-coming 2006-tornado season and will we be on the learning curve regarding these threats also?

In actuality, the military has been preparing for action on the streets of the U.S. (martial law) for many years. A recent example of this training took place in November 2001, and started out by local police cordoning off the historic and picturesque town of Petersburg, Virginia.

As darkness fell across Petersburg, and after an oblivious and shaken children's theater group had to be evacuated from the area, confused residents watched the 22nd Marine Expeditionary Unit from Fort Pickett literally attacked their town.

Unmarked vans rolled onto Sycamore Street unloading heavily armed Marines to block access to the assault area. Then light armored vehicles soon arrived unloading more Marines to train their guns on crucial roadways. Then armed helicopters roared through the darkness as even more marines slid down ropes onto the rooftop of Butterworth's furniture store. These marines then engaged in a fierce, all out machine gun battle throughout the town.[6]

You would expect to see something like this in a Hollywood movie; unfortunately this was no movie. Although technically speaking this was just a 'mock rehearsal,' the mood of this military exercise was deadly serious.

This takeover of Petersburg, Virginia, was not an isolated example of the U.S. Military preparing to wage war on our streets; in recent years this disturbing and rather puzzling phenomenon has been taking place in numerous cities across the U.S.

On 15 February 2002, the *Drudge Report* carried a story entitled: *"Marines To Hold Anti-Terrorist Test Raid In North Little Rock."* According to this article:

> *"Hundreds of Marines will raid North Little Rock, Arkansas, next week for an 'urban experiment' in terrorism response," the Wall Street Journal reported on Friday.*

> *"They will post snipers, stop vehicles, patrol streets, search buildings, and evacuate the wounded, whose gear will beep to signal they have become casualties. Local residents will permit their homes to be searched. The Marines plan later assaults elsewhere, including Boise, Idaho."* [7]

Marines assaulting Little Rock, Arkansas, and Boise, Idaho, and stopping private vehicles and searching civilians' homes? Seems a little overboard in the 'heartland' —don't you think? THIS IS AN DAMN RIGHT !!! OUTRAGE!!

Similar mock 'urban assaults' have also recently taken place in places like Annapolis, Chicago, Birmingham, Jacksonville, outside of Phoenix and in several posh beach communities along the California coast, plus dozens of other communities throughout the United States. The military conducted some of their assaults by day and others by night. Sometimes the Marines arrived in armored vehicles and sometimes they stormed beachside communities by boat.

Our military has been trying to keep these mock urban 'takeovers' as quiet as possible, and has been reluctant to openly discuss these combat drills with the media. The towns are simply blocked off by local police and then the military (involving numerous military branches) rolls in and takes over. Residences that ask these solders 'what is going on' are routinely told to shut up and go inside their houses or they will be immediately arrested (although it's hard to believe). *Does it appear that we must also do battle with our own military and National Guard troops?*

IF NECESSARY. GOD HELP US !.

In the case of the military takeover of Petersburg, Virginia, all the military would say is that the Marines were assaulting this town as part of a mock exercise against terrorists—who were theoretically held up in Butterwoth's furniture store. As stunned as the local residents of Petersburg were over this 'outrageous' display of military firepower in their quiet little town, this was only one such exercise staged in 'thirteen' days of mock urban assaults taking place in other communities throughout southern Virginia.

WHO ARE THE REAL "TERRORISTS"? COULD IT BE OUR OWN GOVERNMENT?

The one constant element that these urban assaults had in common was that they were all done in practice to theoretically 'stop the terrorists.'

In a strange and contradictory statement, the Defense Department recently said that these mock military exercises were officially part of a program called, "Training in the Urban Environment," and were totally unrelated to terrorism.[8]

If these mock assaults on the cities of our nation are unrelated to terrorism, then whom exactly are the Marines preparing to wage war against on our American city streets?

To further add to the strangeness of the military's recent behavior, for years now, our military has also been bragging about the realistic towns built on military bases around the country for the expressed purpose of training their troops to engage in urban combat.

Why leave these military bases to send tanks down main street USA, scaring the hell out of our civilian population and unnecessarily disrupting peoples' lives?

The probability of having to send the Marines (or other military units) into 'sleepy-town' USA in order to stop a group of terrorists is also very unlikely. If a local terrorist incident were to take place, federal, state and local law enforcement agencies (who are receiving extensive training and equipment for just such an event), would be more than capable of handling all but the most extreme terrorist threats and/or situations.

Since it is very unlikely the Marines will be sent into our cities due to a terrorist incident, then why would they be sent in at all? So what are the Marines really training for and why are they attacking U.S. cities?

The answer here is painfully clear! You do in 'practice' what you plan on doing in the real 'end game.' The U.S. Military would not be 'practicing' on our nation's streets unless they knew they are going to have to be 'deployed' someday on these very same American streets.

Aside from the troops gaining valuable tactical experience in 'securing' and 'locking-down' urban centers, these mock exercises also psychologically condition both the troops and their officers to move against 'civilian targets.' An act that is sometimes difficult for many soldiers and their commanders to justify. As a soldier, you're taught that you are protecting this country from its 'foreign' enemies. If, on the other hand, you're ordered to storm Phoenix, Arizona, (and if necessary even shoot down American citizens), any soldier might have a difficult time in following and then coping with his commander's military decision against civilians.

If you are a general and you know you're going to have to eventually send your troops into the nation's cities, and in the worst-case scenarios, to fight off your own citizens—you'd have to get your troops and commanders accustomed to this unusual idea. You must also move them into the towns and onto the streets because that is where they will eventually be deployed; and if your goal is to get your troops psychologically ready to storm Los Angeles, San Francisco, Phoenix, St. Petersburg, Chicago, St. Louis, Detroit, Cleveland, New York and Boston—then this is <u>how,</u> <u>where,</u> <u>when</u> and <u>why</u> you must train them.

Once again, if a massive cataclysm were to strike our planet severely damaging and disrupting our society, the government would have little choice but to send the military into our major cities in order to suppress the ensuing chaos that would surely erupt. *(Shades of New Orleans again?)*

If the fragile fabric of our society was to be torn apart at its seams, the military would have to be sent into our cities in order to restore some type of law and order—even by force if necessary. The military will also be needed immediately before the brown dwarf's passage in order to institute martial law. These would be the obvious reasons the Marines (and others) have been practicing mock attacks on our cities—all the while trying to keep the real reason secret.

The public is simply being told that these mock attacks are to 'stop the terrorists.' A convenient 'cover story' to conceal the real reason these military exercises are taking place. Once again, these events have little to do with what the public is 'officially' being told and a lot to do with what they're not. Admittedly this all sounds very conspiratorial—but the facts hold true!

However, in addition to our training and then allowing the U.S. Military to openly participate in domestic law enforcement activities, our government has also made secret agreements with other governments to allow foreign troops to cross our national borders. In other words, troops from other countries can now cross over our 'national borders' and be distributed wherever/whenever they are needed in a time of national emergency.

Earlier in this section we mentioned how countries such as Russia, Canada, Mexico and even Antarctica, are currently under U.S. Military control. To further illustrate why this official exchange of troops and military command has been set into place, we now turn our attention to a newspaper article published on 10 December 2002.

This *Associated Press* piece entitled: *"New Military Cooperation Pact Allows Canadian—U.S. Troops To Enter Each Others' Territory,"* sheds a bright new light on exactly why these bizarre 'behind the scenes' plans are being enacted. This article stated:

> *Under the (new) agreement, either country can request military help from the other…The agreement calls for increased joint operations and exercises against terrorism. It also creates a new planning group to study how both countries would jointly deploy military forces and emergency services in response to a terrorist attack/other natural disasters.* [9]

Once again we must ask ourselves what type of natural disaster would prompt the U.S. to ask Canada to send troops into our cities? What type of 'other natural disaster' could be driving these types of extreme military preparations?

Clearly, there is more to the exchange of troops between countries than just the threat of terrorism, and it would seem from this article that massive, multi-national 'natural disasters' are also being planned for!

As we have already alluded to, this agreement between the U.S. and Canada is only one such agreement of this type. The U.S. and other countries have these same agreements with the United Nations, Mexico, Russia, England, Australia, China and apparently dozens of other countries from around the world.

As we have seen, when the brown dwarf passes our planet, it is more than likely going to leave an awful mess in its wake. The topography of Earth may be radically altered and national boundaries may largely lie underwater or be undeterminable. Therefore, the common exchange of military forces sent between different nations may be necessary—placing troops where they are most needed—in whatever cities or countries are left remaining on their feet!

The Army National Guard

The U.S. Marines have not been the only branch of our military that has found an excuse to train in urban areas. The Army National Guard has also been very busy in recent years. The National Guard, however, has not focused solely on the 'war on terrorism.' The National Guard's 'cover story' of choice has been the ongoing federal 'war on drugs.'

Like the 'war on terrorism,' the 'war on drugs' allows the government to justify all sorts of questionable behavior that would otherwise raise greater suspicions from the public and media. Both issues make great 'cover stories' designed to achieve a specific and often 'hidden agenda.'

The National Guard is now actively campaigning against private citizens in drug eradication sweeps. In 1992 alone, National Guard troops assisted in making over 20,000 arrests on members of the U.S. public. They've searched over 120,000 cars, entered over 1,200 privately owned buildings and trespassed onto private property over 6,500 times.[10]

Like the Marine's 'war on terror,' the National Guard's 'war on drugs' seems to require a massive 'over-use' of force, involving hundreds of combat ready troops, helicopters, armored personnel carriers and tanks. *Once again—this sure sounds like a conspiracy theory, doesn't it?*

Is the Army National Guard, with its automatic weapons and armored personnel carriers really needed to stop cars looking for marijuana, coke and God knows what else? Or could the 'war on drugs' being waged by the Army National Guard—largely be a clever 'cover-up' training story. If the National Guard's 'drug eradication sweeps' are just another 'cover story,' then what's the real reason for all of their recent 'urban warfare' training exercises? Wouldn't it be better if our government begins telling us the truth—even if it means toughing it out?

Like the Marines, the National Guard will also play a critical role in maintaining law and order, both before and after the coming global catastrophes. The experience that the Guardsmen derive from these 'drug eradication sweeps' will be desperately needed when they are rolled out to bring, 'order out of chaos' and to 'enforce U.S. martial law.'

It is also important to note the increase in preparedness taking place on and around most National Guard armories, with dramatic increases in personnel, equipment and combat training in 'urban warfare' being prevalent.

The National Guard is also preparing for something much bigger than we are being 'officially' told—and it has nothing to do with funny looking cigarettes or other drugs, etc!

A federally mandated army

During the late morning hours of 14 January 1997, a team of heavily armed federal agents descended on ropes from a military helicopter onto the small rocky island of Santa Cruz, several miles off the central California coast. As sniper teams moved into position along the ridge-tops to secure a perimeter around the attack area, other agents of this assault team staged a dynamic entry into a small building in the very center of the island.

This was no mock drill however, since the federal agents with their ski masks, machine guns and bullets—were all too real. This commando-style raid was not carried out by the FBI or even the BATF, but by agents from the National Park Service! That's right, The National Park Service, the same nice people in charge of your local neighborhood swimming pools and favorite family vacation spots.

The small building which was the objective of their raid was not a 'crack house' or even the clandestine hideout of 'terrorists,' but a simple civilian bow-and-arrow hunting lodge.

The official government reason for this 'real life' military-style raid was to identify possible suspects on the island who were allegedly stealing Chumash Indian Artifacts, items such as bone fishhooks and flint arrowheads. Upon conducting this raid, the agents found very little in this lodge except for a 15-year-old girl, Crystal Graybeel, who was handcuffed and thrown face down on the floor where she remained in custody for several hours. And as it turns out, no criminal activity or stolen artifacts were ever found—just some very frightened innocent people.[11]

This situation is typical of the extreme 'over-use' of force being exercised by federal agencies in recent years. Unfortunately, situations like this are becoming more and more common as our Federal Government transforms its agencies into militarized assault forces. At last count the Federal Government has over 80,000 armed agents and is currently training another 25,000 each and every year. Most of these federal agents are being trained in the use of military tactics including the use of M16s, (the automatic weapons that military troops carry).

This trend has not gone unnoticed. In 1997 journalist, Joseph Farah, wrote an article entitled: *" Clinton's Militarization of the Government,"* wherein Farah goes on to say:

The last couple of years have witnessed the biggest arms buildup in the history of the Federal Government. The kind of arms that are proliferating in Washington these days are the kind pointed at our own civilian population and carried by a growing number of federal agencies with ever-larger budgets and ever-deadlier arsenals.[12]

Other journalists have also sounded the alarm over this disturbing trend stating that:

The Federal Government is obviously building its own standing army. This type of Militarization of our federal agencies goes far beyond anything in the history of modern-day law enforcement policies.[13]

The federal agencies that are being militarized might surprise most people. Agencies such as the FBI, (which now has over 60 heavily armed SWAT teams and growing), and the DEA, (which has also been drastically increasing its SWAT forces), are alarming enough. But even more surprising is that agencies such as the Internal Revenue Service, National Park Service, Federal Emergency Management Administration, the Department of Transportation, Social Security Administration, Department of Housing and Urban Development, Department of Fish and Game, the Small Business Administration and even NASA, are equipping and training heavily armed commando units *(to do???)*.

When recently asked by the G.A.O. (General Accounting Office of the U.S. Congress), why the Federal Government is undergoing such a drastic and expensive militarization, the Federal Government was strangely silent and to this day has made no 'official' comment as to the true reason(s) for their military-like build-up and training programs.

Why is the Government 'covertly' building its own federal army? Why do so many federal agencies need so much firepower—firepower that goes far beyond anything that would normally be used in the exercise of their day-to-day duties and responsibilities?

Our government is a large and complex organization with numerous agencies that are vital to its efficient operation. Both before and after the global cataclysms occur, the general public will begin to panic—desperately seeking out assistance from any governmental agencies they can find. Each agency will have to try and protect their own assets and personnel if the 'individual parts' of the federal government are to function as a 'whole.' *(Let's remember New Orleans?)*

In other words, each agency will need its own 'individual army' in order to continue functioning as an integral piece of the overall government and not be 'overrun' or 'disabled' by the general public. This is how the orderly 'continuity of any government' will be achieved. These circumstances are the 'real reason' and the only 'reason' that the Social Security Administration, the Department of Housing and Urban Development, and the Small Business Administration—all need heavily armed SWAT teams!

Where does one go to feel safe about one's self—and at what price or sacrifice does one pay for the right or privilege of protecting what is rightfully ours as law abiding citizens? Does this federal arming of the civilian government portend the pathway to control the masses—should "X" reappear? And what if anything can we do if all hell breaks loose in the streets around us?

The militarization of state, county and city police resources

Not only are the military and federal branches of government planning to use combat style weapons, tactics and force against the general population to maintain order and enforce martial law in the wake of the upcoming catastrophes, but local, county and state police forces have also been slated for militarization as well.

An article recently appeared in the popular law enforcement magazine, *Guns and Weapons For Law Enforcement,* encouraging officers to increase their available firepower and training. This article, entitled: *"Your Primary Duty Weapon—Long Gun Versus Handgun, Why You Must Take The Long Gun,"* prompted officers to start using military style rifles as their 'primary' weapons while both <u>on</u> and <u>off</u> duty. *Could this factoid be a valid need to 'out-gun' the bad-guys?*

This article championed the benefits of military style weapons, stating that they were far more accurate, had much greater range, were more harder-hitting and most importantly, had a greater 'psychological impact' on the general public.

This article <u>is not</u> an isolated example of how the paramilitary thinking aspect is slowly creeping into law enforcement departments around the world. Many such units across the U.S. and other continents have already issued military-style weapons to their officers and provided them with combat training conducted by U.S. military Special Forces instructors.

The military has even stepped in and given certain police departments key weapons, tanks and helicopters, as well as the combat training to use this powerful equipment against the enemy—if not the terrorists—*then apparently the general public?*

Other departments have gone as far as asking their officers to purchase high powered military weapons out of their own pockets and to have them on hand just in case they're needed during a sudden 'national emergency operation.'

Why would local, county and state police offices need such massive firepower and military training? Is a routine traffic stop performed on a 68-year-old lady from Pasadena (driving her vintage '57 Chevy convertible), going to result in an armed conflict requiring the use of assault weapons capable of piercing the sides of an armored personnel carrier?

To date, no 'official reason' has publicly addressed the militarization of police departments. But when one considers all of the other measures being put into effect in order to prepare for martial law, the militarization of local, county and state police departments makes perfect sense. The police will be needed to back up the military when society is 'locked down' and placed under martial law. A militarized police department will also be needed in order to enforce any governmental actions following the upcoming destructive events—such as seizing personal property like guns and food or arresting violators of martial law.

One thing is very clear, police departments around the world are transforming themselves into hardened paramilitary units and, whatever the reason for this metamorphosis, the end result doesn't look pretty. Then again—if *Planet-X* is a reality—they've probably 'got it right.'

Walls with cameras and eyes...

Few individuals today have taken the time to notice what's been taking place on our nation's highways. As the public goes about their busy lives, their government has been walling-in the sides of our highways and erecting scores of cameras along most major roads and bi-ways.

All of this is part of a federally mandated program in which individual cities and states have little say. It doesn't matter what city you look at, from Seattle to San Diego, from Houston to New York, from St. Louis to New Orleans; take a closer look at your local highway systems and you'll find these so-called 'traffic walls' and 'traffic-cams' being installed nationwide.

The general public is being told that these 'traffic walls' are for traffic noise reduction and that the 'traffic cameras' are being put in place to monitor traffic conditions—and this is mostly true! Like all good 'cover stories' this one contains at least a small dose of truth. Walls do help reduce highway noise and the cameras do help monitor traffic conditions. Just watch any local evening news program and you'll often see 'grainy/exacting images' taken from one of these so called 'traffic cams' during highway reports/car chases/weather summaries and local news segments.

These traffic cam 'video-feeds' are being deliberately transmitted to all local news organizations in order the get the public accustomed to the presence of these 'see all' cameras and to convince them that those cameras are there only to monitor traffic and/or weather conditions!

There is a lot more to this story, however, that the public is not being told. First is the excessive cost of these highway programs. Erecting concrete and steel walls equipped with sophisticated electronic camera systems (with all of their fiber optic components), additional support materials and construction crews—is costing billions—if not trillions of dollars!

Everyone is for reducing traffic noise, and it's nice to see what the traffic's like on our local highways. *But in a society still facing massive hunger and poverty, deteriorating roads and bridges, crumbling sewage systems, bankrupt counties and cities, a multi-regional health care system in crisis, under-equipped and poorly-staffed school systems, and a host of other problems and shortages from under-funded AIDS and cancer research projects to the problems of balancing the budget, how can we justify squandering billions of dollars on thousands of miles of concrete walls with tens of thousands of cameras and expensive support equipment?*

Even if walls and cameras were needed on our roads and highways (which they are not) why are so many cameras being put in place? In some locations the cameras are so extensive there may be several positioned right next to each other and pointing in all four directions. *Are traffic conditions changing so rapidly that we need multiple cameras all monitoring the same thing?*

There are additional aspects to this equation the public is not being told about. While these traffic cameras do feed into local newsrooms and even public websites, they're also being fed into most Emergency Operation Centers (EOC's). These EOC's as they are called, are modern, bunker-like facilities mostly hidden beneath larger cities, which have been quietly constructed at extraordinary cost to taxpayers. New York City's EOC recently underwent a small renovation that is still costing millions of dollars to complete.

These EOC's have adequate provisions to support hundreds of emergency personnel and are often equipped with 'state-of-the-art' command and communications equipment. Part of this equipment includes large arrays of television screens showing selected feeds from the traffic system cameras. In other words—these EOC's can monitor most (if not all) of the highway systems around the nation from these real-time video images.

Again, how can our government justify this type of expense in the face of everything else that needs to be done? And why do our cities need such elaborate and expensive underground bunkers—many often resembling NASA control rooms in sophistication and design?

The most startling questions regarding these walls/cameras/OEC Ops-centers is—who's really behind providing their funding/implementation/administration/control?

That answer is a joint venture between the Department of Transportation and the Department of Defense. All of these walls, cameras and EOC's are being installed under a sophisticated project code-named: 'ATSAC.' ATSAC is an acronym that stands for **A**dvanced **T**actical **S**upport **A**nd **C**ontrol. *(Although, we believe, another acronym is being unofficially fed to the general public?)*

What the public is also not being told is that all of these walls and cameras are being erected to support the implementation of 'martial law.' That's what the word 'control' means in ATSA**C**.

This is not a new idea! As a matter of fact—it's thousands of years old. By walling up the highways, the Defense Department has essentially created its own version of the Great Wall of China, thus making many of our nation's highways extremely difficult to cross over from one side to the other, or advance in any direction, for any reason.

In other words, if you wanted to cross a particular highway and the overpasses and underpasses are guarded by armed troops—and the highway itself has tall walls on both sides of the road, how would you cross it and where? There are ways, but it would be much more difficult and dangerous than you might think.

Essentially, these 'walled-in' highways seal up portions of the nation's cities. If lawlessness breaks out in one area, these walled-up highways will help to keep such random lawlessness from easily spreading to other areas of these same troubled cities that are now on the increase.

The heavier the population density of a particular area, the more walls have to be installed to keep those areas and their local populations contained. Much like cutting fire breaks through a forest can help contain a forest fire from spreading, walled-up highways act as physical barriers that help to contain the pandemonium, violence and lawlessness that will break out right before and/or in the aftermath of the coming global cataclysms.

Traffic cameras help the Emergency Operations Centers to monitor and control their highways from inside their underground bunkers. Both traffic cameras and walls help to ensure that these highways remain clear of unnecessary vehicles, pedestrian traffic and all illegal access with only authorized vehicles being allowed to travel during martial law episodes. *But we wonder how our fellow Americans will react when federal orders are issued to 'cease and desist' all movements?*

Also, as a general rule of thumb, on most highways you'll find the placement of these cameras 'close' to over and underpasses and 'near' to on and off ramps. Since these high-traffic areas are the most likely points that people will use (attempting to cross the highways), so these areas must therefore, be kept under closer surveillance.

Place multiple military units on the highways, then add in a few helicopters patrolling the skies (helping ATSAC enforce a tightly controlled system of crowd/population/riot control) and suddenly—ATSAC becomes an important/powerful asset in the implementation of martial law.

Not only are cameras and walls being installed on our nations highways to keep them clear of unauthorized traffic, but cameras are also being rapidly placed on most inner-city surface streets and traffic intersections. Simply watch any local news segment noting the number of public scenes being shown utilizing these traffic-cams and highway cameras—way too many to count.

Recently, the government has been installing thousands of fixed cameras on the horizontal poles around surface street intersections. The public is under the assumption that these particular types of cameras photograph the license plates of vehicles that run red lights and will automatically send the driver a traffic ticket and all of this is very true—but....

In reality these cameras become the eyes/ears of a complex system of recorders and computers programmed to detect movement(s) or motion passing through intersections. These cameras and the sophisticated computers that monitor them are actually able to detect any movement within or around these intersections, be it vehicles or people or animals.

Once martial law is declared and the public is ordered off the streets and into their homes, these intersection cameras and their sophisticated computers will start electronically monitoring any unauthorized movements through or around these intersections. If any unusual movements are detected by these very sophisticated monitoring systems (twenty-four hours a day—seven days a week)—armed troops and equipment will be dispatched to that location immediately!

In other words, what all of these intersection cameras and their computers have accomplished is to place an elaborate 'motion-detector' system throughout our cities streets and intersections, similar to the motion-detectors of a home or business security system. Once you are ordered off the streets, that 'system' will be fully activated and you will not be able to go anywhere near or around those intersections without triggering these cameras and being immediately detected.

ATSAC is no joke! It is a very serious and deadly project! When martial law is declared and you are caught outside of your house YOU WILL BE IMMEDIATELY ARRESTED! OR EVEN WORSE—SHOT DEAD!!! Don't delude yourself with any other ideas. Once martial law is declared you're not going anywhere! You could consider 'it' as being under 'house arrest.'

Few people today have any knowledge or understanding regarding the real motivation for erecting and implementing these ATSAC systems throughout our nation and around the world; not even the work crews installing these elaborate systems know what their true purpose is designed for (although some of them are suspicious). Once again, they're only told the official 'cover story' and not the 'real reasons'—the approach of the terrible comet called *Wormwood*!

Gun control—legalization—licensing

The subject of gun control and access is a political hot potato. Both pro-gun and anti-gun people are passionate and adamant about their beliefs and habits. If you ever want to start a heated argument/debate within a group of friendly people—simply bring up the subject of 'gun control.'

The introduction of this topic is not meant to stir up controversy or even to take sides on this volatile issue. Most people today however, have very little understanding about the subject of gun control and especially 'why' it's happening. This section is therefore intended to introduce you to some of the more interesting events that are taking place regarding this volatile subject, of which you may, or may not be aware.

Much of the recent gun control legislation being instigated throughout the world is filled with smokescreens, false information and blatant lies, all of which have confused the general public as to what is 'real' and/or 'not real' involving these gun control actions and policies.

These circumstances dictate that we take a closer look at gun control and once again ask ourselves if we are being given the straight scoop involving this subject? Or could the rationale behind taking away the public's guns have a deeper more profound meaning than the American public is being told? YOU BETTER BELIEVE IT!

Let's make no mistake about it! Governments around the world are systematically removing guns from the hands of ordinary citizens—all of the guns! This intention clearly surfaced on 13 June 2000, when a U.S. Justice Department attorney by the name of William B. Mateja, dropped a bombshell in front of a federal judge in an open court session.

According to Mateja, and in turn the U.S. Justice Department, our nation's constitution no longer ensures ordinary citizens the right to bear arms. These inalienable rights as stipulated in the Second Amendment (the amendment that gives ordinary citizens the right to own firearms), <u>now applies only to members of the nation's National Guard</u>. Mateja went on to say: *"If you are not a Guardsman, (then) you have no right to own a gun of any kind!"* YOU LIE!!!

The stunned federal Judge, William L. Garwood, sought clarification of this extreme statement. The Judge asked Mateja, *"Are you saying that the Second Amendment is consistent with a position that you can take guns away from the public, and that the Federal Government can restrict the ownership of rifles, pistols and shotguns from all people? Is that the position of the U.S. Government?"*

Mateja looked at the judge and calmly said, *"Yes, Sir."* So the judge probed further. *"Is it the position of the United States that citizens who are not in the National Guard, are afforded no protections under the Second Amendment and that they may not own a firearm?"* — *"Exactly,"* replied Mateja.[14]

This attitude of total gun elimination from the hands of the public is reflected in the fact that even though there are currently over 20,000 gun laws on the books (even restricting the ownership of BB guns in some areas of the county), the Federal Government is insisting that we need more and stricter gun laws—immediately! *Hmmmm! Now where have we heard that before?*

Governments have used every trick in the book to steadily rid the public of their firearms, especially this class of automatic firearms arbitrarily placed under the heading of being 'assault weapons.' Whatever your perception of assault weapons might be—it is probably inaccurate. The point however, is that even though the government has gone after this class of firearms with a vengeance, claiming that these weapons are destroying the very society in which we live, in reality, however—statistics support that assault weapons account for very little serious crime.

Most firearms that fall under the heading of assault weapons are very expensive, hard to conceal and are not favored by most criminals. Sure, there are exceptions to this rule, but most criminals prefer cheap, easy to conceal, (small handgun-type) firearms that are anything but assault-class weapons. And yet, the government is relentlessly outlawing any guns/ammo that can possibly be classified as assault weapons. *The question is obviously why and what can we do about it?*

Many states have now made the possession of assault weapons a serious crime requiring five-year mandatory prison sentences if you're caught with one. More and more states every year are following suit and outlawing these high-powered guns. The State of New Jersey for example has some of the most severe penalties regarding assault weapons in the county.

But according to the New Jersey State Police:

> *Since we have started keeping records, assault weapons have been used in an 'over-whelming' .026 of 1% of crimes in New Jersey. This means that our officers are more likely to be confronted by an escaped tiger from the local zoo, than they are to be confronted by an assault weapon in the hands of a criminal loose on the street.*[15]

The state of New York has also outlawed assault weapons, claiming that its police officers are in grave danger from these weapons. But the facts show that no New York police officer has been shot with an assault weapon in over ten years.[16]

Even in the State of California, the home of some of the most drastic gun laws prohibiting the ownership of assault weapons, this contradiction is also apparent. According to the California Bureau of Forensic Services' recent 'confidential' report:

> *It is obvious to those of us in the state crime lab system that the presumption that assault weapons constitute a major threat in California is absolutely wrong.*[17]

This is not to say that crimes, and unfortunately even deaths, don't occur with these weapons. But the true fact is that every year baseball bats kill far more people than assault weapons. Therefore, if we want to make society a safer place, we should start by eliminating the bats!

It would clearly seem that assault weapons are hardly the killing monsters that the public's been deliberately convinced they are. Besides, in many states it's perfectly legal to purchase AR-15's and ammunition to shoot them, assuming of course you can pass the state's background checks.

In 1990, even the FBI had to comment on the misrepresentation of assault weapons saying: *"Despite media concern over Uzi's and AK-47's (two notorious and vilified assault weapons), no law enforcement officers have been killed by these weapons in the previous ten years."* [18]

So why has there been such a firm/effective/concentrated effort to convince the public that these assault weapons are evil? If assault weapons account for very little crime—why is the U.S. government trying so hard to abolish them? So why am I defending my position on them?

Keep in mind that the only true significance that 'assault weapons' have—is that they can be used for military purposes! In other words, assault weapons can be used to counter or match the firepower of military units. Assault weapons have a 'military' significance and are of 'military' value—therefore they play a very small roll in the nation's actual crime rate!

Assault weapons however, have not been the only type of firearms the governments of the world are eliminating from the hands of their populations—all guns are being slated for elimination. One of the main tactics that governments have used to abolish public gun ownership is to convince the public that 'less guns' means 'less crime.' Hundreds of new gun laws have recently been passed under the battle cry, *"Let's make our society safer by getting rid of guns!"*

But almost every study that has ever been done on the relationship between crime and gun ownership, shows that reducing the number of guns in society <u>does not reduce crime</u>—it actually <u>increases it</u>.

This point can be clearly demonstrated in the case of Australia's gun elimination program. In 1996, the Australian Government decided that it was going to ban most firearms and aggressively seized more than 640,000 guns from law-abiding Australian citizens.

In the two years following this gun-grab, armed robberies rose by 73%, kidnappings by 38%, physical assaults by 17%, and manslaughter by 29%.[19] OOPS... —Here we go again!!

According to a recent survey, Australia now ranks number one in violent crimes among industrialized nations. England, who also abolished all of its private gun ownership—now ranks second. Clearly, the reduction of guns doesn't reduce crime and any one who understands this difficult subject clearly knows and understands that.

So why are governments around the world continuing to say that we must eliminate private gun ownership to reduce crime and stabilize society?

The government has also spent a great deal of time and money convincing the general public that defending themselves with guns is dangerous and that criminals will likely take your gun away—and use it against you. As a gun owner—I rather doubt that most 'other' American gun owners would agree with that concept.

But according to Florida State University criminologist, Gary Kleck, U.S. citizens use their guns to defend themselves from criminals at least a million times every year. And in approximately

98% of these cases, no shots are ever fired and the criminals flee at the mere sight of the citizen's gun.[20] *So what part of this 'common sense' conclusion doesn't the government understand?*

In actuality, citizens have had to shoot their attackers in only 2% of these cases and in only 1% of the cases do the attackers manage to take guns away from their intended victims. Women are also two hundred and fifty times more likely to fend off an attacker if they're armed as opposed to being unarmed.[21] Clearly, guns save many lives each year and the American public knows it!

So why are global governments still trying to convince their people that they are much safer in their homes without a gun than with one? Maybe we're right about their collective fears the general public will instinctively resist 'martial law?' AND RIGHTLY SO!!!

Most governments would simply rather you not have a gun, even in your home for protection. Instead, many authorities say that in the event of a criminal breaking into your house, you should call the police and wait for them to show up and deal with your problem. Of course these same governments know however, that in 95% of all 911-type calls placed to police, that specific crime is already over and the criminals long-gone by the time police arrive on the scene.

When governments start to run out of reasons to eliminate firearms, they always fall back on one of their favorite tactics—the loving need to 'save our children.' It is true that some children are tragically killed by firearms each year, but in 1995 for example, 2,900 children died in car crashes, 950 drowned, 1,000 died of burns and less than 200 were killed with guns—and some of them while in the process of committing crimes.[22]

Granted, any child killed is a horrible tragedy, but more children were killed in 1995 by bicycles than by firearms. Therefore, we must ask the question: *Are children really in such danger from guns that we must rid our society of them?*

Or is the safety of our children just a good way to scare people into willingly giving up their firearms? How much of what the public is being told by officials is the truth—and how much is designed to achieve another agenda? So if 'X' comes—do fewer guns mean easier control?

Whatever your views on the subject of guns is your business! But keep one thing in mind, when you give up your rights to legally own a firearm, you are giving up the ability to defend yourself and your family. In the event that something catastrophic goes wrong, the police, most likely, are not going to be there to help you! *You're going to be out there all alone—just you and them!*

Take the horrific looting and riots in Los Angeles as an example. In the summer of 1991, mass riots broke out throughout the Los Angeles area over the acquittal of police officers responsible for the senseless beating of Rodney King. To protect themselves, the police retreated to their homes and precincts, leaving more than 50 people brutally killed, with over 4,000 injured and more than 700 buildings burned to the ground and two billion dollars in property destroyed.

Those who weathered the storm best were the brave storeowners, mostly Korean, who stood guard over their property with pistols, shotguns, and yes, assault weapons. As an ironic side-note, many of these same storeowners were later arrested and sentenced for weapons violations.

In the aftermath of the L.A. riots (which this author photographed), many people tried to sue the Los Angeles police department for not providing solid protection and responding to the public's frantic calls for help. To the surprise of many, the courts unanimously ruled that the authorities have <u>no</u> constitutional obligations to protect the public and most of these cases were immediately thrown out of court. In other riots throughout the years and in many other cities across America like Chicago, St Louis, Detroit, Newark and others—these court decisions were always the same.

In other words the police have no responsibility or obligation to protect you! They are required to 'attempt' to do so, only if their lives or well-being are <u>not</u> placed in jeopardy during the process. You are in <u>no way</u> entitled or guaranteed help from the authorities. When the chips are down, baby—you're on your own! Simply put, if you were stupid enough to give up your guns and your ability to defend yourself—then reality dictates you deserve whatever fate awaits you.

Do guns account for violent crime and accidental deaths? Yes, of course! But so do cars, steak knives, baseball bats, candleholders, fire pokers, Christmas tree stands, automotive tools, shovels and a host of other common household, gardening and sports-related items.

Life is not perfect and unfortunately—tragic things happen with almost every item found in the modern kitchen! When you give up the right to own a firearm you may believe that you're really making the world a safer/better place to live, but what you're actually giving up is the ability to defend yourself and your family! So please think <u>long</u> and <u>hard</u> on this point!

If most governments are aggressively outlawing gun ownership, why are they doing it? If the government's 'cover stories' justifying disarming of the public aren't supported by the facts, then why are they so insistent on eliminating gun ownership? —Maybe they 'all' know about 'X'?

Keep in mind that the U.S. Government is not the only government in the world that appears to be doing this. Most other industrialized countries have either already disarmed their citizens or, like the U.S., are very close to doing so. Recently, the United Nations has even started promoting the disarming of all nations around the world, not only eliminating private gun ownership but also firearms training and instructional materials as well.

By now you should be able to recognize the true motivation behind this urgent need to disarm all populations of the world. *No guns equals no resistance—and no resistance guarantees control!*

The up-coming global cataclysms are likely to produce massive sociological upheavals. Rioting, food shortages, looting and other categories of mayhem will be the order of the day. It is likely that we, as a planet, are in for some hard times in the years ahead! All of the governments around the world, as well as the U.N., are going to have their hands full in trying to maintain law and order—both before and after the brown dwarf's passage.

If armed citizens begin to physically resist martial law or armed mobs started attacking military units for food, equipment or more firearms and munitions—militaries might not be able to regain the upper hand. If an armed 'us against the law' mentality ever gets started between the public and the military itself, governments may never be able to restore law and order, and the United States and other surviving nations would theoretically cease to exist as civilized societies.

Unfortunately, an armed and aggressive mob can rip even the best trained military units to shreds if the conditions and motivations are right, just ask the U.S. Special Forces units that were sent to Somalia a few years back rescuing American hostages held by renegade Alcadian war lords.

We believe this is the real reason behind gun control laws and enforcement. Governments know they must do everything possibly to disarm the public before these cataclysms strike. They must also do it fast, effectively and without incident. The future existence of many governments may depend on 'them' having the guns and the power—not the 'public.'

Even more spending

We've already seen the massive militarization of our federal management agencies. But their having 80,000-armed federal agents (with growing numbers by the day) is apparently not enough to handle whatever 'crisis' may be coming at us from outer space.

The U.S. Government has been dramatically increasing its spending in order to promote an ever-greater level of disaster preparation and training.

On 22 December 2001, the *Washington Post* reported that President Bush would make a dramatic increase in spending for homeland security, more than 'doubling' the 2002 budget for the fiscal year 2003. The *Washington Post* went on to say that the President was also planning to make this increase in spending the 'centerpiece' of his next fiscal budget, which increases spending on all homeland security measures into the 'tens of billions' of dollars every year for the next several years to come.

These budget increases will be accomplished at 'any' and 'all' cost, and the administration has already acknowledged that it will have to cut deeply into other domestic programs paying for these new spending initiatives, i.e., port and airport security plus securing our porous borders.

With all of the extreme preparations that have already been taking place over the past decade, why would the President feel the need to increase spending even more? Even if more money was needed for homeland security, a 'doubling' of the current budget seems a little extreme.

In fact, the current administration is spending money like there's no tomorrow driving up the national debt by billions of dollars every month. The continuing Iraqi war and this huge increase in homeland security spending have alarmed many economists and it's already been suggested that if this current level of expenditure continues—the U.S. will eventually bankrupt itself!

In a seldom seen moment of honesty—the President (George W.), recently announced that the new expenditures are to equip and train 'regional authorities' to respond to national emergencies and to practice 'doomsday rehearsals.' *So who says that 'George' doesn't always tell the truth?*

The government wouldn't spend this money unless they knew 'doomsday' was rapidly approaching! And the sad commentary is it's not only the U.S. that's facing these momentous challenges but all world nations as well! Then add in the deadly factor of global terrorism competing for 'dollar attention' and you've got 'the perfect storm' of financial woe and concern to deal with.

In December 2003, the U.S. Congress announced it was appropriating funds for a considerable increase in the number of men and women in the armed services. This decision will add an additional 40,000 troops to the Army, 29,000 to the Air Force and over 15,000 to the Marines, although the final numbers may eventually run much higher. Large enlistment increases have also been slated for the Army National Guard and the U.S. Coast Guard. Apparently, whatever event is in our immediate future the U.S. Government believes our current military is insufficient—and needs to be increased by 'tens of thousands' of combat-ready soldiers.

In a related story involving 'doomsday' preparations, in September 2003, Russia launched a series of satellites designed to monitor natural disasters that are apparently going to take place on a massive scale. *Reuters News Service* reported:

> *A Russian rocket successfully launched on Saturday half a dozen satellites, including three devoted to monitoring natural disasters throughout the world.*
>
> *Two of the satellites were Russian and the others belonged to organizations in Britain, Nigeria, South Korea, and Turkey.*
>
> *The British, Nigerian, and Turkish satellites were part of the 40 million dollar <u>Disaster Monitoring Constellation project</u>, which its British backers say will provide <u>day-to-day monitoring of disasters</u>.*
>
> *Five ground stations will provide up-to-the-minute data to enable relief agencies to direct their operations more efficiently in tracking droughts, earthquakes, fires, and other calamities. Other countries taking part include Algeria, China, and Thailand.[23]*

At first, most people would not give this story a second thought. But think about what you've just read for a moment.

What type of natural disasters would be so large/pervasive that we need a whole series (constellation) of satellites just to monitor them? What type of disaster needs five ground-based tracking stations positioned around the world providing up to the minute information to help coordinate ground relief efforts? And what could be waiting for us in the future that has Russia, Nigeria, Turkey, Algeria, China, Thailand, South Korea and others, all 'working together' assembling a worldwide disaster monitoring system into place? —They're actually helping each other??

From dramatic increases in disaster preparation spending, to an entire series of satellites and ground-based tracking stations designed to monitor 'global cataclysms,' and from international agreements implemented to exchange military forces between nations planning for martial law— what's going on here? Are many governments of the world secretly working together by quietly preparing Earth for something 'big' happening suddenly—and from the looks of it—soon?

What's FEMA really doing—and why?

FEMA was created in 1979 (at about the same time NASA started frantically searching for hard evidence of the brown dwarf —'Wormwood') established under Presidential Memorandum 32.

In short, FEMA is the primary federal agency now responsible for overseeing and managing all 'national emergencies' regardless of their nature—natural disasters/terrorism/civil unrest! And in recent years FEMA has engaged in a number of interesting activities that may shed more light on what's headed our way and what the government doesn't wish to openly admit.

On 19 June 2002, FEMA posted special 'bid notices' to award the agency's largest contract ever to several U.S. firms. FEMA is reportedly spending billions of dollars to prepare 'temporary' housing facilities for displaced U.S. citizens on a scale never before seen.

According to FEMA, they are asking U.S. firms to provide detailed plans for technical support, consultants and other management resources in order to set up emergency living facilities for millions of fleeing Americans.

On 17 July 2002, *ECTV* carried a *NewsMax* story entitled: *"FEMA Preparing for Mass Destruction on Cities."* According to this article:

> *FEMA, the federal agency charged with disaster preparedness, is engaged in a crash effort to prepare for multiple mass destruction (events)...on US cities—including the creation of sprawling temporary sites to handle millions of displaced persons...*

> *The agency (FEMA) has already notified vendors, contractors, and consultants that it needs to be prepared to handle the logistics of aiding millions of displaced Americans who will flee from urban areas...*

> *The agency plans to create emergency, makeshift cities that could house hundreds of thousands, if not millions, of Americans who may have to flee their urban homes...*

> *Ominously, FEMA has given a deadline of having the cities ready to go by January 20. [Note: New Orleans, Katrina and Rita nearly busted FEMA's resources and staffing.]*

> *FEMA is currently seeking bids from major real estate management firms, and plans to name three firms in the near future to handle the logistics and planning for these temporary cities.*

> *FEMA officials have told these firms they already have tents and trailers ordered. The tents and trailers would provide shelter for displaced populations.*

> *The real estate firms are expected to provide engineers and architects to lay the plans for emergency infrastructure needs, such as sewage and electricity.*[24]

Once again the 'cover story' FEMA is giving the public (as to why they're making these massive relocation plans) is that large American cities might have to be evacuated during a terrorist attack. And this may be, at least in part, true! But according to *NewsMax.com*, when FEMA officials were recently asked why the bid notices that went out to contractors did not mention this potential for terrorism, FEMA said that *"the program's main focus...is (actually) on natural disasters."* [Note: The last several hurricane seasons severely tested FEMA's resolve and duty.]

If fact, upon closer examination, FEMA's actual bid notice says:

> *The Contractors shall be required to provide support capabilities for all types of (natural) disasters with special emphasis on river and coastal flooding, tornadoes, hurricanes, typhoons, earthquakes, and tsunamis.*[25]

In addition to FEMA making plans to house millions of citizens displaced from their homes by natural disasters, FEMA has also set up a number of major relocation centers throughout the nation. From sporadic news reports, FEMA apparently has over 100 of these relocation centers already set up to function and receive disaster victims.

According to *The Final Warning* by Kathleen Keating:

> *These camps are all over the country, with the largest camp located in Alaska. Most of these camps are built to house approximately twenty thousand people, while the camp in Alaska can arguably support five hundred thousand.*[26]

The questions at this point should be obvious. *What type of natural disaster is FEMA preparing for? What type of disaster would involve earthquakes, coastal and river flooding, typhoons, tsunamis (tidal waves) and hurricane force winds? Could these natural disasters be so severe that they would require evacuating millions of individuals into temporary housing? Why is FEMA maintaining so many relocation centers around the nation, capable of housing tens or even hundreds of thousands of people? And mostly—how come we know so little about them?*

Another very interesting part of FEMA's bid notice to potential contractors is their requirement that bidding firms plan for 'typhoons' as part of their bid proposals. Typhoons do not take place in the northern hemisphere. In other words, because of the direction in which the Earth rotates, and the geographic location of the continental U.S. in relation to the planet's rotation, typhoons take place on the opposite side of the equator in the southern hemisphere.

If FEMA is planning for typhoons, could this mean they are planning for an alteration in the rotation of Earth? On the inside—is FEMA considering the possibility of an actual pole shift?

In another recent story, FEMA has been developing a large office complex in the Washington, D.C., area. Even though the construction of these new offices has been expensive, FEMA claims that it desperately needs these new facilities, ASAP.

Then, in December 2001, the agency's director, Joe M. Allbaugh, suddenly announced that FEMA was pulling out of the new facilities at a huge cost of 94 million dollars to taxpayers. *What was that all about and what caused this sudden and expensive change of heart?* According to Allbaugh, FEMA is pulling out of these new facilities because they're located in very close proximity to Reagan National Airport, Interstate 95 and the Potomac River basin.

The first two of these reasons makes little or no sense. All of Washington, D.C., is relatively close to the airport and most buildings are also close to interstates and highways—that's how the employees get to and from work! But it's the third reason that's really puzzling.

You see, the government and the FEMA director obviously know that this forthcoming global catastrophe will produce massive changes in the water levels of the Potomac River—possibly flooding large areas of Washington as it overflows its banks. So in a recent assessment of future damage, Mr. Allbaugh wisely realized that his agency's new building sits in harm's way and so decided to pull out of the immediate area—even if it meant losing 94 million in taxpayer dollars.

These are only a few examples that clearly indicate that FEMA (as a governmental agency) is in the process of properly bracing itself and our nation's resources for what's potentially coming.

Getting ready now

In 2002, under the direction of Secretary Tom Ridge, the U.S. Department of Homeland Security started a massive public information TV ad-campaign called *"Get Ready Now."* In this public awareness project, Director Ridge makes a 30-second commercial telling his fellow Americans to 'get ready' for both <u>man-made</u> and <u>natural disasters</u> and to 'be prepared' for the <u>unexpected.</u>

This advertising program was designed to motivate Americans to prepare for any upcoming national emergency, especially situations in which individuals would have to take care of themselves for a few days, a few weeks or maybe even longer, 30-90 days. (Remember New Orleans)

The public is being urged to put together an emergency supply kit containing water, food, a flashlight and a radio both with extra batteries, a first aid kit, blankets and some warm clothing, dust masks, extra prescription medications, pet foods, cooking utensils and bathroom needs, etc. (We'll look into the specifics of personal preparations later in this book).

Emergency planning was also part of Secretary Ridge's *"Get Ready Now"* program encouraging people to develop a family communications plan in case separated, secure an emergency shelter within your home, working together as a community and by helping other people around you.

Although the main reason given by the government for this preparation leans toward the threat of terrorism, the preparation advice given also applies very nicely toward the passage of the brown dwarf. Of course the government never mentions this scenario—and rightfully so; they would be irresponsible if they did —instead they simply encouraged all Americans to, *"Get Ready Now!"*

The government's *"Get Ready Now"* informational booklet concludes by stating:

> *Be prepared to adopt this (preparation) information to your personal circumstances and make every effort to follow instructions received from authorities on the scene. Above all, stay calm, be patient, and think before you act. (In other words don't go out and loot). With these simple preparations you can <u>be ready for the unexpected</u>.*[27]

Most modern-day astronomers including those at NASA believe that Earth being struck by a large asteroid or comet is one of the gravest threats facing humankind today. At any moment a large space rock the size of a football field could hit the Earth—causing unimaginable damage.

And little do most people know that they're really preparing for some truly unexpected events!

Hiding a brown dwarf — 101

Arecibo, Puerto Rico

For years the large radio telescope known as the Arecibo Observatory in Puerto Rico has been considered the best 'early warning' system for the detection of approaching space objects that our planet has. The large radio dish at Arecibo is perfect for calculating the speed, trajectory and distance of so-called Near Earth Objects (NEOs) that could be rapidly approaching our planet at this very moment.

Several noted astronomers and organizations have recently stated that the search for objects approaching our planet is the highest priority in astronomy today and the use of the Arecibo observatory is vital to this endeavor.

But recently in an unexpected official announcement (that stunned the astronomical community), the Arecibo Observatory and NASA both unexpectedly announced that Arecibo was not going to look into this subject anymore, and furthermore, was pulling the Arecibo radio telescope out of the NEO (Near Earth Object) project altogether.

On 19 December 2001, an article appeared in a number of space publications and news services stating:

> *The Planetary Society (and numerous other scientific groups) strongly condemns NASA's decision, announced today, to terminate radar observations of Near Earth Objects (NEOs) from the Arecibo Observatory In Puerto Rico.*
>
> *Arecibo is the most powerful radio observatory on Earth and is the most accurate instrument we have for studying NEOs...."Arecibo radar observations are critical for determining the exact location, speed and direction of objects that approach Earth," said Louis Friedman, Executive Director of the Planetary Society. "We need this information to know how significant the probability is of any one asteroid hitting the Earth."*
>
> *Radar observations provide the very accurate position and velocity information necessary to determining the orbits and predicting the future paths for objects that come very close to Earth.*
>
> *"The decision to eliminate these Arecibo observations, and not obtain precision data, is very short-sighted," commented Friedman. "If an object is discovered headed toward Earth, we are certainly going to wish we had the ability to track it accurately."* [28]

Why would NASA (and so many other astronomers) place the NEO project as the very top priority in astronomy and then with no reasonable warning—'shut down' the entire project?

And why would NASA be so irresponsible as to remove Earth's best 'early warning' detection system—leaving Earth blind to cosmic collisions? Is someone 'in charge' simply asleep at the switch, or have they decided to ignore the situation altogether—hoping it might just 'go away'?

The answers should be obvious! There is something headed toward our planet that NASA does not want the astronomical community, and especially the general public, to know about. The elimination of the Arecibo Observatory leaves our planet blind in regard to what's approaching us from space—and this is the whole idea behind the Arecibo closure. We're not supposed to see what's coming—that's the whole point!

But Arecibo is not the only observatory in recent years to be taken off line. As a matter of fact, most observatories that are accessible to the public have been closed for remodeling, burned to the ground, or placed under military control over the past year or two. There is some-thing sinister and mysterious approaching us from space, and the governments of the world are going to do everything they can to make sure nobody sees this object until the very last minute.

Bye, bye 'Space Environment Center'

If being hit by a large asteroid is the biggest threat facing humanity (for those that don't know about the approaching brown dwarf)—being struck with a massive solar flare is the second biggest. Today, space scientists admit that if a large solar flare known as a coronal mass ejection (CME) was directed toward Earth, the results could be devastating, knocking out satellites and power grids around the world and causing upwards of a trillion dollars in infrastructure damage.

Thankfully, satellite operators, power companies, and militaries have an 'early-warning' system called the 'Space Environment Center' (SEC). This center is a division of NOAA (the National Oceanic and Atmospheric Administration in Boulder, Colorado) that provides real-time data and pictures of the solar environment. This early warning information allows other agencies to make critical adjustments to their systems in order to limit damage to sensitive equipment in the event that a large solar flare is directed towards Earth.

Then, to the further amazement of space scientists, in the fall of 2003, the government unex-pectedly announced plans to close the entire SEC program and eliminate the reporting of all solar data altogether. Not only is the SEC to be totally eliminated, but it was slated to happen rapidly —even taking place by the end of the month.

Note: At the end of October 2003, just as the U.S. Government is slating the SEC for closure, an unprecedented level of solar activity has erupted, producing the largest and most powerful solar flares and CME's ever recorded by modern science!

Why would the government even consider closing something so important as the SEC? Why would they be doing such an outrageous and irresponsible thing to the American public?

Because the SEC picks up images of the Sun and in turn anything that is nearing the Sun from space—the SEC would certainly have picked up images of this approaching brown dwarf as it comes ever-nearer, giving the world's populations additional/advanced notice of its approach and more time to solve their social/logistical problems—such as panicking and riots in their streets. Once again, the powers that be are determined to keep the exact location and timing of the brown dwarf's approach a closely guarded 'secret' for as long as possible. The less 'advanced warning' the public has, the less time they will have for rioting and looting—and the less time the government will be forced to maintain martial law. Simply put, keep society running 'normally' and 'smoothly' for as long as absolutely possible and only shut things down at the last moment.

Keeping the approaching brown dwarf a TOP-SECRET until the last moment is an important part of the government's overall 'national security' preparedness plans—and they're probably right.

Bunkers, bunkers, everywhere—but built for whom?

In 2000, ground was broken on an enormous underground complex in front of the U.S. Congress in Washington, D.C. Most congressional leaders are calling it one of the most important and exciting new developments in Washington's history and champion this large underground city.

This huge underground complex being called the New Congressional Visitors Center is a massive construction project costing 500 million dollars at present, but almost everyone agrees the final cost will eventually run much higher. *(Some have even suggested the final costs could run into the billions of dollars.)*

This underground congressional city is truly a feat of modern engineering and comes complete with congressional offices, elaborate security systems, tunnels to other parts of Washington and designed with secret escape passages...to??

Even though Congress is elated with their new underground city, the rest of Washington and the nation are understandably outraged!

How can Congress spend so much money on such a seemingly unnecessary project? Even if they did need a new visitors center (which they don't) why place it underground—and why include so many features that seem so unnecessary for simply visiting the Congress?

This is not an isolated example of large underground complexes being built in recent years however. Numerous other news reports have surfaced in recent times about clandestine and quite 'mysterious' underground tunneling and building on the part of other governments around the world. Russia, Japan, England and dozens of other nations have also constructed large underground facilities/bunkers capable of housing many thousands of people. And all of these foreign governments are now quite reluctant to even talk about these massive underground construction projects and routinely go as far as to completely deny their very existence all together. *Hmmm! Now where have we heard ancient accounts like that before?*

On 8 December 2003, the *Jerusalem Post* ran an article entitled: *"National Underground Shelter Being Readied."* This compelling article by Arieh O'Sullivan stated:

> *An underground cavern meant to serve as an emergency National Control Center for the heads of government is reportedly being carved out of the stone in the Judean Hills.*
>
> *Channel 10 revealed what it claimed was one of the "most secret projects in the state." It said that since 2002 tractors have been digging out a network of tunnels and chambers at an undisclosed location.*

> *The project is to house a command complex capable of withstanding an atomic bomb, chemical or biological attack, and earthquakes. The TV station reported that not all of the details were released for publication by the military censor's office.*
>
> *Like similar emergency control centers around the world, this project would be used to host the prime minister and the cabinet in times of peril. It is to be equipped with a hi-tech network that sorts and funnels data onto large video screens for a fuller picture of the battlefield situation (perhaps rioting on the streets of Jerusalem). The cost of this project is estimated to be more than 500 million for the mining (task) alone.*
>
> *MK Yossi Sarid (Meretz) reacted to the report calling the bunker a wasteful and unnecessary expenditure, especially in light of cuts in the defense budget, which is there to protect the entire public and not just the Prime Minister.*[29]

This article points out several important factors that are common with these underground construction projects. All of these facilities cost hundreds of millions or even billions of dollars to construct; are exclusively used for the safety of the rich and politically powerful; are built to withstand nuclear explosions as well as 'natural disasters' such as earthquakes; and all seem to have large video screens to watch the 'mayhem' taking place with the little people above.

Why are all of these underground complexes being built around the world and why do so many of their builders seem reluctant to talk about these elaborate construction projects? Could these underground cities be part of the preparation for the brown dwarf's upcoming passage?

As we have seen earlier in this book, ancient cultures also built large underground complexes capable of housing tens of thousands of people. These complexes, like those in Turkey and other places throughout the Middle East, were lived in for a few years and then mysteriously abandoned. And at the same time these underground cities were being occupied, the above ground cities all around them burned to the ground. Evidence suggests that the underground inhabitants survived while many of the above ground populations did not. —OOPS…

When you consider the massive gravitational effects the approaching brown dwarf is going to have on our planet—generating massive storms, high winds, volcanic fallout, earthquakes and a flammable hydrocarbon tail passing through our atmosphere, is it any wonder why all of these underground governmental facilities are currently being built throughout the world! Future-minded and enlightened governments everywhere are 'digging in' for the rough road ahead.

Is the reality of a one-world government closer now?

Governments, corporations, powerful groups and influential individuals all have intelligence-gathering resources because ultimately—advanced knowledge of upcoming events translates into political, financial and social power structures. Put another way, knowledge of upcoming events provides the ability to be proactive making arrangements for these events before they happen—ultimately placing you in an advantageous situation when these dire events come to pass.

If you knew the sky was falling—would you wait until it hit you before taking evasive action??

As we have already stated, it would be naive to think that powerful governments and research organizations are ignorant of this approaching brown dwarf star. These same institutions are obviously aware of the geologic damage this object's passage is going to cause. They know that even if a full-blown pole shift does not happen, large sections of Earth, including entire countries could end up underwater, or be covered by mountains of hot volcanic ash, or be smashed into muddy rubble by powerful earthquakes.

Dealing with the aftermath of these events will take more than localized efforts; it will take global oversight and coordination if our planet is to fully recover. That is why nations are setting aside their differences and preparing to exchange military troops, building and launching joint disaster monitoring satellites and eliminating barriers to free trade and commerce.

For many years now, global plans have been in effect creating a one-world government—the 'New World Order' if you will. Organizations such as the United Nations, World Bank, World Wildlife Fund, World Trade Organization and other globally oriented entities, are making plans to operate as international managers and if necessary, create a planetary 'take over/recovery' government. In other words, these power groups use their advanced intelligence of this incoming object to place themselves into positions of global power control before the upcoming events.

In reality and in fact—it just may take a globally organized and well-financed political effort to internationally recover from the devastating effects of this approaching brown dwarf's passage.

This agenda of a coming 'global government' was clearly alluded to by none other than former Secretary of State under President Nixon, Dr. Henry Kissinger, who in 1991 publicly stated:

> *Today, America would be outraged if U.N. troops entered Los Angeles to restore order. Tomorrow they will be grateful! This is especially true if they were told that there was an outside threat from beyond...that threatened our very existence.*
>
> *It is then that all peoples of the world will plead to deliver them from this evil. The one thing every man fears is the unknown. When presented with this scenario, individual rights will be willingly relinquished for the guarantee of their well being granted to them by the World Government.*[30]

Once again in the interest of readability, we are going to put the brakes on this chapter. Unfortunately there are dozens of other important news articles that we haven't presented. But like other chapters in this book, this one subject could easily fill an entire volume all by itself.

Suffice to say that plans are in effect to erect a 'one-world government/new world order' in the very near future. This global government will be far different from what most Americans are currently used to. Whether this global government will be a good thing or not—can only be accurately judged in the future. The only thing that can be offered at this time for your added consideration is the old adage: *"Power corrupts, and absolute power corrupts absolutely."*

In conclusion: For hundreds, if not thousands of years, historians/philosophers/scientists have known about the periodic passage of a large celestial object coursing through our solar system.

Within the past several decades, individuals within our own government began to study these ancient records and subsequently learned of this periodic 'cosmic visitor' and the destruction this celestial object is capable of producing. These same individuals also realized that the geologic and archeological evidence uncovered over the past several hundred years supports this ancient history and they accurately concluded our planet is ultimately headed for another catastrophic 'fly-by' in the near future.

It didn't take long for these same individuals to also realize that the large gravitational attraction of this object was pulling on the outer planets of our solar system, and a number of scientists and governmental agencies subsequently began to mathematically calculate the general location of this mysterious outer space visitor. Once the general location of this object had been established, the government began to look for this heavenly body with light and then later infrared telescopes.

To the government's initial elation they found what they were looking for—but then quickly realized the magnitude of their discovery. A brown dwarf star is coming toward us and its passage is more than likely going to cause a substantial amount of destruction to our fragile planet. Realizing this was going to be a global event, preparations had to begin in earnest—so the U.S. informed selected members of the United Nations, then setting up to develop a series of emergency 'stop-gap' measures designed to deal with the massive planetary destruction anticipated.

Major steps were taken in order to preserve the infrastructure of the U.S. Government—forming federal agencies such as FEMA, passing a series of executive orders, preparing the military to invoke martial law and a host of other measures all focused on maintaining the 'continuity of our government' under crisis. Of course, all of these preparations have been conducted 'under the table,' and the public has simply been given a series of 'cover stories' that have allowed for these extensive preparations to begin in earnest and be advanced without 'informing' and/or 'panicking' the general population.

The decision was clearly made to keep people in the dark for as long as possible, thus keeping the normal functioning of society going until the bitter end. Once this object becomes visible in the sky—only weeks (or even days) before the dwarf's actual passage, martial law will be enacted—essentially 'shutting-down' society in order to preserve the economic infrastructure of our modern-day world. If martial law were not enacted, a physically, mentally and spiritually unprepared public would loot and vandalize society right back into the Dark Ages or beyond!

The military, along with federal, state and local police will jointly enforce martial law. Aided by a sophisticated array of highway walls, cameras, OECs and other crowd control measures, the general population will be successfully kept 'locked down' until after the brown dwarf's passage.

So maybe George Orwell's 1984 wasn't as 'far out' as most people reading it came to believe?

The public, of course, will have little choice in this matter for most of their guns have already been stripped away. They will therefore have no effective means of interfering with the will of heavily armed government and law enforcement agencies. Unfortunately, the public will also not be able to defend themselves against each other, and it's likely that individual neighborhoods will be sealed off—many becoming lawless jungles, with raping and pillaging being the order of the day as the brown dwarf makes its final approach. *Considering our nation's past history— maybe so?*

As the brown dwarf nears, its gravitational effects will cause massive coastal flooding at the very least, prompting coastal residents to break martial law and head inland. FEMA has prepared for this eventuality and has made preparations to house these fleeing citizens by the millions. FEMA has also developed a network of relocation centers around the country to act as additional detention/relocation centers and to house critical-need government employees and their families.

Sports stadiums, prisons, auditoriums, convention centers, other large public facilities will also be used as detention centers for those arrested during martial law (like they did in New Orleans.) As the brown dwarf passes, the government hopes that the damage will be minimal, allowing clean up efforts to begin quickly. However, should the destruction become more extensive, the government (through the use of executive orders), is ready to take drastic measures—drafting ordinary citizens for labor, confiscating personal property, breaking up families (like in New Orleans) or just about anything else it has to do in order preserve the 'continuity of government.'

These types of draconian measures are not limited to the U.S. and most other westernized governments around the world have been engaged in passing similar laws and preparation programs. Whatever's going to happen here is going to affect the entire planet, not just the U.S. —and we believe 'the one-world government' is presently/covertly preparing for it.

In the event that individual countries cannot deal with the massive levels of destruction inflicted on them by the brown dwarf's passage, hopefully a series of global agencies such as the U.N., World Bank and World Trade Organization will 'kick in'—helping to restore law and order and rebuild our current 21st century society after the collapse occurs. And hopefully, the greater world community will also work together by sharing/distributing their military units where they are most needed—as well as cooperating on information regarding areas of intense destruction.

The examples of governmental preparations that we have detailed in this section merely scratch the surface of all that is currently being done. There is simply not enough room in this chapter to cover all of the global preparations taking place. Also, we have no way of knowing all of the preparations taking place behind closed doors, and therefore we've only reported on 'the most obvious' of things going on right in front of our eyes and all over the Internet.

Let us also make it perfectly clear that we're not blaming any government for its current actions. We understand why the governments of the world are preparing for the upcoming cataclysms and keeping this critical information from the public. The world in which we live <u>must</u> carry on as long as it can <u>without</u> disruption. If word of these events got out too soon, the general public would certainly panic, drastically interfering with their government's ability to preserve their nation's damaged infrastructures and in turn the future of our global society—whatever happens.

Besides, there simply are not enough available resources (such as food and other survival supplies) on this planet for every man, woman and child to personally prepare ahead of time for the up-coming catastrophic events. The governments of the world have no choice but to selectively utilize these limited resources for their own individual agendas—good or bad!

And they must do so while keeping this proactive allocation a quiet secret from the masses.

Our government and others are definitely getting ready for something! They are making preparations on a massive scale and they are doing it quickly. They are using a host of 'excuses' and 'cover stories' to justify these necessary disaster preparations, while trying to keep the whole situation quietly hidden under the table.

At this point we can only hope the timing of the brown dwarf's passage causes little damage and that all of the government's preparation plans hold together. So let's hope for the best future of our children and society as we know 'it'—praying that we come out of this dire event unscathed.

But what if this is not the case? What if the upcoming passage causes more destruction than currently anticipated? What if our planet undergoes a massive displacement of its crust— causing a horrendous chain of natural disasters to paralyze our world? What if members of the military and police start deserting their stations and going home to defend their own family— leaving society to fend for itself? What if the authorities are totally overwhelmed by the magnitude of the upcoming events? Or what if the 'chain of command' suddenly breaks down and the coordination of inadequate emergency resources become non-existent? And what if society as we know it deteriorates into total anarchy? Or terrorist-like nations start a massive warfare campaign against each other and the world in the shadow of Wormwood's approach?

If we are to believe the prophetic warnings investigated in the last chapter, this is exactly what may happen. Remember that all of the prophecies we presented/reviewed warned us of a massive pole shift taking place, followed by a chain of horrendous natural catastrophes and a subsequent meltdown of our modern-day society!

Since it's highly unlikely the authorities are going to save us, or even provide any meaningful assistance once the *Planet-X* events in question begin, <u>we should 'hope' for the best but 'prepare' for the worst.</u>

If we've learned anything as a nation (under stress) following the last several hurricane seasons and the tragic aftermath of the mega 9.0 earthquake and subsequent tsunamis that ravaged SE Asia in December of '04 (killing over a quarter million people)—we must remove our heads from under the sand and strive to understand that 'things' aren't going to 'suddenly get better.'

And if planet Earth is now entering into a periodic cycle of 'global warming' with its effects on our oceans causing greater and more destructive hurricane seasons—don't we at least owe it to ourselves and our families to 'smarten up,' —thus heeding the warning signs long before its 'fashionably' too late? —Another old adage says: "He who hesitates is often lost!"

We want to remind our readers that this work was not written to scare or intimidate its audience —but rather to educate, prepare and explain the reality of the 'bigger cosmic picture' out there. Some would call it a 'zealot's mission—but I feel it's my responsibility to share this information.

In the next two chapters we'll look at what you can personally do in order to prepare for the worst-case scenario. Hopefully we're wrong about 'X' coming in 2009/2012—but if we're not??

CHAPTER SEVEN ENDNOTES

[1] Watson, Paul Joseph, *Order Out Of Chaos* (AEJ publishing, 2003) p. 268.

[2] http://www.smh.com.au/articles/2002/07/27/1027497418339.html.

[3] http://www.southjerseynews.com?issues/march/m031603e.html.

[4] http://www.newsmax.com/archives/articles/2003/11/20/185048.shtml.

[5] Tyson, Ann Scott, *Military adds U.S. to Unified Command* (Christian Science Monitor, 2001)

[6] Sprengelmeyer, M. E., *Marines Storm Southern Town* (News Washington Bureau, 10 November 2001)

[7] http://www.drudgereport.com/flash2.html.

[8] Farah, Joseph, *Domestic Rapid Deployment Forces* (WorldNetDaily.com, 1998)

[9] Cohen, Tom, Associated Press, 10 December 2002.

[10] Bovard, James, *Lost Rights* (Palgrave, 2000) p. 201.

[11] Foster, Sarah, *Armed and Dangerous, Federal Agencies Expanding Use of Firepower*, WordNetDaily, 15 August 1997.

[12] Farah, Joseph, *Clinton's Militarization of the Government*, WorldNetDaily, 15 August 1997.

[13] Foster, Sarah, *Armed and Dangerous, Federal Agencies Expanding Use of Firepower*, WordNetDaily, 15 August 1997.

[14] Poe, Richard, *The Seven Myths of Gun Control* (Form Publishing, 2001) p. 13.

[15] Bovard, James, *Lost Rights* (Palgrave, 2000) p. 220.

[16] Ibid.

[17] Ibid.

[18] Ibid.

[19] Poe, Richard, *The Seven Myths of Gun Control* (Form Publishing, 2001) p. 100.

[20] Ibid., p. 105.

[21] Ibid., p. 108.

[22] Ibid., p. 122.

[23] http://reuters.com/newsArticle.jhtml?type=scienceNews&storyID=3518018

[24] http://www.earthchangestv.com/secure/0702_3articles/printerfri.../17FEMA.html.

[25] Ruddy, Christopher, NewsMax.com, 7 August 2002.

[26] Keating, Kathleen, *The Final Warning* (Picasso Publishing, 2000), p. 96.

[27] US Department of Homeland Security, www.ready.gov.

[28] http://www.spaceref.com/news/viewpr.html?pid=6951

[29] O'Sullivan, Arieh, *Jerusalem Post*, 8 December 2003.

[30] Watson, Paul Joseph, *Order Out Of Chaos* (AEJ Publishing, 2003) p. 267.

This page provided for reader's notes.

— CHAPTER EIGHT —

SELF SUFFICIENCY — *Good up to a point, but we need the Lord.*

In the preceding chapters of this book we explored a brief snapshot of the extensive information indicating that a 'cosmic' global cataclysm may be inevitable in planet Earth's near future. We investigated the historical records of ancient civilizations and the archeological and geologic evidence supporting these ancient accounts. We reviewed the prophetic visions from a host of gifted clairvoyants and witnessed the manifesting physical signs of this approaching celestial event. We've also investigated how the governments of the world are covertly preparing themselves for this 2012 event/secretly setting the stage for the inevitable declaration of martial law.

All of this information is useless however, if you do nothing with it! Therefore let us now look into how this upcoming global cataclysm may affect the society in which we live, our daily lives and even more importantly—what you can do about it! *Witness for Christ, so that people may "escape all these things". Luke 21:36*

It's a House of Cards

The modern-day society in which we live is a vast and wonderfully complex machine. All of our daily needs such as food, water, heating, clothing, transportation, police protection, communications, electricity and a host of other modern conveniences and services are available to us with little thought as to where these various conveniences come from.

If we need food we have 'mega-market' grocery stores open 24 hours a day filled with every type of food product imaginable. If we need clean water it's as close as the turn of a faucet. Our homes are heated by simply flipping a switch on the wall. To communicate with someone, or call for the assistance of the police or fire department, we simply pick up the phone. Even our clothes are washed for us by placing them in a cleaning machine and then turning it on.

All of these modern conveniences help our society function so efficiently, that we take for granted just how fortunate we really are in 2006.

But all of these conveniences come to us with a 'hidden price.' In order for your local supermarket chain or independent to be open and stocked with food (and thousands of other household items), an extensive array of people, skills and circumstances must all come together functioning in a well-coordinated, precise, by-the-numbers dance involving thousands of key components.

The food in your Kroger, Ralphs or Schnucks stores for example must first be grown, harvested, produced, processed, transported and sold at market. The huge debate currently raging in the House and Senate over illegal immigration and how it could affect the migrant 'farm worker' issue—come into play in this discussion. Unfortunately it's not as simple a task as most people think! For instance—let's take the daily availability of just one head of lettuce or a tomato.

In order to produce just one tomato there are very specific growing seasons, climates and environmental conditions that farmers must contend with. The soil must have the right amount of nutrients, proper chemical composition and precise 'pH balance.' These crops must be provided with the right amount of water, favorable atmospheric temperatures and plentiful sunlight to grow properly. If all of these conditions are met and the crops reach maturity, they must then be harvested, transported to processing centers and eventually distributed to markets. So if all this can be done in a very short time before the tomatoes rot, consumers can finally purchase them.

All of these processes and steps require favorable weather conditions, available transportation and distribution facilities and vast amounts of resources and skilled people to do the harvesting. If any step in this complex chain is missing/or/delayed, the whole process rapidly collapses.

Even though we are only talking about tomatoes, almost every other item in your local grocery store has to undergo a similar 'complicated process' before it reaches you—the consumer. If any of these necessary factors is missing (say transportation becomes impossible because roads and airports are covered in volcanic ash), our whole super-duper modern production machine will come to a grinding halt—producing something most people in the U.S. today are totally unfamiliar with—FAMINE!

The processes that bring us all the other modern conveniences we take for granted are equally complex. Services such as public water systems and sewage disposal, trash collection, telephone and Internet communications, electrical power and natural gas service, gasoline and heating oil and so on, all rely on the 'complex' orchestration of favorable atmospheric/weather conditions, skilled manpower, a modern transportation system, distribution facilities and a viable 'people market' to support the whole complex process.

Unfortunately, it is this complexity that is the 'Achilles Heel' of our modern-day society. Like a finely tuned and complex machine that is rendered 'inoperable' because one small part is broken, our society can be brought to its knees faster and easier than most people 'could' or 'would' ever imagine possible.

When a global cataclysm takes place severely disrupting the normal workings of our complex/interdependent world, our entire society and global cultures will be instantly taken 'off line,' thus dramatically disrupting all the established social/political/religious systems/organizations on this planet that the 'collective' of the United Nations so desperately depends upon for its survival.

Even if the incoming brown dwarf doesn't come directly between the Earth and Sun, causing a full-blown pole shift, its strong gravitational effects are going to create quite a mess down here.

Strong winds and severe climactic conditions will destroy crops and livestock in the fields. Powerful global earthquakes and other geophysical events will crush public water mains, topple power lines and communication/cell phone towers, destroy roads and bridges, and set cities ablaze as natural gas lines rupture. Huge tidal waves will wipe out harbors and flood large parts of coastal areas. Massive volcanic eruptions will spew huge amounts of ash and pumice into the atmosphere, choking people, animals and plants to death as sunlight is blocked out plummeting global temperatures to the extreme. In effect—the entire planet shuts down—everything stops!

If these events were to suddenly happen, 98% of people on this planet would be in for a very 'rude awakening' regarding their ability to survive/plan for the future/rebuild society/or continue living at all.

Once again, keep in mind that when we say global cataclysms—we mean just that; we're not talking about local disasters such as a major hurricane, earthquake, or tornado. As tragic as these events are, they will pale in comparison to the events we are about to face when the brown dwarf passes our planet—events that will be more powerful and dramatic than any recorded in modern history.

What would you and your family do if grocery stores suddenly had no food? What would you do if no water were available from your faucets? And how would you stay warm if your heater no longer worked and outside temperatures were say, –15 degrees? How would you protect yourself and your family if you were being confronted by an armed mob and the police were not responding to your emergency 911 calls for help? And let's not forget—your local/national authorities had already enacted strict 'gun control' policies stripping away your personal stash
✱ *of guns and ammo leaving you defenseless and impotent to carry on everyday?*

✱ INSIST ON KEEPING YOUR 2ND AMENDMENT RIGHTS.

A brief look at your dwindling options

The horrible events that we have been investigating throughout this book might be unthinkable to many, but these images will not prevent them from happening. Once again, you must ask yourself: *If these events were to take place tomorrow, what would I do in order to survive?*

You may at first think of fleeing your area to an area of safety. But as we have already demonstrated, once these approaching events become obvious to the general public, the government will surely invoke 'martial law' across our nation. This fact, along with the ATSAC systems such as cameras and walls that are already in place—will essentially prevent you from going anywhere at all! NOT HERE IN THIS RURAL AREA, THANK GOD!

HEAD FOR THE HILLS, IF POSSIBLE. IF YOUR SITUATION IS DESPERATE
Besides, where would you go? Remember, this is a global cataclysm affecting the entire planet. Even if you could bypass the cameras and the heavily armed troops, how would you obtain gas to travel or have clean water, or defend yourself from armed and desperate looters? Once these events in question start becoming obvious to the general public—going anywhere with anyone will be a truly perilous/bad/impossible mission/option at best.

Secondly, you may think/or pray the government will be take care of you. Don't count on it!

Your local/state/federal officials (God bless them all)—will be desperately struggling to take care of themselves—currently taking steps to preserve the 'continuity of government'. In other words the government's recent actions are directed at preserving the integrity of its current 'power structure' and not necessarily coming to the aid of 'family households' or 'individuals.'

In reality, the government has no other choice! It will have a hard enough time protecting itself, its critical facilities and essential personnel—and that's it! Unfortunately, there isn't the means, time or resources to prepare for the well being of every person in the U.S., much less the world.

Besides, as we pointed out in the last chapter, the government has already asked the public to prepare for what's coming via its Homeland Security's *"Get Ready Now"* program. And if 'you' weren't smart enough/or able to heed their blatant warnings to 'personally' provide for yourself and your family ahead of time—some would say, *"Sorry, you deserve your fate!"* We disagree!!

In addition, most people are unaware that the U.S. no longer has a Civil Defense Program (from the 50s 'cold war' era. This program was totally dismantled/eliminated decades ago. And there are no well-stocked bomb shelters with food and medical equipment, no civil defense volunteers that are going to come to your aid, no emergency provisions that will magically show up at your door one morning. You won't like this scenario but you're going to be alone—out on your own!

A third option that you might take is to exercise your powers of 'denial.' You can choose to dismiss all of the evidence (presented here) concerning the potential of a coming global catastrophe and say, *"It's all just too far out."* Or, *"I just can't believe that something terrible like this could happen to our planet—not at this point in time—and certainly not to me."*

Keep in mind that the universe is a violent place and massive cataclysms happen throughout the cosmos all the time. Nothing makes this planet exempt or immune to these natural catastrophic events. Like it or not, they've happened here before and they'll happen here again—that's just the reality of life on our world and the current situation we find ourselves in. You can choose to live in denial all you'd like—but this isn't going to stop these unfortunate events from happening or to delay the process in progress!

You could also choose to dismiss your involvement in these events. Many people will say things like: *"Well, if it happens, it happens!"* or *"There's nothing I can do about it!"* or, *"I'm not going to live in fear. When it's my time to go, it's my time to go!"*

Unfortunately, such cavalier dismissive attitudes are quite commonplace when people have full stomachs and they're in no immediate danger. We should realize that once these events happen —people (including yourself) are not going to be as 'accepting' or 'carefree' regarding their situation and will likely wish they'd been much more proactive while they had the opportunity to do so. Remember, we're our own best 'reality engineers' responsible for our lives and welfare!

You can choose to dismiss your eventual involvement in the upcoming events now, or you can take the easy way out by saying you're not going to 'worry' about these events—but, dear reader, also realize that you'll pay dearly for this lax attitude should these events transpire!

The last and only choice you have (literally) is to take the information presented in this book and do something to save yourself, your family and your loved ones.

Getting ready

In the next chapter we'll explore the specific skills and items you should consider acquiring as preparation for future events as 2009/2012 arrives. But before we look into the specifics of your personal preparation activities, let's first take a moment to assess your 'current state,' or 'level of readiness,' and the 'basic questions' you should start asking yourself at time ticks by.

First, your most important survival tool is your brain—think! *How will you provide food, water and shelter for yourself and your family when the 'rug of society' is suddenly pulled out from under you? How will you provide for your own security and physical safety? How will you deal with sudden medical/dental/injury problems and how will you stay warm when it's freezing out?*

Remember that when the bad times come, all of these things will have to be accomplished under the most extreme climactic, social, political and family conditions.

Secondly, you must look at the area in which you are currently living. *Is this a good area to ride out the global cataclysms—or should you consider relocating? How close are you to an ocean or other large body of water? And is your immediate group of friends and family mentally, spiritually and physically prepared, or will they 'lose it' when these deadly events occur? Are you living in a geologically active area prone to earthquakes or volcanoes? Are you in an area of high fire danger, flash flooding, heavy snow packs, or wide-open seashores and large lakes?*

Also, *what type of outdoor survival skills do you and your family currently have? Do you know how to survive in the wild, skin a deer/rabbit, or purify contaminated water, fill a tooth, preserve food, treat severe hypothermia, defend yourself/and family against an armed/dangerous mob?*

If these events happened right now/or next month and you and your family had to survive on your own without any of the conveniences of our modern society, how well would you survive?

There is one other consideration that you'll have to make. If you're going to get ready—you're going to have to do it now! Preparation is not difficult, but it takes time, effort and some money. There are specific skills, knowledge and equipment that you and your family must acquire if you're going to survive these upcoming global events.

Keep in mind that the celestial events we've examined in this book may occur with little or no warning. So if you hesitate until these events 'begin to happen'—it'll likely be 'way too late' to effectively prepare for them. You'll never be able to equip/train/prepare yourself and family members adequately at the very last minute before it begins.

Also keep in mind that the majority of humanity isn't 'proactive,' they're 'reactive!' They're not going to do anything about preparing themselves until it dawns on them that they're probably in big trouble with limited, if any, options to help them.

Put another way, the general public will not lift a finger until they realize their well-being is in serious jeopardy. If the events in question happen as evidence suggests they will (suddenly and violently) there will be six billion people on this planet all frantically trying to grab the last few remaining 'scraps' of whatever they can find. This last minute frenzy won't get them very far!

As we've already mentioned, these upcoming events will not be the 'end of the world.' They are
＊ a natural and cyclical part of this planet's journey through space. But these events will 'knock out' our finely tuned modern-day society for some time. The modern conveniences that you and your family rely on so heavily—will be violently and suddenly taken 'off line' before you will have a chance to realize what's hit you. If New Orleans is any example—there's the proof!!

＊ NOT REALLY. GOD IS IN CONTROL, AND HAS HIS PURPOSES. WE HAD BETTER MAKE SURE 273 WE ARE ON HIS SIDE, FIRST AND FOREMOST! THAT IS BY FAR AND AWAY THE BEST PREPARATION OF ALL.

These events are quite survivable however, just as our ancient ancestors survived them many times before us—but we must all be spiritually, mentally, physically and emotionally ready for these cosmic events when they happen (which we hope they don't).

So don't wait, start educating yourself and your family now!! Start preparing for some of the basic knowledge and equipment you might need immediately—because cosmic time is running out and quickly, too!

Think of it in this way. When driving your car you're not planning on getting into an accident or having a flat tire. And you wouldn't want to take your car out on the road without having auto insurance or wearing a seatbelt or not having a spare tire kit. Simply think of your preparation plans as being an insurance policy in life—a cosmic 'one' —you know, just in case the bottom drops out… and there you are!

Even if you're properly prepared and 'God bless'—nothing happens, you've simply acquired some extra food and supplies that you can always eat/wear, and new skills that you can always utilize, and then some great camping gear for the family's next outdoor adventure together.

As we finish writing this chapter it's Friday, 7 April 2006. With the new hurricane season a mere two months away all the talk on the Weather Channel is about the up-tick in violent/high scale (F3 - F5) tornadoes this year. This season has already proved to be deadly with dozens of lives lost and hundreds of millions in damages crossing half a dozen states across 'tornado alley—the mid-south region. The latest count is 416 with intensity and longevity stats setting new records.

Living in the northwestern tip of Mississippi, I had the rarest of opportunities watching/waiting/ wondering if last week's episode of wild tornado weather was going to come—descending on Memphis (our nearest neighbor across the TN state line) and us. When the emergency weather notices first started streaming across the Weather Channel and network stations, sure enough the affected areas included the entire city of Memphis and all adjacent counties to the south, north and east of a line drawn along the Mississippi River from Missouri (to the north) and Louisiana (to the south) —a whopping region that included thousands of square miles across six states.

As dusk was settling in the winds picked up, the sky above turned a swirling dirty gray and the lightning show was unbelievable. Out in the back yard my trees were swaying wildly in the wind and as I looked to the NW—although it must have been thirty miles away—I could clearly see this massive storm system with its typical 'circular motion' weather pattern gearing up for what the forecasters had predicted so accurately—one hell of a tornado-laden event—22 by last count.

What I was witnessing up in the heavens was Mother Nature gone mad—the lightning strikes tearing along the horizon for a hundred or more miles and when the rains finally came—so did the hail stones—some large, some small, most like pebbles. Gathering up a dozen larger hail bits it was time to go back inside for what followed in six states was destruction/devastation/death.

If you don't prepare now and the dire events in question come to pass—you and your family will likely not survive! Of course even if you do prepare—you still may not survive! *Considering the consequences—don't you owe it to yourself and loved ones to at least make an honest try?*

"BE PREPARED" IS THE BOY SCOUT MOTTO — A VERY GOOD MOTTO.

— CHAPTER NINE —

PERSONAL PREPARATIONS

In the last chapter we acknowledged our dependence on modern society and concluded that once the brown dwarf passes our planet—most, if not all, the modern conveniences that we take for granted could be instantly stripped away. If this were to happen, everyone would suddenly be responsible for all of his or her basic needs such as food, water, fuel, protection, warmth, shelter, etc. In the last chapter, we also addressed the importance of taking 'proactive' steps in order to prepare for this totally self-reliant eventuality.

In reality, however, there's no way to effectively tell you how to prepare for the future! <u>Only you can decide what is right for you and your family</u>. This chapter can offer you some general ideas and solid guidelines in order to point you in the right direction, but ultimately you (and only you) will have to be the judge of what actions to take, or not take.

Before we begin addressing your personal preparation for the upcoming global cataclysms, you (the reader) will need to evaluate your particular situation. Everyone's current position in life is different. Since everyone is in somewhat differing circumstances—everyone's preparation plans will therefore differ accordingly. What is right for one person may not be right for another!

In preparing for the upcoming eventualities, you'll need to start out by assessing your current geographic location; your personal financial situation; the skills, talents and mind set of the people around you; your commitment and motivation to survive; your current skills, knowledge and abilities; the natural resources in your area; and a host of other factors, all of which will affect how you should personally prepare for what's approaching.

After reading this book and assessing your personal circumstances, you'll have to estimate how severe <u>you believe</u> *'Wormwood's'* upcoming passage <u>will be</u> and you'll have to place your bets on the table as to how much <u>physical damage</u> could result from the brown dwarf's <u>next passage</u>.

Will the upcoming passage produce only slight damage resulting in a few days to a week of inconvenience with reduced amounts of utilities and public services disrupted or be much worse?

If you decide that the upcoming passage will cause only a small amount of damage and inconvenience, then you can simply follow the government's guidelines in their *"Get Ready Now"* program. All you may need is several days of food and water, along with a radio and batteries, some extra blankets and a few other basic medical/personal/pet necessities. In this scenario you'll only be without the trappings of modern society (electricity, water, grocery stores, etc.) for a few days before things start getting back to normal in your specific geographic area.

Will the dwarf's passage cause more severe problems resulting in a few weeks to a few months of hardships or will its effects thrust you into a long-term 'survival mode' rife with challenges?

If you decide that the brown dwarf's passage will cause more extensive damage (earthquakes, some coastal flooding, a few volcanoes, etc.), you may have to survive without the conveniences of our modern-day society for a few weeks up to a few months. At which point your personal preparations will have to become more involved and extensive.

If you're not sure of what to do, best plan for the worst-case scenario. There is a very good possibility the gravitational effects of the passing brown dwarf will cause Earth's crust to slip around its liquid core, producing a geologic pole shift. If this event takes place, an extreme array of geophysical disasters will befall Earth. Large earthquakes will devastate cities, volcanic ash will cover entire towns, tectonic plates will buckle sending coastal areas to the bottom of the ocean, extremely high winds will devastate buildings, bridges and power lines, and flammable methane will set vast areas of the planet ablaze.

If a pole shift occurs, it will permanently wipe out modern civilization as we know it. The delicate and complex systems that provide our food, water, utilities, police and fire protection, clothing and a variety of other modern conveniences (that we take for granted) will be literally 'wiped out' over night by the violence of the upcoming events.

In planning for the upcoming passage, this book will <u>not</u> assume the brown dwarf's next fly-by will produce only small or limited amounts of damage. We've listened to the accounts of ancient cultures that have all warned us of the total destruction that befell their civilizations. We've also examined the massive archeological and geologic evidence calling to our modern world, telling us of the destructive power of what's coming. We're also paying close attention to the physical signs that are currently taking place all around us. And we've carefully considered numerous prophetic warnings given to the world by gifted visionaries and prophets through the ages. As for the immediate moment—we must diligently 'read between the lines' into the government's recent actions—taking notice of how their preparation plans far exceed anything needed to prepare for a small, isolated disaster—much less a global catastrophe of biblical proportions.

We will therefore focus on preparing for an all-out pole shift! Once again, we're 'hoping' for the best—but we're 'preparing' for the worst.

Also, keep in mind that surviving these events isn't brain surgery, but it does require some basic skills and preparation. This preparation must be done well ahead of time, however. If you wait until these upcoming events start to unfold suddenly becoming obvious to everyone, the general public will be starting to panic—and it will be too late in the game for you to effectively prepare. You must therefore be proactive, 'read between the lines' of what's going on around you and take immediate steps to provide for yourself and your loved ones way ahead of time.

This chapter will inform you of <u>certain</u> basic skills and items that you'll have to obtain if you're going to survive the coming planetary changes. Keep in mind that a 'billion' people around the world <u>may survive</u> these *Earth Changes* because 'millions' of them are currently preparing for the worst. On the other hand, 'billions' of people on this planet may perish because they're either unaware/complacent/or ignorant of the hard <u>facts</u> to wisely prepare in advance regarding *Wormwood's* approach. The purpose of this book is to present the <u>facts</u> as we believe them to be! If we're wrong, great! But if we're right—at least our readers were presented the <u>facts</u> beforehand.

Unfortunately most people will do nothing to save themselves until it's too late. Considering all of the information we currently have regarding these upcoming events—the fact that most people are doing nothing to prepare is an inexcusable tragedy.

Before we look into the specific items you should consider having on hand, let us take a moment and review the overall 'phases' and some other considerations you will likely contend with during a pole shift.

Phases in surviving the pole shift event

In beginning our discussion on how to prepare for the upcoming pole shift let us start out by addressing the different *phases* of what we're likely to experience. There are three distinct 'stages' or 'phases' to surviving the upcoming passage.

The *first phase* involves surviving the actual passage itself. In order to do this you must be situated on an area of a tectonic plate that will not be forced below sea level once the plates begin to buckle. You must also be in a position to survive the destructive earthquakes, volcanoes, tidal waves, violent winds and sociological violence (also known as raping and pillaging) that will accompany the crustal shift. In order to survive this *first phase* of the passage, you preferably want to be situated in a strong underground shelter or basement in a somewhat isolated or unpopulated area, and far away from any large bodies of water like lakes/oceans/bays— (several hundred miles away would be good—a thousand miles even better).

The *second phase* of surviving the upcoming shift is known as the *bunker phase*. The *bunker phase* is the hunkering down period, waiting for the atmosphere to settle, the volcanic ash to dissipate and the Sun to shine once again. This phase could prove to be extensive, lasting a few months or longer—depending on your geographic area and other key factors. This *second phase* is simply a waiting game, remaining in a secure shelter until it is safe to venture outside. Many of your preparation items should be directed towards this 'bunker phase.'

The *third phase* is the *agrarian phase*. This is where and when you come out of your bunker to begin living anew. The upcoming shift will <u>not</u> throw mankind back into the Stone Age, but it will regress mankind back to the more simple, farm-like conditions of a hundred years ago. This 19th century lifestyle will continue until society can technologically rebuild itself. (Or the ETs ✳ step in and rebuild it.) In this *third phase*, basic hunting, fishing, farming and agricultural skills and equipment will be the correct order of the day. DON'T TRUST THE "ETS" THEY ARE MOST LIKELY NOT WHO YOU THINK THEY ARE!

All three of these *phases* will require their own set of skills, knowledge and materials.

Another important consideration has been stated numerous times by survival experts. People should prepare for the upcoming cataclysms from the <u>bottom up</u>—not the <u>top down</u>. In other words, picture yourself lying in a pool of muddy water, freezing and starving—then prepare from that point <u>upward</u>. Considering that if you were in this type of a dire situation: *what would you need to pull yourself up and out of these conditions and in turn—survive?* This is preparation from the <u>bottom up</u>. Starting with the basic necessities of survival and then building your preparations from this foundation would be your best bet scenario in any potential disaster event.

If you prepare by thinking you're going to be sleeping in your own bed, cooking in your own kitchen and all you need to survive is to have some extra food on hand and maybe a few candles you may be in for a rude awakening. This is an example of preparing from the <u>top down</u>—and will likely be still inadequate for the intensity of what's approaching.

These upcoming events will be violent! Once the Earth's crust begins to slip, the powerful geologic upheavals will severely damage most structures and in many cases you may not have a house left standing. Most of the other modern conveniences (that we're all so accustomed to) will also be totally obliterated as well. In reality you may end up camping on the site where your house once stood.

In fact, a good way to look at your basic preparation plans is to think in terms of going on a <u>very extended camping trip</u> to a primitive third-world country with no modern facilities of any kind. If you were to engage in such an endeavor—first ask yourself this! *What will I need to survive and thrive in this type of a hostile/foreign environment?*

Once again, try to prepare from the <u>bottom up</u>, not the <u>top down</u>.

Also be advised that the following list of items and the quantities involved are the <u>minimums</u> that each individual should consider obtaining. We have included only the absolute basics that will give you a realistic chance at survival. If you can elaborate on the following list and be more prepared, that's even better. A wise decision would include you're making up an additional list (above and beyond) what we're suggesting in this tome.

In order to survive these upcoming *Earth Changes* you will not only need to be personally prepared, but preferably be a part of an equally prepared group of people. Understand that surviving these *Earth Changes* is best accomplished as a group activity. The diverse skills and experience of a number of individuals can go a long way in helping the entire group pull through these upcoming events. Keep in mind however, that the larger the group the more personality conflicts can arise, especially when every one is under considerable stress, so keep the size of your group reasonable/the quality of your survival membership high/and be sure to pick a good/ strong Captain to mediate disputes and run the road show.

The following list of personal items is composed of 'three' mainline sections: basic camping/ survival equipment, food/water, medical supplies, body hygiene, personal knowledge/skills and living off the land. A small but inclusive library of reference books—cooking, medical, horti-culture, religious/spiritual, survival, maps, writing paper/pens/pencils, should also be included.

Basic camping/survival equipment and gear

<u>A Good Tent</u>—This item will serve several uses. Besides being one of your few means of privacy, it will serve as your sleeping area and offer you an additional level of protection from the raw elements. When you buy your tent always keep quality in mind. Your tent may have to withstand some harsh environmental conditions, so get a good one. <u>The tent should be self-supporting, have sealed seems, a rain fly and a waterproof floor</u>. Keep in mind that your choices in the tent category must be all-inclusive, meet exceptional standards and be durable and strong.

Your tent will also need to store many of your personal items, so allow extra space for your personal things. Do <u>not</u> plan on having three people all reside in a three-man tent. It is 'highly' recommended that you plan on having a three-man tent for one person, and a five-man tent for two people. At the same time don't go overboard, you may not have the room in a basement or shelter to erect a 'big top circus tent'—so keep it reasonable.

<u>A Sleeping Cot</u>—Pick up a copy of the Cabela's catalog (see list of suppliers at the end of this chapter) and buy one of their heavy-duty army cots and the cot organizers that go along with it, including the nightstand and the cot tree. Also, pick up the self-inflating cot pad. In the *bunker phase* you'll be spending a lot of time on your cot, so make yourself as comfortable and functional as possible within reason and choices.

<u>A 0° Or Better Sleeping Bag</u>—It's quite likely that there'll be some cold, cold times immediately following the shift, so get a good sleeping bag that will handle zero or sub-zero conditions. Also, there is no way to 100% guarantee that a shelter/bunker/tent will not leak, so consider getting a bag with synthetic insulation that will maintain it's insulating ability even when wet. Avoid buying a down-filled bag, for down is not a good insulator when wet.

In addition to a good bag, make sure you have a thin, washable sleeping bag liner. There may not be washing facilities to accommodate a whole sleeping bag, but if you have a removable liner, this can be removed and easily washed. Liners can be purchased or you can simply sew a sheet closed, so it fits into your bag. This will afford some protection to the inside of your bag against perspiration and body oils. Your sleeping bag will have to be used for a long time before you will be able to wash it, so take steps to keep it as clean as possible.

<u>Pillows/bedding</u>—Don't forget to include pillows with removable pillowcases and sheets.

<u>LED Flashlights</u>—Pick up a copy of the C. Crane Company's catalog and order a couple of LED Flashlights. These flashlights are not as bright as normal flashlights but a set of batteries will run an LED flashlight for hundreds of hours. These flashlights are also virtually unbreakable and the LED bulbs will last for thousands of hours. Be sure to get the <u>least</u> number of LED arrays in the light for the longest possible battery life. Long battery life is more important than brightness.

<u>A Portable Radio</u>—This will be important, at least in the beginning of the pole shift, before radio stations are knocked off the air. However, if your radio can receive short-wave bands, ham radio operators may utilize these frequencies after the commercial (AM and FM stations) go down. Therefore get a radio with AM, FM and Short-wave capabilities (and the appropriate batteries).

<u>Batteries, Batteries and More Batteries</u>—You cannot have too many batteries! Have at least <u>five sets of batteries</u> for each LED flashlight and radio. In addition, pick up a few extra packs of assorted sizes such as AA's and D's for general use.

<u>Snap lights</u>—Also known as Cyalume light sticks (also called chem-lights). These are safe, flameless sources of light that give off no heat. Pick up at least 50 of the white ones, they will come in handy. Don't bother with other color sticks over the white ones; they give off the most usable light. Another great alternative are those 'ever-shine' (shake'em up) flashlights on TV.

Candles—Have at least two cases (48 candles) per person, more would be even better. The longer lasting the candles the better. Make sure that each candle will burn for at least 50 hours each. You can purchase longer lasting emergency candles from several locations. Major Surplus and Survival has a case of 24 100-hour candles at a very reasonable price. (See last page)

A Stove—Finding a combination camping and backpacking stove is one option. Portable propane stove with two/or/four burners is another good idea. A nice advantage to portable propane stoves is the availability of additional propane tanks, which Costco sells for around $23.00. If you decide on using propane stoves pick up multiple propane tanks and have them filled immediately. Empty fuel/cooking tanks lying around won't do anyone much good.

A WORD OF WARNING. Whatever stove and fuel you decide on—please be extremely careful with its operation as well as the use and storage of the fuel. If propane is your choice, make sure your tanks are stored outside in a secure and properly ventilated area. All fuels are extremely flammable so use considerable caution when storing and using them. The last thing you want to happen in a survival situation is to have an accident with a large quantity of flammable liquid.

In general, having a stove that utilizes sealed canisters or tanks of fuel such as propane are probably safer than most outdoor stoves that require pouring fuel into their storage tanks. Any time a flammable liquid is poured from container to container the risk of having a fire accident increases. In general, consider using sealed bottles or tanks of propane.

Cookware—While we're on the subject of stoves, you will also need something to cook in. Most people tend to pull out their normal household pots/pans/utensils—then use them on their camping stoves. You might want to also consider picking up a set of heavier old fashioned 'cast iron' cookware to be used over open fires once it's safe to venture outside of your shelter again.

Thermal Underwear—Pick up several pairs of thermals (both thick and thin). Think twice about cotton as it's a poor insulator when wet, consider going with synthetic brands. Cabela's and other clothing catalog companies (Sears, J.C. Penny, Montgomery Ward) all have a wide variety.

Polartec/Fleece Jackets and Pants—Make them lightweight/warm/durable with great insulating ability. Once again always pick up several pairs of jackets/vests/pants. The Cabela's catalog has a wide variety and stick with dark colors for security reasons. Go with black/gray/dark blue/or green and stay away from any/all bright colors such as reds, yellows, pinks, light greens, etc.

Gore-Tex Parkas and Bibs—Waterproof and durable, Gore-Tex provides an excellent outer layer for your clothing system. Pick up both thinsulate insulated and non-insulated types. Once again stay with dark colors such as black, gray, dark blue or green and once again, avoiding bright colors like reds, yellows, pinks, white etc…

Hats and Gloves—Quickly pick up several pairs in each style. Insulated products with Gore-Tex are once again best and Cabela's catalog has a good variety. Remember to stay with dark colors.

Boots—Purchase several pairs of rugged/all weather boots. Danner makes great boots and make sure they're comfortable/waterproof/breathable. A Core-Tex outer layer is preferable and they should have a strong Vibram sole built in. As with all of your personal equipment, you may never get the opportunity to purchase replacements, so always buy quality items that last!

Other Clothing Items—Obtain lots of extra socks, underwear, comfortable/casual shoes, shirts, long pants, short pants, belts, extra shoe and boot laces, bandanas, etc., choosing a nice variety/ with plenty on hand. Clothing items should be rugged yet practical/stylish. Ladies—stick with black combat boots and jeans over high heels and cocktail dresses— (well, maybe one or two.)

Sun Glasses and Goggles—Eye protection will be ultra-important. In addition to several pairs of sunglasses, pick up several pairs of assorted goggles that'll protect your eyes from blowing sand, dust, hot ash, pollens and other small/threatening objects.

Dust/Gas Masks—The high winds and volcanic ash in the environment following the pole shift will make breathing difficult. Have at least 25 dust/particle masks on hand. Northern Tool and Equipment Co. has a good variety and supply. Pick up a box of inexpensive ones (a box of 50 will run you $5.99) but also pick up 10 of the really good ones. The 3M particulate respirator 10 packs are $19.99, they're a little more expensive, but they'll screen out 95% of particles down to .3 microns and have an exhaust valve on them for comfort. For gas masks—visit any military surplus facility and by asking the right questions you'll find the best equipment at the right price.

Once again, these items are only the basics. If you feel the need to include additional personal items (such as gas masks, knives, flares or swimming equipment)—add them to your list.

Food and personal hygiene

Stocking up on food will be one of the most important things that you'll have to do and plan for. Even before the brown dwarf causes our planet to shift its axis of rotation, martial law will shut down most/if not all forms of commerce, including grocery/hardware/fuel/automotive stores.

Based upon the above—it's difficult to know exactly how much food will be needed, so we'll just have to try a best guess. You may have to stay in your shelter for at least a few months, maybe longer. Once the atmosphere settles down enough to venture outside it may still take another 6 months or longer before any usable crops can be grown/harvested/sold. We'll therefore plan for a 12-month food supply (per household person)—a minimum safety margin.

A One-Year Basic Supply System—You could obtain your one-year supply all at once from *Walton Feed*. If you call *Walton Feed* and order their one-year basic unit package you'll get thirteen 6-gallon super buckets. The thirteen 6-gallon pails include wheat, pinto beans, rice, instant milk, oats, corn, sugar, yeast etc. You'll also receive 597 lbs. of basic dry food in thirteen, 6-gallon buckets all sealed for long-term storage—and all for around $300 plus S&H. WOW! A years worth of food for 300 bucks! *What a good deal, right—maybe great?*

It's a very good deal, actually one of the best you're likely to get in your preparation activities. There are some large drawbacks to this system, however. The main drawback to this basic food package is the slow development of a condition known as 'appetite fatigue.' This is a phrase you should become very familiar with. Most people will soon become tired of eating the same foods over and over again—day after day. You'll find that in a rather short amount of time you'll no longer want to eat the same things over and over—even if you're literally starving to death.

It sounds strange but the old adage of *"You'll eat anything if you're hungry enough,"* just isn't true. Go ahead give it a try! Take a particular type of food, let's say beans for example, and try eating them for every meal day after day, after day. You'll soon find that repeatedly eating these beans (every day) will soon make you feel physically ill. This is condition is known as 'appetite fatigue,' and it is a major problem in long-term survival situations. The best way to combat 'appetite fatigue' is to allow for a wide variety of foods from a number of different sources.

Another drawback to this basic food system is that it is composed mostly of uncooked grains. These uncooked grains require a lot of cooking time, and in turn fuel, in order to make them palatable. Even with the use of a pressure cooker, these basic grains are very demanding on fuel usage. Since cooking fuel will be limited, balancing your food program with a variety of other nourishing foods that don't consume as much fuel in their preparation is critical for survival.

You may still consider purchasing this basic 'one-year' supply from *Walton Feed* and utilizing only part of it toward your one-year supply. For example, use half of this basic supply (six-months worth) and then supplement another six-month worth of food from other sources. This will also give you a six-month reserve supply of grains from *Walton Feed*—just in case.

You could also consider purchasing the one-year supply of grains from *Walton Feed* and then splitting it between two people, each taking half of the package. Either way, the *Walton Feed* one-year basic unit can provide a great food base to build on from there.

The *Walton Feed* website is also a good source of information on emergency food storage and other disaster preparation topics. Simply read through their info material utilizing what you feel is appropriate for your individual needs (either individual or family sized).

Assuming that you've decided to use a six-month supply of the *Walton Feed* basic package, the remainder of your one-year supply should come from freeze-dried and store-bought sources.

A Three-Month Supply of Freeze-Dried Storable Food—Always stick with one of the major manufactures such as *AlpineAire, Ready Reserve, Mountain House,* etc. *Walton Feed* also has freeze-dried foods carried under the brand name *Rainy Day Foods.*

A good place to start is on the Internet. Run a search for www.alpine.com. They have a full line of *AlpineAire* and *Ready Reserve* food packages. Scroll down to the bottom of their home page and then click on *Ready Reserve Systems* or *AlpineAire Systems.* There you'll find an interesting assortment of different survival food package options and sizes to choose from.

One of the best packages is the *AlpineAire* gourmet supreme packs. Their three-month package contains over 77 pounds of food (dry weight) and their menu is excellent. Chicken primavera, teriyaki turkey, beef rotini, western style tamale pie, garden vegetables, corn chowder, apple almond crisp, and the list goes on and on. This is exactly what is needed to offset the austerity of the one-year basic system from *Walton Feed.* And because the *AlpineAire* package is fully cooked, all you have to do is add hot water, wait a few minutes and dinner is served! If necessary, you can even use cold water in their preparation process.

The only drawbacks to these freeze-dried food systems are the $ costs.

Arguably, your three-month supply of freeze-dried food should be one of the single most expensive items in your personal preparation plans—so buy the best package selection that you can possibly afford.

If their 'gourmet supreme pack' is totally out of your price range, *AlpineAire* also has several other three-month packages that are lower in cost. Keep in mind, however, that some of their lower cost packages start to include more and more uncooked grains. You'll already have a lot of uncooked grains from the *Walton Feed* one-year supply—so try not to include too much more.

The packages from the *Ready Reserve* and *Mountain House* and *Rainy Day Food* companies are also good, but make sure the package you purchase is mostly composed of foods that require little or no cooking. Most of these foods should be able to be eaten with only the addition of hot water.

A Three-Month Supply of Store-Bought Foods—The remaining food in your 12-month supply plan should be composed of familiar, regular grocery store foods.

Most people have a distorted idea of just how much food they consume on a daily basis. Therefore a three-month supply of food is going to seem like a lot, but that's because you're accustomed to going shopping every week or two. Three-months is 90 days, and at three meals per day—that's 270 meals that you're preparing for. Once you see how much food you normally eat in a three-month period—all stacked up in one place—you'll be shocked.

There are also several important considerations to keep in mind while buying your three-month supply of store-bought food. Obviously the first is a wide variety. Your three-month supply of survival food is an excellent opportunity to further combat your 'appetite fatigue' thus offsetting the austerity of your one-year supply of grains from *Walton Feed*.

Secondly, while purchasing your three-month supply of store-bought foods, try to <u>avoid glass containers as best you can</u>. In some cases you may not have a choice, but the upcoming *Earth Change* events will be violent, and glass containers may break while they're being stored. <u>So try sticking with shatter-resistant plastic containers, cans and boxes whenever possible—keep glass containers to the bare minimum.</u>

Another extremely important consideration when purchasing your store-bought food is to <u>stay away from foods that need refrigeration</u>, both <u>before and after</u> opening the packaging. If you do buy foods that need refrigeration after opening—buy the smallest size that's reasonable in order to reduce waste and food spoilage.

In other words, when you purchase mayonnaise, it's far better to buy <u>three</u> 10-oz squeezable containers than <u>one</u> 30-oz glass container. Yes, the <u>three</u> 10-oz plastic containers will end up costing more money for the same amount of mayonnaise, but the 30-oz glass container will likely break during the violent earthquakes that accompany the pole shift and they'll surely spoil before you can use it all. Keeping this type of thinking in mind is important to remember.

Also, try to purchase foods that require a minimum of both water and cooking time for their preparation. Ideally, most of your store-bought food should require little or no water and only minimal or no cooking for their preparation.

Your three-month supply of store-bought food should include at least:

<u>50 cans of meat/fish</u>—Tuna, corned beef, Spam, chicken, beef stew, Underwood ham/chicken, pink salmon/crab/shrimp etc. This will be one of your most important categories. Besides offering some much needed taste to rather bland tasting grains, your canned meat/fish/poultry will also give you a source of high quality protein, so please, don't skimp in this category. If you can add additional amounts of meats and fish, do so—being cooped up for three months is tough.

<u>Hard salami/Summer sausage/Beef sticks</u>—Pick up a half dozen or so of several types of dried meat products for additional protein and calories. Stick with smaller sizes that can be used quickly.

<u>25 cans of assorted vegetables</u>—Again think variety. Peas, carrots, mixed corns, green beans, beets, sliced mushrooms (technically not a vegetable), diced tomatoes, kidney beans, refried beans, etc. For the most part 15-oz cans are generally best. Remember, there will be no refrigeration for leftovers. However, if you're a member of a larger group you might want to include several larger cans of vegetables from wholesalers like Costco, Sam's Club, etc.

<u>25 cans of fruit</u>—Pears, apricots, fruit cocktail, pineapple, mandarin oranges, berries, peaches, etc. These canned fruits will seem like a godsend after your one-year supply of pinto beans. Once again 15-oz cans are probably best, but a few larger cans might also be a good idea.

<u>25 cans of soup</u>—Campbell's, Progresso, Wolfgang Pucks, etc. Try to get mostly the larger 18 oz cans that <u>do not</u> need water added to them during cooking.

<u>5 boxes of dry soup mixes</u>—Get a good variety in multiple 5-10 pack formats.

<u>10 cans of chili</u>—Think variety, 15-oz. or larger.

<u>10 cans of baked beans</u>—Bush's, Van Camps, with or without pork.

<u>10 cans of canned pasta</u>—Franco American, Chef Boyardee, also try getting some with meat/onion/peppers, etc. 15-oz sizes are generally best—but a few larger cans wouldn't hurt.

<u>Pasta</u>—Get a good variety, regular spaghetti, penne, macaroni, rotini, etc. Pick up several to a dozen packages of each type. And be sure to include pasta-type hamburger-helper products—get a good variety—there's many to choose from—buy half a dozen each. This idea will help to keep your menus <u>fresh</u> and <u>tasty</u> as time ticks by until the 'bunker phase' ends.

<u>Pasta sauce and grated cheese</u>—This so important it needs its own listing. Pick up at least 15 cans/jars of pasta sauce. Once again, try to get shatter resistant plastic jars whenever possible. Take advantage of the variety on the market, traditional spaghetti sauce, Alfredo, meat sauce, garlic and mushroom, green pepper and onion, etc.—be sure to mix up your choices again.

Also pick up at least 6 plastic containers of grated Parmesan or Romano cheese. Better to get the smaller ones as opposed to the larger ones especially if they require refrigeration after opening.

<u>25 packages of Top Ramen</u>—Assorted flavors, chicken, beef and shrimp. Costco and Sam's Club have 36 package cases for around $5. This would be one item worth picking up in extra quantity. A big bag for the buck—and Top Ramen feeds a lot of hungry kids/people!

<u>Bouillon Cubes</u>—a very versatile item. Pick up several jars of each flavor: vegetable, beef and chicken. While you're at it, pick up a dozen cans each of chicken and beef flavored broth. This stuff will come in handy. Get a few small cans and a few larger 1-quart sizes as well.

<u>5 'large' boxes of instant mashed potatoes</u>—Easy and quick to make. Try Costco and Sam's club for great deals on their larger boxes. Then add in 25 packages or cans of gravy as a topping.

<u>5 'large' boxes of assorted instant rice</u>—Quick and easy to make.

<u>10 boxes of Kraft macaroni and cheese dinners.</u>

<u>5 'large' containers of powdered drink mix favorites</u>—Kool-Aid, Country Time lemonade, Tang, Gatorade, Crystal light, etc. While you're at it, pick up a few cases of soft drinks and a couple of cases each of V-8 juice, orange juice, apple juice, Kerns nectar, Arizona ice tea, etc. Mix it up!

<u>5 jars of applesauce</u>—Try to get these in <u>plastic</u> as opposed to <u>glass</u> containers.

<u>5 'large' boxes of cold milk cereals</u>—once again think variety. Rice Crispies, corn flakes, granola, shredded wheat, Cheerios, Kix, etc. Again, mix it up with a good variety for taste!

<u>5 'large' boxes of instant oatmeal/cream of wheat/farina</u>—Get the largest boxes available.

<u>5 'large' boxes of bisquick pancake mix and several plastic bottles of pancake syrup.</u>

<u>Powdered milk</u>—One of the most versatile items on your list. Pick up at least 5, 64-oz boxes. More would be even better.

<u>Protein bars</u>—Cliff, Balance, Harvest, Power, etc. Pick up boxes of several different types.

<u>Coffee/Tea/Hot Chocolate</u>—Pick up several 'large' assorted cans/tins/boxes of each. Adding in some flavored coffee creamer products might also be a good idea as well—mixing it up again. In terms of including teas—there's a great variety available and most of them come packaged in amounts varying from 15-100 units per container. Soft drinks, juices, milk, beer and health-drink brands will be hard to keep/obtain—so we suggest that coffee and tea make great alternatives.

<u>Baking supplies</u>—All purpose flour, baking soda, baking powder, yeast, corn meal, corn starch, molasses, sugar, potato flour, rice flour, bread mixes, cake mixes, etc., —will make the joy of cooking less stressful and more enjoyable—so pick up several boxes/packages of each item.

<u>Cooking oil</u>—At least 5, 48-oz assorted brands/uses in plastic containers is best. Also add in a few larger units of 64-oz. lard or vegetable shortening.

<u>Snacks</u>—Pop Tarts, instant pudding, nuts, dried fruit, cookies, Goldfish, Cheez-it's, pretzels, beef jerky, popcorn (several varieties), Doritos, corn chips, hard candy, trail mix, etc. These will be important 'feel good' or 'comfort zone' foods. Pick up several boxes/packages of each type.

Most major markets have large packages of dried fruits and shelled nuts at reasonable prices. Pick up several packages each of raisins, apricots, plums, dates, apple chips, etc., as well as several packages each of pecans, walnuts, pistachios, macadamias, peanuts, etc. Try to stay away from items with lots of chocolate, as it tends to melt creating a clean-up mess in the process.

<u>Spices</u>—Pepper, lemon pepper, garlic salt, butter flavoring, cheese flavoring, vanilla extract, cinnamon, nutmeg, oregano, thyme, Lawry's seasoning salt, cayenne pepper, minced onion, garlic, salt, sage, chili powder, accent, etc. This variety of spices will further help to battle your family's 'appetite fatigue' syndrome, so try picking up several of each. Once again, Costco, Sam's Club and most 'dollar an item' thrift stores can be a great resource to help stock up spices.

<u>Condiments</u>—Pace picante sauce, mustard (in several varieties), hot sauces, steak sauces, ketchup, relish, pickles, hot/sweet peppers, olives, chutney, salad dressings (both bottled and dry), hollandaise sauce mixes, cheese sauce mixes, etc. are great to have. Pick up several of each choice (again try for plastic containers). Stick with smaller sizes if refrigeration is required after opening. Restaurant supply companies such as Smart & Final, also carry cases of some condiments in the small packets—which keep indefinitely if stored properly.

<u>Mayonnaise</u>—Pick up at least 5, easy squeeze 8-10-oz. containers suggested.

<u>Vinegar</u>—White, cider, red wine, tarragon and balsamic pick up a 1-gallon container of each.

<u>5 jars honey</u>—Plastic as opposed to glass containers. Costco and Sam's club are great sources.

<u>5 jars assorted jams/jellies</u>— Shatterproof containers if possible—8-10-oz. suggested.

<u>5 jars assorted peanut butter</u>—Shatterproof containers if possible—8-10-oz. suggested.

<u>10 boxes assorted crackers</u>—Saltines, grahams, Ritz, Club, Triscuit, or variety packs, etc.

<u>5 cans of Easy Cheese/ cheese-type spreads</u>—Choose a healthy and tasty variety.

<u>Paper plates, bowls, cups and eating utensils</u>—Water may have to be carefully conserved. You may not have enough water for washing dishes and therefore should rely on disposable plates and utensils while in the shelter. Paper goods are disposable/plastics are washable and reusable.

A 1-year period involves 365 days; you will need at least two of everything each day. Therefore you'll need 730 each of plates, cups, bowls, forks, spoons, etc. Costco and Sam's Club have great deals on large boxes of these items. 1,200 plates for $9.00, 500 forks for $4.99, 1,200 cups for $13.00, etc. If you have a few extra around that's great—there's always company.

10 roles of paper towels—Used for an incredible amount of things.

10 boxes of Kleenex—Assorted sizes.

5 large rolls of aluminum foil—heavy duty and regular weight.

5 boxes of assorted sizes/uses plastic zip-loc bags.

5 boxes of saran/cling wrap—Assorted sizes and uses.

10 'large' boxes of matches and several bags of Bic lighters—A very important item. Unless you are an expert at rubbing two sticks together and producing a flame (which is much harder to do than most people think it is), you'll need a generous supply of matches and small lighters.

A final word on food choices/uses/purchases

You may be asking yourself why should I have chocolate pudding and Pace picante sauce around in such a dire, survival situation. Well, the answer is quite simple. A good tasting variety of food will be one of your only anticipated luxuries and comforts while in the 'bunker phase.'

Also, these *Earth Changing* events will be physically and psychologically disturbing. A good hot meal will prove to be one of the most important salvations to your emotional and physical well being. That's why an important emphasis has been placed on a healthy variety of food.

Besides, bunker living is boring and mealtimes will be looked forward to with great anticipation.

Water—Is the 'Achilles heel' of most survival situations. A good source of water is vital to maintaining life. In the *bunker phase* it may or may not be possible to get to an outside water source, therefore a large supply of fresh water must be taken into your shelter in order to hold you over until an outside source can be obtained. You will need a minimum of 1-gallon per day, more would be better and be sure to get plastic jugs/larger containers or small packet 12-24 units.

You should therefore plan on having at least 100 gallons per person in your shelter—more would be better. Water can be stored in several different ways. You might consider a mixture of water storage drums and cases of bottled water. Either way make sure you have enough water on hand for at least several months until you can safely venture outside of your shelter to seek fresh water supplies. The human body can only last several days without water, especially when under stress or injury. Therefore have plenty of it around and learn to create daily rationing for everyone.

Most disaster preparedness websites and stores sell water storage drums and sanitary equipment. It's important to properly prepare the sanitation of both the drums and the water before filling.

Once you're able to venture out of your shelter you'll need to find a fresh water source. At this time a really good water filter will also be necessary and there's a number of good ones available on the market. Most disaster preparedness Websites offer articles on water storage and purification. Read and learn all that you can about this important topic it may save your life one day.

Multi-vitamins—Pick up a large (500 tablet) bottle of a multi-vitamin/mineral supplement for each person. Sam's Club and Costco—both offer larger bottles of them under their house brand names. In addition, having a few extra bottles of supplements and herbs around couldn't hurt.

An extensive First-Aid kit—Pick up a few boxes and bottles of just about everything your local drugstore carries. Band-Aids, aspirin, Tylenol, antiseptics, antibiotic ointment, laxatives, gauze pads and rolls, first-aid tape, antacids, Pepto-Bismol, calamine lotion, thermometers, anti-fungal cream, cold medicine, cough drops, decongestants, etc., etc. Select choices of everything on the shelves. If you don't need it—someone in your group will, and don't forget your medical books.

Personal Medications—Stock up on any personal medications or specialized medical supplies that you'll need. In addition, have any critical/chronic medical problems and/or dental work addressed before the shift occurs—as doctors, hospitals and emergency rooms will all be scarce.

Personal hygiene—Soap, Purel, tooth paste and brushes, towels, Chap Stick, dental floss, razors, scissors, nail clippers, sewing kit, comb, deodorant, Q-Tips, feminine products, etc. Get as much as you'll need for a year. Be sure to include several 'large' containers of 'handy-wipes' per person in order to keep your hands clean without having to use any water.

In addition, be sure to include plenty (a case of each would be nice) of insect repellent, sunscreen and dry skin lotion. Some mosquito netting and repellant products would also be a good idea.

Toilet paper—Another item that deserves it's own section. Like batteries, you simply can't have too much toilet paper. There are substitutes for T.P.—but there are no good substitutes. Have at least 50 rolls per person on hand. Get the larger value-pack brands from Costco/Sam's club. 24 roll packages average between $7.50 and $9.00.

Tradable items—Keep in mind that many 'millions' of people will survive these upcoming *Earth Changes*. As the atmosphere settles down and people begin to venture out of their shelters, a 'barter economy' will likely be set up. No doubt there'll be other people around to trade or barter with as they, too, hopefully begin to put normalcy back into their fragmented lives.

Pick up several cartons of cigarettes/tobacco products and several bottles of assorted spirits, a few sets of steak knives, extra boxes of matches or lighters, and any other small items you think might make for good 'big trading wampum' items for use after things outside calm down a bit.

What about hoarding currency (both change and paper bills)? It's probably a good idea to start putting away loose change and stray dollar bills. Currency of any kind will become invaluable and remember—keep your paper currency down to $1.00 and $5.00 denominations. If you have the ability to keep gold or silver (in coin formats)—keep them small and well-hidden, as these valuables will attract the 'worst elements' of a shattered society wanting to steal or obtain them.

A final word on your mega-shopping spree

Once you make the big decision to begin your survival preparations—be thinking as you move through the stores or page through the catalogs (in the process of putting together your survival supplies), to keep in mind that this might be the last opportunity you'll have to purchase these items for quite some time. Therefore, if you <u>think</u> you'll need a specific item then <u>get it</u>—cause you'll not likely to have a <u>second chance</u> at making these important purchases and choices.

Think that this could be the <u>last time</u> you'll have casual access to a supermarket, drug store or hardware outlet. Whatever you're going to need of a manufactured nature you'll have to get it now, or forever hold your peace. So keep this in mind when shopping and buy plenty of everything you think you'll need before hand. As we've said: *"we believe the 'X' clock is ticking..."*

Once again, keep in mind that the preceding shopping list is just a recommended or sample list. Feel free to alter any of the above information to suit your particular budget, tastes and life style. For example, you may decide to eliminate all of the uncooked grains from the above list and stock up entirely with freeze-dried meals. Or you may not like canned vegetables, therefore you should add in extra varieties of canned fruit—and get creative—only you know what you like.

Remember to obtain a plastic, waterproof container suitable for your personal and family I.D.s, legal documents, business papers, currency, cherished photographs and other personal items.

Training, knowledge and living off the land

If you survive the shift itself (phase one)—which is largely a matter of being in a safe location and having a good shelter or basement; and you make it through the bunker phase (phase two)—which is simply a matter of having a good shelter and being properly prepared, and then one day 'halleluiah'—all of a sudden you'll find yourself cast into (phase three)—the agrarian phase.

Canned goods/pre-packaged foods won't last forever and eventually batteries will run out. The high winds and hot volcanic ash will settle down and soon you'll be thankful that you can finally get out of your shelter. It's at this point that <u>life</u> for you and your loved ones will <u>begin anew</u>!

It doesn't take a lot of brains to move inland before the shift takes place. It doesn't take a lot of skill to sit in a bunker and eat peanuts. In the 'third phase' however, training, knowledge and practical skills will take center stage. You'll now have to grow your own food, raise and process and cure your own meat, treat your own illnesses, build your own house, make your own clothing, find and purify your own water, etc. The conveniences of modern society will surely be stripped away and you'll have to emerge from your shelter becoming truly 'self-sufficient.'

Therefore, all of the self-sufficient skills, training, knowledge and equipment that you can obtain <u>before the shift</u>—will be vital/critical to <u>your survival</u> (and that of your loved ones) in the new world that emerges; 'reality engineering' begins and ends with each individual regardless of age.

Pick up free copies of the <u>Lehmen's Non-electric</u> and <u>Cumberland General Store</u> catalogs. In the front and back sections (respectively), there are numerous books on farming, gardening, raising animals, canning and preserving, woodstove cooking, bread making, soap and candle making, root cellaring, basic country skills, wood working, beer/wine making, etc. Remember, the more your family learns before hand and the more information you take into your bunker… the better.

Pick up several books on survival skills, primitive wilderness skills and living off the land. Most disaster and emergency preparedness websites and supply-type stores have dozens of titles for sale. Many emergency/disaster preparedness websites also have great articles and other information on everything from water storage and purification, to food rotation programs and survival information. Read and learn all you and your family can while they have the chance.

Get copies of magazines like *Countryside*, *Wilderness Way*, and *Mother Earth News*. Read the articles, order back issues, scan the ads for additional books, products, and classes. Learn as much as you can about being self-sufficient—it just might be your survival ticket into the new world that cometh.

That is also why making it through the upcoming *Earth Changes* with a group of like-minded people is so important. You'll greatly benefit from the 'collective skills' and 'knowledge' of a group of 'trained' and 'prepared' friends. In this manner—different people can study 'specific skills,' then teach the rest of the group 'different aspects' of what they've learned in the process.

In addition to your training, knowledge and acquired skills, you'll also need to put away hand tools for gardening such as shovels, spades, picks, axes, etc. You will also need additional hand tools such as saws, hammers, nails, hand drills, crowbars, etc. *Lehman's* and *Cumberland* catalogs (as well as many super hardware stores) are good sources for non-electric tools/supplies.

In addition, put away a good supply of seeds and other gardening supplies. Root crops such as potatoes, carrots, beets, onions, lettuce, cabbage, etc., will be best to plant at first—due to the lingering high winds after the shift. Once things settle down a little more, other types of food crops will be helpful—so set aside a good variety of different seed types and varieties.

A word of warning about seeds! International corporations such as Monsanto, ADM and others have created so called 'terminator seed' products over the past several years. These seeds produce crops but do not produce any viable seeds that can be planted the next year. When you buy your seeds make sure they'll produce viable offspring with additional seeds and bulbs.

Herb growing and sprouting kits will also come in handy, as will Mason Jars and other canning supplies. Have a beer-making kit on hand and you'll soon become a very popular person.

Fishing and hunting equipment/skills will also be in high demand. Set aside a supply of fishing poles, tackle, extra fishing line, lures, etc. Most fishing and hunting books will also come in handy. As a general rule of thumb, try to select a subject or two—then become an expert at it.

Some additional considerations in your planning

Battery usage—try to keep battery-operated devices to a minimum. Batteries are used-up quickly and once they're gone, they'll leave your devices without power and largely useless. It's best to take an inventory of what batteries are needed—then create a good plan to utilize them properly.

<u>Firearms/ammunition</u>—There's no real way (in good conscience) that we could <u>not advise</u> you to include firearms in your personal preparation plans. This is a big decision that people must make for themselves. The one thing that we can say about this subject however, is that if you do decide to own/include firearms/ammunition, —<u>please seek out professional training in their use.</u>

Most large gun stores offer firearms safety classes and other instructional programs to teach people how to 'effectively' / 'safely' use their weapons. A firearm in the hands of an 'untrained' and 'unknowledgeable' person can be just as dangerous to themselves and the people around them, as is a vicious criminal. So please get adequate/professional training for yourself and loved ones if you travel down this road. Personally, we've included firearms/ammo in our preparations.

<u>Limited space</u>—You'll have to wrestle with what you'll need, what you'll want and what you'll have room for in your shelter. These three considerations are something you'll have to contend with. Most shelters, in order to be structurally strong, must also be kept relatively small. So most of your shelter space will be taken up with your survival provisions and vital equipment needs. The remaining space will be rapidly taken up with sleeping, living and cooking space.

Keep your preparations simple; stick to the necessities that you'll need to support your well-being, i.e., food, water, clothing, tools, fuel, toiletries, essential books, etc. And don't fill your shelter with items that you don't absolutely need/want. *Your pets must be carefully considered!*

<u>Pets</u>—Food, potty pads and newspaper/kitty litter, chew toys, extra water, medicines, etc., at least a year's worth! If you're willing to make the investment—bring them along with love.

<u>Psychological Considerations</u>—This will be an important category both <u>before</u> and <u>after</u> the shift begins to take place—choosing your shelter mates will also be critical for you to survive in tact.

As mentioned earlier, bunker living can and will get boring, so make sure to include a number of board games, decks of cards, books (especially farming and agriculture subjects), puzzles, coloring books and crayons for the kids, etc. These items will help to pass some of the leisure time spent living in the 'bunker phase,' so stock up on a good/mixed supply of them.

Also, <u>screening the people that you'll be 'bunkering' down with is very important</u>. Just one 'bad apple' personality—that's either 'disagreeable' or 'argumentative' can ruin an otherwise peaceful, cooperative and happy-faced group. So be extra careful whom you include in your survival plans. Teamwork will be crucial to the survival of the entire group, so try to include <u>only cooperative, good-natured team players into your bunker environment; 3 - 6 months is a long time.</u>

<u>Physical conditioning</u>—An individual that is in 'good/sound' physical condition can withstand the physiological effects of stress much better that an 'out of shape/weak' individual. Because the upcoming *Earth Changing* events will be stressful, try getting yourself into good physical condition beforehand. Hiking, running, weight training, aerobics, stretching, etc., is suggested.

<u>Being properly prepared</u>—Admittedly, this preparation list appears a bit daunting and expensive at first—but this is the price you'll pay for being a modern-day Noah. *Now imagine (if you will), what 'his' shopping list and choice of 'ark mates' must have been like? Talk about having pets??*

Even though all the items on your preparation list could fill a small moving van, nevertheless they could be put together relatively quickly and cheaply under the right planning/conditions.

You may already have many of the items on your list—extra clothing, camping gear, tools, food, spices, toiletries, etc. First take stock of what you already have. Then carefully go through your home/basement/garage/attic making a list of everything you don't have. Next start by organizing/ putting together these supplies in a safe/designated place. Most people have more survival items around their homes than they think—besides a little old-fashioned house cleaning never hurts.

The rest of the items can be put together relatively fast. Put aside a few items one week and then a few the next and the next—before you realize it you'll have most of the supplies you'll need.

The key component here is that you must get started <u>now</u>. If you wait until the general public's figured out that they, too, need to start preparing, food and other critical supplies will evaporate from store shelves instantly. Most stores/suppliers <u>don't carry</u> a lot of reserve stock these days. So if there's a run on a particular item, that item won't be available on the shelves very long.

Even in the best of times, 'backorders' and 'out of stock items' are very common. If there are even a few people ahead of you in obtaining certain critical items on your list, you may find that you're unable to obtain those items you need. So don't delay in obtaining your needed supplies.

Our recommendation is to put together all of your camping gear first. This gear will not spoil while sitting on the shelf and you can always use it for family vacation/camping trips.

At the same time start your reading and skills acquisition. Get the skills you and your family will need to survive on their own after the shift. Practice/develop your hunting/fishing skills and read up on basic country survival knowledge and other self-sufficiency topics. Start acquiring your hand tools and then learn gardening/cultivating/farming skills/techniques/methods.

And while you're acquiring your camping equipment/supplies and survival skills, also get your one-year food supply from *Walton Feed* and your freeze-dried provisions. Both of these food sources have long shelf lives keeping fresh for years if stored properly in a dry, moisture proof, low heat environment. Large water containers (if prepared correctly) will also last indefinitely.

Also, pick up all of your non-perishable store bought items such as toilet paper, paper plates, paper towels, container spices, etc., early—they won't spoil or rust or grow roots.

Some store-bought foods have a limited shelf life. After a year or so, many store-bought items begin to loss their taste, nutrition, and general palatability. The best method to adopt regarding your store-bought foods is to keep several of the items you normally use on hand and then rotate these items for consumption—replacing what you've used.

For example, if you like canned peaches, keep a dozen cans on hand and then rotate through them. Every time you open a can, replace it with a new can placed at the back of the line. This not only keeps extra amounts of the foods you normally use on hand—but will keep your canned supplies fresh when needed. Once you get the 'hang of it'—food management becomes easy.

It's recommended you accomplish most of your preparations <u>before</u> it becomes obvious that it's <u>necessary</u>. Once this celestial object becomes visible—the public will start to panic. Stores will be quickly overrun and stripped bare. And soon the military steps in closing roads and declaring martial law—and then you'll be stuck in the ultimate 'bad situation.' So start your basic preparations now. Remember—forewarned is forearmed. Good luck and may God be with you.

List of suppliers, magazines and books:

Cabela's
400 E. Avenues A
Oshkosh, Nebraska. 69190
1-800-237-4444
www.cabelas.com

Northern Tool and Equipment
P.O. Box 1499
Burnsville, MN. 55337-0499
1-800-533-5545
www.Northerntool.com

C. Crane Company
1001 Main Street
Fortuna, Ca. 95540-2008
1-800-522-8863
www.ccrane.com

Lehman's Non-Electric Catalog
One Lehman Circle
P.O.Box 41
Kidron, Ohio, 44636
1-888-438-5346
www.lehmans.com

Cumberland General Store
#1 Highway 68
Crossville, TN. 38555
1-800-334-4640
www.cumberlandgeneral.com

A.M. Leonard
241 Fox Drive
P.O. Box 816
Piqua, OH. 45356
1-800-543-8955
www.amlgardener.com

Major Surplus and Survival
435 W. Alondra Bl.
Gardena, CA. 90248
www.MajorSurplusNSurvival.com

Walton Feed Stores and Supply
135 north 10th
P.O. Box 307
Montpelier, ID 83254
1-800-847-0465
www.waltonfeed.com

Suggested Magazines and Books:

Wilderness Way Magazine
P.O. Box 621
Bellaire, TX. 77402-0128
713-667-0128
{ HYPERLINK http://www.wwmag.net}

Countryside Magazine
W. 11564 Hwy. 64
Withee, WI. 54498
1-800-551-5691
www.countrysidemag.com

Mother Earth News Magazine
1503 SW 42nd St.
Topeka, KS. 66609
1-800-678-5779
www.motherearthnews.com

Home Power Magazine
P.O. Box 520
Ashland, OR. 97520
1-800-707-6585
www.homepower.com

This page provided for reader's notes.

— EPILOGUE —

PRELUDE TO OUR 2012 PLANET-X COUNTDOWN

Dear Readers, please refasten your safety belts! Your cosmic ride isn't over yet...!
Earth date: Friday 04/08/06... The Mission: Create the Epilogue... Time: 10:15 AM...

Planet Earth...(spiritual name—Urantia): is a small watery world cast upon an intrepid journey hurtling through the vastness of outer space in the Milky Way galaxy as we ponder the ultimate question: *Are we truly alone drifting through the universe?* The human race, 6.5 billion strong, lives and dies upon this glorious world as we enter into the 21st century of mankind's existence.

Hi, again! It's Dr. Jaysen Q. Rand, author of this timely *Planet-X Survivor's Manual* based upon the history, research, background and science concerning the return of *Planet-X* in 2009/2012.

You've just finished reading the written results of several years of our researching/assembling the many scientific papers/magazine/newspaper items/*Planet-X* Internet articles producing our text/graphics/illustration package. This edition was carefully designed to present the accurate mission/scope/message of our research featured within its exhibits/illustrations/and bibliography sections. We know this read hasn't been a 'joy ride'—but then again—it's not a 'love and romance' novel, either! Our decision to produce this book came after deep thought and resolve.

Humans cling to this tiny space rock totally preoccupied with their day-to-day agendas. Meeting life's immediate 'needs' and 'wants' is overwhelmingly paramount in most people's daily existence. So engrossed are we in our immediate environment that few people realize what's really going on around them. Even fewer people are privy to this 'larger picture,' a 'real life picture' affecting <u>every</u> life form's intelligence level/reality for their individual experience in this world.

And although most people don't see this 'larger picture' of what's going on around them, many are just beginning to 'wake up'. Today, evermore individuals realize that 'something's not right about Earth's normal environment patterns! Everybody's talking about her erratic weather, the dramatic increase in hurricanes, floods, earthquakes and active volcanoes, and the massive solar flares that are exploding from the surface of the Sun sometimes directed right towards Earth with ever-greater frequency. Today's feature films/television specials/documentaries are exploring the prophetic warning signs regarding these upcoming *Earth Changes* and bookstores offer us best-selling titles on *Earth Changes*. Thankfully but surely, people are beginning to 'tune' in to this 'larger picture!' Even children love learning from 20th Century Fox's *Ice Age I & II—rated PG*.

Humans are also waking up to the reality of the UFO/ET phenomena. Numerous books/magazine articles/radio/television shows are captivating the public's attention—all dealing with this serious subject on a much more frequent basis. Most major cities now have support groups and frequent lectures on the contactee/abductee phenomenon—with folks from all walks of life beginning to openly discuss their ET experiences regarding apparent 'genetic manipulation' at the hands of these other worldly beings. It should be noted that <u>this aspect</u> of our research soon proved to be

IMPORTANT: THE ET'S ARE FALLEN ANGELS IN OPPOSITION TO GOD. HAVE NOTHING TO DO WITH THEM!

much more involved/interesting/daunting than we ever imagined. We suggest to our readers they investigate this UFO/ET phenomenon with an open mind—linked to our concept that the 'larger picture' of our *Planet-X* saga may well involve a connection to the UFO/ET hypothesis. There are literally thousands of books written on the subject available in bookstores, libraries and the Internet. I firmly believe UFOs/ETs are intricately connected to our unfolding *Planet-X* drama.

Ultimately, this book must focus upon one aspect of this 'larger picture'—the approach and passage of a spent brown dwarf star (*Wormwood—see Revelations Chap. 8, Vs. 11*). Within the preceding pages we've reviewed the catastrophic accounts of ancient cultures leaving rubble littering this planet—both above and below the watery abyss. And we've also seen the case evidence for our 'pole shift theory' and how these catastrophic events are brought about by a routine slippage of the Earth's crust around its fluid-like mantle on a cosmic cyclical schedule.

We've also investigated the astronomical evidence supporting the approach of this brown dwarf star and the increasing physical changes manifesting on Earth as a direct result of its approach. And we've also peered into the future through the eyes of gifted prophets and previewed how world governments are currently bracing themselves for these upcoming 2009/2012 calamities.

And lastly—we've just reviewed the necessity of being spiritually, physically and emotionally prepared for these upcoming planetary events. The next passage of the brown dwarf will likely cause considerable physical damage to our planet destroying many major world cities, their agriculture, utilities and bursting water mains, eliminating highways/roads/bridges, knocking out electrical power grids disrupting public services instantly. Unfortunately, once our modern-day world is abruptly taken off line, most people will be in for a very harsh—rude awakening!

And it's highly probable that a billion people will survive the passage of the brown dwarf itself, but because few people will actually take the time to prepare/provide for their own personal self-sufficiency, many will likely perish after the initial wave of destruction sweeps over and across Earth. Simply put, millions of people won't be able to fend for, or defend themselves, once most of our 'taken for granted' 21st century conveniences and pleasures are suddenly eliminated.

As tragic as these approaching events are however, they are in reality, simply only one isolated part of what's really going on! This incoming celestial object and the destruction it's going to cause represent only *one chapter* of an even more mysterious unfolding cosmic drama. This entire book represents only that *one chapter* of a much 'larger work' in *Earth Changes* literature.

What about this larger picture in which the brown dwarf's passage plays its supporting role?

At this point in time you should be able to answer that question yourself. Think about it for a moment. We believe a brown dwarf is approaching, and it's going to inflict significant damage on our world when it passes. We also believe it's possible that an ET race has been busy creating a hybrid 'replacement' population they'll set in place once the majority [50-75%] of humanity is eliminated in the pole shift event. And at the same time, the major governments and capitals of the world are bracing themselves for this upcoming event by taking steps to 'lock down' and 'preserve' as much of society as possible—ultimately attempting to remain in control by retaining their weakened dominance over planet Earth after the pole shift events of 2012. All Vegas bets are off as the many sides jockey into position for what could be the final end games!

Don't you now see certain conflicting 'agendas' hidden within this unforeseen cosmic tragedy? For unbeknownst to most people, Earth is currently engaged in a power struggle of galactic proportions. In the near future this planet is slated for great changes with a multitude of different/ competing power groups (both on/off the planet), frantically laying plans to become the newest 'top dog' once the smoke/death/destruction clears from the upcoming terrorist holocaust.

You could say that a 'cosmic battle' is currently being waged on battlefield Earth. This conflict takes place right in front of our eyes, as most humans appear 'out of touch' with what's really happening around them—thus failing to realize this conflict is even happening. Unfortunately, this evil battle is for ultimate control of our planet and the future of all humans inhabiting it.

On one side of this cosmic battlefield, stands a group of alien entities that has (through intelligent genetic manipulation of our species), created a new race of Homo-hybrid beings that are scheduled to 'replace' much of the human population living on Earth at this time. And in reality, these same aliens are also replacing the current 'power structures' governing this world. They are doing it 'covertly' and in a manner that is largely going 'unnoticed' by the general public. This 'good-guy' Homo-hybrid race will repopulate our planet after much of present-day humanity is eliminated during the pole shift event (2012). If these Homo-hybrids are successfully merged into place in the near future, planet Earth will become a far different place than it is today.

On the other side of this battlefield stands a conglomerate of powerful individuals and governments (the Illuminatis) jockeying for their complete 'positions of control' once dreaded events of the brown dwarf's passage come to life. They're also preparing themselves and their respective societies covertly, in a clandestine manner that's also going unnoticed by the public. If these current power structures manage to maintain and later coordinate their all-powerful control across this planet, we may also awake to find/face a world that's far more different than today.

The global public is utterly oblivious to this raging 'power struggle' and is unfortunately caught up within their one-sided objectives. Once again, because the average person is so 'caught up' / 'distracted' by family matters, their daily jobs, hobbies, sports, fantasy football leagues, the latest consumer electronics and play games (including their 'must see' reality-based TV) that they've become totally unaware of this clandestine cosmic battle currently raging all around them.

Needless to say, since both sides in this galactic 'chess game' use their general populations to further their objectives (dominate control of the planet), it's in the vested interest of both parties keep the public as ignorant as possible regarding what's really going on within global politics.

Truth of the matter is that we're waging the biblical battle of Armageddon, the cosmic struggle for planet Earth, an unholy war based on good/evil, notwithstanding the threat of global terrorism. The upcoming passage of the brown dwarf star *Wormwood* is simply the 'cosmic catalyst' that sparks all sides into initiating their 'final control moves' on this living space rock—Earth.

Who will ultimately win this cosmic battle is still unclear. All warring sides have not yet played out their cards—and these many-sided factions still have powerful aces hidden up their sleeves. We believe that the global war on terrorism is a many-faceted threat with implications that reach far beyond ethnic/fundamentalist/religious or political factions all vying for power as *'X'* arrives.

297

The universe in which we live—is truly a strange mixture of creative and destructive forces. Everywhere we look throughout the cosmos we see miraculous birth and great beauty indelibly mixed with unbridled destruction. Throughout the cosmos countless worlds are created and destroyed on a constant basis. Large interstellar clouds of gas and dust are giving birth to new stars while other, older stars are exploding in massive supernovas. Some planets, we believe, are being evacuated/abandoned forever while others are being repopulated and colonized—all part of the cosmic ebb and flow of the universe, the yin and the yang of God's eternal creation!

The bigger picture as presented here must include the most recent aspects of what appears to be a growing escalation in the degree and severity of natural disasters that include abnormal seasonal weather patterns with much warmer winters/burning summers with extended seasonal periods.

Since 2001 the yearly uptick in earthquakes, tornadoes, tropical Atlantic storms and unusual Pacific typhoon activity (coupled with numerous tsunami events), signals a changing planetary pattern to what we've come to accept as normal natural disasters. We must also include an additional uptick in the frequency and new eruption patterns of hundreds of old and newly formed volcanoes and, not surprisingly, much of this new volcanic activity is occurring beneath the surface of the world's oceans—slowly heating them up/disturbing global weather patterns.

The volatile subject of 'global warming' has been hotly debated across the world, with a variety of theories and conclusions—most of them inconclusive and unprovable. Following this chapter we've included a fascinating look into the subject of global warming through a dissertation we've prepared on the Kyoto Accord. This presentation should help illuminate our theory that: *Earth's molten core center appears to be rotating (spinning) much faster recently causing increased heating, thus triggering eruptions of hundreds of new undersea volcanoes warming the planet's oceans. Could this be the reason for the Atlantic and Pacific's yearly storm patterns gone awry?* We believe these answers lie deep <u>within</u>—not <u>above</u> the planet's surface!

Quoting from *USA Today* 29 August 2005*: "The giant iron ball at the center of Earth appears to be spinning slightly faster than the rest of the planet. The solid core, which measures about 1,500 miles in diameter, is spinning about one-quarter to one-half degree faster per year than the rest of the world, scientists from Columbia University and the University of Illinois at Urbana-Champaign report in the current issue of* <u>Science</u>*. Scientists are interested in the spin (aspects) of Earth's core because of its role in generating the magnetic field that protects the planet from solar blasts and its involvement in (the role of) volcanoes and earthquakes. The researchers base this conclusion on their analysis of travel times and shape of earthquake waves as they passed through the planet." – END –*   *[See the feature film: An Inconvenient Truth]*

In closing our *Planet-X* discussion, we'd like to recap highlights of what we believe are truly alarming global disaster statistics facing our world in the near future. Once again the axiom that "our past reflects our future" is best demonstrated in the following outline of disaster events and numbers of natural catastrophes striking Earth from the near past to present-day 2007.

Geologically speaking, we're living in the *Cenozoic era* which began 65-million years ago. The start of this geologic period seemingly happened to coincide ('by chance') with what's believed to be one of the greatest of all natural disasters to ever strike Earth, that being a gigantic asteroid that theoretically smashed into what is now the Gulf of Mexico near the Yucatan Peninsula. It's further believed this asteroid event also caused the demise of the dinosaurs, a momentous catastrophe that signaled a dramatic new beginning for the evolution of most, if not all, life forms that were finally freed from this extreme predatory reptilian beast stalking/terrorizing/controlling this planet for nearly 365 million years. *(Who hasn't seen Steven Spielberg's Jurassic Park trilogy?)*

We believe it's vitally important for our readers to understand the relationship between Mother Nature and the world she rules over with its human inhabitants. And in doing so—we'll review historical perspectives on the history of natural disasters ravaging mother Earth in the past. We believe this review is important because of the current dramatic up-tick in the degree, severity and recurrence of natural disasters presently afflicting this planet in record numbers since 1972.

These newly presented statistics reflect once again what can be found throughout the recorded history of past civilizations. In truth, we know very little about our actual history—the real history of the human race that has been in existence long before the start of our meager 'modern-day' recorded history, a fragmented/documented antiquity of less than 7,000 years! *Why is that?*

Quoting selected excerpts from chapter three may answer this question of— *"Why?"*

"The destructive events that have taken place in our past have cut us off from our ancestry however—and we do not hear their warnings. These past cataclysmic events are so geologically powerful and destructive that (like the ancient Egyptians said) they force us to "start over again as children," every several thousand years. – END –

"But once again, as centuries turn into millennia, these historical accounts start becoming vague and many of these important 'oral traditions' are simply forgotten –or discarded by future generations as foolishness. Unfortunately "ignorance of the past equals ignorance of the future." – END –

"Then, thousands of years later, these 'new world' civilizations are once again revisited by the "usual inundation" caused by Earth Changes and caught off guard tragically destroyed just like the 'old world' civilizations before them and those before them. – END –

"And so it goes again once again—over and over and over. Destruction, followed by rebuilding, followed by destruction again! The ancient cultures were right when they said that, "We live in the 'fourth world' and that the preceding 'three worlds' have all been destroyed by global cataclysms." – END –

"The shattered remains of ancient buildings scattered over the many landscapes of our planet are screaming at us to 'wake up' and tune into the 'bigger picture' of what has transpired on our world in the past, and what will possibly transpire again in the near future. – END –

"The enormous piles of human and animal remains (chaotically entombed in so many locations throughout the world) are a blatantly telegraphed warning—spelling out for us the reality of the dire situation we are once again about to experience. – END –

"Our planet is littered with the remains of violently destroyed civilizations! The ruins lying underwater off present-day Egypt, Malta, Japan, India, Cuba, the Bahamas and many other locations around the world, are also calling out—trying to send us a clear warning of the great 'cycles of destruction' and the "usual inundation" that has claimed the lives of so many hundreds of millions in the past—and is (once again) rapidly headed our way. We have therefore 'lost our legacy' and the ability to 'understand our past destinies'—we humans are truly a species aimlessly adrift in space, unwitting victims of a cosmic drama far and away beyond our comprehension and acceptance!" – END –

The following statistics offered here aren't meant to scare our readers, but to warn them not to make the same mistakes that past civilizations/cultures have made before. And we believe the *Planet-X* issue (existing as an actual threat to our solar system and planet Earth), seems to have been lost in the information shuffle and a possible cover-up not only by our government and NASA—but also by most major free-world governments also dealing with the threat of *Planet-X*. Quoting from a 23 October 1996 *Associated Press* article entitled:

New Rebel Planet Found Outside The Solar System...

A new planet that breaks all the rules about how and where planets form has been identified in the orbit of a twin star about 70 light-years from Earth in a constellation commonly known as the Northern Cross. This new planet has a roller coaster like orbit that swoops down close to its central star then swings far out into frigid fringes, following a strange egg-shaped orbit that is unlike that of any other known planet. – END –

Is it so far fetched then—that Planet-X could well be another example of a rogue planet, or in this case, a brown dwarf star that follows this same type of irregular orbit around its own sun?

As our several Websites come on line we will be providing our readers with viable updated and scientifically oriented material extracted from the Internet, newspapers, magazines (both scientific and non) and a host of related references. [<returnofplanet-x.com>/<surviveplanet-x.com> /<futureworldmedia.com>] Note: Additional Internet Websites may be added in the future.

If a major pole shift is in our future, maybe we should begin by revealing the fact that Earth's magnetic pole appears to be drifting/shifting more quickly than ever before. *Could this be another dramatic sign that Mother Earth is about to recreate herself?* Quoting from a 2005 *Associated Press* article appearing on the *American Geophysical Union's* Internet site (http://www.agu.org):

Earth's Magnetic Pole Is Shifting

Earth's north magnetic pole is drifting away from North America and toward Siberia at such a clip that Alaska might lose its spectacular Northern Lights in the next 50 years, scientists said.

Despite accelerated movement over the past century, the possibility that Earth's modestly fading magnetic field will collapse is remote. But the shift could mean Alaska may no longer see the sky lights known as auroras, which might then be more visible in more southerly areas of Siberia and Europe.

The magnetic poles are part of the magnet field generated by liquid iron in Earth's core and are different from the geographic poles... the surface points marking the axis of the planet's rotation. Scientists have long known that magnetic poles migrate and in rare cases, swap places. Exactly why this happens is a mystery.

"This may be part of a normal oscillation and it will eventually migrate back towards Canada," Joseph Stoner, a paleomagnetist at Oregon State University, said at a recent American Geophysical Union meeting. Previous studies have shown that the strength of the Earth's magnetic shield has decreased 10 percent over the past 150 years. During the same period, the north magnetic pole wandered about 685 miles out into the Arctic, according to a new analysis by Stoner.

The rate of the magnetic pole's movement has increased the last century compared to fairly steady movement in the previous four centuries, the Oregon researchers said. At the present rate, the north magnetic pole could swing out of northern Canada into Siberia. If that happens, Alaska could lose its Northern Lights, which occur when charged particles streaming away from the sun interact with different gases in Earth's atmosphere.

The north magnetic pole was first discovered in 1831 and when it was revisited in 1904, explorers found that the pole had moved 31 miles.

For centuries, navigators using compasses had to learn to deal with the difference between magnetic and geographic north. A compass needle points to the north magnetic pole, not the geographic North Pole. For example, a compass reading of north in Oregon is about 17 degrees east of geographic north.

In the study, Stoner examined the sediment record from several arctic lakes. Since the sediments record the Earth's magnetic field at the time, scientists used carbon dating to track changes in the (planet's) magnetic field. They found that the north magnetic field shifted significantly in the last thousand years. It generally migrated between northern Canada and Siberia, but it sometimes moved in other directions, too. – END –

Let us now turn our attention to the subject of global earthquakes and a look at major earthquake activity during the last century as compiled by a 2005 *Associated Press* article. The following statistics dramatically detail the destructive power and potential devastation caused by the affects of tectonic plate movements seen across most of Earth's continental landmasses.

Global earthquakes represent one of the major factors governing the overall picture of natural disasters occurring on Earth. They are currently up more than 400% over those of past centuries.

Major Earthquakes Around The World Since Early Last Century

Date	Location	Magnitude	Fatalities
07/19/06	Jakarta, Indonesia	6.8	525
07/19/06	Jakarta, Indonesia	Giant Tsunami	273 Missing
07/18/06	Sunda Straits, Java Island	6.2	Unknown

Major Earthquakes Around The World Since Early Last Century (continued)

Date	Location	Magnitude	Fatalities
05/27/06	Indonesia (Java)	6.7	6,000
12/18/05	Pakistan/India/Afghanistan	7.6	25,000
12/13/05	Northeast Afghanistan	6.7	Many thousands
10/08/05	Pakistani Kashmir	7.6	87,000
03/28/05	Sumatra/Indonesia	8.7	1,000
12/26/04	Sumatra/Indonesia	9.0	176,000
	Fatalities from 11 different countries following earthquake/tsunamis		
12/26/03	Bam, Iran	6.5	26,000
05/21/03	Northern Algeria	6.8	2,300
03/25/02	Northern Afghanistan	5.8	1,000
01/26/01	India	7.9	2,500
09/21/99	Taiwan	7.6	2,400
08/17/99	Western Turkey	7.4	17,000
01/25/99	Western Colombia	6.0	1,171
05/30/98	Northern Afghanistan/Tajikistan	6.9	5,000
01/17/95	Kobe, Japan	7.2	6,000
01/14/95	Los Angeles, CA (Northridge)	6.8	87
09/30/93	Latur, India	6.0	10,000
06/20/90	Northwest Iran	7.3-7.7	50,000
12/07/88	Northwest Armenia	6.9	25,000
09/19/85	Central Mexico	8.1	9,500
06/16/78	Northeast Iran	7.7	25,000
07/28/76	Tangshan, China	7.7-8.2	655,000
02/04/76	Guatemala	7.5	22,778
05/21/70	Mt. Huascaran, Peru	7.8	20,000
03/27/64	Anchorage, Alaska, US	9.2	141
02/29/60	SW Atlantic Coast of Morocco	5.7	12,000
04/18/1906	San Francisco, CA, US	7.7	3,000+
1811-1812	3 Quakes/New Madrid, MO, US	8.0+	Thousands

Major Hurricanes On Record

Storm	Location/Category	Damage (In 1990 $$)	Deaths
2005 Wilma	Gulf Coast/NE / CAT 2	$ 35,000,000,000	Hundreds
2005 Rita	Gulf Coast/NE / CAT 3	$150,000,000,000	Dozens
2005 Katrina	Gulf Coast / CAT 5	$285,000,000,000	1,150
08/12/04 Bonnie	Caribbean/US / CAT 3	Not Available (NA)	NA
08/11/04 Charlie	FL / CAT 4	$14,000,000,000	NA
09/01/04 Frances	FL / CAT 2	$ 8,860,000,000	NA
09/09/04 Ivan	FL/LA/AL / CAT 3	$ 13,000,000,000	NA
2003 Isabelle	NC/VA/MD / CAT 2	$ 3,370,000,000	NA
09/25/04 Jeanne	FL / CAT 3	$ 6,500,000,000	NA
2001 Allison	TX/LA / Trop Storm	$ 5,000,000,000	NA
1999 Floyd	NC / CAT 3	$ 4,666,807,360	NA

Major Hurricanes On Record (continued)

Storm	Location/Category	Damage (In 1990 $$)	Deaths
1998 Georges	PR/MS / CAT 5	$ 6,300,000,000	NA
1996 Fran	NC / CAT 3	$ 3,670,400,000	NA
1995 Opal	NW FL/AL / CAT 3	$ 3,520,596,085	NA
1995 Marilyn	Virg Isl/PR / CAT 3	$ 1,624,110,320	NA
1992 Andrew	SE FL/SE LA / CAT 5	$ 34,954,825,000	NA
1992 Iniki	H / CAT ?	$ 2,100,600,000	NA
1991 Bob	NC/NE U.S. / CAT2	$ 2,004,635,258	NA
1989 Hugo	SE / CAT 4	$ 9,739,820,675	NA
1985 Elena	MS/AL/NW FL/CAT 3	$ 2,015,663,203	NA
1985 Juan	LA / CAT 1	$ 2,418,795,844	NA
1983 Alicia	N TX / CAT 3	$ 3,421,660,182	NA
1979 Frederic	NE U.S. CAT 3	$ 4,965,327,332	NA
1972 Agnes	NE U.S. / CAT 1	$ 8,602,500,000	122
1970 Celia	S TX / CAT 3	$ 2,015,663.203	NA
11/13/1970	Bangladesh, Pakistan	NA	500,000-1,000,000
1969 Camille	MS/ LA CAT 5	$ 6,992,441,549	256
1965 Betsy	FL/LA / CAT 3	$ 6,500,000,000	75
06-07/1965	Bangladesh, Pakistan	NA	35,000-40,000
05/28-29/1963	Bangladesh, Pakistan	NA	22,000
1961 Carla	TX / CAT 4	$ 2,550,880,095	46
1960 Donna	FL/Eastern US/CAT 4	$ 1,823,605,000	50
1957 Audrey	SE U.S. / CAT 4	$ 696,091,000	390
1955 Diane	NE US / CAT 3	$ 5,640,676,187	NA
1954 Hazel	SC/NC / CAT 4	$ 1,910,582,732	95
1954 Carol	NE U.S. / CAT 3	$ 3,134,443,597	NA
1944 NE USA	CAT 3	$ 25,055,000	390
10/16/1942	Bengal, India	NA	35,000+
1938 New England	CAT 3	$ 4,748,580,000	NA
1926 Florida	Miami / CAT 4	$ 1,738,042,353	NA
1938 New England	CAT 3	$ 3,593,853,000	600
1935 Florida Keys	CAT 5	NA	408
1928 Lake Okeechobee	CAT 4	NA	1,836
1926 Miami FL	CAT 4	$ 1,315,397,000	243
1919 Florida Keys	CAT 4	NA	600-900
1915 Galveston TX	CAT 4	$ 1,177,937,000	275
1909 Grand Isle LA	CAT 4	NA	275
1900 Galveston TX	CAT 4	$ 707,762,000	6,000+
06/06/1882	Bombay, India	NA	100,000+
1881	Haiphong, Vietnam	NA	300,000
1876	Bengal, India	NA	200,000
10/05/1864	Calcutta, India	NA	50,000-70,000
10/10-12/1780	Caribbean Islands	NA	20,000-30,000
10/07/1737	Bengal, India	NA	300,000+

Total Damages........$1,655,328,750,975

At best guess—a whopping sum of one trillion, six hundred fifty-five billion, three hundred twenty-eight million, seven hundred fifty thousand, nine hundred seventy-five dollars was this country's price tag from the year 1900 through 2005 for hurricanes devastating the U. S.

Once again… as the troubled weather-year 2006 finally reached its dramatic end, '06 posed an ominous and bold question: *Was planet Earth and the United States currently facing a cosmic struggle against the forces of Mother Nature for their continued existence?*

Badly battered by no less than 28 tropical storms in 2005 alone—with 13 tempests turning into category 1/2/3 hurricanes—and no less than four of them being listed as category 4/5 (by their severity/intensity/destruction) begs the question: *What's going on here and what've we missed?*

Reported every year since 1992 when hurricane Andrew (a CAT/5) devastated south Florida—the nation's natural disaster price tag continued rising dramatically—billions of dollars at a time.

Katrina, a huge (CAT/5), was deemed the most powerful hurricane ever recorded in the Atlantic Ocean/Gulf of Mexico in modern-day times. It not only flooded/destroyed 85% of New Orleans, but also decimated more than 90,000 square miles of the region's vulnerable Gulf Coast, killing more than 1,150 people with its fury and causing the repair/rebuild/repopulation costs to soar over the estimated $65 billion+ mark. And then a mere three weeks later, hurricane *Rita* struck next—a CAT/3 event that further tore apart the region instantly rescattering *Katrina* evacuees to nearly ever state in the union. These two storms represented the worst and most costly natural disasters to strike this country in its entire history… *But is the end of this nightmare in sight—or is it just now beginning?* That's one of the basic questions we've strived to answer in this tome!

In addition to the previously named 21 tropical storms in 2004 (a number that had stood since 1933), tropical storm *Alpha* formed in late fall in the Caribbean setting the record for the most named storms in any Atlantic hurricane season—thus marking it the first time that hurricane forecasters had turned to the Greek alphabet for additional names. *Alpha* was the 22nd event to reach tropical storm strength in 2005 especially with the season lasting until November 30th.

Since 1995 forecasters reported the Atlantic has been in a period of higher hurricane activity, a cycle now expected to last at least another 10 years. Scientists say the cause of this increase is a rise in ocean temperatures (another sign of global warning?) and a decrease in the amount of disruptive vertical wind sheer that rips hurricanes apart. Forecasters at the nation's Hurricane Center in Miami went on to say these upcoming hurricane seasons (2006-2007)—may be part of a natural cycle that can last for at least 20 years or possibly 40 to 50—and that current global weather conditions are similar to those experienced in 1933-35 and again in the 1950s and 60s.

In 2005, the U.S. Gulf Coast was battered by hurricanes *Dennis* (the earliest storm to ever reach a category 4 hurricane status in the Caribbean basin last year), followed by *Katrina, Rita* and *Wilma*—with *Wilma* being the 21st hurricane on the list of tropical storms named in 2005. The letters Q, U, X, Y and Z are traditionally skipped when naming yearly tropical storms.

Was Mother Nature trying to tell us something new in her 2005 bigger/badder bag of tricks? And what should we be expecting as the 2006 hurricane season begins in earnest on June 1st.

Last year for the very first time, the Greek alphabet provided a continuation for the list, but it had never been used in six decades of regularly naming Atlantic storms. It should be noted that storms *Alpha, Beta, Gamma, Delta* and *Epsilon* made the list, with the 2005 season obliterating many long-standing records. In 154 years of hurricane record keeping, 2005 had the most named storms (28), including tropical storm *Epsilon*, citing the most hurricanes, the highest number of major hurricanes hitting the U.S. (4) and the *most top-scale* category 5 hurricanes (3).

The Bush administration was bitterly criticized for what appeared to be its slow response to *Katrina* with Michael Brown, Director of the Federal Emergency Management Agency (FEMA), losing his job and the President's approval ratings sinking rapidly. In the aftermath of last year's hurricane season, the President ordered the nation's Homeland Security Department to review all of its disaster plans for every major metropolitan area in harm's way. FEMA is also pledging to manage the flow of personnel, supplies and security—better/faster/more efficiently.

The feeling of relief at the end of the fierce 2005 season may not last very long. Forecasters at the Miami Hurricane Center say that 2006/2007 may be brutal years because the Atlantic is in a period of frenzied hurricane activity that began in 1995, and which could last at least another decade. Government hurricane experts are quick to say this increase is due to a natural cycle of higher global sea temperatures, lower wind shear and other complicating factors—although some scientists strongly blame global warming. *But why are global sea temperatures rising so fast?*

Whatever the future holds including the upcoming hurricane seasons of 2006/2007 and beyond, one thing appears certain. Mother nature will have her way and if *Planet-X* (playing into this deadly equation) becomes a reality as the years 2009-2012 approach, we had better begin our national, state, local and personal preparations against these recurring disasters in a meaningful serious and smart way—the sooner, the better for all concerned especially in this country.

— *A Brief History of U.S. Tornadoes* —

Source information from: U.S.A. Today, Thursday, 2 June 2005 - Reported by Patrick O'Driscoll

Over the past decade, an average of 1,274 tornadoes strike the nation each year. For the first five months of 2005, the count was 365, far below normal. In another twist, Oklahoma, in the heart of Tornado Alley, and home to the prediction center, had zero tornadoes in May, a new record.

Five people have died in tornadoes since January 1st, matching the lowest total recorded. In 1992, there were five tornado deaths and none in April or May.

The National Weather Service's Storm Prediction Center, reported Wednesday that only 129 tornadoes struck the U.S. last month. There were more than 500 in May both last year and in 2003.

Tornadoes have killed an average of 51 people a year since 1990. May is usually the deadliest month. An average of 19 people were killed in May each year from 1997 to 2004. Deaths generally are down and sightings of tornadoes are up over the past two decades. Factors include better-trained tornado spotters in the field and better forecasting techniques. Improved warning systems have also helped.

A key factor in the low number of tornadoes so far in 2005 was a large low-pressure system that persisted over the Great Lakes and Northeast this spring.

This low pressure blocked the usual parade of storms from forming on the Plains and Midwest; those weather systems draw moist air from the Gulf of Mexico that can spawn deadly tornadoes. Fortunately no one died in a tornado in April or May of this year. These are two of three busiest months for the storms. – END –

— *Final Food For Thought Regarding Global Warming* —

HINT: IT'S <u>NOT</u> MAN MADE, AND IS NO LONGER HAPPENING AT PRESENT.

***Source information from:** Anchorage Daily News, http//www.and.com via the Associated Press*

Continuing global warming and climate change could melt the top 11 feet of Alaska permafrost by the end of this century, according to a new study. A federal study applied one supercomputer climate model to the future of permafrost.

Under the most extreme scenario outlined, warming temperatures could thaw the top 11 feet of permafrost near the ground surface in most areas of the Northern Hemisphere by 2100, altering ecosystems across Alaska, Canada and Russia.

"If that much near-surface permafrost thaws, it could release considerable amounts of greenhouse gases into the atmosphere, and that could amplify global warming," said lead author David Lawrence, with the National Center for Atmospheric Research. "We could be underestimating the rate of global temperature increases."

A permafrost researcher at the University of Alaska, Fairbanks, however, disagrees that the thaw could be so large. "Alaska's permafrost won't melt that fast or deep," said Vladimir Romanovsky, who monitors a network of permafrost observatories for the Geophysical Institute.

"If air temperatures increase 2 to 4 degrees over the next century, permafrost would begin thawing south of the Brooks Range and start degrading it in some places on Alaska's Arctic slope," he said. "But a prediction that melting will reach deeply over the entire region goes too far," he added.

The computer climate model didn't consider some natural factors that tend to keep the permafrost cold, Romanovsky said. For example, deeper permafrost, largely untouched by recent warming at the surface, would have an influence.

Lawrence said he hopes to collaborate with Romanovsky to fine-tune future studies to deal with those deeper layers.

Permafrost – earth that remains frozen year-round – lies under much of Alaska, Canada and Siberia. It can be more than 1,000 feet deep on the arctic slope.

Ground melting is only one clue that Arctic climate change may be speeding up. In September, the polar ice cap shrank to its smallest extent in 25 years of monitoring by satellite. Tundra has been greening up. NASA recently reported that 2005 may top 1998 as the Earth's warmest year on record.

"The permafrost simulations came from some of the most detailed climate models ever made," Lawrence said. "Using supercomputers in the United States and Japan, it calculated how frozen soil would interact with air temperatures, snow, sea ice changes and other processes." The study was published December 17, 2005, in the Journal's Geophysical Research Letters and presented earlier in the month at a science conference in San Francisco. – END –

Reflections on Earth's unknown future—2009 through 2012

Whatever fate awaits us—Mother Earth is about to reveal her secrets regarding the reality of *Planet-X* coming in 2009/2012. One thing is absolutely certain!! *Something 'BIG" is radically wrong with the normal functioning of planet Earth's global operating systems and mankind's ability to either control or understand these cosmic forces/dynamics... And time, we believe... is rapidly running out in the landscape of human life as we presently live it here on Earth in 2007.*

The world today is a truly dangerous place. The global threat of Islamic fundamentalist terrorism appears to be only the tip of the iceberg. On 5 November 2005—the cruise ship *Seabourn Spirit* with 151 guests aboard was attacked by modern-day pirates off the coast of Somalia. Two boatloads of mean-spirited pirates approached the *Spirit* about 100 miles off the Somali coast and opened fire with grenade launchers and high-powered machine guns. This luxury liner escaped attack by shifting to a higher speed and then rapidly changing course as the vessel's passengers, mostly American and European were gathered together in the ship's main lounge for their safety.

According to the *International Maritime Bureau*, a division of the *International Chamber of Commerce* (that tracks trends in piracy)—there's been a dramatic rise in piracy along Somalia's nearly 2,000-mile coastline in 2005. 15 violent incidents were reported between March and August compared with just two for all of '04. Last June a U.N. chartered ship carrying 935 tons of rice bound for Somalia victims of the Asian tsunami on 26 December 2004, was also hijacked by pirates who held its crewmembers hostage for over three months before releasing them.

With political turmoil/instability/fear of nuclear proliferation dominating affairs in the Middle East, plus Iraq/Iran, high gas/fuel prices, corporate greed, congressional scandals, wild fires, national/regional/global natural disasters on the rise—who needs pirates in the 21st century??

And *Planet-X* may not be the only outer space visitor threatening Earth in the near future!

According to a 29 August 2005 *USA Today* news article written by Dan Vergano: *Astronomers are now debating what to do about Earth's close encounter with a huge asteroid in 2029 and again in 2036—near Earth passages that might be way too close for comfort. The key question about Apophis is whether its 2029 trajectory will go through a roughly 2,000-foot-wide region called a "keyhole," an important component for Earth.*

Apophis, a 1,059-foot-wide asteroid, has excited astronomers since it was first spotted last year. After observing it for a while, scientists concluded that it has only a 1-in-8,000 chance of ever smacking Earth. But even that slim chance has them talking and NASA pondering how to keep track of it—just in case. This asteroid passes close to Earth *(within 22,600 miles) every seven or eight years, but the 2029 trajectory is expected to be its closest approach ever. If the asteroid were to strike Earth, scientists say the impact would be felt somewhere on a line stretching from Japan to the Caribbean creating a roughly 2-mile-wide crater probably causing a devastating global tsunami.*

According to NASA scientists, this asteroid should be visible, about as bright as the stars in the Big Dipper constellation, to observers in Europe. Such a close asteroid flyby comes only once every 1,500 years—certainly a profound scientific opportunity. – END –

It's easy to understand why many writers, news commentators and religious leaders are now beginning to agree that as a modern-day global society—we may be approaching the *End Times*. Our bibliography section lists a number of well-written books on the subject with the same theme being repeated in hundreds of current news magazines, videos and Hollywood motion pictures.

This book wasn't written with a doomsday theme—but rather as a sober wakeup call to what appears to be dramatic changes coming to our planet's political, social, religious aspects and in its global weather patterns. What we've tried to demonstrate in our work is the 'larger picture' of what appears to be a cosmic agenda in place for planet Earth—perhaps our *End-Times Prophecy*.

As a subject of scientific interest both *Newsweek* and *US News & World Report* carried stories on *"X."* Quoting first from *Newsweek* covering this topic in its <u>28 June 1982</u> article entitled:

Does the Sun Have a Dark Companion?

A 'dark companion' could produce the unseen force that seems to tug at Uranus and Neptune, speeding them up at one point in their orbits and holding them back as they pass…the best bet is a dark star orbiting at least 50 billion miles beyond Pluto. It is most likely either a brown dwarf, or a neutron star. Others suggest it is a tenth planet, since a companion star would tug at the other planets, not just Uranus and Neptune. – END –

Quoting from the second article in *US News & World Report* <u>10 September 1984</u> entitled:

Planet-X – Is It Really Out There?

Shrouded from the sun's light, mysteriously tugging at the orbits of Uranus and Neptune, is an unseen force that astronomers suspect may be Planet-X – a 10th resident of the Earth's celestial neighborhood. Last year, the infrared astronomical satellite (IRAS), circling in a polar orbit 560 miles from Earth, detected heat from an object about 50 billion miles away that is now the subject of intense speculation. – END –

Regardless of what your personal beliefs are regarding the true reality of *Planet-X*, religion, the subject of UFOs and ETs, global warming, partisan politics and terrorism—our daily existence and continued life on this world is affected every day by what happens *to* and *around* us as a global community. Hopefully this book offers you a second chance to understand the *bigger picture* of life and existence here on spaceship Earth, our home planet in the Milky Way galaxy.

As I write this last section of the book—both the Senate and House are engaged in bitter partisan debate over the parameters/language of pending legislation surrounding the *how/where/what* to secure along our nearly 2,000-mile long border with Mexico—another part of this *bigger picture*.

A closing statement regarding *Planet-X* prophesies in 2006 and beyond

Although I don't profess to be a prophet in any sense of the word—I do have certain ideas and viewpoints to share about future events on planet Earth as we speed towards 2009 / 2012. The great academic genius Albert Einstein once said: *"Imagination is more important than knowledge."* We'd like to comment on his statement by saying: *"We completely agree 100%!"* However, once forewarned with the knowledge and information about *Planet-X* as contained in this book—your imagination should take over creating your own prophecy about Earth's future.

We should also point out that the Internet offers a rich array of websites/blogs/commentary and research (both professional and non) covering the subject of *Planet-X/Nibiru/Wormwood* and a host of related material on topic. We encourage you to seek other ideas/viewpoints and opinions on *Planet-X*— thus rounding out your understanding of the <u>facts</u> and <u>non-facts</u> in your discovery.

Planet-X is admittedly a volatile/argumentative/controversial/and in many cases—a politically/socially/and religiously charged subject. By keeping an open mind, heart and spirit—your vested interest level will provide rich rewards both surprising and plentiful to all seekers of the truth.

My contactee mission to write this book BEWARE OF SUCH DECEPTIONS!

Jumping back in time to September 1950, a single event in my life forever changed its direction mission/scope/intent. In another book currently under writing entitled: *The Reality Engineer*, this author details how at age eleven, his life was saved by a young ET and how he spends nearly five hours aboard their landed 'flying disc' more commonly known today as a UFO / 'flying saucer.'

Details of the *what, when, where* and *why* of that story weren't as significant as was the result of my 'life's mission role' they had offered me. Their ET offer came as the direct result of my real-life contactee encounter with A-Lon and his ET family in the wilds of Manitoba, Canada.

The writing of this book (and others), my career as a record, TV and media producer, and my lecturing and educating activities on topic—fulfilled their 'destiny call' for my *Planet-X* teaching role from that day forward to now. These Fourth-Racer ETs correctly predicted that I would be a musician/producer, a writer and teacher—they were right on <u>all counts</u> and in the <u>right order</u>.

While aboard their landed spacecraft that stormy afternoon, I was given a classroom learning session wherein I was shown an hour-long program detailing the origin of the universe, including our sector of the galaxy and solar system, and a prophetic look at *Wormwood* as seen through its billion-year history with her recurring role as Earth's cosmic nemesis throughout the ages.

When asked 'why' <u>I was shown</u> this special program—their response was that I was chosen (along with thousands of others across the planet) to become part of their ET 'end-times' mission to help save our planet and everyone on it who would <u>listen to</u> and <u>learn from</u> Mother Nature's warning signs (both Earthbound and celestial)—then immediately taking the appropriate steps to prepare for a <u>worst case</u> *Planet-X* scenario (while actively praying for the <u>best case</u> outcome).

As I pressed on for more information I was then shown planet Earth in the aftermath of 2012!

So, I agreed to their offer and to play by their rules. 56-years later after successfully fulfilling their career prophecies (forecasted in 1950)—the last segment of my *Planet-X* mission required me to produce the book you're now reading. So there you have it; this was the scope of my role!

[Sure sounds like another *Universal Pictures*—Steven Spielberg ET-II blockbuster—only this time *Kathleen Kennedy's* screenplay isn't fiction—and these ETs don't look like nor act like their lovable (child-like) space creatures did. And thanks to Director Spielberg—it suddenly became quite fashionable (during the late 70s/early 80s) talking about ETs—visiting Earth like they'd already landed—which of course they already had—let's not forget *Close Encounters*!]

Armageddon: Is the place where the final battle between good and evil will be fought (probably a reference to the battlefield of Megiddo)—an ancient city in N. Israel, on the plain of Esdraelon most often identified with the Biblical Armageddon prophecy in—*Rev. 16:16: And he (the Lord) gathered them together into a place called in the Hebrew tongue Armageddon.* This place called Megiddo is perhaps the world's most contested piece of territory and Bible prophecy tells us that once again it will become the focal point for a spiritual battle fought beyond our comprehension.

Didn't that come full-circle and doesn't that passage qualify for the End-Times best reading list?

This author believes we've already entered the time period identified by modern-day Christians as the End-Times heralding the return of Jesus Christ to his faithful Church on planet Earth—Rome and Salt Lake included. Although the word "Rapture" never appears in the Bible—many Christians profess the belief that Christ himself will return with his legions of angels to first remove his flock from this world (via the "Rapture" scenario for safekeeping), then proceed to destroy the forces of hell in the final battle between good and evil—Armageddon. So, here's my personal prophecy and forecast for Earth's near future and beyond heading towards 2009/2012:

Phase one:

RECOMMENDATION: JUST READ THE BIBLE, GOD'S WORD!

Will it (Armageddon) happen in our lifetime? Yes! *When exactly?* We believe that clock's been ticking for several years now. And our best-guess estimate lines up with 2009 as the start of real hostilities (notwithstanding global terrorism with Iran as the fuse)—then escalating into a global war with NUKES flying every which way until the planet really gets toasted—or until some extraterrestrial intervention arrives (be it spiritual *{the Lord}* or celestial *{Planet-X}* or both at the same time). *Will the so-called "Rapture" really happen?* Probably, and for all the reasons previously stated—although the actual facts/scenarios/details may vary slightly from prevailing wisdoms of the day and various Christian faith interpretations of the Bible's sacred 'Word.'

Phase two:

Will planet Earth continue to suffer growing numbers and more severe natural disasters as 2009/ 2012 approaches? You bet! *And do we believe that Planet-X is the likely culprit here?* You bet we do! *Is there any chance this 'bitter cup' will pass our way?* Sure!! Anything's possible—but it's highly unlikely with all the warning signs we see everywhere! Chapters 8-9 are a great start and using your 'God-given imagination' is the next logical step. *Will mankind survive a pole shift (should one occur in 2012)?* Absolutely! But don't expect things to be the way they were: bye, bye modern-day civilization with all its conveniences! *When should you begin preparing and will it help?* <u>AS SOON</u> as you feel it's right for you to begin the process and <u>YES</u> it will!

<u>Phase three</u>: Long range forecasts include: **o** A continuing escalation of more severe/dramatic *Earth Changing* events sweeping across the globe approaching 2009/2012 with specific focus on powerful tropical storms/hurricanes/tornadoes/earthquakes/volcanoes/flooding/wildfires. Governments of the world (although well-meaning and sincere) will be overwhelmed with the scope and tragedy of these mega-natural disaster events (shades of New Orleans and the Gulf Coast). Momentarily they will seemingly all band/joining together—all the while secretly planning their individual conquests over the remaining few survivors still strong enough to defend themselves.

o Once the first series of major *Earth Changes* strike the North American continent approaching 2009—Canada, the US, Mexico and Central America will patch up their social/political/financial differences as we see a unified continental society develop with little or no border restrictions with a practical/working/operational philosophy—one designed to keep all of these 'democratic societies' in 'accord' as 'things' start to get truly problematic for their terrified populations.

o As these global events manifest—the planet's major population centers will begin to experience over-crowding/food/water/utility shortages/government disruptions/with public disturbances/great civil disobedience and wide spread marshal law declared by the governments in power.

o Global terrorism remains a constant/deadly threat moving past 2009 with the probability of continued escalating terrorist acts committed against the weaker/more damaged western nations/ cultures as these *Earth Changing* events manifest into reality worldwide; 'suicide bombers' and 'dirty bombs' are sent against selected U.S. targets like Washington, D.C., New York, Chicago, Los Angeles, New Orleans, St. Louis, Boston, San Francisco, Portland, Seattle, Minneapolis, St. Louis, Kansas and Oklahoma City, Memphis, Atlanta, Jacksonville, Tampa, Miami for starters.

o Japan, Australia, Great Britain, Israel, Canada and several other European nations will continue their coalition of friendship/cooperation/security as the *Earth Changing* 'bottom drops out' around them. France, Germany, other European and Scandinavian countries soon follow suit, all out of dire necessity and fear of internal collapse, financial weakening and mass civil disorder.

o In regard to our recently crumbling relationships the U.S. maintains with Venezuela, Bolivia, Cuba and other Central/South American and Caribbean nations—those prospects continue disintegrating eventually becoming openly hostile to the common welfare and security of their North American neighbors. They'll also test our naïve/peaceful willingness in seeking viable/workable solutions to their mostly left-wing/liberal/socialist/communistic ideals/and propaganda programs.

o Russia, China, North Korea, Iran, Syria, quite possibly Saudi Arabia, Egypt, Yemen and the Palestinians create the new format of a deadly terrorist 'cold war' era. This time their weapons of choice are oil/industrial terrorism/dirty bombs/suicidal Muslim fanatics—take your choice!!

o The final battle of Armageddon has begun as the Biblical account of 'tribulation' starts unfolding and the world braces for what promises to be the worst period of war and unrest imaginable!! The war in Lebanon with Israel defending against HEZBOLLA and HAMAS signaled the start.

○ As expected by the western world—the United Nations (U.N.) continues to remain impotent/corrupt/gutless/incapable/useless by their not achieving any meaningful measure of respect/control/dignity/honesty/leadership or discipline in guiding world affairs now or in the future. NATO remains in tact but is greatly stressed/torn/conflicted by regional/religious/cultural politics surrounding these *Earth Changes*. For the moment the U.N./NATO remain stable *but for how long?*

○ A recent book entitled *The U.N. Exposed (How the United Nations Sabotages the Security of the U.S.)* written by Eric Shawn (a *Fox News* journalist), takes on the current-day U.N. with his scorching expose of their sins—both large and small. Except for the global humanitarian work financed (in large part) by the mega-millions of yearly U.S. tax dollars donated to the U.N.'s dishonest coffers—many Americans question why we continue to support 'it' by throwing away cash resources on a dysfunctional organization boldly conducting its shady business on U.S. soil.

○ Poor Africa as always, is tragically left 'out there on her own'—more like 'the survival of the fittest.' Those dozen 'Island Nations' (at least the ones surviving the giant tsunamis now stalking them) will also be 'left on their own' to endure. We should add that all of the world's major city coastlines remain extremely vulnerable as well as those located on major rivers and inland lakes.

○ The use of military force—regardless of <u>who</u> starts the conflict—will be limited. If the entire planet is suddenly sent 'off line,' merely surviving will become paramount with military options remaining marginal and rogue dissident nations quickly humbled and/or destroyed in the process.

○ If Iran succeeds in producing nuclear weapons (while seriously threatening Israel and the West with arms proliferation and continued terrorist support)—all bets are off!! Best guess is that the Israelis will strike first—drawing in the U.S., U.K., Australia and a loose cast of European and Asian coalition members—with some/or most reluctant at first jumping into the fray. And don't count out Israel using 'first strike' low-yield NUKE weapons—THEY <u>remember</u> the 'holocaust.'

○ Expect major Middle East earthquakes in 2009/2012 that bring down the 'Dome of the Rock' and other sites sacred to both warring factions. Once again—all bets are off should these natural disasters occur. Biblical prophecy calls for the rebuilding of the 'Temple Mount'—and if this is accomplished by the Jewish state—all hell breaks loose in this already volatile/war-torn region.

○ Concerning U.S. politics—the November '06 Congressional elections shook up the GOP ranks as the power curve in Washington shifted to the DEMS. Long shot presidential tickets include a *Juliani/Rice* pairing, a *Clinton/Obama* match-up, and the chance the GOP may lose even more Congressional seats if their core issues of global warming, immigration and Iraq aren't resolved. Whatever the outcome—the '08 election promises to be volatile, lethal, hotly debated, steamy!

○ Sad to say—political/Congressional bickering and mutual name-calling continues to rankle the American public with no clear pathway developed or legislated (in the near future) for either <u>our controlling the country's borders</u> or its <u>out-of-control illegal immigration problems</u>. President Bush's prime-time speech on Monday, May 15, 2006 was certainly a step in the right direction —albeit a year late and dollars short in the Administration's attempt at dealing with the border problems which former Administrations (of both parties) have simply ignored for the past 20 or more years. The general amnesty law enacted in 1986 by then President Reagan set the tone for judicial reforms but failed to achieve any meaningful results as 10-12 million illegals flooded in.

○ Gasoline prices finally settle in at around $3.85 for regular and $4.25 for premium grades and diesel. Alternative fuels and hybrid vehicles remain a slow transition in the U.S. with other smarter countries like Brazil bravely leading the way by gaining foreign oil and natural gas independence. The U.S. lacks an unconditional will and unwavering commitment to kick in, for we possess the greatest ability to open new oil fields/grow corn and develop other Ethanol based products allowing the U.S. to pursue its own energy independence programs by 2012 or before.

○ As President Bush recently stated—*"Don't expect federal or local governmental agencies to bail out or totally protect the public from any sudden/catastrophic natural disasters."* Recently, Senator Susan Collins, R-Main (Chairwoman of the Homeland Security Committee) and Senator Joe Lieberman, D-CT (top Democrat on that same committee)—stated in a 04/27/06 *USA TODAY* feature article that in their opinion: *"FEMA is a failure and should be replaced with a more powerful disaster-response agency."* That won't happen soon! Michael Chertoff, new head of the Department of Homeland Security (DHS), said: *"A new departmental agency is not needed,"* repeating FEMA's familiar mantra: *"Are You Ready?"* The key question should be: *Are They?*

○ Fully expect harsh rhetoric/heated debate to continue swirling around the 'global warming' issues now gaining world attention. Former VP Al Gore has been a long time advocate of adopting immediate U.S. policies/procedures reducing the threat of what Gore perceives as massive global warming issues on a planet-wide scale. He's recently thrown his support into promoting what the industry calls 'his movie,' a Hollywood-style feature film titled: *An Inconvenient Truth.* Screening reviews appear strong stating Al Gore's film project boldly takes on the global warm-issue head on (and he should win the OSCAR), challenging the 'usual administration suspects' caught up in this on-going battle between <u>die-hard environmentalists</u> pitted against <u>big-business interests</u>—with the Republican administration weighing-in/defending their mainstream agenda.

○ Speaking of recent films—Hollywood just released a remake of *The Poseidon Adventure* (1972) naming the new flick—*Poseidon.* Same story, same plot—but far better 'special effects.' I couldn't help but overhear audience reaction as they were gasping and commenting on the real horror of what had happened to that sleek ultra-modern ocean liner as it was struck by a rogue 100-foot wave totally capsizing the giant ship and killing almost everyone onboard. *Could this happen?* Absolutely!! *Is this scenario <u>pure storytelling</u> or a <u>now truth</u>?* Anything's possible!!

○ Other recent box office hits like *The Day After Tomorrow, CORE, The Perfect Storm, Twister, Armageddon, Deep Impact, Super Volcano,* and TV network specials like *NBC's* earthquake thriller, *10.5* and *CBS's* hurricane drama *Category '6'* all seemingly share a common theme— Mother Nature gone mad. Even the *Weather Channel* and the *History Channel* are now featuring weekly serialized programs detailing the reality/probability/severity/scope of the most current weather disasters and global events now savaging the planet with no reprieve or escape in sight.

○ The real burden of public/family survival rests with the individual head of each family household, or the single person responsible for his, her or their own safety and welfare in the future. Ultimately, your future and that of your loved ones lies in your own hands—so prepare for it! *Reality Engineering* your survival for whatever future awaits our planet is an individual responsibility to be taken seriously. We believe that every man/woman/child deserves a glorious safe 'future.' We've tried to present the facts as we believe them to be. —The rest is now up to you!

In closing, let us look back at the prophecies of Mother Shipton—revisiting this 16th century seer who appears to have had a completely lucid understanding of this cosmic drama in which we are currently embroiled. Many hundreds of years ago coming from a society barely digging itself out of the Dark Ages, Shipton was able to communicate more about Mother Nature's wild ways than most people are capable of understanding today in the early years of this 21st century.

Mother Shipton's haunting insight prompted her to sacrifice her own life by writing for us her messages of warning and hope—a prophetic futureworld vision from across the permeable fabric of time and space. As Confucius once said…*"Study the past if you would divine the future."*

Remembering what Mother Shipton wrote to us back in England's Dark Ages:

For seven days and seven nights
Man will watch this awesome sight.
The tides will rise beyond their ken
To bite away the shores and then
The mountains will begin to roar
And earthquakes split the plain and shore.

Not every soul on Earth will die
As the dragon's tail goes sweeping by.
Not every land on Earth will sink
But these will wallow in stench and stink.

And before the race has built anew
A silver serpent comes to view
And spew out men of like unknown
To mingle with the Earth now grown.

Cold from its heat and these men can
Enlighten the minds of future man
To intermingle and show them how
To live and love and thus endow.

The children with the second sight
A natural thing so that they might
Grow graceful, humble and when they do
The 'Golden Age' will start anew.

The dragon's tail is but a sign
For mankind's fall and man's decline
My body singed and my soul set free
You think I utter blasphemy
You're wrong these things have come to me
The prophecy will come to be. – END –

Thank you sincerely for reading our book—please pass on its <u>title</u> and <u>message</u>.

May God bless and keep us all.

314

THE RETURN OF PLANET-X

EXHIBITS

-- THE RETURN OF PLANET-X EXHIBITS --

-- SHOULD PLANET-X ARRIVE TO TERRORIZE EARTH –
Color graphic: Random Arts – Los Angeles

Our Global Warming Issue Segment
Courtesy of the following sources and Internet Websites:

-- A Common Sense Review of the Kyoto (Greenhouse Gases) –
Accord Debate

Review Commentary by Dr. Jaysen Q. Rand
Reference commentary courtesy: Roedy Green from Kyoto Accord [1]
Ice Core Measurements of CO_2 and Scripps Institute Measurements of CO_2
At Mauna Loa, Hawaii Courtesy: Roedy Green

-- Global Warming, Globalization and the Kyoto Accord –
Opinion – and – Conjecture
Reference Commentary Courtesy: bcast.html[2]

-- "Why the Kyoto Greenhouse Gases Accord Is Full Of Hot Air" –
(An edited abstract) courtesy: Roger Phillips Website - May 1999[3]

-- "Addressing The Kyoto Accord" --
(An edited abstract) courtesy: Commentar Website[4]

Edited Abstracts Drafted by: Dr. Jaysen Q. Rand

Website Reference Data:
1) http://mind prod.com/Kyoto.html
2) http://www.k5kj.net/gwarming.htm
3) http://www.enterstageright.com/archive/articles/0599kyoto.html
4) http://www.truehealth.org/kyoto.html

SHOULD PLANET-X ARRIVE TO TERRORIZE EARTH, LIFE HERE WOULD NEVER BE THE SAME AGAIN.

-- THE RETURN OF PLANET-X EXHIBITS --

– *Evidence Mounts For Companion Star To Our Sun* –

Article/Graphics Courtesy: Stellar Chemistry/Dr. Hal Puthoff wtzechel@yahoo.com

*Front / Back Book Cover Planet-X Color Graphics and Additional
Planet-X Custom Air Brush Portraits by: Shusei Nagaoka, Japan and Los Angeles*

*The Integratron and Giant Rock Photographs
courtesy: George VanTassel Estate and Dr. Doris VanTassel*

*Additional Giant Rock/Integratron Commentary
by: Dr. Jaysen Q. Rand*

*E.T. true believers to descend on desert 'UFO-ville' article
courtesy: USA TODAY 04/27/06 P.3-A*

*We also wish to acknowledge and thank all of the many contributors who
graciously shared their valued ideas and commentary for this creative writing project.*

---

*Here I am in this small room
which is in a minor portion of this building
which is a tiny dot on the map of this country,
which is only a small corner of this planet,
which spins around unnoticed within this vast solar system,
which appears almost as if it were a mere nothing
within this never ending galaxy and expanding universe.*

—— Author Unknown

A Common Sense Review of the Kyoto (Greenhouse Gases) Accord Debate

Mr. President, our review of critical data gathered here in the Epilogue highlights our *Future-Day Hypothetical Overview of Earth Changes—2007*. We believe it prudent to offer you a common sense review of the *Kyoto Accord (greenhouse gases)* debate connected to our *Planet-X* dilemma.

We've prepared the following discourse on global warming for review and commentary taking on the task of editing this 'global key issue' analysis for your review. Certainly one of the hottest political/economic/social issues facing the planet today are the planet's complicated global warming issues. At present—the United States has declined to sign onto the *Kyoto Accord* (as currently written) and, for good reasons. These reasons will be covered later within this section.

More importantly let's discuss the possibility there may be an even more sinister reason why planet Earth and its oceans appear to be heating up. One working hypothesis centers around the fact that Earth's molten core center appears to be rotating (spinning) much faster recently causing increased heating, thus triggering eruptions of hundreds of new undersea volcanoes warming the planet's oceans. *Could this be the reason for the Atlantic and Pacific's yearly storm patterns gone awry?*

The Kyoto Accord Is A Problem-Solving Dilemma Within Itself.

What is the Kyoto Accord? Reference commentary courtesy Roedy Green from Kyoto Accord 1:

"The Kyoto Accord is an international treaty whereby countries mutually agree to reduce the amount of greenhouse gases they emit if their neighbors do likewise. It (the Accord) is an extremely complex multi-layered agreement that allows for trading off pollution credits. If it's cheaper to reduce emissions in country 'A,' then country 'B' can buy out the unused pollution credits (from 'A'), thereby having them count toward 'B's' own quota of (usually higher) emission reduction figures.

"Happily, the global atmosphere does not 'care' where the greenhouse gas reduction numbers originate from. The present-day Kyoto Accord document currently calls for a greenhouse gas emission reduction of 6% in Canada and 5% in the United States.

"A MAJOR QUESTION: —Why ratify the Kyoto Accord, Mr. President?

"After millions of years of remaining constant, greenhouse gas levels, particularly CO_2, started to climb sharply at the beginning of the industrial revolution." [Editor's note: This was a challenging time of complex social and economic changes resulting from the mechanization of early pioneering industries that began in England in the 1750s].

"The most recent global count of greenhouse gases suggests they are almost certainly higher than they've ever been in 20 million years. This is not a natural fluctuation but rather a side effect of modern-day humans diligently burning fossil fuels like oil, coal, gas, wood and Earth's forests. These greenhouse gases (CO_2) trap 'heat' in the planet's atmosphere much like what a professional 'greenhouse' operation does. This planet-wide heating phenomena is called 'global warming.'" (END) [See following (CO_2) graphics]

Hawaiian-type shield volcanoes like Mauna Loa, are of gigantic proporations & represent the largest volcanic formations on Earth, apart from huge basaltic plateaus. Mauna Loa, including its underwater part, is about 10,000 metres (33,000 feet) in height with a base diameter of 250 miles. It has been an active venting volcano for the past 75 years.

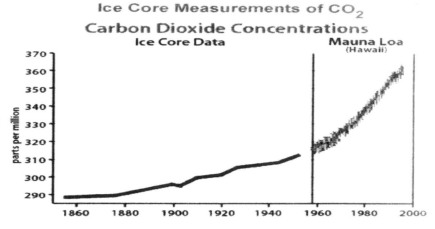

319

A Common Sense Review of the Kyoto (Greenhouse Gases) Accord Debate

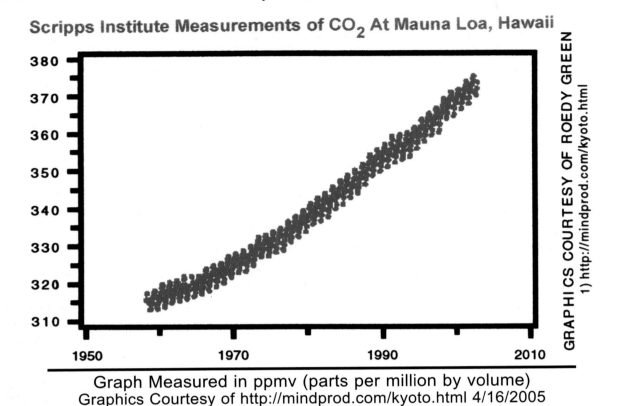

Scripps Institute Measurements of CO_2 At Mauna Loa, Hawaii

GRAPHICS COURTESY OF ROEDY GREEN
1) http://mindprod.com/kyoto.html

Graph Measured in ppmv (parts per million by volume)
Graphics Courtesy of http://mindprod.com/kyoto.html 4/16/2005

The hotly debated issues surrounding the pros and cons of the Kyoto Accord take on many faces as we continue to examine several differing viewpoints from opposing sectors arguing the debate.

This commentary, Mr. President, doesn't mean to focus/nor take a positive or negative stance on the issues, but rather to provide you, Sir, a well-rounded dissertation in its process of discovery.

It is understood that the official US Government White House position rejects the demands of the European, Asian and African nations claiming that we are acting irresponsibly in this debate by not signing the Kyoto Accord on record. Let us now continue with our submission, Mr. President, presenting the 'remarks' of a bold Website identifying itself only as bcast.html[2] smartly entitled:

"Global Warming, Globalization and the Kyoto Accord
Opinion - and - Conjecture

"Another item of general interest is the growing debate on Global Warming. One must look at the Kyoto Accord with its obvious favorable treatment of 'third world developing economies' and equally obvious unfavorable treatment of 'developed polluting economies,' under the light and intent of International Globalism.

*My definition of Globalism: The movement of manufacturing facilities and jobs from high cost, highly regulated (e.g., OSHA) labor markets (generally located in the West) to less expensive, more poorly regulated and easily manipulated labor markets generally located in the third world. This movement is also designed to circumvent and avoid much stricter environmental regulations which presently exist in the West. [Editor's note: It seems grossly unfair to set unreasonable emission reduction standards for the Western economies when emission reduction standards remain unchecked for third world emerging nations with their increasingly polluting economies i.e., China/India/Japan/Russia].

A Common Sense Review of the Kyoto (Greenhouse Gases) Accord Debate

"The present Kyoto Accord version directly favors the movement of manufacturing from the US and other Western nations to the so-called 'third world.' Was the Kyoto Accord a real attempt to stem 'global warming,' or only another political tactic in the strategy to move manufacturing from expensive Western labor markets to lower cost, less regulated locations in 'third world countries'? Regardless, the side effect over time will be to weaken the US and the Western Hemisphere's hold on the profits of capitalism.

"The fact is that world climate has always varied and will likely continue to change and go through its cold/warm cycles. Based upon scientific studies, the world's climate would have been warming now whether or not human influences were present." (END)

Further discussion of Earth's periodic climate changes is offered by Canadian Roger Phillips in a Web piece posted May 1999[3] entitled: *"Why The Kyoto Greenhouse Gases Accord Is Full Of Hot Air.* His interesting commentary offers us a fair and balanced viewpoint discussing the reality of modern-day global warming and its relationship to the raging Kyoto Accord debate.

"Why the Kyoto Greenhouse Gases Accord Is Full Of Hot Air." (An edited abstract)

"I hope you all enjoyed last summer (1999). Reports show it was one of the best in recent memory for most parts of Canada. Some attribute this to El Nino, the somewhat mysterious effect of periodically changing seawater temperatures in the Pacific Ocean off Peru. Still others suggest it's a manifestation of the so-called 'global warming' trend.

"Scientific studies tell us that over the past 2.5 billion years there have been seven ice ages, times when North America/Europe was covered in ice up to 9,800 feet thick. The annual average temperature over the globe today is about 15G. When ice ages occur, the average temperature falls to about BC, or 7-8 degrees below that of today.

"But between ice ages, things warm up. Going back three billion years, we can see that four lengthy periods when Earth was much colder than today occurred in the period up to 225 million years ago. But much of that earlier time saw warmer periods.. .almost all of the past 225 million years have been warmer than today, with the recurrence of ice ages about 750,000 years ago (for about 50,000 years duration), and then repeating about 330,000 years ago and again about 60,00q years ago.

"Scientists believe that the alternate periods of colder and warmer weather are chiefly related to changes in the position of Earth's yearly orbit relative to the sun, the ultimate source of Earth's warmth. However, the periodic changes in the sun's brightness (the brighter the sun, the warmer the Earth), change in the concentration of carbon dioxide and methane in the atmosphere for natural reasons, and volcanic activity is also thought to play a major role.

"Long-term weather is just as complex, it seems, as is short-term forecasting. Looking at the past 65 million years you might conclude the trend is a 'cooling one,' with ice ages occurring more frequently over time.

"But looking at the past 20,000 years (a relative 'second' in celestial time), one might conclude things are warming up. Looking at only 1,000 years of history, we note that between about 1400 AD and 1650 AD --the average global temperature fell one full degree. During the earlier 1000-1300 AD warmer period, Vikings colonized Greenland, so named for its then green pastures on its SE coastlines while grapevines grew in southern Britain. In the colder period that followed, the Seine river froze over in winter and grapevines disappeared from Britain. The grapevines have since returned...

1) Earth's overall weather and temperature patterns vary between ice ages and warming periods. 2) The cause of these changes is not completely understood, but certainly they have not been due to man, since the extensive use of fossil fuels is a recent development, and in any event, we have only been around for roughly 250,000 years. 3) Where exactly we are in this never-ending cycle is unclear because it takes centuries to accurately discern a statistical trend or changing pattern in global weather dynamics.

We know that the average temperature in the world today, despite current warming trends, is somewhat lower than it has been for most of the time mankind has walked on planet Earth. Left to its own devices, the weather will warm up before it eventually cools off again and we experience an all-but-certain future ice age.

"If natural forces have the world locked into unchangeable cold and warm weather cycles, what was the basis for all the international glamour' regarding 'global warming,' which lead up to the Kyoto Accord protocol being drafted in December, 1977? (END)

In closing this section devoted to the subject of 'global warming' and the Kyoto Accord, we wanted to include this last offering coming to us from a Website calling itself the *Commentar.*[4] We found their commentary to be both insightful and positive -- a refreshing approach to say the least!

"Addressing The Kyoto Accord" (An edited abstract)

"Every scientific paper ever written which deals with causes of the greenhouse effect (and there are acres of them) —recognizes carbon dioxide emissions and deforestation as the principal causes of the greenhouse effect. For some baffling reason, every such paper then considers the immense problems of reducing carbon emissions, while dismissing/ ignoring the 'no problem,' 'low cost solution' of global reforestation as impractical--as is currently thought in the US, for instance.

"The concept of 'reforestation' presents few problems, costs next to nothing, doesn't disrupt the everyday flow of people, global business and lifestyles and results in vast and immeasurable benefits: ● it ends the greenhouse effect ● it closes the ozone holes ● it tempers and stabilizes global climates ● it results in abundant water supplies ● it purifies water ● it absorbs many pollutants and ● it beautifies the natural global landscape.

"It is universally thought that doubling forested areas in the U.S. is impractical; it would require far too much land now used for farming and urban centers. This is only partially true! We can, for instance, plant trees/hedges along all high ways, inside the dividers and cloverleaf interchanges, along all country and urban roads, streets, parking lots and back alleys in every city and town, easily doubling the trees/shrubs/ground cover on our business and residential properties. This would substantially increase the green cover not only in the continental US but on all continents and islands," (END)

Having reviewed the hotly debated issues surrounding the concept of global warming and the world's concern driving it to adopt what has become known as the Kyoto Accord, do any of these factors play against our basic thesis that planet Earth may be in for a rough ride, a lot rougher than our just worrying about global warming and its after-effects covering many years post 2012??

The answer is quite obviously, Mr. President, YES! Given the urgency of the actions necessary to offset the lethal effects of *Planet-X*, the US can take the lead (without signing the Accord) utilizing reforestation as the single most effective way to restore Earth's fragile 'air manufacturing system.'

Now is the time for our federal government and governments of all nations to begin the teaching process using the issue of 'global warming' as a pilot program helping the planet to heal itself by restoring the environment whenever/wherever possible. Global reforestation as previously stated would be a great start. Educating the public is another major step followed by local, state, federal and planetary programs to jump-start the process. The 'future' is only as bright as the wisdom of mankind to fashion 'it' and time as we know it waits for no man, or issue, or problem. The primary concern isn't simply 'global warming,' Sir, but what comes 'next' for planet Earth.

1) http://mindprod.com/kyoto,html -- 2) http://www.k5kj.net/gwarming.html
3) http://www.enterstageright.com/archive/articles/0599kyoto.html
4) http://www.truehealth.org/kyoto.html

Subj: **"Evidence mounts for companion star to our Sun"SPX, retransmit by WT Zechel,D/Ops**
Date: 4/25/2006 4:38:07 P.M. Central Daylight Time
From: wtzechel@yahoo.com
To: director@eyepod.org

STELLAR CHEMISTRY

Evidence Mounts For Companion Star To Our Sun

by Staff Writers
Newport Beach CA (SPX) Apr 25, 2006

Artist conception of the planetoid Sedna.

The Binary Research Institute (BRI) has found that orbital characteristics of the recently discovered planetoid, "Sedna", demonstrate the possibility that our sun might be part of a binary star system. A binary star system consists of two stars gravitationally bound orbiting a common center of mass.

Once thought to be highly unusual, such systems are now considered to be common in the Milky Way galaxy.

Walter Cruttenden at BRI, Professor Richard Muller at UC Berkeley, Dr. Daniel Whitmire of the University of Louisiana, amongst several others, have long speculated on the possibility that our sun might have an as yet undiscovered companion. Most of the evidence has been statistical rather than physical.

The recent discovery of Sedna, a small planet like object first detected by Cal Tech astronomer Dr. Michael Brown, provides what could be indirect physical evidence of a solar companion. Matching the recent findings by Dr. Brown, showing that Sedna moves in a highly unusual elliptical orbit, Cruttenden has determined that Sedna moves in resonance with previously published orbital data for a hypothetical companion star.

In the May 2006 issue of Discover, Dr. Brown stated: "Sedna shouldn't be there. There's no way to put Sedna where it is. It never comes close enough to be affected by the sun, but it never goes far enough away from the sun to be affected by other stars Sedna is stuck, frozen in place; there's no way to move it, basically there's no way to put it there - unless it formed there. But it's in a very elliptical-orbit like that. It simply can't be there. There's no possible way - except it is. So how, then?"

"I'm thinking it was placed there in the earliest history of the solar system. I'm thinking it could have gotten there if there used to be stars a lot closer than they are now and those stars affected Sedna on the outer part of its orbit and then later on-moved away. So I call Sedna a fossil record of the earliest solar system. Eventually, when other fossil records are found, Sedna will help tell us how the sun formed and the number of stars that were close to the sun when it formed."

Walter Cruttenden agrees that Sedna's highly elliptical orbit is very unusual, but noted that the orbit period of 12,000 years is in neat resonance with the expected orbit periodicity of a companion star as outlined in several prior papers. Consequently, Cruttenden believes that Sedna's unusual orbit is something indicative of the current solar system configuration, not merely a historical record

SATURDAY, APRIL 29, 2006 AMERICA ONLINE: PUTHOFF

"It is hard to imagine that Sedna would retain its highly elliptical orbit pattern since the beginning of the solar system billions of years ago. Because eccentricity would likely fade with time, it is logical to assume Sedna is telling us something about current, albeit unexpected solar system forces, most probably a companion star".

Outside of a few popular articles, and Crultenden's book "Lost Star of Myth and Time", which outlines historical references and the modern search for the elusive companion, the possibility of a binary partner star to our sun has been left to the halls of academia. But with Dr. Brown's recent discoveries of Sedna and Xena, (now confirmed to be larger than Pluto), and timing observations like Cruttenden's, the search for a companion star may be gaining momentum.

Related Links

Binary Research Institute

Solar System

Total Solar Eclipse

Planets Venus

Planets Wallpaper

STELLAR CHEMISTRY
Observations Reveal Origin Of Dust Around Nearby Star

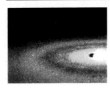

Tokyo, Japan (SPX) Apr 23, 2006
Japanese astronomers report they have employed a combination of observing strategies and advanced imaging technologies to produce the most detailed picture yet of a dusty disk surrounding a nearby star.

SATURDAY, APRIL 29, 2006 AMERICA ONLINE: PUTHOFF

A Brief History of Giant Rock and *VanTassel's* ET Inspired Integratron Machine

Giant Rock is located approximately 175 miles NE of Los Angeles near the small Mojave Desert community of Landers, CA. Giant Rock itself covers *5,800* square feet, is seven stories high and is estimated to weigh about 13,300 tons--thus becoming the largest free-standing rock in the world. At present, Giant Rock stands on Government owned land operated by the Bureau of Land Management (BLM), currently under Southern California jurisdiction. [Note: This same rock suddenly and mysteriously cracked on its east-facing side a number of years ago fulfilling a longstanding Indian prophecy stating that: *"When the 'Great Stone' of our fathers cleaves itself in two--the 'beginning of the end' is near! Beware the 'Great Spirit' that abides here--for he signals the next passage of the coming 'Comet of Death.']* Once again we believe this Indian prophecy foretells the coming of *Planet-X Wormwood~*

The rock as you see it pictured here was photographed by this author in April 1978. At the time, I was visiting with noted UFO contactee and researcher George VanTassel and his 2nd wife, Dr. Dorris VanTassel. I had been invited to meet the VanTassel's on their property which contained the Integratron machine pictured below. A mutual friend in Miami, Dr. J. Manson Valentine, arranged the visit knowing that I was researching a new book on the extraterrestrial hypothesis and wanted to interview George and his wife and take pictures for our forthcoming book.

Dating back into antiquity from about the 16th century to around 1877, it's widely believed that most native California American Indian tribes of that region considered this giant rock and most of the adjoining area around it to be sacred and holy ground. These Indian tribes of the north and south Mojave deserts would meet annually (during the fall months) at the 'Giant Rock' site, which they called the 'Great Stone,' because to them it metaphysically symbolized the "Great Spirit" as the largest single object found in the area.

The Indians would peacefully come together with their families to shed their differences for three days of non-stop joyous meetings, meditations, food feasts and sporting games. During these meetings, however, only the tribal chieftains were allowed to be physically close to the 'Giant Rock' or to touch its gleaming surface while all others had to camp some distance away in respect of this spiritual symbol.

It was believed by the Indians that the small mountains rising dramatically to the south and SW of Giant Rock was holy ground to them and was protected by Quetzalcoatl--the principal Aztec god symbolized as a great plumed serpent, a powerful mythological figure of the Meso-American pantheon denoting the blending of heaven and Earth.

George W. VanTassel stated that on the night of 24 August *1953,* he had personal physical contact with extraterrestrials who had landed on the desert near Giant Rock seeking him out in the middle of the night. An ET named Solganda, visited VanTassel at the rock off and on during seven years giving him specific information on how to build a special machine called the Integratron. The machine's purpose was, for the most part, kept secret--but was widely believed to be a human regeneration and time-traveling device that may have never been completed (by design/intent).

This machine is pictured on the reverse page and stands 38 feet high and is 58 feet in diameter. It's a non-metallic structure whose top dome is an electrostatic, magnetic generator with a series of rotating armatures over four times larger in diameter than any in existence. The energy field created by this electromagnetic field generator encompasses the entire machine and beyond it, up to 100 feet in every direction. The human body can instantly detect this strong electromagnetic field.

After VanTassel passed away in 1978, I was invited by his widow, Dorris, to come live on the Integratron site to help her maintain it. I spent a year out there (1983-84) recording a diary of metaphysical events revealed in a follow-up book entitled: *The Reality Engineer*. Those events and experiences helped shape the landscape, contents and direction of the book you are now reading.

GIANT ROCK IS THE LARGEST FREE STANDING STONE IN THE WORLD, COVERING
5800 SQUARE FEET, IS SEVEN STORIES HIGH AND ESTIMATED TO WEIGH 13.300 TONS.

THE INTEGRATION IS LOCATED 175 MILES NE OF LOS ANGELES NEAR THE SMALL MOJAVE DESERT
COMMUNITY OF LANDERS, CA. THIS MACHINE IS A NON-METALLIC STRUCTURE THAT STANDS 38 FEET
HIGH AND 58 FEET IN DIAMETER. THE DOME ITSELF IS AN ELECTROSTATIC, MAGNETIC GENERATOR
WITH ARMATURES FOUR TIMES LARGER THAN ANY OTHERS IN EXISTENCE. THE DOME DOES NOT
CONTAIN ANY NAILS, BOLTS OR OTHER METAL ASSEMBLY, YET THE DOME IS SIX TIMES STRONGER THAN
COMMERCIAL BUILDING CODES REQUIRE AND IT IS HELD TOGETHER MUCH LIKE A CHINESE JIG-PUZZLE.

326

E.T. true believers to descend on desert 'UFO-ville'

53 years after alleged sighting, alien 'contactees' among those returning to tiny Landers, Calif.

By Benjamin Spillman
USA TODAY

LANDERS, Calif. — "E.T." has been back home for years, and now earthlings claiming contact with space aliens are planning a homecoming of their own Saturday in a section of the Mojave Desert that looks a lot like the moon.

Nearly three decades after a free-thinking Californian named George Van Tassel hosted his final gathering to honor alien visitors, pioneers of the UFO culture are coming back to the site of the nation's earliest extraterrestrial rallies.

They will be coming to see the Integratron, a dome-shaped building said to have been commissioned in 1953 by creatures from outer space; to view the Giant Rock, site of the early rallies; to hear tales by those who say they've had experiences with extraterrestrials; to see demonstrations of "new technologies" by UFO experts; and to enjoy a UFO-themed opera and art exhibits.

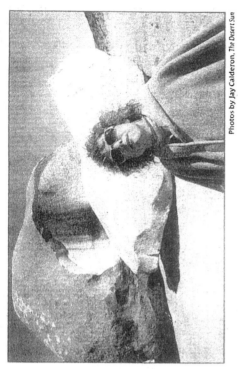

Photos by Jay Calderon, *The Desert Sun*

Real-life *X Files*: Barbara Harris, is organizing the first formal reunion of "contactees" near Giant Rock, in rear, alleged site of an alien visit.

The Integratron: Barbara Harris and Bob Benson inside structure built by George Van Tassel allegedly at the direction of aliens.

327

THE INTEGRATRON IS LOCATED 175 MILES NE OF LOS ANGELES NEAR THE SMALL MOJAVE DESERT TOWN OF LANDERS, CALIFORNIA. ABOUT A MILE AWAY ON BLM LAND SITS 'GIANT ROCK' -- THE LARGEST FREE-STANDING STONE IN THE WORLD.

"This is where the x-files were talked about before there was *The X Files*," said Barbara Harris, who is organizing the first formal reunion of alien "contactees" at the site since Van Tassel died in 1978.

"I did not want this history to pass away," she said.

Harris, her husband, Rob, and those helping her want to rekindle the spirit that from 1954 to 1977 attracted thousands annually to this remote desert area about 150 miles east of Los Angeles.

Harris said the philosophy of peace and harmony with aliens fostered during the old rallies is an important counterweight to today's portrayals of extraterrestrials as hostile invaders — E.T., of course, being an exception. Earthling contactees describe "alien people who were here to help humanity," Harris said.

Harris said as many as 500 people — some from as far as British Columbia, Canada, and Montgomery County, Md. — have registered for the reunion, which costs up to $195 and will include a recording studio for early contactees to recount their experiences.

Van Tassel was a test pilot who left Southern California's booming aerospace industry for the desert in 1947. He and his family lived a simple existence in a home a prospector had dug under a seven-story-tall boulder called Giant Rock.

In 1953 Van Tassel claimed to

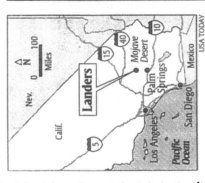

USA TODAY

have been visited by aliens who instructed him to build a structure aimed at extending human life to help people take advantage of the wisdom acquired through age. He called it the Integratron, and it became his mission for the next 25 years.

"The Mojave Desert has been UFO-ville since 1947," said Joseph Trainor of Attleboro, Mass.

From 1996 to early 2006, Trainor operated a website about UFO sightings.

Trainor counted the Mojave Desert rallies and sightings among significant postwar developments that still influence UFO culture today. They include alleged UFO sightings in Washington state, Idaho and New Mexico in the late 1940s and early 1950s.

"Giant Rock, I would say, is probably one of the key UFO hot spots in the U.S.A.," Trainor said.

Welcome, earthlings: Outside of the Integratron in the Mojave Desert, where this weekend's UFO convention will be held.

The highlights of the original rallies were speeches by Van Tassel and others who claimed not only to have seen extraterrestrials but to have communicated with them.

Witness accounts and TV documentaries indicate that at their peak, the rallies attracted as many as 10,000 people. Guests trekked to the desert by car or landed airplanes on a small strip called Giant Rock Airport.

There, Van Tassel and other speakers regaled audiences with tales of flying saucer rides and attempts to channel alien messages through their bodies.

"They came from all over. It wasn't just from the United States," said Robert Short of

Cornville, Ariz., who attended the early rallies, claims to have been in contact with aliens since the early 1950s, and will be on hand Saturday.

Short, a Christian minister who makes appearances to detail his alien claims, says the gathering Saturday is an important homage to early believers who by speaking publicly risked ridicule from others.

"A lot of them are gone now," Short said. "People are paying tribute to what took place out there."

"It is one of the best things that ever happened as far as an event in my life," Bob Benson, 60, of Wildomar, Calif., said of the reunion, which he plans to attend.

Benson lived near Giant Rock from 1972 until Van Tassel's death. He says he didn't see any UFOs but he believed in the healing power of the Integratron, which he helped build.

The reunion, Benson says, is validation that the work he and Van Tassel did is still relevant.

"You finally realize it is for people," said Benson during a recent visit to the building and Giant Rock. "It is for everybody, it is not just for myself."

The proceeds from the Retro UFO Space Convention will go to a local historical society and to preserving the Integratron, which despite being built without nails, survived a magnitude-7.3 earthquake in 1992.

In addition to raising money, Harris said she expects the reunion will bring new energy to the Integratron by highlighting its UFO past for a new generation of people who still want to learn about the phenomena.

Dan Woodman, 56, of Anaheim, Calif., says he's looking forward to the event.

Woodman, who has had five generations of relatives living full or part time in Landers, remembers Van Tassel and the early rallies.

"I'm seeing the next generation enjoying the story," Woodman said.

Spillman reports daily for *The Desert Sun* in Palm Springs, Calif.

328

"WHAT A LONG STRANGE TRIP IT'S BEEN"

THE GRATEFUL DEAD

A WISE MAN HAS SAID: "DON'T BELIEVE EVERYTHING YOU READ".

Bibliography

THIS BOOK IS VERY INTERESTING AND CONTAINS A GOOD DEAL OF TRUTH, BUT IS A VERY MIXED BAG.

FOR THE WHOLE TRUTH, WITHOUT ANY MIXTURE OF ERROR, READ FROM GOD'S WORD, THE HOLY BIBLE.

MOUNTAIN MAN JIM

The Return of Planet-X – Its Research, Background and Science

BOOKS ON PLANET-X COSMOLOGY

The 12th Planet (Book 1 of the Earth Chronicles)
By – Zecharia Sitchin, © 1976
Published by: Avon Books (Imprint of HarperCollins Publishers) New York, NY
ISBN: 0-380-39362-X

Underworld (The Mysterious Origins of Civilizations)
By – Graham Handcock, © 2002
Published by: Crown Publishers, New York, NY
ISBN: 1-4000-4612-2

Ancient Mysteries
By – Peter James and Nick Thrope, © 1999
Published by: Ballantine Books, New York, NY
ISBN: 0-345-43488-9

Atlantis in America (Navigators of the Ancient World)
By – Ivar Zapp and George Erickson, © 1998
Published by: Adventures Unlimited Press, Kempton, IL
ISBN: 0-932813-52-6

Atlantis (Insights From A Lost Civilization)
By – Shirley Andrews, © 1997
Published by: Llewellyn Press, St. Paul, MN
ISBN: 1-56718-023-X

Maps Of The Ancient Sea Kings
By – Charles H. Hapgood, © 1997
Published by: (Scribner & Sons) Div. Of Adventures Unlimited Press, Kempton, IL
ISBN: 0-932813-42-9

The Origin of Humankind (The Evidence In Time)
By – Richard Leakey, © 1994
Published by: Basic Books, A Division of HarperCollins, Inc., New York, NY
ISBN: 0-465-03135-8

National Geographic Magazine
    1) Coral Eden (Coral In Peril) Vol. 195, No. 1 – January 1999
    2) In Search of Vikings (Denmark's Mystery Ships) Vol. 197, No. 5 – May 2000
    3) Wrath of the Gods (Catastrophe Hunts A Cradle Of Civilization) Vol. 198,
        No. 1 – July 2000
    4) The Planet's Weather History – September 2004
Published by: National Geographic Society, Washington, D.C.

Before The Flood
> By – Ivan Wilson, © 2001
> Published by: Saint Martins Press, New York, NY
> ISBN: 0-312-30400-5

Epics of Early Civilizations (Myths of the Ancient Near East)
> Contributions By -   Michael Kerrigan, (The Hittites), © 1998
>   Alan Lothin, (The Ancient Near East), & (A Land of Champions),
>   & (The Legacy of the Mesopotamians), © 1998
>   Piers Vitebsky, (A Divine Realm, The Kingdom of Baal), © 1998
> Published by: Duncan Baird Publishers – Castle House 75-76 Wells Street,
>   London, England, W1P-3RE
>   And Time-Life Books, BV, Amsterdam, Netherlands
> ISBN: 0-7054---3553-9

The Book Of Knowledge, The Keys Of Enoch
> By – J. J. Hurtak, Ph.D., © 1977
> Published by: The Academy For Future Science, Los Gatos, CA
> Library of Congress Catalog Card No. 76-55939

The Maya
> By – Michael D. Coe © 1967
> Published by: Praeger Paperbacks/Frederick A. Praeger Pub., New York, NY
> Library of Congress Catalog Card No. 66-25117

The Mayan Prophecies
> By – Maurice M. Cotterell, © 1995
> Published by: Element Books, Rockport, Mass
> ISBN: 1-85230-692-0

When Time Runs Out (Prophecies of the New Millennium)
> By – Tom Kay, © 1997
> Published by: Hampton Roads Pub. Co., Inc., Hampton Roads, VA
> ISBN: 1-57194-059-7

BOOKS ON PLANET-X SCIENCE AND EARTH CHANGES

Planet-X, Comets and Earth Changes
> By – James M. McCanney, © 1980
> Published by: James M. McCanney (SELF), Minneapolis, MN
> ISBN: 0-972-2186-0-2

BLINDSIDED (Planet-X Passes in 2003 – Earthchanges)
> By – Mark Hazelwood, © 2001
> Published by: FIRSTPUBLISH (A Div of the Brekel Group, Inc.) Orlando, FL
> ISBN: 1-931743-40-1

The Return of Planet-X Bibliography

The Origin of the Universe
By – John D. Barrow. © 1994
Published by: Basic Books, (A Division of HarperCollins Publishers) New York, NY
ISBN: 0-465-05354-9

Catastrophobia (The Truth Behind Earth Changes in the Coming Age of Light)
By – Barbara Hand Clow, © 2001
Published by: Bear and Company, Rochester, VT
ISBN: 1-879181-62-2

Technology of the Gods (The Incredible Sciences of the Ancients)
By – David Hatcher Childress, © 2002
Published by: Adventures Unlimited Press, Kempton, IL
ISBN: 0-932813-72-9

Earthquakes (Planet Earth)
By – Bryce Walker and The Editors of Time-Life Books, © 1982
Published by: Time-Life Books, Inc., Chicago, IL
ISBN: 0-8094-4300-7

Earth Under Fire (Humanity's Survival of the Apocalypse)
By – Paul Laviolette, © 1997
Published by: Starburst Public, Schenectady, NY
ISBN: 0-9642025-2-2

Volcanoes (On Planet Earth)
Edited By – George G. Daniels and The Editors of Time-Life Books, © 1982
Published by: Time-Life Books, Inc., Chicago, IL
ISBN: 0-8094-4304-X

Comets (Creators and Destroyers)
By – David H. Levy, © 1998
Published by: Touchstone Books, (A Division of Simon & Schuster, Inc.) New York, NY
ISBN: 0-684-85255-1

Pole Shift (The Coming Catastrophe)
By – John G. White, © 1985
Published by: A.R.E. (The Edgar Cayce Foundation Press), Virginia Beach, VA
ISBN: 0-87604-162-4

The Delicate Balance (Coming Catastrophic Changes On Planet Earth)
By – John Zajac, © 19899 & 1990
Published by: Prescott Press, Inc., Lafayette, LA
ISBN: 0-910311-57-9

The Earth Changes Survival Handbook ("How to" Survive The Earth Changes)
By – Page Bryant, Foreword by Brad Steiger, © 1983
Published by: Sun Publishing Co., Santa Fe, NM
ISBN: 0-89540-150-9

The Mars Mystery (The Secret Connection Between Earth and Mars)
By – Graham Hancock, © 1998
Published by: Crown Publishers, Inc., New York, NY
ISBN: 0-609-60086-9

Stars and Planets (A Field Guide to the Stars and Planets)
By – Jay M. Pasachoff, © 2000
Published by: Houghton Mifflin Company, New York, NY
ISBN: 0-395-93432-X

The Coming Global Superstorm
By – Art Bell and Whitley Strieber, © 2000
Published by: Pocket Books, New York, NY
ISBN: 0-671-04190-8

Cataclysm!! (Compelling Evidence of a Cosmic Catastrophe in 9500 B.C.)
By – D. S. Allan and J. B. Delair, © 1997
Published by: Bear and Company, Rochester, VT
ISBN: 1-879181-42-8

Path of the Pole
By – Charles Hapgood, © 1958
Published by: Adventures Unlimited Press, Kempton, IL
ISBN: 0-93283-71-2

BOOKS ON THE PLANET-X PARANORMAL CONNECTION

The Bermuda Triangle (The Triangle Of Death)
By – Charles Berlitz and J. Manson Valentine, Ph.D., © 1975
Published by: Avon Books, an Imprint of The Hearst Corporation, New York, NY
ISBN: 0-380-00465-8

Paradox (A Round Trip Through The Bermuda Triangle)
By – Nicholas R. Nelson, © 1980
Published by: New Horizon Printing, Summerland, B.C., Canada
ISBN: 0-8059-2707-7

The Philadelphia Experiment (Project Invisibility)
By – William L. Moore, © 1994
Published by: Random House, Inc., New York, NY
ISBN: 0-449-2147-1-0

The UFO Encyclopedia (The Complete A-Z Guide to Extraterrestrial Phenomena)
 Compiled and Edited by – John Spencer, © 1991
 Published by: Avon Books (A division of The Hearst Corporation), New York, NY
 ISBN: 0-380-76887-9

Scientific Study Of Unidentified Flying Objects (The Final Report/Univ. of CO)
 By – Dr. Edward U. Condon (Scientific Project Director), © 1968 & 1969
 Published by: Bantam Books, Inc., New York, NY
 ISBN: 533-047477-195

The Report On Unidentified Flying Objects (Official Project Blue Book Report)
 By – Edward J. Ruppelt, (Former Head of Project Blue Book) © 1956
 Published by: Ace Books, Inc., New York, NY 10036
 ISBN: No Listing

Project Blue Book (The Top Secret UFO Findings of the U.S. Air Force)
 Edited by – Brad Steiger, © 1976
 Published by: Ballantine Books (a Division of Randam House, Inc.), New York, NY
 ISBN: 0-345-34525-8

*Symposium On Unidentified Flying Objects (Hearings before he Committee
 On Science and Astronautics – U.S. House of Representatives –
 Ninetieth Congress – Second Session – July 29, 1968 – No. 7)*
 U. S. Government Printing Office, Washington, D.C.

UFO Sightings (The Evidence)
 By – Robert Sheaffer, © 1998
 Published by: Prometheus Books, Amherst, NY
 ISBN: 1-57392-213-7

The Illuminati Papers (Revealing The Secret World Government)
 By – Robert Anton Wilson, © 1980
 Published by: And/Or Press, Inc., Berkeley, CA
 ISBN: 0-915-904-52-7

China Lake (The Naval Weapons Testing Center at Ridgecrest, California)
 By – Anthony Hyde, © 1992 – A Novel
 Published by: Fireside, Rockefeller Center, New York, NY
 ISBN: 0-679-41084-8

The Threat (Revealing the Secret Alien Agenda)
 By – David M. Jacobs, Ph.D., © 1998
 Published by: Fireside, Rockefeller Center, New York, NY
 ISBN: 0-684-84813-9

Project Moondust (Beyond Roswell)
(Exposing the Government's Continuing Covert UFO Investigation Cover-ups)
By – Kevin D. Randle, Captain, U.S.A.F.R., © 1998
Published by: Avon Books, Inc., New York, NY
ISBN: 0-380-72692-0

Talking With Extraterrestrials (Communicating With Enlightened Beings)
By – Lisette Larkins, © 2002
Published by: Hampton Roads Pub. Co., Charlottesville, VA
ISBN: 1-57174-334-0

A Magical Universe (Exploring The Cutting Edge of Human Consciousness)
Edited by: Jerry Snider and Michael Peter Langevin, © 1996
Published by: Swan/Raven & Co. (An Imprint of Blue Water Pub. Inc.) Mill Spring, NC
ISBN: 0-926524-39-9

The Real Truth About UFO's and the New World Order Connection
By – William Josiah Sutton, © 1997
Published by: The Institute of Religious Knowledge
ISBN: 0-917013-00-X

The World of Strange Phenomena
By – Charles Berlitz, © 1988
Published by: Ballantine Books (A Fawcett Crest Book), New York, NY
ISBN: 0-449-21825-2

Witnessed... (The True Story of the Brooklyn Bridge UFO Abductions)
By – Budd Hopkins, Ph.D., © 1996
Published by: Pocket Books (A Division of Simon & Schuster, Inc.), New York, NY
ISBN: 0-671-57031-5

Communion (A True Story of Alien Abduction)
By – Whitley Streiber, © 1987
Published by: Avon Books (A Division of The Hearst Corp.), New York, NY
ISBN: 0-380-70388-2

The Infinite Concept of Cosmic Creation
By: Ernest L. Norman, © 1998
Published by: Unarius, Science of Life, El Cajon, CA
ISBN: 0-935097-41-4

Infinite Contact
By: Ernest L. Norman, © 1960
Published by: Unarius, Science of Life, El Cajon, CA
ISBN: 0-935264-11-X

BOOKS ON PLANET-X RELIGIOUS AND SOCIAL ASPECTS

Now You Can Understand The Book of Revelation
    By – Jim McKeever, © 1980
    Published by: Omega Publications, Medford, OR
    ISBN: 0-931608-07-4

Shrouds of the Seventh Seal (The Anti-Christ Whore of Babylon!)
    By – Gyeorgos Ceres Hatonn, © 1981
    Published by: America West Publishers, Tehachapi, CA
    ISBN: 0-922356-34-3

Armageddon, Oil and the Middle East Crisis (What The Bible Has To Say)
    By – John F. Walvoord, © 1989 & 1990
    Published by: Zondervan Publishing House, S.E. Grand Rapids, MI
    ISBN: 0-310-53921-8

The 1980[s Countdown to Armageddon
    By – Hal Lindsey, © 1980
    Published by: Westgate Press, Inc., King of Prussia, PA
    ISBN: No Listing

The Coming World Climax (A Planet in Crisis)
    By – James C. Hollenbeck, © 1943
    Published by: James Carlton Hollenbeck, Chicago Repository, Chicago, IL
    ISBN: No Listing

The Millennium Book of Prophecy
    (777 Visions and Predictions from Nostradamus, Edgar Cayce, Gurdijeff,
    Tamo-san, Madame Blavatsky, Old/New Testament Prophets/89 Others)
    By – John Hogue, © 1994
    Published by: Harper (A Division of HarperCollins Publishers), New York, NY
    ISBN: 0-06-251498-9

Millennium Prophecies (Predictions For the Year 2000 and Beyond)
    By – Stephen Skinner, © 1994
    Published by Carlton Books Limited, Denver, CO
    ISBN: 1-85868-034-1

Signs Of The Times (Biblical Prophecy and Current Events)
    By – A Skevington Wood, © 1970
    Published by: Baker Book House, Grand Rapids, MI
    ISBN: 0-8010-9518-2

The Promise (An Account of Biblical Prophecy and Future Events)
    By – Hal Lindsey, © 1982
    Published by: Harvest House Publishers, Eugene, OR
    ISBN: 0-89081-351-5

The Holy Bible (Containing the Old and New Testaments), © 1975
    Published by: The National Bible Press, Philadelphia, PA
    ISBN: No Listing

Time Has An End (A Biblical History Of The World 11,013 BC – 2011AD)
    By: Harold Camping / Family Radio © 12005
    Published by: Vantage Press, New York
    ISBN: 0-533-15169-4

RE-Discovering The Sacred (Spirituality in America)
    By: Phyllis A. Tickle © 1995
    Published by: The Crossroad Publishing Company, New York
    ISBN: 0-8245-1460-2

Wheat and Tares
    By: Harold Camping © 2001
    Published by: Family Stations, Inc., Oakland, CA
    ISBN: No Listing

The End Of The Church Age… And After
    By: Harold Camping © 2002
    Published by: Family Stations, Inc., Oakland, CA
    ISBN: No Listing

What Has Religion Done For Mankind?
    By – Watchtower Bible and Tract Society, Inc., © 1951
    Published by: International Bible Students Association, Brooklyn, NY
    ISBN: No Listing

Predictions For The Year 2000 & Beyond (Nostradamus & Other Experts)
    By – Gus Vandermeer © 1998
    Published by: Micro Mags, Inc., Lantanna, FL
    ISBN: No Listing

The Bible Code
    By: Michael Drosnin © 1997
    Published by: Simon & Schuster, New York
    ISBN: 0-684-81079-4

The Treasury of Scripture Knowledge
>Edited by: Homer Heater, Jr., Ph.D. © 1982
>Published by: Hendrickson Publishers, Washington, D.C.
>ISBN: 0-917006-22-4

Wormwood
>By: G. P. Taylor © 2004
>Published By: G. P. Putnam's Sons, New York
>ISBN: 0-399-24257-0

MISCELLANEOUS PLANET-X REFERENCE BOOKS

THE AREA 51 SCIENCE-FACT/FICTION NOVEL SERIES
>By – Robert Doherty (see © dates below)
>Published by: Bantam/Doubleday/Dell Books, New York, NY
>Series includes the following selections:

AREA 51, (The novel)	© 1977	ISBN: 0-440-22073-4
AREA 51, The Reply	© 1998	ISBN: 0-440-22378-4
AREA 51, The Mission	© 1999	ISBN: 0-440-22381-4
AREA 51, The Grail	© 2001	ISBN: 0-440-23495-4
AREA 51, Excalibur	© 2002	ISBN: 0-440-23705-X
AREA 51, The Sphinx	© 2000	ISBN: 0-440-23494-8
AREA 51, The Truth	© 2003	ISBN: 0-440-23706-8

Domain
>By – Steve Allen, © 2001
>Published by: Tor Books, Inc., New York, NY
>ISBN: 0-812-57956-9

ATLANTIS
>By – Greg Dunegan, © 1999
>Published by: Berkley Fiction Classics, New York, NY
>ISBN: 0-425—16936-7

1990 Guinness Book of World Records (The Most Incredible Compendium Ever of Astonishing, Authenticated Facts and Figures From Around the Globe)
>Edited by – Donald McFarlan and Norris D. McWhirter, Editorial Advisors
>Published by: Bantam Books (Div. Of Bantam/Doubleday/Dell Group, Inc.), New York, NY
>ISBN: 0-553-28452-5

NOTE: In addition to the above listed reference works, the Futureworld Entertainment Group maintains a complete reference library of over 2,375 selected volumes devoted exclusively to the subjects of metaphysics, UFOs and ETs, geo-political/physical/environmental and religious topics that are available upon request and as needed for future Planet-X radio/TV series production requirements.

About the Author

THE RETURN OF PLANET-X
And Its Effects Upon Mother Earth

A Natural Disaster Survivor's Manual

Dr. Rand received his Honorary Ph.D. in the field of Energyinformative Sciences, from the *Academy of Energyinformative Sciences,* conducted with Moscow University, Russia.

His contributions in the study and pursuit of Extraterrestrial Communications, research into UFO phenomena, cosmology and his representing the United States at *The First World UFO Congress* (Tucson, AZ -1991) – earned him distinctive recognition and his Doctorate from their Russian Academy of Sciences on December 18, 1992 in Moscow.

Jaysen Rand also attended the University of Illinois (Chicago Campus), Palmer School of Business, the National College of Chiropractic and earned three U.S. Army (MOS) school diplomas from (1963-1966).

He's also a gold/platinum, multi-award winning music producer/recording artist/songwriter/publisher and recording studio manager being a music A&R executive with real hands-on corporate industry experience.

As a Grammy nominated record producer, Rand received significant industry recognition from *RIAA, NARAS, NATRA, Billboard, Record World* and *Cashbox* magazines, a *Readers Digest* article on hot dance music, a *60-Minutes* TV disco dance special, and 3 *Dick Clark LA Music Award* nominations earning him 35 gold and platinum records. Dr. Rand now resides in Horn Lake, MS.

In support of Doctor Rand's creative writing projects based on his *Planet-X* entertainment concepts, he's written three Teleplays all designed as TV Pilots for weekly series. He believes that these exciting Planet-X adventure themes would easily translate into major contemporary film studio projects followed by several weekly TV series.

The author is currently completing a 4-CD set of demo sound tracks designed for his writing projects based upon *Planet-X* and are currently available upon request for audition and production purposes.

"Reality, as perceived by each human being, is the sum total of their cumulative life experiences —moment to moment."

Dr. Jaysen Q. Rand

Jaysen Q. Rand has authored three books including *The Extraterrestrial Hypothesis, The Cosmic Blueprint For After* and *The Reality Engineer. Dr.* Rand continues his writing, accepting select speaking engagements/film/TV consultations and has written feature articles for the *UFO Library Magazine,* Studio City, CA. Rand travels widely establishing close ties with his fellow UFOlogists and paranormal researchers especially in Russia where Rand has close ties with Lt. Col. Marina Popovich and her former husband, Army General Pavel Popovich, who both live in Moscow. Marina and Pavel remain active in the UFO field representing Russia.

Tomorrow is a dream that leads me onward.
Tomorrow is a pathway I've yet to choose,
it is a chance I've yet to take,
a friend I've yet to make,
it is a talent I have yet to use.

Tomorrow is a dream that leads me onward,
always just a step ahead of time.
And it is a choice I have yet to know,
a love I have yet to show...
For it is the one I am yet to be.
--Author Unknown